Queenship and Pow

Series
Charles
University of Nort
Pembroke, NC,

Carole Levin
University of Nebraska
Lincoln, NE, USA

This series focuses on works specializing in gender analysis, women's studies, literary interpretation, and cultural, political, constitutional, and diplomatic history. It aims to broaden our understanding of the strategies that queens—both consorts and regnants, as well as female regents—pursued in order to wield political power within the structures of male-dominant societies. The works describe queenship in Europe as well as many other parts of the world, including East Asia, Sub-Saharan Africa, and Islamic civilization.

More information about this series at
http://www.palgrave.com/gp/series/14523

Estelle Paranque
Editor

Remembering Queens and Kings of Early Modern England and France

Reputation, Reinterpretation, and Reincarnation

palgrave
macmillan

Editor
Estelle Paranque
New College of the Humanities
London, UK

Queenship and Power
ISBN 978-3-030-22346-5   ISBN 978-3-030-22344-1   (eBook)
https://doi.org/10.1007/978-3-030-22344-1

This Palgrave Macmillan imprint is published by the registered company Springer Nature Switzerland AG
The registered company address is: Gewerbestrasse 11, 6330 Cham, Switzerland

*To my grandmother, Henriette Comte, a true queen who
will always be remembered.*

Acknowledgments

This volume started because of my ongoing interest in both *Game of Thrones*' character Daenerys and Elizabeth I of England. It was then an interest shared with my colleague Dr Valerie Schutte who helped me put together this collection. Thank you!

I am incredibly indebted to all the contributors of this collection who have worked so hard on their chapters. It has been a pleasure to be working with them. I am extremely proud of their chapters and very glad of what we have accomplished.

I would also like to thank the two anonymous reviewers who have made insightful suggestions and have helped make this edited collection stronger.

I would like to thank the series editors of Queenship and Power, Carole Levin and Charles Beem, for their support and faith in this collection. I would also like to thank my two editors Megan Laddusaw and Christine Pardue. I genuinely enjoy working with you two.

I am so grateful for all the support I received from my family and friends. Putting together an edited collection is not an easy task and requires lots of hard work. I could not have done it on my own and I would like to thank everyone who has supported me in this endeavor.

CONTENTS

NOTES ON CONTRIBUTORS

Sarah Betts is a PhD candidate at the University of York. Her thesis is entitled "Wrong but Wromatic: Remembering and Representing Royalists and Royalism 1642–Present" and examines cultural representations and memories of the Cavaliers in England. She has wider research interests in memories of the Civil War, in the Stuart Dynasty and the British Monarchy, as well as representations of history and monarchy in popular culture. She has published chapters on matriarchy in the Stuart Dynasty and on televising the seventeenth century in BBC drama. She also has forthcoming projects and publications on English Civil War Memorials, dynasty and queenship in early-modern and modern Britain, monarchy in historical drama on film and television, popular consumption of history, and the interplay between imagination and memory in Public History.

Imogene Dudley is in the final stages of her PhD at the University of Exeter, which has involved researching women's waged work in the southwest of England in the seventeenth century. This was funded by the Leverhulme Trust as part of a wider project on women's work in early modern England headed by Professor Jane Whittle. She also has a Master's degree in Medieval History from St Hilda's College, Oxford, and a BA in History from Swansea University. Her wider research interests include fifteenth- and sixteenth-century England, the Wars of the Roses, the House of York, and the histories of gender, family, and dynasty more widely. Imogene is under contract to write a biography of the princesses of the House of York for Amberley Press, which is scheduled for publication in late 2020.

Susan Dunn-Hensley is a visiting assistant professor at Wheaton College and the author of *Anna of Denmark and Henrietta Maria: Virgins, Witches, and Catholic Queens* (2017). Her other publications include "Return of the Sacred Virgin: Memory, Loss, and Restoration in Shakespeare's Later Plays," in Dominic Janes and Gary Waller, eds., *Walsingham in Literature and Culture from the Middle Ages to Modernity* and "Whore Queens: The Sexualized Female Body and the State," in Carole Levin, ed., *"High and Mighty Queens" of Early Modern England*. She has contributed biographical entries to *A Biographical Encyclopedia of Early Modern Englishwomen: Exemplary Lives and Memorable Acts, 1500–1650*, edited by Carole Levin and Anna Riehl Bertolet, and she has published in *Religions*. She is at work on a book on queenship and sexual violence.

Benjamin M. Guyer is a lecturer in the Department of History and Philosophy at the University of Tennessee at Martin, USA. His articles have been published in *The Sixteenth Century Journal* and he is the author of essays in several edited collections. Most recently, he is co-editor with Paul Avis of *The Lambeth Conference: Theology, History, Polity and Purpose* (2017).

Courtney Herber is a doctoral candidate in the Department of History at the University of Nebraska-Lincoln studying under Dr. Carole Levin. Courtney's research centers on foreign consort queens in the early modern British Isles with an interest in the performative nature of queenship and how women were represented on the early modern stage. She has presented work on Anna of Denmark's early masquing, comparative papers on the tenures of Katherine of Aragon and Henrietta Maria of France, and work on early modern Irish theater and the women of the Geraldine family. Some of her recent publications include "En un infierno los dos: Katherine of Aragon and Anne Boleyn in Shakespeare and Fletcher's *Henry VIII* and Calderón's *La cisma de Inglaterra*" in *The Palgrave Handbook of Shakespeare's Queens* and she is co-creating a role-playing game titled "Empire and Resistance: Prelude to the Wars of the Three Kingdoms" set in early 1640s Dublin, which is under review by *OneShot*, a critical gaming journal.

Carole Levin is Willa Cather Professor of History at the University of Nebraska. She was the co-founder of the Queen Elizabeth I Society. She has won awards for her teaching from SUNY/New Paltz and the University of Nebraska. She is the author or editor of 19 books including *The Heart and Stomach of a King: Elizabeth I and the Politics of Sex and Power* (second edition, 2013) and *Dreaming the English Renaissance* (2008). Her most recent books are the edited collection, *Scholars and Poets Talk about Queens* (2015), the co-edited (with Anna Bertolet and Jo Carney) *A Biographical Encyclopedia of Early Modern Englishwomen: Exemplary Lives and Memorable Acts, 1500–1650* (2016) and (with Anna Bertolet) *Creating the Premodern in the Postmodern Classroom* (2018). She has held long-term fellowships at both the Newberry Library in Chicago and the Folger Shakespeare Library in Washington DC, and in 2015, she was a Fulbright Scholar at the University of York in England.

Elizabeth Ann Mackay is an assistant professor in the University of Dayton's English Department, where she teaches courses in early English literature, Shakespeare, early modern women writers, and composition. Her scholarly projects attend to intersecting representations of early modern rhetorics and gender, with a particular focus on sixteenth- and seventeenth-century English women writers. She has published articles in *Tulsa Studies in Women's Literature, Rhetoric Review*, and *Journal for Early Modern Cultural Studies*. She is completing a book project that explores early modern mother-daughter instructional relationships and how maternity intervenes in the traditions of intellectual education, pedagogy, and rhetoric.

Estelle Paranque is Lecturer in Early Modern History at New College of the Humanities and an Honorary Research Fellow within the Centre for the Study of the Renaissance at the University of Warwick. She holds her PhD in Early Modern European History from University College London and she is the author of *Elizabeth I of England Through Valois Eyes: Power, Representation, and Diplomacy in the Reign of the Queen* (2019). She has written extensively on Elizabeth I, Henri III of France, Catherine de Medici, and other early modern European queens. She is working on her next project focusing on royal mistresses in France and England as shadow queens.

Imogen Peck is a historian of early modern Britain, with particular research interests in memory, the experience of civil war and post-conflict societies, and social and cultural history. She is employed as a teaching fellow at the University of Warwick and her articles have been published in *Historical Research, Northern History,* and several edited collections.

She is working on her first book, *Recollection in the Republics: Memories of the British Civil Wars in England, 1649–1659*, which explores the ways the British Civil Wars were remembered by successive governments, their opponents, and the wider populace between the execution of Charles I and the collapse of and the Purged Parliament (forthcoming with Oxford University Press, 2021).

Kelly D. Peebles is Associate Professor of French and Director of Language & International Health at Clemson University. Her research focuses on sixteenth-century French literature and culture, in particular women and gender issues, the French Calvinist network, book history, and the health humanities. She is the editor and translation of Jeanne Flore's *Tales and Trials of Love*, vol. 33 in the series The Other Voice in Early Modern Europe (CRRS/Iter, 2014), and she has published several articles on Renée de France, in *Literary Encyclopedia, Women in French Studies*, and the volume *Royal Women and Dynastic Loyalty*, edited by Caroline Dunn and Elizabeth Carney in the Palgrave Macmillan Queenship & Power series (2018). She is completing *Portraits of Renée de France: Letters, Documents, and Literary Works* with Gabriella Scarlatta (The University of Michigan-Dearborn).

Stephanie Russo is a senior lecturer in the Department of English at Macquarie University, Sydney, Australia. She has written widely on women's writing of the long eighteenth century in journals such as *SEL: Studies in English Literature, Women's Writing, Tulsa Studies in Women's Literature, Gothic Studies* and *Persuasions*, and is the author of the book *Women in Revolutionary Debate: Female Novelists from Burney to Austen* (2012). Her research interests include representations of queenship, monarchy, and revolution, women's writing, feminism, romance, and historical fiction. She is working on a monograph on the literary afterlife of Anne Boleyn for Palgrave Macmillan's Queenship and Power series, which will cover 500 years of writing about Anne Boleyn, from the poetry of Thomas Wyatt in the sixteenth century, through to a wide range of contemporary literary and televisual texts. Her Twitter handle is @DrStephR.

Valerie Schutte holds her PhD in History from the University of Akron. She is author of *Mary I and the Art of Book Dedications: Royal Women, Power, and Persuasion* (2015) and editor or co-editor of four volumes of essays on queenship, heirs, and Shakespeare. She has also written articles and book chapters on royal Tudor women, history of the book, and Shakespeare. Forthcoming publications include an essay on loyalty to King Henry VIII as expressed in books and her career as an independent scholar. She is completing a monograph comparing Princesses Mary and Elizabeth Tudor and plans to undertake a large-scale investigation into the life and afterlife of Anne of Cleves.

Jurriaan van Santvoort holds a PhD from University College London, awarded for a thesis entitled "The Ideas of Chivalry in Eighteenth-Century Britain." He has written articles and book reviews in numerous journals, including *History of European Ideas, English Historical Review,* and *Journal of British Studies.* He held the 2016–2017 Jacobite Studies Trust Fellowship at the Institute of Historical Research at the University of London and has taught at University College London and Boston University's Study Abroad Program in London. He now teaches history and politics at Brighton College.

Benjamin L. Wild PhD, FRHistS, is a course director at the Victoria and Albert Museum and teacher at Sherborne School. A decorative arts historian, his research focuses on the history of dress. He is preparing a cultural history of fancy-dress costume for Bloomsbury Academic.

CHAPTER 1

Introduction: Remembering, Forgetting, and the Power of Memory

Estelle Paranque

"The historian's representation is indeed a present image of an absent thing; but the absent thing itself gets split into disappearance and existence in the past."[1] Historians, sociologists, philosophers, and other thinkers have spent centuries wondering about how to represent something that is absent, that no longer occurs, that is, the past. Even though history seems to disappear as soon as it unfolds itself, historians have for many centuries aimed and still aim to understand, analyze, and reimagine that past in part to make sense of the present, but also distinguish something that is unimaginably different, but has potentially familiar fragments.

Political rulers in particular continue to attract the attention of historians who seek to understand them not just within the context of their own

I am incredibly indebted to Jo Eldridge Carney and Carole Levin, who have revised drafts of this introduction. Thank you so much for your help.

[1] Paul Ricoeur, translated by Kathleen Blamey and David Pellauer, *Memory, History, Forgetting* (Chicago: Chicago University Press, 2004, paperback edition 2006), 280.

E. Paranque (✉)
New College of the Humanities, London, UK

© The Author(s) 2019
E. Paranque (ed.), *Remembering Queens and Kings of Early Modern England and France*, Queenship and Power,
https://doi.org/10.1007/978-3-030-22344-1_1

1

time period and reigns, but in their afterlives. Understanding how rulers in the past have been represented, remembered, and reimagined not only allows us to grasp the different and complex representations of leadership that have existed but also enables us to examine the social construction behind these reputations and their influence on collective memory and shared identity. Moreover, we are often compelled to position our knowledge of previous rulers with and against current political leadership, and the comparison is often mutually informative.

This collection of chapters focuses on early modern English and French kings and queens, examining past representations, the shaping of rulers' reputations in premodern literature, their reinterpretation in art, and their reincarnation in popular culture. It is invaluable to examine memories of French and English kings and queens as the histories of these two countries, particularly in the period the chapters discuss, were so intertwined with alliances, wars, and intermarriage between the royal houses. As a result, the political landscape often featured family fighting family, cousins trying to destroy other cousins—or members of both countries collaborating for a common goal. Among those who are discussed in this collection, Henry VIII's younger sister Mary became, at least briefly, Queen of France, and Henry IV's youngest daughter Henrietta Maria became Queen of England. Henry VIII's second wife Anne Boleyn spent much of her formative youth in France and her daughter Elizabeth was courted by a series of French princes.

It is undeniable that European early modern rulers still garner enormous interest and influence our understanding of modern societies. In her work on how representations of modern monarchies allow the rise of nationalist movements, Milinda Banerjee argues "spectres of dead kings are haunting the world today."[2] Historians' attempts to understand an era are not confined to the study of great rulers, but a particular reign is often where such a study begins as we try to learn how they influenced their time and shaped it. These rulers accomplished things we might celebrate or deplore; they may have promoted admirable advances culturally or

---

[2] Milina Banerjee, "Spectral sovereign and divine subalterns," https://jhiblog. org/2018/11/07/spectral-sovereigns-and-divine-subalterns/?fbclid=IwAR3Yx-CQa-oz1I1twhkQGHLWO2IFfCpjaYczFLkGnRnJX6Ogi2Aw6Tv_z0LU, last accessed on November 10, 2018.

politically, and they may have also shaped hierarchal and oppressive political systems and ideologies. Historians seek to understand how rulers acted not as an isolated phenomenon, for their actions inevitably influenced what followed. Centuries after their death, these political figures and leaders that have shaped France and England remained part of our common history and have helped us build a shared identity. Historians endeavor to make sense of their reign for our present society.[3]

Why is it so important to remember early modern monarchs? First, because the ways in which they were represented after their death show us how societies have evolved and shaped their ruling model from premodern monarchs' own style of rulership. Second, it also demonstrates that representations are intertwined with reputations and influence, shedding light on the cult of power but also on the cult of personalities. European premodern kings and queens were important political players and were remembered as such, but through memory other images take form and are remembered as celebrities in their own right.

Remembering can take place through different spectrums: reputation, reinterpretation, and reincarnation. This collection features a series of case studies that offer new examinations of particular historical monarchical figures through these various lens: reputation through literature, reinterpretation through arts, and reincarnation in popular culture.

Remembering Through Reputation

While the *Oxford English Dictionary* defines reputation as "the beliefs or opinions that are generally held about someone or something,"[4] one only has to look at the play Othello to see concerns and anguish about reputation in the early modern period. In part of it was Othello's reputation—

---

[3] On the importance of representations, see: Thomas N. Corns (ed.), *The Royal Image: Representations of Charles I* (Cambridge: Cambridge University Press, 1999); Carole Levin, "Elizabeth's Ghost: The Afterlife of the Queen in Stuart England," *Royal Studies Journal* 1 (2014): 1–17; Janice North, Karl C. Alvestad, and Elena Woodacre (eds.), *Premodern Rulers and Postmodern Viewers* (New York: Palgrave Macmillan, 2018). On the link between monarchy and national identity, see Milinda Banerjee, "The Royal Nation and Global Intellectual History: Monarchic Routes to Conceptualizing National Unity," in Milinda Banerjee, Charlotte Backerra, and Cathleen Sarti (eds.), *Transnational Histories of the 'Royal Nation,'* (New York: Palgrave Macmillan, 2017), 21–43.

[4] Oxford Dictionary Online, https://en.oxforddictionaries.com/definition/reputation, accessed on July 13, 2018.

"his honors and his valiant parts" (1.3.288) that led Desdemona to fall in love with him. While Cassio wails "Reputation, reputation, reputation! Oh, I have lost my reputation! I have lost the immortal part of myself, and what remains is bestial" (2.3.281–2), the cynical villain Iago responds that "[r]eputation is an idle and most false imposition" (2.3.287–8). But Iago does not know how significant reputation—the reputation for honor—is, and it is that knowledge that leads him to destroy Othello's reputation and eventually his life. At the end of the play Othello decries "I am not valiant neither," and questions why honor should outlive honesty (5.2.291) Those especially in the public sphere are deeply aware how important it is to create a good reputation and fear the political and social impact if that reputation is harmed. Sometimes reputations become so dominant it is difficult to reassess them. While early modern queens and kings shaped their own reputations through speeches, letters, and portraits, often events helped develop their reputations for good or ill in ways that were beyond control. And the ways in which their reputations were remembered after their deaths varied and evolved.

In the first part of this volume, five chapters tackle rulers' reputations through premodern literature and examine how in the decades and even centuries following a queen or a king's death some reputations emerged and took hold in our modern preconception of that said queen or king. Carole Levin focuses on the parallels between two iconic queens: Boudicca and Elizabeth I. Through meticulous research, Levin examines how Boudicca was remembered in the centuries after her death, including during Elizabeth I's reign, and then reveals the parallels that can be drawn between the two queens regarding how they were both remembered in the seventeenth and eighteenth centuries.

Chapter 3 discusses Mary Tudor, queen of France's romanticized reputation in a seventeenth-century love story written by Jean de Préchac, a courtier and author at the French court. Valerie Schutte demonstrates that a sixteenth-century French queen and English princess were still part of a shared identity and a focus of interest over a century after her death. In Chap. 4, Stephanie Russo explores how Anne Boleyn was remembered by three female writers in the long eighteenth century, whose works represented the English queen in a new light. More complicated than previous depictions of "whore or martyr," Anne Boleyn remained a subject of interest centuries after her execution and has drawn attention of novelists and historians alike, making them reassess her fatal demise and reshape her reputation.

Chapter 5 focuses on Edward VI of England's legacy regarding the English Reformation and how his reputation as a king influenced it in the second half of the sixteenth century and in the seventeenth century. This reassessment of Edward's reputation is paramount to understanding the foundational narratives of the Reformation and to what extent Edward's actual political power played a role in his posthumous representation. The last chapter of this section examines how Richard Hurd presented Elizabeth's reign to his contemporaries, emphasizing the importance of the nobility during her reign and reimagining an Elizabethan England where the last Tudor queen was only a voice among her chivalric nobles.

This section of the volume provides complementary chapters on how English and French kings and queens were represented in premodern literature. Boudicca, Elizabeth I of England, Anne Boleyn, Edward VI of England, and Mary Tudor queen of France remained part of a shared identity, and their memory was used as a means to understand and cross bridges between societies that kept evolving throughout centuries. Their reputations also evolved and changed over time; being remembered in premodern literature could mean having reputations distorted or romanticized, but more importantly it showed that these monarchs were still part of a collective memory.[5]

Remembering Through Reinterpretation

Following the death of those who are powerful, politicians, scholars, artists, and others have found a variety of ways to commemorate and represent. As the person being commemorated moves more and more into the past, especially in popular culture, the cultural reconstructions often romanticize, embellish, or make the life more dramatic in sensationalized ways. These depictions often tell us more about the cultural values of the time they were created as opposed to presenting historically accuracy. Some commemorations could be contested by a range of political perspectives. Commemorations could be theater, art, and even costumes.

In the next section, the chapters examine the reconstruction of various rulers through art and culture. Performing plays enabled people to gather and enjoy an artistic and social experience. In plays, the actors brought

---

[5] On the links between collective memory and history, see Jeffrey Andrew Barash, *Collective Memory and the Historical Past* (Chicago and London: The University of Chicago Press, 2016), 168–210.

past characters to life and in many ways they were able to connect with the public on a different level.[6] In Chap. 7, Estelle Paranque analyzes Charles IX's terrible reputation after his death in chronicles and plays during the seventeenth and long eighteenth century. He is the embodiment of an anti-king and his reign served as a reinterpretation of monarchy as a whole and a cautionary tale of what a king should never do.

In her case study, Imogen Peck discusses the fraught commemoration in Interregnum England of the anniversary of Charles I of England's death. This chapter aims to reassess the challenges that such a memory posed to the English state. Such a death was problematic to commemorate and yet Charles I was part of England's past and history. His regicide profoundly influenced England's relations to monarchy, and as Peck demonstrates, the complexities behind choosing to remember or forget a date to fit into a historical narrative would promote certain political ideas or agendas.

The next chapter focuses on reinterpretations of Henrietta Maria's representations through visualized means, such as image and performances in the nineteenth and twentieth centuries, and how they influenced national and international history and memory. Sarah Betts also makes interesting parallels between emotional and historical representations of Henrietta Maria and how this influenced our own perception of the late queen of England and princess of France.

In Chap. 10, Benjamin Wild takes a new approach to look at monarchs' representations and explores how British people from the eighteenth century revived the Stuart dynasty by dressing as the Stuarts at social and entertaining events. Influenced by contemporary literature and plays, dressing up like a Stuart enabled people to self-reflect and reinterpret their knowledge of the seventeenth century as well as participating in and reinterpreting their memory of it.

Reinterpretation through any artistic forms allows the next generations to discover and remember their past. Plays, visual arts, commemorations of a particular event, and fancy dressing entertainments all actively recreate history and in so doing contribute to the construction of a broad, collective cultural identity.

---

[6] See Julie Sanders, *The Cambridge Introduction to Early Modern Drama, 1576–1642* (Cambridge: Cambridge University Press, 2014), 1–16.

REMEMBERING THROUGH REINCARNATION

From the twentieth century, with the invention of the video camera, directors and creators of movies and television shows have returned again and again to the early modern period for their subject matter. In the 1930s, films covering past events and royal figures are prominent. *Fire Over England* (1937), *The Private Life of Henry VIII* (1933), *The Private Life of Louis XIV* (1935), and *Remontons les Champs-Elysées* (1938) are only a few of the films that focus on English and French monarchs who are said to have made the history of their country.

Adapting a historical event or a past reign into a movie, a television show, or a novel requires "recognition and remembrance."[7] In other words, popular culture is an important component of our shared identity and how we remember the past, often through reincarnation and shedding light on new facets of a historical character. In this section of the collection, the chapters engage with remembering through reincarnation in popular culture.

Imogene Dudley examines Margaret of Anjou's representations and reincarnation in modern novels, ranging from 1980s to 2016, and how these fictional works have contributed to or challenged the queen's dreadful reputation as She-Wolf. Through Margaret's personality, drive for power, and sexuality, Dudley reveals how historical fiction and academic history can influence one another to offer a more balanced opinion of a historical character who has suffered from a negative reputation for centuries.

Chapter 12 focuses on how Francis II of France has been reincarnated in historical fiction, in both novels and television shows. Kelly Peebles confronts these popular representations through reincarnation and reveals how Francis II was depicted right after his death and what kind of portrayals dominate our perception of him in our modern society.

In the next chapter, Estelle Paranque argues that the fictional heroine Daenerys Targaryen of *Game of Thrones* is the spiritual daughter of Elizabeth I of England. Through comparisons involving their relationships with their councilors and suitors, and their use of power and authority, a strong resemblance can be drawn between the fictional and historical queens. This comparison also invites comparisons with our understanding of powerful political women today.

[7] Linda Hutcheon, *A Theory of Adaptation* (New York: Routledge, 2006), 4. Also see, Marc Ferro, "Film as an Agent, Product and Source of History," *Journal of Contemporary History*, 18, 3 (1983): 357–364.

In Chap. 14, Elizabeth Mackay discusses the complexities behind writing historical fiction, focusing specifically on Elizabeth I and how she has been portrayed in popular fiction. In her chapter, Mackay does not aim to engage with historical accuracy but instead examines how these novels whose authors claim to "do" history are actually participating in reincarnating new Elizabeths to the public. In the next chapter, Henrietta Maria's paradoxical and conflictual reputations are examined as Susan Dunn-Hensley looks at how Henrietta Maria's persona was revived in popular culture. She examines both academic writings and historical fictions and argues that despite feminist trends, Henrietta Maria's negative reputation from the seventeenth century still persists today. In both chapters, the use of historical fiction through novels to reimagine and reincarnate historical figures is at the heart of their arguments.

In the last chapter, Courtney Herber focuses on Marie-Antoinette's popular representations in historical movies and Japanese anime. She focuses on the ways in which Marie-Antoinette's character is used to fit into another historical narrative. Popular culture is a powerful tool to remember historical characters; through reincarnation, screenwriters, writers, and novelists reveal their own understanding of a historical figure and often distort the reality to fit their artistic purposes or imagination.

THE POWER OF MEMORY AND HISTORY

Remembering Queens and Kings of Early Modern England and France offers chapters that deal with the complexities behind concepts that are intertwined with one another: remembrance, memory, and reputation. The different case studies engage with how remembering can lead to reassessing reputations, reinterpreting, and reincarnating historical characters and events and how they are what is at the core of collective memory. Furthermore, these chapters demonstrate how French and English rulers' memory and legacy keep crossing bridges between people and nations—even today, as societies struggle to define their national identity. Perhaps national identity can only be enhanced and more completely understood alongside another nation's identity and culture. Perhaps our fascination with these characters means that somehow we keep reinterpreting their historical impact on our modern society to make sense of the present day.

This collection has chosen to focus on England and France, but all these bridges and comparisons can be drawn with other nations around the world, as in the end one might point out that the power of memory has no bounds and no borders. In all, rulership or what we today call leadership and how it is perceived is clearly not a concept of the past and our current leaders will also be remembered—how well they are remembered and whether it is as more heroic or more villainous is in part due to their actions but also how the world responds to them. In reading this collection, we can see that to be true with premodern rulers who have made history part of our collective memory we have to engage with their complex reputations. And so the process continues.

BIBLIOGRAPHY

Banerjee, Milinda. "The Royal Nation and Global Intellectual History: Monarchic Routes to Conceptualizing National Unity," edited by Milinda Banerjee, Charlotte Backerra, and Cathleen Sarti, *Transnational Histories of the 'Royal Nation*,' 21–43. New York: Palgrave Macmillan, 2017.

Barash, Jeffrey Andrew. *Collective Memory and the Historical Past.* Chicago and London: The University of Chicago Press, 2016.

Cannadine, David. "The Context, Performance and Meaning of Ritual: The British Monarchy and the 'Invention of Tradition', c. 1820–1977," edited by Eric Hobsbawm and Terence Ranger. *The Invention of Tradition*, 101–164. Cambridge: Cambridge University Press, 1983.

Corns, Thomas N. ed. *The Royal Image: Representations of Charles I.* Cambridge: Cambridge University Press, 1999.

Ferro, Marc. "Film as an Agent, Product and Source of History." *Journal of Contemporary History*, 18, 3 (1983): 357–364.

Hutcheon, Linda. *A Theory of Adaptation.* New York: Routledge, 2006.

Levin, Carole. "Elizabeth's Ghost: The Afterlife of the Queen in Stuart England." *Royal Studies Journal* 1 (2014): 1–17.

North, Janice, Alvestad, Karl C. and Woodacre, Elena, eds. *Premodern Rulers and Postmodern Viewers.* New York: Palgrave Macmillan, 2018.

Ricoeur, Paul. Translated by Kathleen Blamey & David Pellauer, *Memory, History, Forgetting.* Chicago: Chicago University Press, 2004, paperback edition 2006.

Sanders, Julia. *The Cambridge Introduction to Early Modern Drama, 1576–1642.* Cambridge: Cambridge University Press, 2014.

ONLINE SOURCES

Banerjee, Milinda. "Spectral sovereign and divine subalterns." https://jhiblog. org/2018/11/07/spectral-sovereigns-and-divine-subalterns/?fbclid=IwAR3Yx-CQaoz1I1twhkQGHLWO2IFfCpjaYczFLkGnRnJX6Ogi2Aw6Tv_z0LU

"Danny Boyle calls for beaches tribute for Armistice centenary." https://news.sky.com/story/danny-boyle-calls-for-beaches-tribute-for-armistice-centenary-11518362

Oxford Dictionary Online, https://en.oxforddictionaries.com/definition/reputation

"Souvenons-nous, pour demain" (let's remember, for tomorrow). http://www.centenaire.org/fr

PART I

Reputation in Premodern Literature

CHAPTER 2

Boudicca and Elizabeth Rally Their Troops: "Two Queens Both Alike in Dignity"

Carole Levin

Fifteen hundred years separated them, but two British queens, both known for their long brightly colored hair, encouraged their troops against foreign invaders, with what was reported to be stirring rhetoric. The queens were Boudicca, head of the Celtic Iceni tribe, and Queen Elizabeth I. We know far less about Boudicca than we do about Elizabeth, but in both cases we do not have definitive evidence about the speeches they gave. We do know that the early modern representation of Boudicca and the reign of Elizabeth I did much to engender English nationalism.[1]

My thanks to Jennifer Hammond for the help with the title. A version of this chapter was presented at the In the Light of Gloriana Conference, London, November, 2016. I am grateful to the organizers, particularly Estelle Paranque, who is also the editor of this collection.

[1] Other scholarship on Boudicca in the early modern period includes Jodi Mikalachki, *The legacy of Boadicea: gender and nation in early modern England* (London and New York:

C. Levin (✉)
University of Nebraska, Lincoln, NE, USA

© The Author(s) 2019
E. Paranque (ed.), *Remembering Queens and Kings of Early Modern England and France*, Queenship and Power,
https://doi.org/10.1007/978-3-030-22344-1_2

With Elizabeth, many scholars are convinced that the version of the 1588 Tilbury speech as presented by Leonel Sharpe is roughly accurate. As Janet Green has pointed out, Sharpe was chaplain to Robert Dudley, Earl of Leicester, who had been the commander of the camp at Tilbury, and Sharpe, then 28, was with him at the camp.[2] The version Green found in the Harleian Manuscripts appears to be his copy from the time. It is dated late sixteenth/early seventeenth century. It may well have been his job to read out the speech to those who did not hear Elizabeth give it. Over 30 years later he sent the speech to George Villiers, Duke of Buckingham, in a letter meant to encourage the duke.[3]

Boudicca's speeches meant to rally the troops against the Romans, however, come from Roman historians well after the events. But especially as provided by the victors, the speeches are impressive in representing female heroism and British nationalism. The sources we have are from the Roman historians Tacitus and Dio Cassius. As the Romans under the Emperor Nero were attempting to dominate Britain, Boudicca led a revolt that, while ultimately unsuccessful, would be known many centuries later as an example of British patriotism, as a leader who fought the invaders of a different religion.

Tacitus was the first to write about Boudicca. His father-in-law, Agricola, as a young man, was with the Roman general Seutonius in 60 CE, so Tacitus did have access to an eyewitness, though it was many years after the events took place. He wrote about Boudicca about 98 in his study of his father-in-law, and again with far more detail in 109 CE in *The Annals of Imperial Rome*.[4] Dio Cassius, a Roman statesman of Greek origin, wrote his Roman History sometime between 214 and 226, and we do not know what sources, now lost, he used. Nor do we have his direct account. Though some of his history has survived, the section on Boudicca comes from the work of the late eleventh-century monk Xiphilinus of Trapezus, who produced what were known as "epitomies" of the work for public reading.

Routledge, 1998), and Samantha Frenee-Hutchins, *Boudica's Odyssey in Early Modern England* (London: Routledge, 2014).

[2] Paul E. J., Hammer, "Sharpe [Sharp], Leonell (bap. 1560, d. 1631), Church of England clergyman and author." Oxford Dictionary of National Biography, 2008. Accessed on August 21, 2018.

[3] Janet M., Green, "'I My Self': Elizabeth I's Oration at Tilbury Camp," *The Sixteenth Century Journal* 28, 2 (summer, 1997): 421–45.

[4] Richard Hingley and Christina Unwin, *Boudica: Iron Age Warrior Queen* (London: Hambledon, 2005), 43.

As well as those learned enough to read these texts in the original Latin for Tacitus and Greek for Dio Cassius, Tacitus's *Annales* was translated into English by Sir Henry Savile and published in 1591. It went through six more editions by 1640. In the sixteenth century it had also been available in French. *The Epitomies of Cassius Dio's Roman History* was available in Elizabethan England in Latin, Italian, and French translations.

Boudicca, also called Boudica, Bundica, Boadicea, Voadicia, Voida, and several other spellings as well, was apparently of royal lineage and married to King Prasutagus of the Iceni tribe. She may have come from a neighboring tribe or more likely to have been a relative of Prasutagus before she married him. They had two young daughters, probably in their early teens at the time of their father's death. Prasutagus's reign was known for its peace and prosperity, and he had made the Iceni a client-kingdom to the Romans, who had invaded under Claudius in 47 CE. The Romans had never conquered the Iceni as Prasutagus had made a deal with the Romans that had left them their liberty. As he was dying he left half of his wealth to the Romans, to keep his people and family safe, and half to his wife, asking her to rule until her daughters were of the age to do so.

But while the Romans may well have respected Prasutagus, they had no respect for the woman who succeeded him, and saw this as their great opportunity. The Procurator Catus Cecianus, who was the Roman administrator of the British province, ordered his men to seize all of the dead king's estate and treasure, and also commandeered the hereditary estates of Iceni nobles.

But the most terrible thing, not only in itself but for its symbolic resonance, was what was done to Boudicca and her daughters. As Tacitus stated, "Boudicea was whipped, & [her] daughters defloured."[5] Deliberately done in public, this was an act of policy and intended as an enormous public insult. The plan was that by this outrage the Iceni would be cowed into submission. But instead, Boudicca responded by encouraging the Iceni tribes—and other neighboring tribes as well—to rebel. According to Tacitus and Dio Cassius, she gave powerful speeches before the battles to inspire and hearten those following her. The tribes took over and violently destroyed Camulodonum [Colchester], and after the general Seutonius refused to protect it, Londinium [London] and eventually Verulamium [St. Albans]. But in the final battle the Roman general

[5] Cornelius Tacitus, *The annals of Cornelius Tacitus. The description of Germanie.* (London, 1598), 209.

Seutonius bottled up the Celtic troops and then slaughtered them. Some claimed that Boudicca survived the battle and died of natural causes soon after, but others, such as Tacitus, believed she poisoned herself rather than be a slave and laughing stock in Rome.

The purpose of this chapter is to analyze depictions of Boudicca and how she is compared with Elizabeth, particularly as queens encouraging their troops, in Elizabeth's reign. Both were powerful women who ruled on their own—Elizabeth as an unmarried woman ruling in her own right and Boudicca as a widow ruling for her young daughters. Both fought foreigners of a different religion. The way sixteenth-century authors described Boudicca was sometimes ambivalent and stressed her violence, but even then those who wrote during Elizabeth's reign were positive about her, in part because of the parallels between the two queens. In the following century that ambivalence is even more extreme, but more of the Elizabethan authors found Boudicca praiseworthy. I also argue that Boudicca was not only a parallel for Elizabeth but that her patriotic speeches were a possible source for Shakespeare's *Henry V*.

When we look at Boudicca in the Tudor age, we find that she had vanished from the historical records for some centuries. She is referred to by the sixth-century monk, Gildas, in *The Ruin of Britain* written between 516 and 547. His view of the native peoples of Britain was negative, portraying them as weak and deceitful. He described how the Romans "imposed submission upon our island without resistance, and entirely reduced to obedience its unwarlike but faithless people."[6] The Romans thought they had conquered the British but then, with no warning, "the treacherous lioness killed the rulers who had been left behind by them."[7] This treacherous lioness, certainly not weak at all, was clearly Boudicca. But the British were such that they still could not successfully fight the Romans.

> There was no preparation of a fighting fleet on sea to make a brave struggle for country ... nor any other warlike equipment on land. They present their backs, instead of their shields, to the pursuers, their necks to the sword, while a chilling terror ran through their bones: they hold forth their hands to be bound like women.[8]

[6] J.A. Giles (ed.), *Six Old English Chronicles* (London: H. G. Bohn, 1848), 301.
[7] Giles, *Six Old English Chronicles*, 301.
[8] Giles, *Six Old English Chronicles*, 301–02.

After Gildas' hostile description of the British and his reference to the "treacherous lioness," there are centuries of silence, with no reference to Boudicca in Geoffrey of Monmouth or Bede. But at the end of the fifteenth century, there was a far more positive image of Boudicca emerging as well, coming not from England but from Venice. Lodovico Ponticus Virunnius was a man of letters, a poet, and a translator. In 1490, the year of his death, he published a compilation of British history using a range of sources, especially Geoffrey of Monmouth. But unlike Monmouth, he added material on Boudicca. Most likely, as Samantha Frenne-Hutchins suggests, his source was Dio Cassius.[9] His patrons were a powerful Venetian family, the Badasri, who were descended from Britons. His work covers British history until the Romans deserted the island. His Boudicca is a national champion who takes the battle against the invaders almost to gates of Rome.[10] Virunnius's work became more available to the English people when David Powel published it in 1585,[11] but John Bale used Virunnius much earlier, as I will later discuss.

In the reign of Henry VIII, Polydore Vergil wrote a history of England up to that current year 1513 and included Boudicca. In Vergil's history her story is briefly told and put into the context of disorderly pagan women, "as it were intoxicate with madness, did prophesie in songes."[12] After the death of her husband the king she is banished and her "doughtors disteined with lecherie."[13] As the British were becoming unhappy under Roman rule, Boudicca "didde chieflie exasperate their minds with great plainte of her wrongs ... persuadinge the men ... to refuse their dutie and homage." Boudicca was captain and at first victorious but then "the Romans Skattered [them] in great slaughter."[14] But the re-emergence of Boudicca in Henry VIII's reign, while interesting, is far from the more significant aspect of the reign, which was the break with the Catholic

[9] Frenee-Hutchins, *Boudica's Odyssey*, 20.

[10] Carolyn D., Williams, *Boudica and Her Stories: Narrative Transformations of a Warrior Queen* (University of Delaware Press, 2009), 40–41.

[11] David Powel, *Pontici Virunnii viri doctissimi Britannicae historiae libri sex magna et fide et diligentia conscripti: ad Britannici codicis fidem correcti, & ab infinitis mendis liberati: quibus praefixus est catalogus regum Britanniae* (London, 1585).

[12] Henry Ellis (ed.), *Polydore Vergil's English History: From an Early Translation Preserved Among the Mss. of the Old Royal Library in the British Museum: Containing the First Eight Books, Comprising the Period Prior to the Norman Conquest*, Vol. 1 (London: Printed for the Camden Society by J.B. Nichols and Son, 1846), 70.

[13] Ellis, *Polydore Vergil's English History*, 70.

[14] Ellis, *Polydore Vergil's English History*, 70.

Church in order to secure a legitimate male heir. At his death he had his daughters Mary and Elizabeth, both of whom he had declared illegitimate earlier in the reign restored to the succession. In the reign of his successor the boy-king Edward VI of England became more Protestant.

The connections between Elizabeth and Boudicca started early in Elizabeth's lifetime in the reign of Edward VI. We have at this time a far more sympathetic view of Boudicca than Polydore Vergil's readily available to the English: John Bale's edition of the young Elizabeth's translation, *The glasse of the synnefull soule*, of a work by Marguerite of Navarre that Elizabeth had done as a New Year's gift for her step-mother Katherine Parr several years earlier when she was 11 years old. Though in her dedication to the queen, the young Elizabeth had asked her not to show the translation to others who might see its faults, Diane Watts argues that copies "must have been in circulation in the royal court,"[15] and that one of the women of Katherine's circle could have then provided it to Bale; Marc Shell cogently argues that the queen herself sent it to Bale after Henry VIII's death.[16] In 1548 Bale published the work as *A Godly Medytacyon of the Christen Sowle.*

Bale added a long "conclusion" that described the great women of Britain's past, many of them women who ruled in their own right or as regents until their sons were old enough. This is a remarkable document, as other early defenses of women were far more focused on religious achievements and experiences, while, though Bale discusses that, he also emphasized political and military accomplishments. In a clearly nationalist perspective, Bale's examples come from the histories and legends of Britain. Bale addressed many earlier historical women, though claimed as impressive as they are, the women in his own age were even more so.

One issue with the history of Boudicca is how many different ways her name could be spelled, with this sometimes leading to Boudicca actually being described as two different women. In some cases this has led to a "good" Boudicca and a "bad one." But with Bale, it meant that he had yet one more strong woman example. "Bundwyca" was tall with golden hair. She was a woman not only of high status, "of most noble linage amonge

---

[15] Watt Dianne, *Secretaries of God: Women Prophets in Late Medieval and Early Modern England* (Rochester: Boydell & Brewer, 2001), 90.

[16] Marc Shell *Elizabeth's Glass: The glass of the Sinful Soul (1544) by Elizabeth I, and Epistle dedicatory and Conclusion (1548) by John Bale* (Lincoln: University of Nebraska Press, 1993), 3.

the Brytaynes,"[17] but also high stomach, meaning she was a woman of "Spirit, courage, valour, bravery,"[18] making us also think of Elizabeth many years later describing herself as having the heart and stomach of a king.

Bundwyca recognized the havoc "which the Romans daily made in this land." With a group of worthy warriors Bundwyca fought the Romans and in this version, conquering as she went into Gaul, and "followed the remnant of them to the very Alps of Italy."[19] Finally, all the toils of war were too much for her and she became ill and died, but at her death she represented the "very glory of women," states Bale, giving his source as the Italian Virunnius.[20]

Bale next describes a new woman, Voada, the wife of Aruiragus, but she is also clearly Boudicca, wife of Prasutagus. This version of Boudicca is "a woman of wonderfull force and hart."[21] This version of the story is much more concerned with women, as Voada not only "strongly armed herself," but also her two daughters and a thousand more women of "Britannysh bloude." They battled against the "fearce Romanes," because of their "tyranny and execrable fythynesse in abusynge maydes, wyves, and wydowe," clearly a reference to the flogging of Boudicca and the gang rape of her daughters.[22] When her people were defeated, she poisoned herself. Bale also celebrated her younger daughter Voadicia's bravery and effectiveness in battle until she too died violently. In other texts Voadicia is also a name used for Boudicca. When in 1581 the cleric Stephen Batman published his translation of Konrad Lykosthenes's work into English as *The doome warning all men to the iudgemente wherein are contayned for the most parte all the straunge prodigies hapned in the worlde* he added substantial additions included word for word Bale's descriptions of Bundwyca, Voada, and Voadicia.[23]

---

[17] John Bale, (eds.), A *godly medytacyon of the christen sowle, concerning a love towards God and hys Christe compiled in frenche by lady Margarete queen of Naverre, and aptely translated into Englysh by the right vertuouse lady Elyzabeth doughter to our late soverayne Kynge Henri the viii.* (Wesel, 1548), 43v.

[18] http://www.oed.com.libproxy.unl.edu/view/Entry/190736?rskey=29cCqW&result= 1&isAdvanced=false#eid

[19] Bale, A *godly medytacyon,* 44–44v.

[20] Bale, A *godly medytacyon,* 44–44v.

[21] Bale, A *godly medytacyon,* 44v.

[22] Bale, A *godly medytacyon,* 44v.

[23] Rivkah Zim, "Batman, Stephan (*c.*1542–1584)," in *Oxford Dictionary of National Biography,* H. C. G. Matthew and Brian Harrison (eds.) (Oxford: OUP, 2004); online ed.,

While we do not have a direct statement by Elizabeth about what she thought of Bale's edition, she most likely approved it, since as soon as she became queen, she appointed Bale prebendary of Canterbury, and late in her reign in 1590 this edition was reprinted. Another edition by James Cancellar had been published earlier in her reign.

Though Bale was describing earlier powerful women, sometimes queens such as Cordelia, he was not specifically writing this to support queens in their own right, as, at the beginning of Edward VI's reign everyone expected he would grow to adulthood, marry, and produce an heir. No one then thought either of his half-sisters would be ever be queen of England. But while Boudicca was represented as a great queen, she was the regent for her young daughters, and Bale may have wanted public support for Queen Dowager Katherine Parr to play a role in the young king's reign. But by the time of this publication, Katherine had married the Lord Admiral, Thomas Seymour. She thus, argues Janel Mueller, very much damaged her reputation "as the third-ranking 'public benefactor' after King Edward and the lord protector."[24] But, Marc Shell argues, the history Bale appended, in the end, helped "prepare Elizabeth and the English people for her monarchy."[25]

In Elizabeth's own reign Boudicca also became a powerful parallel in terms of fighting off the foreign aggressor of a different religious and political system and engendering nationalism. Boudicca's battle with the Romans allowed her in some ways to become an earlier parallel and stand-in for Elizabeth, a Protestant heroine.

In the reign of Elizabeth Raphael Holinshed goes into far more detail than Bale and aspects of his presentation of Boudicca was more impressive and sympathetic to her than Polydore Vergil. In Holinshed the rising she led was much more a nationalist movement. Holinshed used both Tacitus and Dio Cassius as sources for the speeches he provided of Boudicca, but as Richard Hingley and Christina Unwin have argued, these speeches were "subtly updated to reflect the political concerns of late sixteenth-century England."[26]

ed. David Cannadine, May 2011, http://0-www.oxforddnb.com.library.unl.edu/view/article/1704 (accessed June 3, 2017); Batman, *The doome* warning, 348.

[24] Janel Mueller (eds.), *Katherine Parr: Complete Works and Correspondence* (Chicago: University of Chicago Press, 2011), 29.

[25] Shell *Elizabeth's Glass*, 64.

[26] Hingley and Unwin, *Boudica*, 119.

The first edition of *Holinshed's Chronicles* was published in 1577, and, unlike its successor a decade later, had over a thousand illustrations printed from 212 woodcuts. This text was read widely and not only was an important source of information about England's past but helped to shape the way that past was viewed. Holinshed devotes considerable length to the story of Boudicca, whom he referred to as Voadicia, and how she became the leader to fight against the Romans. Before even mentioning Boudicca, however, Holinshed makes clear the terrible conditions for the British under Roman rule. The British "began to conferre togither of their great and importable miseries, of their grievous state of servitude, of their injuries and wrongs, which they dailie sustained."[27] Holinshed explains because of the wrongs Boudicca had endured, and her hatred of the Romans, the British chose her as their captain, explaining "for they in rule and government made no difference ... whether they committed the same to man or woman." Holinshed's Boudicca is tall, with long yellow hair, and her "brave and gorgeous apparel also caused the people to have hir in greate reverence."[28] Her words, Holinshed using here Dio's *Roman History* as his source, to encourage the British were "full of prudence and spirit."

> I doe suppose ... that there is no man here but doth well understand howe much libertie and freedome is to bee preferred before thraldome and bondage.... Therefore (my welbeloved Citizens, friendes, and kinsfolke) for I think we are all of kinne, since we were borne and dwell in this Ile.[29]

Boudicca's speech referring to all who listen as kinfolk of hers echoes Elizabeth's 1559 declaration that "every one of you and as many as are English, are my children and kinsfolk."[30]

---

[27] Raphael Holinshed, *The firste [laste] volume of the chronicles of England, Scotlande, and Irelande: Conteyning the description and chronicles of England, from the fist inhabiting unto the conquest: the descriptin and chronicles of Scotland, from the first original of the Scottes nation till the yeare of our Lord 1571: the description and chronicles of Yrelande, likewise from the first originall of that nation untill the yeare 1571* (London, 1577), 60.

[28] Holinshed, *The firste [laste] volume of the chronicles of England*, 61.

[29] Holinshed, *The firste [laste] volume of the chronicles of England*, 61.

[30] Leah S. Marcus, Janel Mueller, and Mary Beth Rose, (eds.), *Elizabeth I Collected Works* (Chicago: University of Chicago Press, 2000), 59.

Holinshed also gives a summary of Boudicca's speech and action before the final battle that destroys British independence. Mounted in a chariot, and having her daughters with her,

> as she passed by the souldiers told them … she was not now come foorth as one borne of such noble ancestors … to fight for hir kingdome and riches; but as one of the meaner sort … to defend hir lost libertie, and to revenge hir selfe of the enimie, for their crueltie shewed in [the]shamefull deflouring of hir daughters.[31]

Though some scholars such as Jodi Mikalachki argue that Holinshed presented Boudicca as representing "savage female excess,"[32] while Holinshed does show violent actions of the Iceni, he actually makes her and the British she leads quite sympathetic with the repeated description of what actually happened to Boudicca and her daughters in this final moment, by portraying her, from Tacitus as a source, as seeing herself as "one of the meaner sort … [defending] her lost libertie." Moreover, if the British had behaved savagely, so did the Romans after their victory, for they slew everyone: "forbare not the execution so much as of the women: the very horses and draught beasts, were thrust through with darts, which made the heape of dead bodies the greater."[33]

The illustration of Boudicca looks like Holinshed's reigning queen Elizabeth. In the 1577 edition every English and Scottish ruler except Elizabeth has a woodcut portrait inserted in the text. Elizabeth is the only monarch not to have a picture—instead her coat of arms is used. James Knapp in *Illustrating the Past* argues that because of her 1563 proclamation against the use of her image until a pleasing one was done, the printer Henry Bynneman made the choice in this one instance to substitute Elizabeth's arms for her portrait, as arms could also represent the queen.[34] While Roy Strong sees the proclamation as a "fundamental document," he says "there is no evidence that [it] was ever put into effect."[35] Moreover,

---

[31] Holinshed, *The firste [laste] volume of the chronicles of England*, 64.

[32] Mikalachki, *The legacy of Boadicea*, 13.

[33] Holinshed, *The firste [laste] volume of the chronicles of England*, 64.

[34] Paul Hughes and James F. Larkin (eds.), *Tudor Royal Proclamations, Volume II: The Later Tudors (1553–1587)* (New Haven and London: Yale University Press 1969), 240–41; James A. Knapp, *Illustrating the Past in Early Modern England: the Representation of History in Printed Books* (Burlington, Vt: Ashgate, 2003), 87n41.

[35] Roy C. Strong *Gloriana: The Portraits of Queen Elizabeth I* (London: Thames and Hudson, 1987), 12, 14.

it is 14 years between this draft and the publication of the Chronicles and certainly images of Elizabeth during these years were available to be copied and used. I am not sure why this decision was made but I would argue that in this case, this portrait of Boudicca is very much the stand-in for queen.

Two years later in 1579 Stephen Gosson,[36] when he was about 24, wrote about Boudicca and compared her to Queen Elizabeth in his work against the theater, *Schoole of Abuse, containing a pleasant invective against Poets, Pipers, Plaiers, Jesters and such like Caterpillars of the Commonwealth.* Gosson had been a scholarship student at Oxford, but because of financial difficulties left without receiving his degree and moved to London. He tried his hand at writing, both poetry and plays, but his work was intentionally didactic, such as the play *Catalins Conspiracies*, which was to demonstrate the evils caused by tyranny. None of Gosson's plays were successful, nor have they survived. While Gosson believed in writing that would improve ethical behavior he described himself appalled by art that encouraged people to give way to their passions, and so was strongly opposed to the theater, and how it caused danger to women and effeminacy in men. In this text, Gosson wanted to demonstrate his education and show his knowledge of the classics and history. His concern was that the English of his time were weak and dissolute, wasting their time in idle past times, while both men and women of the past were strong and disciplined.

It is interesting that Gosson stressed strong and courageous historic women as well as men, and one example was "Bunduica a notable woman and a Queene of Englande."[37] Gosson presented Boudicca as a great queen fighting the invaders, whose eloquent speeches roused her subjects. The Romans, however, were, as Boudicca contemptuously described them, "smoothly appareled, soft lodged, daintely feasted, bathed in warme waters, rubbed with sweet oyntments, strewd with fine poulders, wine swillers, singers, Dauncers, and Players"—which Gosson feared was more and more true of the English in his own time. Gosson then compared Boudicca with Elizabeth, explaining how

---

[36] For more on Gosson, see Arthur F. Kinney, "Gosson, Stephen (bap. 1554, d. 1625), anti-theatrical polemicist and Church of England clergyman." *Oxford Dictionary of National Biography* (2007). Accessed on November 22, 2018. http://www.oxforddnb.com.libproxy.unl.edu/view/10.1093/ref:odnb/9780198614128.001.0001/odnb-9780198614128-e-11120

[37] Gosson, 21.

God hath now blessed *England* with a Queene, in vertue excellent, in power mightie, in glorye renowmed, in governmente politike, in possession rich, breaking her foes with the bent of her brow, ruling her subjects with shaking her hand, removing debate by diligent foresight, filling her chests with the fruites of peace, ministring justice by order of law, reforming abuses with great regarde: & bearing her sword so even, that neither the poore are trod under foote, nor the rich suffred to loke too hye, nor *Rome*, nor *France*, nor Tyrant, nor Turke, dare for their lives too enter the List.[38]

Gosson's Boudicca was heroic and a parallel to his own queen. If Holinshed had suggested that while Boudicca was a strong British queen, she was also violent, Gosson's work demonstrated that for at least some of the English, Boudicca was the great early queen whose virtues would shine even more brightly in Elizabeth.

There is also a possibly sympathetic description by William Camden in study of Britain, originally published in Latin in 1586 and later translated into English; he again put what happened both within the context of the Roman treatment of Boudicca and her daughters specifically and the more general beliefs of the British of "the miseries of servitude ... that no other good was to be looked for but sufferance, but that more grievous burdens should be imposed upon them still ... so that now there was nothing safe from their unsatiable avarice, nothing freed from their unbridled lust."[39] While Camden described the "killing, hanging, burning, and crucifying" of those in the town they sacked, he also did not mention Boudicca in that context. At the final battle he described Boudicca as the leader "for it was the custome verily of the Britans to make warre under the conduct of women," but has her tell the British, as did Holinshed, about the horrors she and her daughters, and many others, had endured, and that she was one of them.

> That she was come then, not as a Lady descended of so noble progenitors, to make either Kingdome or riches her quarrel, but as one of the common people, in revenge of her libertie lost, her body sore whipped, and her

[38] Gosson, 21.

[39] William Camden, *Britain, or A chorographicall description of the most flourishing king-domes, England, Scotland, and Ireland, and the islands adjoyning, out of the depth of antiqui-tie: beautified vvith mappes of the severall shires of England: vvritten first in Latine by William Camden Clarenceux K. or A. Translated newly into English by Philémon Holland Doctour in Physick: finally, revised, amended, and enlarged with sundry additions by the said author* (London, 1637), 49.

daughters chastity assailed by uncleane handling: that the Romans lust and concupiscence, was growne to such a passe, that they spared no body, no not aged persons, nor left their Virgins undefiled.[40]

Camden also gives the strong woman part of her speech: "for her owne part, being but a woman," she was resolved to fight to the death. "The men might live as they pleased, and serve as slaves." Moreover, if the British had behaved savagely, so did the Romans after their victory, for they slew everyone: "forbare not the execution so much as of the women: the very horses and draught beasts, were thrust through with darts, which made the heape of dead bodies the greater."[41]

It is tempting to wonder what Elizabeth thought of this earlier queen and the rousing speech that she gave to her army as they were fighting the foreign aggressor, especially as about a decade after the first edition of Holinshed she was doing the same thing. I have found no evidence of Elizabeth ever mentioning Boudicca, but we do know that Elizabeth read both Tacitus and Holinshed, and Bale having written about Boudicca in the afterward to her translation was very probably something of which the queen was aware. And it does seem ironic that in the 1577 Holinshed the illustration of Boudicca is the stand-in for Elizabeth, and a decade later at the time of the Spanish invasion, Elizabeth addresses her troops in a way that paralleled Boudicca.

In 1588 Philip II of Spain sent his Armada against England. English naval skill and the fortunate weather allowed the English to defeat the Spanish. Instead of staying safely in London, Elizabeth went to Tilbury to cheer on her troops. Leicester encouraged her. "What comfort not only these shall receav who shalbe the happiest to behold you self, I can not express.... You shall make glad many thousands, both here and not farr of[f]."[42] Elizabeth did go to Tilbury, despite the fears of advisors such as William Cecil, Lord Burghley, and Sir Francis Walsingham. The Sharpe version of the speech stated:

We have been persuaded by some that are careful of our safety, to take heed how we commit our selves to armed multitudes, for fear of treachery; ... Let tyrants fear ... I am come amongst you, as you see, at this time, not for my

---

[40] Camden, *Britain*, 51.
[41] Camden, *Britain*, 52.
[42] State Papers Dom, Eliz, xxxiv, no. 34 in Miller Christie "Queen Elizabeth's Visit to Tilbury in 1588," *The English Historical Review* CCIX (1919), 47.

recreation and disport, but being resolved, in the midst and heat of the battle, to live and die amongst you all; to lay down for my God, and for my kingdom, and my people, my honour and my blood, even in the dust. I know I have the body but of a weak and feeble woman; but I have the heart and stomach of a king, and of a king of England too.[43]

Mikalachki argues that the descriptions of Elizabeth at Tilbury depict her in opposition to Boudicca. "As typical of early modern misogyny in her wild savagery as Elizabeth was exceptional in her self-contained chastity, Boadicea was indeed the frightful 'woman at the bottom' who revealed misogynist anxieties about 'women on top' in early modern England."[44] I argue instead that depictions of Boudicca's bravery and nationalism against her Rome, augment Elizabeth's power against her modern Rome. Moreover, though Boudicca was a wife and mother and Elizabeth a Virgin Queen, another way that the two queens parallel each other is we only see Boudicca when she is widow and thus acting alone.

Soon after the Armada victory, the silk weaver and writer Thomas Deloney, famous for his popular topical ballads, published some pamphlets. *The Queenes visiting of the campe at Tilsburie with her entertainment there* is often discussed as an alternate version of Elizabeth's speech, though as Miller Christie pointed out many years ago and Thomas Healey argued more recently, it is highly unlikely that Deloney was actually there; rather he wrote it from reports from others.[45] What is more interesting for this project is his *A New Ballet of the strange and most cruel whips, which the Spaniards had prepared to whip and torment English men and women.* Deloney described the evils the Spanish planned for Elizabeth and the English had they succeeded. The vivid descriptions of violence, much of it sexual, almost have a pornographic nature.

These holy men, these sacred saints,
And these that think no ill:
See how they sought, against all right,
To murder, spoil and kill!
Our noble Queen and country first
They did prepare to spill.

[43] Marcus, Mueller, Rose, *Collected* Works, 325.
[44] Mikalachki, *The legacy of Boadicea*, 129.
[45] Christie, 47; Thomas Healy, "Elizabeth I at Tilbury and Popular Culture," *Literature and Popular Culture in Early Modern England*, Matthew Dimmock and Andrew Hadfield, eds. (Surrey, England: Ashgate, 2009), 168.

But after a lengthy description of the whips and instruments of torture devised by the Spanish, and the rapes and murders planned, including of pregnant women, Deloney then compares them to the earlier Romans.

> Did not the Romans in this land
> Sometimes like practice use
> Against the Britains bold inheart,
> And wondrously abuse.

Deloney then goes on to describe what happened to Boudicca and her daughters in more detail.

> The good Queene Voadicia,
> And eke her daughters three;
> Did they not first abuse them all
> By lust and lechery;
> And, after, stripped them naked all,
> And whipped them in such sort,
> That it would grieve each Christian heart
> To hear that just report?

Deloney then makes the comparison between ancient Rome and contemporary Spain explicit:

> And if these ruffling mates of Rome
> Did Princes thus torment;
> Think you! The Romish Spaniards now
> Would not show their descent?[46]

If Deloney wanted to use the story of Boudicca as a way to emotionally involve his readers in the potential horrors of Spanish rule, James Aske was more interested in Boudicca the English nationalist fighter. Soon after the victory Aske wrote a poem about her speech, which was published on November 23, 1588, on the eve of the service at St. Paul's organized to officially give thanks for the victory. There is no way to know if Aske actually witnessed the speech but for the purpose of this essay that is really not a concern.[47] Aske's poem was intended to not only to commemorate

---

[46] Thomas Deloney, *A New Ballet of the straunge and most cruell whipeps, which the Spanyards had prepared to whippe and torment English men and women.* (London, 1588), 1.
[47] Green, "'I My Self'," 426n24.

Elizabeth's speech at the time of the Spanish Armada; Aske was actually far more concerned with the Pope than with Philip of Spain, and he presented the history of the evil Catholics since the beginning of Elizabeth's reign. He explained that his poem is about "the wiked attempts of the divelish Pope.... This ravening Wolfe, this foule deceiptfull Pope" against Elizabeth and how she overcame them. Like Boudicca, Elizabeth is a queen with "courage stout."[48]

Aske made a specific comparison of Boudicca and his own "thrise renowned Queene ... an Amazonian Queene." He described Elizabeth coming into the camp to give her speech and suggested that she brings to mind Boudicca "once Englands happie Queene."[49] In his version Aske described the earlier queen as pursuing her foes "with honor of the day." With Boudicca was her daughter Vodice who also showed "constant courage" until her death. Both mother and daughter "are now reviv'd, their vertues lie (I say) / Through this our Queene, now Englands happie Queene." Though Boudicca lost against the Romans, she and her daughter demonstrated valiant acts of bravery that heralded the "courage wonderfull" of "our sacred Queene."[50] For Aske, there was no ambivalence about Boudicca; her heroism mirrored and anticipated the heroism of Aske's own queen.

Edmund Spenser's *The Faerie Queene*, first published in 1590, also mentioned Boudicca when discussing famous historical women, and again presented her as a strong and brave woman, and used some of the same adjectives other writers had used. Spenser described her as "stout Bunduca" who took up arms and gathered the Britons around her, "she marched strait against her Foes." While he then discussed her eventually defeat by the Romans, he discussed her "fresh corage," while in the battle and that after the defeat, "Rather then fly, or becaptiv'd, her selfe she slew."[51] When Spenser again brings up Boudicca later in the poem, he ignored the defeat, referring to her as

> The bold Bunduca, whose victorious
> Exployts made Rome to quake[52]

---

[48] James Aske *Elizabetha Triumphans* (London, 1588), 1, 2.
[49] Aske, 23.
[50] Aske, 24.
[51] Edmund Spenser, *The Faerie Queene Disposed into Twelve Books, Fashioning XII, Morall Vertues* (London, 1590), 340.
[52] Spenser, *The Faerie Queene*, 441.

While Holinshed and Camden, who were more specifically presenting the history of Britain, praised Boudicca but recognized her violence, these writers such as Gosson and Spenser, who more briefly write about Boudicca, presented her in a heroic manner. Writers such as Gosson and Aske used Boudicca as the precursor of Elizabeth, who was then shown as an even greater queen.

The last example under discussion is the final one chronologically though it comes between Boudicca and Elizabeth historically. And that is Henry V as characterized by Shakespeare. The nationalistic Henry fighting the French against long odds also, like Boudicca, can be read as a stand-in for Elizabeth against powerful Spain and Rome. *Henry V* was not composed until 1599, more than ten years after the victory, and at the end of a decade of bad harvests, inflation, the return of the plague, and worry over the succession.[53] While there were fears of further invasion throughout the 1590s, it was particularly intense in 1599. So the play both celebrated England's past and represented a concern for the present. As David Bevington has persuasively argued, in the years following the Armada, "dramatists preferred to invoke the memories of Crecy and Agincourt rather than deal face-to-face with the Armada victory itself."[54] And the king's speech before the battle of Agincourt is also, as Anny Crunelle Vanrigh argues, a historical looking back at that victory,[55] as Henry exclaims using the future tense:

> He that shall live this day, and see old age,
> Will yearly on the vigil feast his neighbours,
> …
> his story shall the good man teach his son;
> And Crispin Crispian shall ne'er go by,
> From this day to the ending of the world,
> But we in it shall be remember'd; (4.3.44–45, 58–61)

The source for Henry V's speech is *Holinshed's Chronicle*. And we certainly have the "I would not wish a man more here than I have." But Holinshed's description of that speech gives no mention of the most moving part.

---

[53] William Shakespeare, *Henry V*, Barbara A. Mowat and Paul Werstine, eds. (New York: Simon & Schuster, 1995). All lines quoted are from this edition.

[54] David Bevington, *Tudor Drama and Politics: A Critical Approach to Topical Meaning* (Cambridge: Harvard University Press, 1968), 301.

[55] Anny Crunelle Vanrigh, "Henry V as a Royal Entry," *SEL: Studies in English Literature, 1500–1900*, 47 (2) (2007), 367.

> We would not die in that man's company
> That fears his fellowship to die with us.
> …
> We few, we happy few, we band of brothers;
> For he to-day that sheds his blood with me
> Shall be my brother; be he ne'er so vile,
> This day shall gentle his condition. (4.3.41–42, 62–65)

But Shakespeare's depiction of Henry's speech does reflect what Boudicca told her troops earlier in Holinshed: "for I think we are all of kinne, since we were borne and dwell in this Ile." And before the final battle Boudicca also states that "she was not now come foorth as one borne of such noble ancestors…; but as one of the meaner sort … to defend hir lost libertie, and to revenge hir selfe of the enimie."[56]

The nationalistic Henry fighting the French against long odds is also, like Boudicca, a possible stand-in for Elizabeth against the powerful Spanish and Rome.[57] Interestingly enough, however, Boudicca's speech also has a further reflection of Shakespeare's play. The night before the battle as the French Dauphin and his nobles are elegant in their tent, the disguised Henry is among his people, making a clear differentiation between the French Dauphin and his supporters and the English king.

Boudicca also makes a clear distinction between the British and the Romans. "In their houses also and tentes, they make much accounte of theyr baked meates, wine, Oyle, and … if any of these do fayle them, they eyther die forthwith, or else in time they languish…: whereas to us every herbe and roote is meate, every juyce an Oyle, all water pleasant wine, and every tree an house." She further refers to the Romans with their "warme bathings, delicate fare, hot wines, sweet oiles, soft beds, fine musicke, and so unkindlie lusts who are altogither given to covetousnesse and crueltie, as their dooings doo declare."[58]

Holinshed's Boudicca also suggests the feminization of the Romans in their leader Nero, "who is called by the name of a man but is in deed a verie woman, as doth appeere by his voice, his harpe, and his womans attire." The character Henry pulls these themes together as he ended his speech in a rousing fashion.

---

[56] Holinshed, *Chronicle*, 62, 64.

[57] For example, Robert Mathew paired Elizabeth "the Brave Queene" and Henry V, who "lead valiant" men into battle. *Musarum Oxoniensium* (1654), 66.

[58] Holinshed, *Chronicle*, 63.

And gentlemen in England now-a-bed
Shall think themselves accurs'd they were not here,
And hold their manhoods cheap whiles any speaks
That fought with us upon Saint Crispin's day. (4.3.66–69)

The manliness of the English suggests in contrast the feminization of the French.

Like Henry V, Boudicca is also inspiring as she brings her speech to a close. She calls to the goddess Andraste, "thou woman of women ... I beséech thée ... victorie, health, and libertie, against these contentious, wicked, and unsatiable men." Then she encourages her soldiers: "Wherefore with hope and good luck, let us set upon them couragiously and teach them to understand, that since they are no better than hares and foxes, they attempt a wrong match, when they endevour to subdue the Greyhoundes and the Woolfes."[59] And then Boudicca, who had a hare hidden about her, let it run free among the troops, who saw it as a great omen. After this speech the British have a great victory over the Romans. While we can never know if Boudicca was in Shakespeare's mind as he drafted the St. Crispian speech, we do know that he read the history of early Britain in Holinshed.

An early queen such as Boudicca, a widow without a man, leading her people into battle, was a potent parallel to Elizabeth, an unmarried queen who was struggling to keep her country safe from formidable invaders. She, like Henry V and Elizabeth, powerfully inspired the people in a time of war. Boudicca in the end was defeated and was said to have died by her own hand. Despite the great victory at Agincourt, only seven years later the Chorus states at the end of the play, "this star of England" was gone, and "Henry the Sixth, in infant bands crowned king." The decade after the Armada was difficult, but Elizabeth, with her "heart and stomach of a king," expressed, in Robert Aske's words, a "courage wonderfull," and these earlier antecedents could only aid in the development of English nationalism.

BIBLIOGRAPHY

PRIMARY SOURCES

Aske, James. *Elizabetha Triumphans* London, 1588.
Anon., *Musarum Oxoniensium*. Oxford, 1654.
Bale, John, ed., A *godly medytacyon of the christen sowle, concerning a love towards God and hys Christe compiled in frenche by lady Margarete queen of Naverre, and*

---

[59] Holinshed, *Chronicles*, 62.

aptely translated into Englysh by the right vertuouse lady Elyzabeth doughter to our late soverayne Kynge Henri the viii. Wesel, 1548.

Batman, S. *The doome warning all men to the iudgemente wherein are contayned for the most parte all the straunge prodigies hapned in the worlde, with diuers secrete figures of reuelations tending to mannes stayed conuersion towardes God.* London, 1581.

Camden, William. *Britain, or A chorographicall description of the most flourishing kingdomes, England, Scotland, and Ireland, and the islands adjoyning, out of the depth of antiquitie: beautified vvith mappes of the severall shires of England: vvritten first in Latine by William Camden Clarenceux K. or A. Translated newly into English by Philémon Holland Doctour in Physick: finally, revised, amended, and enlarged with sundry additions by the said author.* London, 1637.

Deloney, Thomas. *A New Ballet of the straunge and most cruell whipeps, which the Spanyards had prepared to whippe and torment English men and women.* London, 1588.

Ellis, Henry, ed. *Polydore Vergil's English History: From an Early Translation Preserved Among the Mss. of the Old Royal Library in the British Museum: Containing the First Eight Books, Comprising the Period Prior to the Norman Conquest* (London: Printed for the Camden Society by J.B. Nichols and Son, 1846), Volume 1.

Holinshed, Raphael. *The firste [laste] volume of the chronicles of England, Scotlande, and Irelande: Conteyning the description and chronicles of England, from the fist inhabiting unto the conquest: the descriptin and chronicles of Scotland, from the first original of the Scottes nation till the yeare of our Lord 1571: the description and chronicles of Yrelande, likewise from the first originall of that nation untill the yeare 1571.* London, 1577.

Powel, David. *Pontici Virunnii viri doctissimi Britannicae historiae libri sex magna et fide et diligentia conscripti: ad Britannici codicis fidem correcti, & ab infinitis mendis liberati: quibus praefixus est catalogus regum Britanniae* (London, 1585).

Tacitus, Cornelius. *The annals of Cornelius Tacitus. The description of Germanie.* London, 1598.

SECONDARY SOURCES

Bevington, David. *Tudor Drama and Politics: A Critical Approach to Topical Meaning.* Cambridge: Harvard University Press, 1968.

Christie, Miller. "Queen Elizabeth's Visit to Tilbury in 1588," *The English Historical Review* CCIX. 1919.

Frenee-Hutchins, Samantha. *Boudica's Odyssey in Early Modern England.* London: Routledge, 2014.

Giles, J.A., ed. *Six Old English Chronicles.* London: H. G. Bohn, 1848.

Green, Janet M. "'I My Self': Elizabeth I's Oration at Tilbury Camp," *The Sixteenth Century Journal* 28, 2 (summer, 1997), 421–45.

Hammer, Paul E. J. 2008 "Sharpe [Sharp], Leonell (bap. 1560, d. 1631), Church of England clergyman and author." *Oxford Dictionary of National Biography.* 21 Aug. 2018.

Healy, Thomas. "Elizabeth I at Tilbury and Popular Culture," *Literature and Popular Culture in Early Modern England,* Matthew Dimmock and Andrew Hadfield, ed. Surrey, England: Ashgate, 2009.

Hingley, Richard and Christina Unwin, *Boudica: Iron Age Warrior Queen.* London: Hambledon, 2005.

Hughes, Paul L and James F. Larkin, ed. *Tudor Royal Proclamations, Volume II: The Later Tudors (1553–1587).* New Haven and London: Yale University Press 1969.

Kinney, Arthur F. 2007 "Gosson, Stephen (bap. 1554, d. 1625), anti-theatrical polemicist and Church of England clergyman." *Oxford Dictionary of National Biography.* 22 Nov. 2018. http://www.oxforddnb.com.libproxy.unl.edu/view/10.1093/ref:odnb/9780198614128.001.0001/odnb-9780198614128-e-11120.

Knapp, James A. *Illustrating the Past in Early Modern England: the Representation of History in Printed Books.* Burlington, VT: Ashgate, 2003.

Marcus, Leah S., Janel Mueller, and Mary Beth Rose, ed. *Elizabeth I Collected Works.* Chicago: University of Chicago Press, 2000.

Mikalachki, Jodi. *The legacy of Boadicea: gender and nation in early modern England.* London and New York: Routledge, 1998.

Mueller, Janel, ed., *Katherine Parr: Complete Works and Correspondence.* Chicago: University of Chicago Press, 2011.

Shakespeare, William. *Henry V,* Barbara A. Mowat and Paul Werstine, ed. New York: Simon & Schuster, 1995.

Shell, Marc. *Elizabeth's Glass: The glass of the Sinful Soul (1544) by Elizabeth I, and Epistle dedicatory and Conclusion (1548) by John Bale.* Lincoln: University of Nebraska Press, 1993.

Spenser, Edmund. *The Faerie Queene Disposed into Twelve Books, Fashioning XII, Morall Vertues.* London, 1590.

Strong, Roy C. *Gloriana: The Portraits of Queen Elizabeth I.* London: Thames and Hudson, 1987.

Vanrigh, Anny Crunelle. "Henry V as a Royal Entry," *SEL: Studies in English Literature, 1500–1900* (2007); 47 (2).

Watt, Diane. *Secretaries of God: Women Prophets in Late Medieval and Early Modern England.* Rochester: Boydell & Brewer, 2001.

Williams, Carolyn D. *Boudica and Her Stories: Narrative Transformations of a Warrior Queen.* University of Delaware Press, 2009.

Zim, Rivkah. "Batman, Stephan (*c.*1542–1584)," in *Oxford Dictionary of National Biography,* ed. H. C. G. Matthew and Brian Harrison (Oxford: OUP, 2004); online ed., ed. David Cannadine, May 2011, http://0-www.oxforddnb.com. library.unl.edu/view/article/1704 (accessed June 3, 2017).

CHAPTER 3

Princess, Duchess, Queen: Mary Tudor As Represented in a Seventeenth-Century French Love Story

Valerie Schutte

On March 3, 1515, Mary Tudor married Charles Brandon, duke of Suffolk. Five hundred years later, their love match is still the most notable fact about Mary, and hers and Charles's narrative has become the quintessential Tudor love story. This chapter examines one printed novel in the seventeenth century that perpetuated their love story and helped to distort the facts of their courtship and marriage into the myth that it has become. First, I briefly overview their actual courtship and marriage. Then, I analyze Jean de Préchac's 1677 novel, *La princesse d'Angleterre, ou La duchesse-reyne*.[1] Finally, I conclude with Préchac's possible sources, including other fictional accounts of their love affair printed before Préchac's novel.

Mary Tudor was born c. 1495, the youngest living child of King Henry VII of England and Elizabeth of York. By age 13, she was betrothed to

---

[1] Jean de Préchac, *La princesse d'Angleterre, ou La duchesse-reyne* (Paris: Estienne Loyson, 1677).

V. Schutte (✉)
Beaver Falls, PA, USA

© The Author(s) 2019
E. Paranque (ed.), *Remembering Queens and Kings of Early Modern England and France*, Queenship and Power,
https://doi.org/10.1007/978-3-030-22344-1_3

Prince Charles of Castille, confirmed by a treaty dated December 21, 1507.[2] On July 30, 1514, Mary rescinded her betrothal to Charles, only to marry Louis XII of France by proxy on August 13 of the same year.[3] Mary married Louis at Abbeville on October 9, 1514, yet the marriage only lasted three months as Louis died on January 1, 1515.

Charles Brandon was the only surviving son of Sir William Brandon and Elizabeth Bruyn. He was a childhood friend of Henry VIII, who granted him many titles and rewards. Brandon married a total of four times, the third of which was to Mary Tudor. Mary and Charles married on March 3, 1515, without the consent of Henry, yet in the presence of Francis I, who helped to organize the marriage and promised to intervene with Mary's brother.[4] The couple returned to England and eventually regained Henry's favor, often appearing at court.

What is perhaps best known about Mary is that she chose to marry for love, knowing that her first marriage was done out of duty to her brother and her country.[5] However, Mary's posthumous reputation has been distorted solely because of this action. She has often been relegated as having only a very minor role in Tudor politics—a brief, three-month foreign marriage—as well as construed as a woman ruled by her emotions.[6] Only in the most recent historiography has it been demonstrated that Mary had an active political life in both France and England, and continued to act in her role of dowager Queen of France until her death in 1533.[7]

Perhaps the most dominating reason why Mary has been remembered this way is because her marriage to Brandon has been romanticized in various novels and poems for the last 500 years, all of which leave out most other aspects of her life.[8] However, Erin Sadlack suggests that the myth of

[2] Erin A. Sadlack, *The French Queen's Letters: Mary Tudor Brandon and the Politics of Marriage in Sixteenth-Century Europe* (New York: Palgrave Macmillan, 2011), 27.

[3] Sadlack, *The French Queen's Letters*, 50.

[4] Letter from Brandon to Wolsey dated 3 February 1515. *Letters and Papers, Foreign and Domestic, Henry VIII*, Vol. 2, 1515–1518, ed. J.S. Brewer (London, 1864), entry 106.

[5] See British Library, MS Cotton Caligula D.VI, fol. 255r-156v and British Library, MS Cotton Caligula D.VI, fol. 253r-254v for letters written by Mary to Henry on her potential marriage of her choosing after the death of Louis. See also Sadlack, *The French Queen's Letters*, 91–117.

[6] Sadlack, *The French Queen's Letters*, 2, 13.

[7] Walter C. Richardson's biography of Mary argues that she "has never been properly assessed" as a typical Renaissance princess, yet at the same time denies her any dynastic importance. Richardson, *Mary Tudor: The White Queen* (London: Peter Owen, 1970), vii.

[8] Sadlack, *The French Queen's Letters*, 1–3, 13, 15, 91, 96–97, 119–120, 160.

Mary's romance has persisted and been repeated because it was a trope she first employed in her own letters, in which Mary framed herself as the protagonist in a romance in which lovers fought for her attention and her hand in marriage.[9] Sadlack notes that "from almost the moment of her death, writers began to fashion Mary as the heroine of an epic love story, claiming that true love triumphs over aged kings, selfish brothers, and even court politics."[10] Sadlack calls these fictional depictions "troubling" because they obscure Mary's life and behaviors as queen and dowager queen.[11] Romanticized versions of Mary "make it all too easy to marginalize Mary, to ignore her as a minor figure of little historical importance."[12] While it is not the job of this chapter to assess the historicity of Préchac's novel or make larger conclusions of the historical Mary versus the fictional one, it is the purpose of this chapter to ask why Préchac chose to write about Mary. Why did Préchac write about Mary in 1677/1678? Why did he focus on Mary and Brandon's courtship and conclude his story shortly after their marriage? And finally, how was Préchac's novel received? All of these questions are difficult to answer, but an inquiry into them will illuminate and reinforce Sadlack's idea that Mary was more politically important than her current reputation allows.

Jean de Préchac and Mary Tudor

Not much is known of Jean de Préchac (1647?–1720), other than him being author of several novels published in the 1670s and 1680s, many based on specific historical people, such as Cara Mustapha, the late Grand Viser and military commander of the Ottoman Empire, and Yolanda of Sicily, who in the 1690s turned to writing fairy tales. He was a parliamentarian who had "excellent court connections" with at least two of his works being "panegyrics of Louis XIV's court."[13] Préchac's novels were all printed in France first, yet many of them migrated to England and were

---

[9] Sadlack, *The French Queen's Letters*, 10, 91.

[10] Sadlack, *The French Queen's Letters*, 160.

[11] Sadlack, *The French Queen's Letters*, 160.

[12] Sadlack, *The French Queen's Letters*, 160. David Loades, *Mary Rose: Tudor princess, Queen of France, the extraordinary life of Henry VIII's sister* (Stroud: Amberley, 2014), 13. Loades notes that the "real woman has been largely lost sight of among these stories and legends."

[13] François Gevrey, *Contes Moins Contes Que les autres: Précédés de L'illustre Parisienne* (Paris: Société des Textes Français Modernes, 2012), 5. Lewis C. Seifert, "Jean de Préchac,"

printed in English translation. According to the online English Short Title Catalogue, at least 13 of Préchac's novels were printed in England in English translation.[14] With the rise of the biographical novel in the mid-seventeenth century, it is not surprising that Préchac's novels reached a widespread audience because of both their subject matter and Préchac's talent for telling stories. Novels were an incredibly popular literary genre during the seventeenth and eighteenth centuries.[15] A novel in French about a beautiful French queen would have found a welcome audience. Another such novel, *La Princesse de Clèves* was published anonymously in March 1678 by Madame de La Fayette and was wildly successful. It was published in English translation in 1689.

Préchac wrote the first novel describing Mary and Brandon's love story, first printed in France in 1677 and then in England in English translation the following year.[16] Préchac's novel was printed a second time in England in English translation in 1686, this time with a variant title—*The Illustrious Lovers, or Princely Adventures in the Courts of England and France.*[17] Like the 1678 version, there is no mention of Préchac on the frontispiece, which was not an uncommon practice for translations not to mention the original author on the frontispiece, yet the first page of the novel gives the original title of the book—*The English Princess, or the Dutchess Queen.*[18]

---

in *The Oxford Companion to Fairy Tales: The Western fairy tale tradition from medieval to modern*, ed. Jack Zipes (Oxford: Oxford University Press, 2000), 400.

[14] http://estc.bl.uk

[15] Patricia Meyer Spacks, *Imagining a Self: Autobiography and Novel in Eighteenth-Century England* (Cambridge and London: Harvard University Press, 1976); Michelle M. Dowd and Julia A. Eckerle, *Genre and Women's Life Writing in Early Modern England* (Aldershot: Ashgate, 2007); Felicity A. Nussbaum, *The Autobiographical Subject: Gender and Ideology in Eighteenth-Century England* (Baltimore: Johns Hopkins University Press, 1989); Sybil Oldfield, *Collective Biography in Britain, 1550–1900: A Select Annotated Bibliography* (London: Mansell, 1999).

[16] Jean de Préchac, *The English Princess, or the Dutchess-Queen. A Relation of English and French Adventures. A Novel. In Two Parts* (London: Printed for Will. Cademan and Simon Neale, 1678).

[17] Préchac, *The Illustrious Lovers, or Princely Adventures in the Courts of England and France. Containing Sundry transactions relating to the love intrigues, noble enterprises, and gallantry: being an historical account of the famous loves of Mary sometimes Queen of France (daughter to Henry the 7th) and Charles Brandon the renown'd Duke of Suffolk: discovering the glory and grandeur of both nations. Written original in French, and now done into English* (London: Printed for William Whitwood, 1686).

[18] This printing includes both parts of the novel and the postscript.

As for why Préchac specifically chose Mary when he could have chosen any French royal person to write about, that is a bit more difficult to discern. *La princesse d'Angleterre* was one of Préchac first novels. However, England and France were still closely connected in 1677–1678 and Mary still held interest in both countries. Around the time Préchac wrote his novel, French King Louis XIV's youngest illegitimate daughter, Françoise Marie de Bourbon, was born on May 4, 1677, and English King Charles II was actively having illegitimate children. With the birth of French and English potential princesses happening, Préchac himself may have been interested in one of the most popular French queens of the previous century, well aware that the monarchies of England and France would continue to intermarry their children. Also, Charles II's mother, Henrietta Maria of France, often travelled between England and France, returning to France for good in 1665, and her daughter, Henrietta Anne, was married to Philippe I, duke of Orléans, so both were famous women who united the English and French thrones and could have served as Préchac's inspiration. While this is entirely circumstantial, it is possible that Préchac understood that his audience, in both England and France, already knew of Mary and he wanted to revive people's interest in her importance for their interconnected histories.

What is perhaps even more difficult to determine is the novel's readership and popularity. It was published twice in English, whereas many of Préchac's other novels were only printed once in English, although some were also printed in Dutch translations in Amsterdam. The 1678 version is currently only held in nine libraries between the United Kingdom and United States, while the 1686 version is only held in four libraries, one in Australia and three in the United States. With so few extant copies of the novel, it does not seem like that it would have been a cherished book passed down within families. Nonetheless, Préchac's novel did have international interest and capitalized on Mary and Brandon's marriage being a popular Tudor romance, especially as Mary and Brandon's story concluded with the lovers being united in marriage, while her brother's more popular marital exploits never really had any happy endings.

THE ENGLISH PRINCESS, OR THE DUCHESS QUEEN

Préchac's work on Mary is an interesting biographical novel, broken into Book I and Book II, that retells the life story of Mary Tudor, while focusing on the men surrounding Mary and their actions more so than on Mary herself.[19] It begins with the accession of Henry VIII and his marriage to Catherine of Aragon, setting the stage for Mary's story to become dependent upon the goodwill of the men around her. Immediately thereafter, Préchac relates how Princess Mary "excelled in Quality, so she exceeded the rest in Beauty," and how she unknowingly attracts the love and attention of all men around her, especially that of Charles Brandon (4). Initially, she is too young to understand Brandon's feelings for her, yet she comes to love him too, at an early age. Their mutual feelings for one another incur the wrath of many other men who constantly try to tarnish Brandon's reputation, and when they cannot, they try to tarnish Mary's instead so that she cannot make a good marriage.

From the beginning, the novel is more about Brandon, whom Préchac portrays as a weak, lovesick fool, while Mary is more level-headed about their relationship. Henry VIII is also aware of their mutual attraction and encourages them to spend time with one another. The largest twist of the novel comes at only 38 pages in, when it is revealed that Brandon is not the biological son of his parents, but his blood father is the son of the Duke of Clarence and his mother is Anne Hemlock, meaning that he has royal blood, is actually fit to marry Mary, and that he is a contender for the throne. Anne Hemlock, his birth mother, died in childbirth, so Lady Brandon substituted him for one of her children who was just born but died.[20] This way, Brandon was not killed as an infant for being an alternative for the throne. It is Brandon's secret royal identity that causes him to make such valiant sacrifices for Mary throughout the novel, as well as always act chivalrous and true to his monarch and his lady love.

In addition to incurring the wrath of Mary's many rival suitors, such as the Irish Earl of Kildare, Brandon also becomes an enemy of Thomas Wolsey, who throws him in the Tower. Henry VIII has Brandon released and the two vow that their chief concern is the welfare of Mary, as "she fell into a Fever, but so dangerous, as put every one in fear of her life" upon hearing he was imprisoned (71). Although Henry is aware of their love, he never offers to unite them in matrimony, likely waiting to make her a political match instead. Brandon himself did not "find it even reasonable,

---

[19] All quotations from Préchac's novel come from the 1678 English translation. Page numbers for quotations will be noted within parenthetical references after each quote.

[20] Secret love children of royal birth were also frequent tropes used in fictional portrayals of Queen Elizabeth I. Michael Dobson and Nicola J. Watson, *England's Elizabeth: An Afterlife in Fame and Fantasy* (Oxford: Oxford University Press, 2002), 26–27.

that he himself should desire it" (85). Brandon continuously offers to leave England so that Mary will agree to a politically advantageous match; he constantly tells her that she deserves to be queen somewhere. Here, Préchac has Brandon show his love for Mary by running away from his own feelings for her. This both depicts Brandon as a weak man who lacks control of his emotions to the point that he must hide from them and increases the mythology around Mary that any man who came near her instantly fell in love with her. Exchanges such as these add drama to Préchac's retelling of already dramatic events.

The war with France takes up a large section of Préchac's novel, especially as he describes how Brandon fought valiantly even after he was wounded, setting up both Mary and Brandon's relationships when they are in France in Book Two. The second half of Préchac's novel shifts focus to Mary's marriage to the French king, time at the French court, and return to England. Again, Préchac adds in dialogue and represents events not in the order in which they actually occurred, yet his story mostly follows Mary's actual betrothal and marriage to Louis. It begins with the Duke of Longueville, a French prisoner in England though allowed to live at court, falling in love with Mary. When he realizes he cannot have Mary for himself, he suggests that she marry Louis XII of France because "his greatest happiness would be to see her Queen of France," like Brandon, desiring that she should be queen somewhere (129). All of Europe becomes involved in the potential match between Mary and Louis, so Henry breaks off her betrothal with Spain and agrees for her to marry the elder Louis XII.

The marriage negotiations and ceremony quickly take place, and Mary immediately gains as many admirers in France as she has in England. Brandon accompanies her to France and again has rivals for Mary's affections, who all realize that Mary and Brandon are in love. Now those whom Brandon defeated in battles in France conspire to tarnish his and Mary's reputations, just as his rivals in England had done. The Duke of Longueville goes so far as to catch Mary and Brandon together, but his plot is thwarted. Brandon returns to London only to immediately return to France with the death of Louis XII. He was to bring Mary back to England. However, the new French king offers to oversee their marriage and get Henry VIII to consent to it, as "one day, when her beauty so surprised him, that he forgot some of his measures, thinking to take her on the right side, he told her, That since he himself could not expect to be happy, it behoved him at least to endeavour to make her so" (231). The two arrive back in England as happily married lovers and are accepted by Henry.

Here the novel ends, but Préchac adds an eight-page postscript which he intends to be a factual account of the remainder of Mary's life for those not satisfied with his novel ending so abruptly. According to Préchac, upon their return to England, Wolsey truly held power, not Henry VIII, and since Wolsey regarded Brandon has his enemy, he had the marriage condemned and banished Mary and Brandon to the countryside in addition to paying heavy fines. They lived in the country for three years and did not return to court until Henry asked them to accompany him to France for the Field of Cloth of Gold. At the French/English meeting, Francis I makes efforts to see her again, as he too had fallen in love with her, and went so far as to make Brandon a knight in France. Mary died in her twentieth year of marriage with Brandon. Together they had five children, their two boys dying the same day of the sweating sickness. They had three daughters (Préchac only mentions the eldest, Frances, mother of Lady Jane Grey, by name), and Brandon died attending to Frances when she was sick, and that because she looked exactly like her mother, he favored her most. Often, in historical and fictional sources of Mary printed after Préchac's novel, this fact is often mentioned, tying Mary's historical reputation to only her love story and that she was grandmother to the nine-day queen, who herself has a very interesting afterlife, often appearing as a Protestant martyr and figure to be admired. Brandon never revealed that he was Prince of York so that he could keep his family safe. So even though Préchac offers his postscript as factual and not part of his novel, in it he still blends fiction with reality, citing Brandon's lineage as a Prince of York. As this rumor does not seem to have actually floated around in the sixteenth century, perhaps Préchac just could not let go of this fantasy that he had created in his novel.

This depiction of Mary and Brandon's marriage and later life actually differs greatly from the newest historical evidence which suggests that Wolsey mediated Henry's anger at the couple for marrying without his permission. In fact, after Louis's death, Mary wrote to Wolsey before she even wrote to her brother.[21] An extant letter draft written by Mary to Henry from April 30/May 1, 1515, details her first marriage and then

---

[21] Sadlack, *The French Queen's Letters*, 91–117. Sadlack has demonstrated how Mary crafted letters to both Wolsey and Henry that show her political awareness of her marital situation, her know-how to manipulate her brother into forgiveness for marrying without his permission, and her recognition of her value as a queen dowager of France.

takes full responsibility for her second marriage.[22] Cardinal Wolsey, who was acting as intermediary with Henry on the couple's behalf, actually wrote in his own corrections to the letter "to add more phrases praising and exonerating Brandon."[23] Aware that this letter was going to be shared with a broader audience, Mary took pains to remind Henry and his council how she had previously married to advance the cause of England and now humbly married for her own satisfaction.[24]

What is interesting about this postscript is that Préchac spent the entire novel telling of the love affair between Mary and Brandon, yet only spent a few pages of the novel and the brief postscript detailing their relationship once they were married. This suggests that writers and readers were much more interested in the story leading up to their union, rather than reading about their relatively uneventful married life. It was the love story that and Mary's fight to marry of her own choosing that captivated readers in the seventeenth century and continues to do so today. Perhaps it was even stories such as Mary's that served as inspiration for the fairytales that he wrote in the 1690s.

Préchac's novel, while largely fictionalized, does closely follow Mary's life, even if some events take place out of order and private conversations are entirely made up. Yet, in his portrayal Brandon wants nothing more than to be with Mary, while Mary must navigate two kings and two courts, along with rivals and detractors who are all aware of her feelings for Brandon and want to make her lose her prestigious positions for it. According to Préchac, Mary begins as a naïve princess, but turns into a politically aware young woman and queen who understands her duty to both her brother and her (first) husband, only marrying Brandon once she has fulfilled those duties. However, no matter her actions, Mary is never as important to the politics of England as are her brother as King of England, her first husband as King of France, and her second husband as a military hero.

Préchac's novel, then, contributes to Mary's posthumous reputation as a lover by focusing more on Brandon, Henry VIII, and Francis I and minimizing her political agency. It is Mary's beauty and charm that give her power and make the men around her listen to her. For example, after Brandon's release from the Tower, Mary recovers from her illness so that:

---

[22] NA SP 1/10/79-80. Reprinted in Sadlack, *The French Queen's Letters*, 182–184.
[23] Sadlack, *The French Queen's Letters*, 114.
[24] Sadlack, *The French Queen's Letters*, 113.

the tranquillity [*sic*] of her mind recalled so effectually her bodily health, that she recovered from her sickness more beautiful than before. But as the King had only delayed his expedition to the War of France for her sake; so he hastened his departure, so soon as he knew her to be out of danger, and used the more precipitancy, because knowing better than any other the trouble that she and Brandon would have to bid adieu, he would not have them have time to prepare for it, nor to revive their passions. (94–95)

Here, Mary's health was so important to Henry that he delayed his war in France, yet her beauty increasing was the only noteworthy outcome of Brandon's imprisonment and release. At Mary's entry into France, Préchac writes, "yet that admirable Beauty, which had so soveraingly [*sic*] triumphed over the subjects of the King her Brother, to his continual disquiet, had no less efficacy of those of the King her husband" (167). Again, Mary's beauty made all those around her immediately fall in love with her and desire her. She gained instant queenly status in France not because of her marriage to its king, but because her beauty made her new subjects desire her to be so.

There are a couple of other things to note about Préchac's novel that increase the elusiveness of both the author and his sources. During the novel itself, Préchac does not seem to be a sympathizer of either England or France, at times telling of the virtues of Henry VIII and condemning the Duke of Longueville for political machinations. Also, Préchac mentions Anne Boleyn (Ann of Bolen) as one of Mary's attendants in France and even one of Mary's "confidents" who knew of her relationship with Brandon (189). As Anne really was one of Mary's attendants, and then stayed in France to serve Queen Claude after Mary left, it is entirely possible that Anne facilitated meetings between Mary and Brandon. If she did, that does room for much speculation as to why Mary sided with Catherine of Aragon during Henry's divorce.

One final thing to mention about Préchac's novel is that there is no mention of Mary telling Henry VIII that she would marry Louis because he commanded her to as long as she could choose her second husband. As already mentioned, Sadlack suggests that this myth was probably one started by Mary herself, as her letters mention marrying of her own choosing. Yet, Préchac did not include this detail in his novel. Perhaps this was not information that was available in France, or maybe Mary, knowing that she was going to marry Brandon all along, would have taken away from the drama of their courtship that Préchac spent so many words building up.

POSSIBLE SOURCES OF PRÉCHAC

Préchac's novel obviously is not historically accurate. Major events are out of order, such as when Henry VIII sought to divorce Catherine of Aragon, and several details are incorrect or wholly made up, such as Brandon's rivalry with the Earl of Kildare. However, Préchac must have consulted some sources on both Mary and Brandon to give him the level of detail he had about both of their lives before their marriage. There are too many details that are historically accurate to suggest that Préchac simply wrote his novel based upon passed down legend about Mary and Brandon.

Not only would Mary and Brandon's courtship have been of interest to Préchac's readers, but sources for this period of Mary's life (especially in France and in French) would have been more available for this period of Mary's life. It is not known what languages Préchac was able to read; however, it seems likely that he had access to both French and English sources, and as a parliamentarian may have even had interactions with English-speaking people at court. Préchac most likely consulted epistolary sources, those by Mary and Brandon, as well as ambassadorial accounts from both the English and French courts. From an early age, Mary's beauty and abilities were often remarked upon in both England and abroad. For example, on February 6, 1512, Erasmus wrote to Anthony of Bergen of Mary's beauty and wisdom, recording that Charles was lucky to have her as his spouse, and Préchac often focuses on Mary's beauty being so powerful that every man who meets her cannot help but fall in love with her.[25] As for depictions of Brandon, perhaps Préchac was familiar with Brandon and Mary's own letters. At least one letter by Brandon, written on April 22 from Montreuil before Mary and Brandon returned to England, uses language asking Henry for forgiveness and takes a tone that presents himself as entirely indebted to Henry.[26] If copies of Mary and Brandon's letters written in France existed in France, Préchac could have extrapolated from these letters that Brandon was a weak man because Mary was depicted as the primary instigator of the marriage and dealing with its after effects, even though the letters were meant to exonerate Brandon because penalties for committing the marriage would have been much worse for him than his wife.

[25] *Letters and Papers, Foreign and Domestic, Henry VIII*, Vol. 1, 1509–1515, ed. J.S. Brewer (London: 1920), entry 1050.

[26] See Sadlack, *The French Queen's Letters*, 112. British Library, Cotton Vespasian F.XIII, fol. 80r.

Another possible source includes a book by Pietro Carmeliano, Henry VII's Latin secretary, who wrote a description of Mary's proxy marriage to Charles that was printed by Pynson in 1508.[27] A copy was sent to King Ferdinand of Aragon.[28] This Latin version could have circulated widely proclaiming the marriage or have been in a library accessible to Préchac. Carmeliano's version constructed Mary as a virtuous, wise, well-spoken, beautiful princess ready for the international stage, even though she was only 13 years old.[29]

As for sources of Mary's life in France, the most obvious seems to be Pierre Gringore's *Pageants for the Entry of Mary Tudor into France*, printed in 1514.[30] Préchac devotes a sizable portion of his novel to Mary's entry and the pageants, probably because Gringore's work was easily accessible. Additionally, both French and Venetian accounts of the tournaments following Mary's coronation mention Brandon's military prowess, earning him the respect of Louis, another aspect Préchac focuses heavily on.[31]

Most likely, Préchac's own work is derivative of other fictional portrayals of Mary. Within a couple of decades after Louis's death, Mary as a lover was mythologized through poems and fictionalized letters that were written from her point of view and expressed her grief over the loss of her husband, while also lamenting the good treatment she received at his court.

Guillaume Crétin's, *Les poesies de Guillaume Crétin* is a letter-poem written from the point of view of Mary to Marguerite d'Alencon, Francis I's sister, and depicts Mary's grief at the loss of her husband.[32] The original date it was written is uncertain, but Crétin died in 1525. In Jean Bouchet's *Epistres Morales et Familieres du Traverseur* (1517), he offers a "letter" from Mary to

---

[27] Pietro Carmeliano, *Hoc presenti libello…Honorifica gesta solemnes cerimonie et trium-phi…Pro sponsalibus matrimonio inter prefatum illustrissimum principem Karolum, et illus-trissimam ac nobilissimam principem Dominam Mariam* (London, 1508).

[28] Bodleian Library, Douce MS 198, fols. 145–57. See James Gairdner's introduction to "the Spousells" for print history. Gairdner, "Spousells of Princess Mary," in *The Camden Miscellany*. Vol. 9 (New York: Johnson Reprints, 1895). See *Letters and Papers*, Vol. 1, entry 6 for confirmation that Ferdinand received a copy of Carmeliano's poem, which he ordered to be translated into Castilian.

[29] Sadlack, *The French Queen's Letters*, 30.

[30] Mary's presentation copy is British Library, Cotton Vespasian B.II. Charles Read Baskerville, ed., *Pierre Gringore's Pageants for the Entry of Mary Tudor into Paris* (Chicago: University of Chicago Press, 1934). Cythia Brown, ed., *Les entrées royales à Paris de Maria d'Angleterre et Claude de France* (Geneva: Librairie Droz, 2005).

[31] Richardson, *Mary Tudor*, 119. Steven Gunn, *Charles Brandon: Henry VIII's Closest Friend* (Stroud: Amberley 1988, 2015, 2016), 34–35.

[32] Guillaume Crétin, *Les poesies de Guillaume Crétin* (Paris, 1723), 191–198.

her brother, in which she praises Louis and his treatment of her.[33] Both of these sources were written in French and printed in France, so Préchac should have had access to both of them, and likely consulted them for his novel.

In 1597, more than 60 years after Mary's death, Michael Drayton printed a collection of poetry in the form of letters and included a letter written by "Marie the French Queene, to Charles Brandon, Duke of Suffolke."[34] In "Mary's" letter, she is in France immediately after the death of Louis and beckons Brandon to come to her aid and retrieve her. At points in the poem, Mary is angry that Brandon is not with her, expresses her jealousy of Margaret of Savoy, and even describes how Louis had her virginity, but as a weak man was barely able to perform. "Brandon" then pens a response to Mary in the next letter in Drayton's collection.[35] Brandon's letter is equally filled with sentiments of his love for Mary, his desire to be with her although King Henry has commanded him to be in London, and the hopelessness he felt at her marriage to Louis. He constantly recounts her beauty, which had the power to make the bedridden Louis walk again and participate in a marriage and post-nuptial tournament. Never is Suffolk angry at his and Mary's situation, rather he is presented as lover who must accept that his love is out of his reach. Préchac may not have read Drayton's poems, but in many aspects, both works are very similar, in that Brandon is lovesick and helpless and Mary's beauty is her most notable characteristic.

While it cannot be proven that Préchac did or did not consult chronicles, letters, or previously published accounts of Mary's two weddings, yet in the areas where Préchac offers much detail (that are not private conversations between Mary and Brandon), it is clear that he must have consulted some type of material that covered Mary and Brandon.

Conclusion

Perhaps David Loades's suggestion that "Mary has always been of more interest to the purveyors of fiction than to historians" rings of some truth.[36] Mary's actual character has been distorted and lost mainly due to the prevalence and popularity of fictionalized accounts of her. It seems that of all the fictional accounts of Mary, "A Song of an English Knight"

---

[33] Jean Bouchet, *Epistres Morales et Familieres du Traverseur* (Poitiers, 1545), letter 14.
[34] Michael Drayton, *Englands Heroical Epistles* (London: Printed by I.R. for N. Ling, 1597), fol. 61v–65v.
[35] Drayton, *Englands Heroical Epistles*, fol. 66r to 69v.
[36] Loades, *Mary Rose*, 13.

in the *Suffolk Garland* (1818) has remained the most popular. It is only eight stanzas long each consisting of eight lines, but in its brevity, it depicts Mary's beauty, her love for Charles Brandon, their marriage, and mentions Lady Jane Grey as Mary's granddaughter. With all of the growing scholarship in queenship studies and renewed interest in Lady Jane Grey, likely scholarship on Mary will continue also, as she serves as an excellent example of a princess, duchess, queen who understood her society and her role within it, yet managed to captivate 500 years of attention because her true self has not yet been fully uncovered.

Préchac's novel, *La Princess d'Angleterre*, although printed in France only once and in England twice, was the version of Mary's mythologized past that was told in the seventeenth century. It demonstrates that Mary remained a popular female figure in both France and England, and the numerous historical and literary sources published about her, both before and after Préchac's novel, show the popularity and relatability of her love story with Brandon. The love story proliferated in Préchac's novel, among other printed sources, might have its origin in truth, but all of these six-teenth-, seventeenth-, and eighteenth-century versions seem to lack appreciation for and agency of Mary, who did not act lovesick, but to her own advantage so neither Henry nor Francis could marry her to whom they chose. However, what is interesting is that Mary is often presented as having a wider range of emotions and abilities than Brandon; he is always a military hero, yet otherwise love sick, while Mary is a princess, queen, and dowager queen who can navigate her enemies and suitors, all while remaining true to Brandon. Préchac's influence can be felt all the way down to twentieth-century portrayals of Mary and Brandon, such as that in Disney's motion picture *The Sword and the Rose* (1953), in which it is Mary who must navigate the treacheries of both the English and French court, while Brandon tries to flee to the New World rather than manage his feelings for Mary.

BIBLIOGRAPHY

PRIMARY SOURCES

British Library
MS Cotton Caligula D.VI
MS Cotton Vespasian F.XIII
MS Cotton Vespasian B.II
Bodleian Library
Douce MS 198

Bouchet, Jean. *Epistres Morales et Familieres du Traverseur.* Poitiers, 1545.

Carmeliano, Pietro. *Hoc presenti libello...Honorifica gesta solemnes cerimonie et triumphi...pro sponsalibus matrimonio inter prefatum illustrissimum principem Karolum, et illustrissimam ac nobilissimam principem Dominam Mariam.* London, 1508.

Crétin, Guillaume. *Les poesies de Guillaume Crétin.* Paris, 1723.

Drayton, Michael. *England's Heroical Epistles.* London: Printed by I.R. for N. Ling, 1597.

Godwin, Francis. *Annales of England Containing the Reigns of Henry the Eighth, Edward the Sixth, Queen Mary written in Latin by the Right Honorable and Right Reverend Father in God, Francis Lord Bishop of Hereford.* Trans. Morgan Godwyn. London, 1630.

Hall, Edward. *The vnion of the two noble and illustre famelies of Lancastre and Yorke, beeyng long in continual discension for the croune of this noble realme with all the actes done in bothe the tymes of the princes, bothe of the one linage and of the other, beginning at the tyme of kyng Henry the fowerth, the first aucthor of this deuision, and so successiuely proceadyng to the reigne of the high and prudent prince kyng Henry the eight, the vndubitate flower and very heire of both the sayd linages.* London: Richard Grafton, 1548, 1550.

Letters and Papers, Foreign and Domestic, Henry VIII, Vol. 2, 1515–1518, ed. J.S. Brewer. London, 1864.

Letters and Papers, Foreign and Domestic, Henry VIII, Vol. 1, 1509–1515, ed. J.S. Brewer. London: 1920.

Préchac, Jean de. *La princesse d'Angleterre, ou La duchesse-reyne.* Paris: Estienne Loyson, 1677.

———. *The English Princess, or the Dutchess-Queen. A Relation of English and French Adventures. A Novel. In Two Parts.* London: Printed for Will. Cademan and Simon Neale, 1678.

———. *The Illustrious Lovers, or Princely Adventures in the Courts of England and France. Containing Sundry transactions relating to the love intrigues, noble enterprises, and gallantry: being an historical account of the famous loves of Mary sometimes Queen of France (daughter to Henry the 7th) and Charles Brandon the renown'd Duke of Suffolk: discovering the glory and grandeur of both nations. Written original in French, and now done into English.* London: Printed for William Whitwood, 1686.

SECONDARY SOURCES

Baskerville, Charles Read, ed. *Pierre Gringore's Pageants for the Entry of Mary Tudor into Paris.* Chicago: University of Chicago Press, 1934.

Brown, Cynthia, ed. *Les entrées royales à Paris de Maria d'Angleterre et Claude de France.* Geneva: Librairie Droz, 2005.

Dobson, Michael and Nicola J. Watson. *England's Elizabeth: An Afterlife in Fame and Fantasy.* Oxford: Oxford University Press, 2002.

Dowd, Michelle M. and Julia A. Eckerle. *Genre and Women's Life Writing in Early Modern England*. Aldershot: Ashgate, 2007.

Gairdner, James. "Spousells of Princess Mary." In *The Camden Miscellany*. Vol. 9. New York: Johnson Reprints, 1895.

Green, Mary Anne Everett. *Lives of the Princesses of England*. Vol. V. London: Henry Colburn, 1854.

Gunn, Steven. *Charles Brandon: Henry VIII's Closest Friend*. Stroud: Amberley 1988, 2015, 2016.

Loades, David. *Mary Rose: Tudor princess, Queen of France, the extraordinary life of Henry VIII's sister*. Stroud: Amberley, 2014.

Nussbaum, Felicity A. *The Autobiographical Subject: Gender and Ideology in Eighteenth-Century England*. Baltimore: Johns Hopkins University Press, 1989.

Oldfield, Sybil. *Collective Biography in Britain, 1550–1900: A Select Annotated Bibliography*. London: Mansell, 1999.

Richardson, Walter C. *Mary Tudor: The White Queen*. London: Peter Owen, 1970.

Sadlack, Erin A. *The French Queen's Letters: Mary Tudor Brandon and the Politics of Marriage in Sixteenth-Century Europe*. New York: Palgrave Macmillan, 2011.

Seifert, Lewis C. "Jean de Préchac." In *The Oxford Companion to Fairy Tales: The Western fairy tale tradition from medieval to modern*, edited by Jack Zipes, 400. Oxford: Oxford University Press, 2000.

Spacks, Patricia Meyer. *Imagining a Self: Autobiography and Novel in Eighteenth-Century England*. Cambridge and London: Harvard University Press, 1976.

CHAPTER 4

Virtue Betray'd: Women Writing Anne Boleyn in the Long Eighteenth Century

Stephanie Russo

The immediate posthumous reputation of Anne Boleyn was largely inscribed by men whose religious and political interests shaped their representations of her personality, relationship with Henry VIII, and the causes of her downfall.[1] From the Catholic propaganda of Nicholas Sander to the Protestant hagiography of John Foxe, a vision of Boleyn as either monstrous or saintly emerged.[2] However, as women started to write about the rise and fall of Anne Boleyn, a more complex figure emerged, prefigur-

---

[1] Eustace Chapuys's diplomatic dispatches have done much to shape the posthumous reputation of Anne Boleyn, given that they are some of the few first-hand accounts of events in the Tudor court of the 1530s. Chapuys was a staunch Catholic and close to Katherine of Aragon and Mary Tudor, and he consistently refers to Boleyn as "the Concubine." See Lauren Mackay, *Inside the Tudor Court: Henry VIII and His Six Wives Through the Writings of the Spanish Ambassador Eustace Chapuys* (Stroud: Amberley, 2014).

[2] John Foxe, *The Unabridged Acts and Monuments Online* or *TAMO* (HRI Online Publications, Sheffield, 2011). Available from: http://www.johnfoxe.org [Accessed: 31 July 2017]; Nicholas Sander, *The Rise and Growth of the Anglican Schism*, edited by D. Lewis (London: 1877).

S. Russo (✉)
Department of English, Macquarie University, Sydney, NSW, Australia

© The Author(s) 2019
E. Paranque (ed.), *Remembering Queens and Kings of Early Modern England and France*, Queenship and Power,
https://doi.org/10.1007/978-3-030-22344-1_4

51

ing contemporary representations of Anne Boleyn as a proto-feminist figure trapped and preyed upon in a rigidly patriarchal world. This chapter compares a number of accounts of Anne Boleyn's life by women in the long eighteenth century: Madame d'Aulnoy, Sarah Fielding, and Mary Hays. Each writer resists representing Boleyn as straightforwardly either whore or martyr. While d'Aulnoy, Fielding, and Hays differ markedly in the focus of their accounts, they all stress Boleyn's status as victim of the tyranny of men, with Fielding, in particular, demonstrating that her victimization at the hands of men commenced well before Henry entered her life. However, at the same time, the Boleyn constructed by these women emerges as an intelligent, perceptive political operator, only finally undone by a system that both rewards and destroys women for exerting the only power they possess: their sexuality. Exploring the symbolic significance of Anne Boleyn to three of her earliest female biographers sheds new light on both the development of the posthumous reputation of Anne Boleyn, and the ways in which perceptions about women and history were transforming during the period.

There are few English queens whose biographies have been as contested as that of Anne Boleyn. As the woman who prompted the English Reformation, insofar as the King's "great matter" was the cause of the split from the Vatican, Boleyn was useful to Protestants as a martyr to the reformist cause. She accordingly appears in John Foxe's *The Acts and Monuments of the Church* (known as the *Book of Martyrs*), in which she is deified as one of the heroines of Protestantism. However, Boleyn's interest in reform was also convenient to Catholic propagandists, as they could attribute what they saw as the blame for the Reformation to her pernicious sexual influence over Henry. Nicholas Sander's *The Rise and Growth of the Anglican Schism* is a notorious example of such polemic, and it is in this text that some of the most notorious myths about Boleyn arose: namely, that she had a goiter on her chin and an extra finger, and that she was Henry's daughter through an affair he had with her mother, Elizabeth Boleyn. Since her execution in 1536, Boleyn's body had become a site upon which competing religious, political, and sexual ideologies were inscribed, a practice that continues to this day. In her 2017 Reith Lectures, Hilary Mantel, author of *Wolf Hall* and *Bring Up the Bodies*, in which Boleyn plays a key role, addressed the ongoing fascination of the story of Anne Boleyn, arguing that, "you can tell that story and tell it. Put it through hundreds of iterations. But still, there seems to be a piece of the puzzle missing."[3] The story of the rise and fall of Boleyn, Mantel suggests, is so fundamentally strange and compelling that it resists inscription, even as it has been constantly revisited and reinterpreted by historian and novelist alike.[4]

One of the most popular eighteenth-century representations of Anne Boleyn was John Banks's popular 1682 play *Vertue Betray'd; or, Anna Bullen*. As the title suggests, this play was somewhat interested in Boleyn's personal experiences and was designed to elicit emotion in the viewer. However, Susan Bordo also describes the play as "an undisguised grenade in the Protestant/Catholic culture wars," emphasizing the play's intervention into religious debates by stressing Boleyn's place as Protestant martyr.[5] However, despite the emphasis that the play places on the affective qualities of the Boleyn story, the Boleyn presented in the play is still little more than a tool through which to stage sectarian interests. As she is about to be executed, for example, she proclaims that "I both forgive, and bless him, and think him as my kindest Benefactor," and emphasis is placed on the legacy of Protestantism that is fulfilled by her daughter Elizabeth.[6]

While this vision of Anne Boleyn prefigured later sympathetic accounts, it was women's representations of Anne Boleyn over the course of the long eighteenth century that present the most interesting, nuanced versions of Boleyn's biography to this point in history, as well as shaped subsequent representations of the executed Queen. It was also women writers who were among the first to consider the effect of Henry's tyranny upon the emotional lives of the women who surround him. What unites these accounts is their representation of Boleyn as a victim of Henry's appetites. As such, they anticipate Karen Lindsey's argument that "[t]oday, Henry's

---

[3] Hilary Mantel, "The BBC Reith Lectures: The Day Is For the Living," 13 June 2017, http://www.bbc.co.uk/programmes/b08tcbrp

[4] Retha Warnicke provides a valuable summation of Boleyn historiography, from the sixteenth century to quite recent interpretations, in her *Wicked Women of Tudor England: Queens, Aristocrats, Commoners* (New York: Palgrave Macmillan, 2012), 15–44. The most commonly consulted biography of Boleyn in recent years has been Eric Ives, *The Life and Death of Anne Boleyn* (Malden: Blackwell, 2004). Warnicke's more recent *Elizabeth of York and her Six Daughters-in-Law: Fashioning Tudor Queenship, 1485–1547* (New York: Palgrave Macmillan, 2017), is also useful in its comparison of the queenship of Anne to those of Henry's other queens. However, my focus here is on literary representations of Boleyn, which often deviate sharply, and often inexplicably, from the historical consensus.

[5] Susan Bordo, *The Creation of Anne Boleyn: A New Look at England's Most Notorious Queen* (Boston: Mariner, 2014), 143.

[6] John Banks, *Vertue Betray'd: or, Anna Bullen* (London: R. Wellington, 1715), 62.

approach to Ann would be instantly identifiable as sexual harassment."[7] As Lindsey writes, the only recourse for Boleyn was to "continue...to dodge her pursuer's advances while sparing his feelings."[8] Women understood the limited options available to Boleyn, who had observed through her sister's example how quickly a royal mistress could fall from favor. D'Aulnoy, Fielding, and Hays consistently stress how incessant Henry was in his pursuit of Boleyn, and the extent to which her emotions were either engaged elsewhere, or were entirely unmoved by the King. In no account is Boleyn in love with the King, but all three women stress the extent to which Boleyn was trapped by Henry's desire, despite what she may have wanted.

It is hardly surprising that it was the long eighteenth century in which more psychologically nuanced portraits of Boleyn began to be written, given that this was the period that saw the rise of the novel and the cult of sensibility. While historical writing was still gendered male, and novels were largely associated with a female readership, Mark Salber Phillips writes that in the eighteenth century, "there is evidence that many writers reconceived the reader's engagement with the historical narrative in more inward and sentimental terms."[9] As such, two of these accounts deploy fictional apparatuses in order to frame their affective accounts of Boleyn. All three of these accounts, too, emphasize the private life of Anne Boleyn. However, none of the texts consider the nature of Boleyn's religion faith.[10] While they all represent Boleyn as a virtuous woman to varying degrees, the nature of her belief is not a central issue in any of the texts, which are far more interested in the way Boleyn's life has been shaped and destroyed by men. D'Aulnoy, Fielding, and Hays thus all neatly sidestep the Catholic-Protestant war that had been played out in previous representations of the body of the Queen. Fielding's Anne even complains from beyond the grave about the fact that she has been made, "the continual Subject of the Cavils of contending Parties."[11] As Christopher Johnson writes of Fielding's

[7] Karen Lindsey, *Divorced, Beheaded, Survived: A Feminist Reinterpretation of the Wives of Henry VIII* (Reading: Addison-Wesley, 1995), 58.

[8] Ibid, 58.

[9] Mark Salber Phillips, *Society and Sentiment: Genres of Historical Writing in Britain, 1740–1820* (Princeton: Princeton University Press, 2000), 103.

[10] G. W. Bernard considers the nature of Anne's interest in reform in: G.W. Bernard, "Anne Boleyn's Religion," *The Historical Journal* 36, no. 1 (1993): 1–20.

[11] Sarah Fielding, "Wherein Anna Boleyn relates the History of Her Life," in Henry Fielding, *A Journey from This World to the Next*, edited by Ian A. Bell and Andrew Varney (Oxford: Oxford University Press, 1997), 102.

account, "this most other-worldly of texts is, ironically, concerned entirely with this world and Boleyn's mortal experiences."[12] The women who wrote about Boleyn were much less interested in religious conflict than their male predecessors, instead focusing on Boleyn's experience as a woman in the patriarchal world of the Tudor court. We see in these accounts, therefore, a much closer interest in Boleyn's childhood, with both D'Aulnoy and Fielding focusing on Boleyn's life prior to her relationship with Henry. Only Hays takes Boleyn's downfall as her focus. Fielding, in particular, attempts to answer the question that is perhaps the most interesting to modern readers, and the question which fiction is most equipped to answer: what did it feel like to be Anne Boleyn? Boleyn's first words in Fielding's narrative—"I am going now truly to recount a Life"—suggest that this is a private confession, told to the reader in the manner of unfolding a secret, and thus Fielding draws the reader into a close relationship with Boleyn.[13] The affective nature of fiction allowed a closer consideration of the imagined interiority of Boleyn.

The earliest of the female biographers examined here was Marie-Catherine Le Jumel de Barneville, known as Madame d'Aulnoy. D'Aulnoy was famous amongst early eighteenth-century readers for her fairy tales, but she also specialized in "secret histories" of historical figures.[14] Her use of this genre perhaps accounts for why a French woman was so interested in the life of an English queen—a queen executed for sexual transgression is tailor-made for the secret history genre, with its focus on uncovering the supposed "truth" behind history's most notorious scandals. Indeed, Bordo describes d'Aulnoy's biography of Boleyn as "a 'real life' dystopian version of the fairy-tale form she favoured – clever, generous and beautiful girl, wicked king, but no happy ending."[15] Indeed, so popular were d'Aulnoy's fairy tales that Jack Zipes writes that she "set a trend in France that became epidemic among her acquaintances and other readers of her

[12] Christopher D. Johnson, "History, Fiction, and the Emergence of an Artistic Vision: Sarah Fielding's Anna Boleyn Narrative," *New Perspectives on the Eighteenth Century* 6.1 (2009): 29.

[13] Fielding, 102.

[14] Melvin D. Palmer describes d'Aulnoy as occupying "an important place in the history of French-English prose fiction in the formative years that saw the rise of the modern novel." Melvin D. Palmer, "Madame d'Aulnoy in England," *Comparative Literature* 27.3 (1975), 237.

[15] Bordo, 147.

class."[16] Banks lifted many plot elements from d'Aulnoy for *Vertue Betray'd*, most notably the relationship between Boleyn and Henry Percy, and the role of Elizabeth Blount in the downfall of Boleyn. While a prior relationship of some description between Boleyn and Percy is widely accepted, even if the exact nature of that relationship remains unclear, there is no historical evidence that Blount had any role in the downfall of the Queen.[17] D'Aulnoy's memoir of Anne Boleyn is found in the deceptively titled *The Novels of Elizabeth, Queen of England, Containing the History of Queen Ann of Bullen*. While Elizabeth might appear to be the focus of the text, she appears only in the framing device that surrounds the biography of Boleyn. Elizabeth has, rather improbably, been shielded from an awareness of the fate of her mother, and entreats the Duke of Northumberland to help her understand why her father executed her mother. The fact that the recipient of the tale of Anne Boleyn is Elizabeth immediately suggests a highly flattering account will ensue. D'Aulnoy protests that Northumberland, as narrator, is "exempt from Partiality," although it is not clear why this might be.[18] It should be noted, however, that while Northumberland is consistently positive in his portrayal of Boleyn, the portrait of Henry that unfolds is hardly flattering, which might not have been pleasing to the historical Elizabeth. D'Aulnoy thus clearly signals that this is a woman's story, about a woman and intended for a female listener: Elizabeth seeks her mother's story, saying, "she should be very glad that the Duke of *Northumberland* would relate it, he having been a Witness to the great of those things which did conduct to that wicked Action."[19] As such, it is a complex and nuanced representation of the ways in which male power shaped the lives of the women around them, from the perspective of a woman whose sexuality precipitates both her rise and her fall, and directed toward a woman whose denial of sexuality became central to her power. It is also significant that d'Aulnoy's account foregrounds the triumph and majesty of Queen Elizabeth so

---

[16] Jack Zipes, "The Meaning of Fairy Tale Within the Evolution of Culture," *Marvels & Tales* 25.2 (2011), 223.

[17] Bessie Blount was married off to Gilbert Tailboys after the dissolution of her affair with the King, and had little further role in the Tudor court. See Elizabeth Norton, *Bessie Blount: Mistress to Henry VIII* (Stroud: Amberley Press, 2011).

[18] D'Aulnoy, Madame. *The Novels of Elizabeth, Queen of England, Containing the History of Queen Ann of Bullen. Faithfully Rendered into English by S.H.* (London: Mark Pardoe, 1680), 3.

[19] D'Aulnoy, 3.

explicitly. As Julie Crane has argued of contemporary representations of Anne Boleyn, Boleyn functions as "an achievement finally realised in her daughter Elizabeth, who is implicated in her mother's disgrace but is also triumphant in the face of it."[20] Boleyn may have fallen, but Elizabeth is the manifestation of her posthumous victory. D'Aulnoy thus transforms a narrative of disgrace and execution into one of triumph and power: the end of the account affirms that "the Princess *Elizabeth* her Daughter, who now governs *England* with so great splendour and glory, inherits her Vertue as well as the Crown, which is her undoubted right."[21]

In d'Aulnoy's biography of Anne, which bears little relationship to the historical record throughout, it is Henry Percy (here spelt Piercy) who is Boleyn's true love. It is unclear why, specifically, d'Aulnoy deviates from the historical record in the specific ways she does, but evidently her concern here was not fact, but instead, the construction of a suitably romantic tale. The tragedy of Boleyn's life is therefore amplified by her separation from the man she loves. When Piercy contrives to sacrifice himself during a tournament out of despair, Anne is overcome: "a mortal grief rob'd her of her Soul, and that Love which was lodged in her heart, in spight [*sic*] of all her attacks to chase it thence, made her feel his power at this time more than in the whole course of her life."[22] D'Aulnoy's Boleyn only gives into marriage with Henry because the King of France, her parents, and Percy himself signal that she must consent to the will of the King: "she could no longer oppose so great difficulties."[23] D'Aulnoy is thus the first of Boleyn's memoirists to suggest that Henry's pursuit of Boleyn might have interfered with her own sexual desires. By stressing Henry's overwhelming power over Boleyn, d'Aulnoy shifts the focus of earlier representations from an examination of Boleyn's behavior to a critique of untrammeled masculine authority. Henry thus becomes the cruel tyrant of fairy tale: the man who has separated Boleyn from her true love. D'Aulnoy even invents a letter expressing Boleyn's heartache at her separation from Percy: "It is forbidden me to see you it is a cruel Necessity unto which I am forced to obey."[24] D'Aulnoy's representation of Anne as tragic lover also anticipates

---

[20] Julie Crane, "Whoso list to hunt: The literary fortunes of Anne Boleyn," in *The Female Figure in Contemporary Historical Fiction*, edited by K. Cooper and E. Short (Basingstoke: Palgrave Macmillan, 2012), 84 (76–91).
[21] D'Aulnoy, 133.
[22] D'Aulnoy, 101–2.
[23] D'Aulnoy, 83.
[24] D'Aulnoy, 53.

a broader shift from Boleyn as avatar of religious tension to heroine of romance fiction, which would become an increasing focus in literary representations of Anne into the eighteenth and nineteenth centuries.

Unlike earlier one-dimensional portraits of Anne Boleyn, d'Aulnoy represents Boleyn as possessing both moral fortitude and intense sexual appeal. The King of France notes that she is worthy of the position of queen, while also admitting he has hardly been immune to her charms: "she had vertue [*sic*] [which] made her worthy of that honour he decreed for her."[25] In this account, so free is Boleyn of any kind of political ambition that she does not even register jealousy when the King transfers his affections to Jane Seymour, telling Norris that "she should be so far from perplexing her self with an incommodious Jealousie, that she should be joyful to see him search his satisfaction."[26] However, while Banks's Boleyn, following earlier representations, is a flat character in her flawlessness, d'Aulnoy's Boleyn is more psychologically complex. She persists in loving Percy, and declaring that love, even after her marriage to the King. In an enlightening incident, too, she accuses Percy of inconstancy in love, not recognizing that he married another woman in order to protect her from the King's jealousy.[27] Boleyn is a woman capable of jealousy and anger but not, crucially, over Henry. By the eighteenth century, it seems that most could no longer believe that Boleyn's relationship with Henry was based on love.

Despite d'Aulnoy's interest in the mechanisms of patriarchal power, she nevertheless makes a woman responsible for Boleyn's downfall. Elizabeth Blount, Henry's mistress, is consumed by jealousy and hatred toward Anne, and "caused a hundred things to be published against the Vertue of this Princess," despite the fact that the historical Blount's affair had ended by the time Henry became involved with Anne Boleyn.[28] Blount, who is, ahistorically, here the former lover of George Boleyn, is also responsible for the rumors about the incestuous relationship of the Boleyn siblings. Henry Norris, too, is responsible for placing Jane Seymour before the King, and for telling Anne of the affair, in the hopes that it will prompt Anne to betray the King by sleeping with him.[29] The King then intercepts

[25] D'Aulnoy, 83.
[26] D'Aulnoy, 89.
[27] D'Aulnoy, 66–7.
[28] D'Aulnoy, 91.
[29] D'Aulnoy, 88.

a letter that Norris has sent to a confidant confessing his love for Anne, and he is thus undone. D'Aulnoy thus resists representing women solely as helpless victims of male tyranny. However, crucially, it is once again Boleyn's sexual appeal, and the ways in which men feel authorized to act upon this desire, that leads to her downfall. Norris essentially tries to trick Boleyn into an extramarital affair. Everywhere Boleyn went, it seems, she was at risk from men who would not resist acting upon their sexual desire for her, despite what she may have wanted or desired.[30]

This Boleyn might be at consistent risk of sexual harassment, but she is also intelligent and determined. D'Aulnoy represents Boleyn as demonstrating an almost inhuman fortitude in the face of despair, as she "submitted to the King's orders without suffering the least murmur against his injustice to escape out of her mouth."[31] When she writes to the King before her death, she tells him that "I do earnestly desire, that the knowledge of my innocent Conduct may never interrupt or disturb your tranquillity, and for a recompence of those felicities you are now going to procure me, I heartily pray you may enjoy perpetual ones."[32] As befits a story narrated to her grown daughter, Boleyn's final thoughts are for her daughter, as she implores the crowd to "assist one day (if there be occasion) those legitimate Rights which her Condition hath given her."[33] While Boleyn might have been defeated by the machinations of jealous, aggressive men and scheming women, it is Elizabeth who is a living testament to Boleyn's worth as a woman and as queen: d'Aulnoy even explicitly says that she "was altogether worthy of that Grandeur to which she was raised."[34] It is an account that affirms both the danger that women constantly found themselves in within the Tudor court, as well as one that celebrates women's power by stressing the female lineage that passed from Anne Boleyn to Elizabeth.

Sarah Fielding's account of Anne Boleyn is an interesting example of writing about the Queen, because for the first time, Boleyn is allowed to speak for herself: Fielding uses the first-person to allow Boleyn to appear

---

[30] This representation of Boleyn as constantly preyed upon was probably a deliberate attempt to counteract accusations made at her trial that she possessed inordinate sexual desires. As Lindsey notes, "it is ironic that Henry would choose to believe this, since it had taken him seven years of courtship to get Ann into his bed" (Lindsey, 126).

[31] D'Aulnoy, 105–6.

[32] D'Aulnoy, 117.

[33] D'Aulnoy, 128

[34] D'Aulnoy, 133.

to narrate her own story. While this narrative of the life and death of Anne Boleyn constitutes one of the final chapters of Henry Fielding's *A Journey from This World to the Next*, this chapter has been persuasively attributed to Sarah Fielding, and her authorship is now widely accepted.[35] The conceit of Henry Fielding's novel is that of a journey through the afterlife, and this contrivance allows Sarah Fielding to allow Boleyn to speak to her own experiences from beyond the grave. Fielding's account is thus far more intimate than previous biographies, and, unusually, takes as its focus Boleyn's childhood and life before her marriage to Henry. Fielding is apparently less interested in Boleyn's later life, with her downfall covering less than two pages of a 16-page chapter. The motivations for the inclusion of Anne Boleyn's story in Fielding's brother's novel must, then, lie beyond the machinations of power in the Tudor court.

Like d'Aulnoy, Fielding was interested in uncovering the psychology of Boleyn, and accordingly, while her Boleyn is also an innocent victim of Henry's tyranny, she is also not completely flawless. Christopher Johnson has explicitly connected Fielding's short account of Boleyn's life to her interest in the novel's capacity to capture psychological realism: "Fielding's largely – and recognizably novelistic – purposes, [were] to explore the inner workings of her characters' minds and to offer her readers a clear warning against the dangers of vanity and pride."[36] The use of the first-person narrative voice is thus clearly central to Fielding's endeavor, as it allowed her to focus on the affective experiences of Boleyn in ways that a third-person account could never accomplish. However, Fielding's Boleyn also anticipates contemporary representations of Boleyn as a femme fatale. At the age of 14, Fielding's Boleyn admits that she became vain: "my Vanity grew strong, and my Heart fluttered with joy at every Compliment paid to my Beauty."[37] Her first love is an unnamed nobleman of the French court (who appears to be the invention of Fielding) who "gave every thing he said and did such an Air of Tenderness, that every Woman he spoke to, flattered her self with being the Object of his Love."[38] However, Boleyn soon learns that men quickly tire of what they possess, and the man grows cold.[39] This rejection, then, is an early lesson about what happens to

---

[35] F. J. Burrows and A. J. Hassall, "*Anna Boleyn* and the Authenticity of Fielding's Feminine Narratives," *Eighteenth-Century Studies* 21 (1988): 429–45.

[36] Johnson, 24.

[37] Fielding, 102.

[38] Fielding, 103.

[39] Fielding, 104.

women who succumb too easily to the men who pursue them—the reader is prompted to recognize here that this early disappointment lies behind her infamous deferral of Henry's attentions. Boleyn also discusses her aptitude in the art of pleasing men: "I observed that most Men generally liked in Women what was most opposite to their own characters."[40] She begins to cultivate artifices designed to attract the attention of men, but she does so not as a manifestation of her lust for power, but because she has learnt through experience that such stratagems are necessary in order to navigate the world of which she is a part. Boleyn's legendary power over men thus becomes a survival strategy. Again, as with d'Aulnoy, Boleyn's story is one of incessant sexual harassment, but Fielding's Boleyn had developed ways to manipulate and hold off the men who pursued her.

What Fielding effectively does, then, is use Boleyn as a means by which to stage a critique of marriage and courtship in a rigidly patriarchal social order. Elizabeth Goodhue has thus read Fielding's work as satirical, and writes that she represents Boleyn as, "neither angel nor whore, she speaks as a woman whose experience on the marriage market makes her justified in satirizing coquettish men and critiquing the patriarchal political system that confers value on women solely for their beauty."[41] Percy, in this account, is the architect of his own misfortune, for when he asks Boleyn to meet him at court, she catches the eye of the King, and two days later he is told by Wolsey never to think of her again. Percy's love for Boleyn seems rather limp, as he quickly renounces his claim on Boleyn, a move which prompts her to consider that "if he could part with me, the matter was not much."[42] Percy has appealed to Boleyn because of his apparent difference from the coquettish men of the French court, but what Boleyn finds is that there is little difference between French and English men when it comes to the marriage market. She is a valuable commodity of exchange, and so can simply be passed along to the most powerful man who expresses interest in possessing her.

It is noteworthy, too, that Henry is all but absent from Boleyn's narration of her life story. He is simply described as "amorous," and all but elided except insofar as he facilitates her rise and fall.[43] What is clear is how

---

[40] Fielding, 106.
[41] Elizabeth Goodhue, "At the Margins of Menippean Dialogue: Sarah Fielding's "History of Anne Boleyn" and the Muted Female Figures of Lucian's Satiric Underworld," *Tulsa Studies in Women's Literature* 29.2 (2010), 266.
[42] Fielding, 111.
[43] Fielding, 112.

deftly Boleyn manages him, prompting her to ruefully reflect that "nothing is easier than to make a Man angry with a Woman he wants to be rid of, and who stands in the way between him and his Pleasures."[44] While Fielding's Boleyn is initially virtuous, she does become rather manipulative, as she admits that whenever the divorce is mentioned, "I used such Arguments against it, as I though the most likely to make him the more eager for it."[45] Boleyn has no real regard for Henry, but is eager to secure the divorce because it will ensure her position, despite the fact that she admits to actually hating the King: "the Aversion I had naturally to the King was much more difficult to dissemble after Marriage than before, and grew into a perfect Detestation."[46] As Goodhue writes, "Fielding allows England's most famous surrogate queen to voice concern about the degree to which marital and political economies depend on reducing women to the status of silent objects and encouraging women's complicity with that reduction."[47] Boleyn feels nothing but hatred for the King, yet she must capture and hold his interest in order to win the marital game that ultimately destroys her when a new, younger player enters the fold. It is a representation of marriage and courtship that would have been well understood by a female reader of the eighteenth century. As Lawrence Stone has famously argued, the eighteenth century saw the gradual shift in public perceptions toward marriage, so that it was transformed from an economic arrangement to the affective union we understand today, although some of Stone's assertions have been challenged by later historians.[48] Much of women's writing from across the eighteenth century, most notably that of Frances Burney, Jane Austen and Mary Wollstonecraft, was interested in staging a similar critique of marriage and courtship as that of Fielding. Even while definitions of marriage were shifting, then, it was clear that many women still saw themselves as objects of exchange within the marriage market, and could therefore relate to Boleyn's struggles with men.

Fielding's interest in the psychological complexity of Boleyn is again manifested in her shifting relationship to her own queenship. Boleyn is initially negative in her attitude toward the possibility of becoming queen,

---

[44] Fielding, 114.
[45] Fielding, 112.
[46] Fielding, 115.
[47] Goodhue, 279.
[48] Lawrence Stone, *The Family, Sex, and Marriage in England, 1500–1800* (London: Weidenfeld & Nicolson, 1977).

largely because of her experiences in the French court: "I would not live in a Court again to be the greatest Queen in the World."[49] However, as her coronation draws nearer, her attitude changes as, "my Heart fluttered, and my Eyes were dazzled with the View of being seated on a Throne."[50] Her initial hesitancy about her role in the court is overcome as soon as she gets a taste of the power and majesty of queenship. Boleyn's own assessment of her behavior is that "the chief Things that lay on my Conscience, were the Arts I made use of to induce the King to part with the Queen, my ill Usage of Lady *Mary*, and my jilting Lord *Peircy*."[51] However, at the end of her account, Boleyn is welcomed into Elysium, as the judge Minos considered that "whoever had suffered being a Queen for four Years, and been sensible during all that time of the real Misery which attends that exalted Station, ought to be forgiven whatever she had done to obtain it."[52] Fielding's interest is the real bodily experience of Anne Boleyn the woman. Anne Boleyn may have played a high stakes game in attempting to shore up her own power, but Fielding suggests, she should be exonerated because the position of queen carries with it so much inherent misery. It is a remarkably balanced view of the Queen, which neither brushes aside Boleyn's least attractive behavior, nor casts blame on Boleyn for those actions she felt compelled upon to take.

Mary Hays's account of the life of Anne Boleyn is found within her landmark 1803 multi-volume work of feminist history, *Female Biography*, the first history of women to be to be written since Christine de Pizan's *City of Ladies* in 1405.[53] In the preface, Hays explains that "my pen has been taken up in the cause, and for the benefit, of my own sex."[54] She thus

---

[49] Fielding, 110.
[50] Fielding, 110.
[51] Fielding, 117.
[52] Fielding, 117.
[53] Anne Boleyn is also featured in Matilda Betham's *Biographical Dictionary of Celebrated Women*, published in 1804. However, Betham's entry on Boleyn is focused on Henry's attempts to secure a divorce, as well as the circumstances of her downfall, and is less interested in Boleyn herself. Betham does note, however, that Boleyn's innocence can be seen in "her serenity, and even cheerfulness, while under confinement and sentence of death" (Matilda Betham, *Biographical Dictionary of Celebrated Women* (London: B. Crosby & Co, 1804), 139).
[54] Mary Hays, *Female Biography; or, Memoirs of Illustrious and Celebrated Women, Of All Ages and Countries. Alphabetically Arranged* (London: Richard Phillips, 1803), I.iii. All forthcoming page references to this text are from this edition and are cited by volume and page number.

explicitly positions the text as part of an attempt to celebrate the biographies of prominent women, as well as to educate her female readers about women's history. As Adrianne Chernock has noted, authors of "women worthy" literature during the period of the American and French Revolutions often used biographies of notable women to "tout women's intellectual capabilities and to underscore their nation's continuing obligation to serve and promote women's interests."[55] Hays is thus situating her work squarely within the revolutionary "rights of women" debate of the 1790s. Similarly, Gina Luria Walker has written that *Female Biography* is significant as "Hays sought to arouse enthusiasm for women's achievements, irrespective of conventional prejudices towards a political party or religious persuasion, endorsing figures that did not conform to traditional moral codes."[56] *Female Biography* is consciously modeled on Pierre Bayle's *Historical and Critical Dictionary* (1697), in which he tried to recuperate the life stories of those figures whose lives were either ignored or distorted by history.[57] However, in focusing on female lives, Hays extends Bayle's project to uncover how "women attested in historical records had been criticized, ignored, trivialized, manipulated and mistrusted."[58] This interest in recuperating the lives and reputations of historically maligned, morally dubious woman renders Boleyn an ideal candidate for examination as part of Hays's corpus of women, although it should be noted that her biography of Boleyn is relatively short compared to other entries. What the inclusion of Boleyn amongst Hays's "women worthy" collection anticipates is Boleyn's contemporary appeal to young women as a kind of proto-feminist icon, a subject canvased at length by Susan Bordo.[59]

Hays was known as a radical dissenter in the 1790s, and much of the recent criticism of *Female Biography* has centered on the extent to which that text is an extension of Hays's radicalism, or a capitulation to a more

---

[55] Arianne Chernock, "Gender and Politics of Exceptionalism in the Writing of British Women's History," in *Making Women's Histories: Beyond National Perspectives*, edited by Pamela S. Nadell and Kate Haulman (New York: NYU Press, 2013), 122.

[56] Gina Luria Walker, "Women's Voices," in *The Cambridge Companion to British Literature of The French Revolution in the 1790s*, edited by Pamela Clemit (Cambridge: Cambridge University Press, 2011), 157.

[57] Hays lists Bayle as one of the primary sources for her biography of Boleyn.

[58] Gina Luria Walker, "The invention of Female Biography," *Enlightenment and Dissent* 29 (2014), 87 (79–136).

[59] Bordo, *The Creation of Anne Boleyn*, 246–259.

conventionally domestic mode of representing female experience.[60] Hays spends barely any time accounting for Boleyn's life prior to her involvement with the King, with the marriage of Henry and Boleyn occurring by the third page of Boleyn's biography. An engagement to Henry Percy, represented by Fielding as the love of Boleyn's life, is here clearly only concocted by Henry as a means by which to justify annulling his marriage to Boleyn. What is of interest to Hays, unlike D'Aulnoy or Fielding, is the downfall of Boleyn, and her biography is interested in accounting for both the historical circumstances of her trial and execution. Like the Henry represented by d'Aulnoy and Fielding, Hays's Henry is a man who cannot accept sexual rejection and yet, is titillated by the thrill of the chase: "Anne quickly perceived her influence over the heart of the monarch, whose passion, either from principle or policy, she absolutely resisted."[61] Remarkably, Hays believes that "in becoming the concubine of the king, she would perhaps have committed an action less reprehensible, than in being the cause of the dethronement and humiliation of the queen."[62] What unites all three accounts is their understanding of the uniquely difficult circumstances Boleyn faced in dealing with the unwanted sexual advances of the King, but here Hays goes one step further in suggesting that an illicit sexual liaison would have been the wiser path.

Hays is also very clear about what lay behind the downfall of Boleyn, arguing that, "with the removal of these obstacles, his love, which opposition had served but to inflame, began to languish and visibly decay."[63] Hays's assessment here recalls the Boleyn of Fielding's account recognizing that men tire of women who they have obtained. Hays's emphasis is on the crimes of Henry as man and as tyrant. Her assessment of Boleyn's character is that she was simply too enthusiastic a player in the game of courtly romance: "no real stigma has been thrown on the conduct of

---

[60] Mary Spongberg has argued that *Female Biography* represents a shift in Hays's writing and that, "following More, Hays maintained that women's influence was best used in the domestic rather than the public sphere" (Mary Spongberg, *Writing Women's History Since the Renaissance* (Basingstoke: Palgrave Macmillan, 2002), 117). However, as Andrew McInnes convincingly argues, "Hays devotes the longest, and most detailed, biographies to women who in no way fit early nineteenth-century ideals of the domestic heroine" (Andrew McInnes, "Feminism in the Footnotes: Wollstonecraft's Ghost in Mary Hays' *Female Biography*," *Life Writing* 8.3 (2011), 279).

[61] Hays, *Female Biography*, II.10.
[62] Hays, *Female Biography*, II.10.
[63] Hays, *Female Biography*, II.12.

Anne, but a certain levity of spirit and gaiety of character...rendered her manners unguarded."[64] While Fielding emphasizes the effect that coquettish men have had upon Boleyn's behavior, Hays insists that "more vain than proud, she took a coquetish [sic] pleasure in beholding the effect of her charms."[65] Indeed, Hays's argument here anticipates the assessment of Greg Walker, who argues that "the kind of flirtatious gossip that seemed to flourish in [Boleyn's] household was in the end her undoing."[66] However, Hays's final assessment of the accusations against Anne is that "such absurdities were, in those times, admitted, as a justification for sacrificing an innocent woman and a queen to the caprice of a cruel and arbitrary tyrant."[67] Hays's Boleyn is neither flawless nor culpable, and again, like Fielding, she avoids representing Boleyn as an icon of religious conflict to focus on human behavior and emotion.

In 1821, Hays produced another account of the life of Anne Boleyn, which appears in her *Memoirs of queens, illustrious and celebrated*. This account repeats the themes of Hays's earlier biography, with Hays commenting that Henry's interest in Boleyn was "stimulated by [her] opposition," and indeed, much of the biography that appears in *Memoirs of queens* is lifted verbatim from *Female Biography*.[68] Hays repeats, for example, her uncertainty about why Boleyn rejected the attentions of the King, saying that, "she perceived her power over the passions of the monarch, and, whether from principle or policy, appeared to discourage his attentions."[69] Hays's emphasis on Henry as a sexual aggressor is confirmed again in *Memoirs of queens*, as she notes that "[Boleyn's] most effectual justification was the marriage of the king with Jane Seymour on the day following her immolation."[70] Boleyn's execution was not about her moral failings, but instead maliciously concocted to facilitate Henry's speedy marriage to her replacement; another reminder of women's powerlessness in the marriage market.

---

[64] Hays, *Female Biography*, II.14.

[65] Hays, *Female Biography*, II.13.

[66] Greg Walker, "Rethinking the Fall of Anne Boleyn," *The Historical Journal* 45.1 (2002), 26 (1–29).

[67] Hays, *Female Biography*, II.21.

[68] Mary Hays, *Memoirs of queens, illustrious and celebrated* (London: T. & J. Allman, 1821), 78. All forthcoming references to this text refer to this edition and are cited by page number.

[69] Hays, *Memoirs of Queens*, 58.

[70] Hays, *Memoirs of Queens*, 86.

While d'Aulnoy and Fielding couch their accounts of Boleyn in some kind of fictional apparatus, Hays's representation is far more obviously "historical" in its deployment of biography. However, even within the apparently non-fictional genre of biography, Hays demonstrates an interest in going beyond known facts and representing something of the personality of the Queen. Hays acknowledges what she perceives as the importance of character in attracting women to history, saying that women's "understandings are principally accessible through their affections: they delight in minute delineation of character" (*Female Biography*, I.iv). Hays makes no attempt to embody Boleyn's voice within the mechanisms of fiction, as d'Aulnoy and Fielding do, but still focuses on the affective experience of the Queen. As Miriam L. Wallace writes, *Female Biography* "stands as an overt intervention in expanding the political sphere to include personal life, affect, and female embodiment, and to cast back into history with this reconfiguration."[71] As such, Hays's interest in her biography of Anne Boleyn goes beyond the recitation of historical fact, or a summation of a didactic message that can be construed by an account of her rise and fall.[72]

Both of Hays's accounts of Boleyn seem calculated to generate sympathy from the reader. Boleyn is represented as an intelligent, measured woman whose only fault was her propensity to adopt the mode of courtly flirtation that she had been exposed to as a lady-in-waiting at the French court. Hays insists on Boleyn's intelligence, which enabled her to meet her accusations in court calmly: "Anne, unassisted by counsel, defended her own cause with a clearness and presence of mind that, on every one not pre-determined to find her guilty, produced conviction of her innocence."[73] Hays is also psychologically astute enough in her representation of Henry to recognize that it was precisely this French glamour and wit that had initially attracted Henry to Boleyn. To an audience of women readers who understood exactly how this double bind in relation to female sexuality operated, Hays's portrait of Boleyn would have been instantly recognizable.

---

[71] Miriam L. Wallace, "Writing Lives and Gendering History in Mary Hays's *Female Biography* (1803)," in *Romantic Autobiography in England*, edited by Eugene Stelzig (Farnham: Ashgate, 2009), 66 (63–78).

[72] Hays thus anticipates Victorian biographies of queens written by women, such as those by Agnes Strickland, which Rohan Maitzen argues are "somewhere in the no-man's land between politics and romance" (Rohan Maitzen, "This Feminine Preserve: Historical Biographies by Victorian Women," *Victorian Studies* 38.3 (1995), 373 (371–393)).

[73] Hays, *Memoirs of Queens*, 84.

As Felicity James writes, "Hays's narratives suggest that the power of sympathy can work across [cultural and historical] boundaries, enabling the reader to appreciate the particular circumstances of the individual, and indeed to break down the 'finality' of history."[74] She thus stresses the sympathetic dimensions of Boleyn's story at the same time as she asserts Boleyn's ongoing capacity to enthrall and beguile: female readers are invited to react to the tale of Hays's spirited, magnetic Boleyn in the same way as they would the heroines of their favorite sentimental novels.

The accounts of d'Aulnoy, Fielding, and Hays prefigure sympathetic nineteenth- and twentieth-century representations of Anne Boleyn, which were largely written by women. A copy of *Female Biography* was in the library of Jane Austen's sister-in-law at Godmersham.[75] It is tempting to speculate that Hays's account of Boleyn's life influenced Austen's juvenile work *The History of England*.[76] Elizabeth Benger's 1821 *Memoirs of the Life of Anne Boleyn, Queen of King Henry VIII* retreads pro-Protestant ground in its depiction of Boleyn's role in the Reformation, but also goes to some length to explore the gendered dynamics of the relationship between Henry and Boleyn.[77] This impulse to make Boleyn relatable, despite the distant glamour and violence of Tudor history, has persisted into contemporary representations of the Queen. The complex and clever Anne Boleyn who appears in contemporary cultural products from the

[74] Felicity James, "Writing *Female Biography*: Mary Hays and the Life Writing of Religious Dissent," in *Women's Life Writing, 1700–1850: Gender, Genre and Authorship*, edited by Daniel Cook and Amy Culley (Basingstoke: Palgrave Macmillan, 2012), 127 (117–132).

[75] Gina Luria Walker, "Pride, Prejudice, Patriarchy: Jane Austen reads Mary Hays," Fellows' Lecture, Chawton House Library (2010) https://www.southampton.ac.uk/english/news/2010/03/11_pride_prejudice_patriarchy.page (accessed 8 August 2017).

[76] Austen declares of Boleyn that "this amiable Woman was entirely innocent of the Crimes with which she was accused, of which her Beauty, her Elegance, and her Sprightliness were sufficient proofs" (Jane Austen, *The History of England*, in *The Cambridge Edition of the Works of Jane Austen: Juvenilia*, edited by Peter Sabor (Cambridge: Cambridge University Press, 2006), 181).

[77] Bordo argues that "where Benger breaks new ground...[is] in her explicit – and surprisingly sophisticated – analysis of the role played by gender expectations in the breakdown of Anne and Henry's relationship" (Bordo, 151). However, Fielding's account of these gendered expectations of relationship pre-dates Benger's work by more than 70 years.

television series *The Tudors*, to Hilary Mantel's *Wolf Hall* and *Bring Up the Bodies*, has her origins in eighteenth-century women's writing about the Queen. The women who first inscribed Boleyn's story refused to make her either angel or whore; instead, they made her a woman.

BIBLIOGRAPHY

PRIMARY SOURCES

Austen, Jane. *The History of England from the reign of Henry the 4th to the death of Charles the 1st by a partial, prejudiced, and ignorant Historian.* In *The Cambridge Edition of the Works of Jane Austen: Juvenilia*, edited by Peter Sabor, 176–189. Cambridge: Cambridge University Press, 2006.
Banks, John. *Vertue Betray'd: or, Anna Bullen. A Tragedy Acted at His Royal Highness the Duke's Theatre*. London: R. Wellington, 1715.
Betham, Matilda. *Biographical Dictionary of Celebrated Women*. London: B. Crosby & Co., 1984.
Bradley, Mary Hastings. *The Favor of Kings*. New York: D. Appleton and Company, 1912.
D'Aulnoy, Madame. *The Novels of Elizabeth Queen of England, Containing the History of Queen Ann of Bullen. Faithfully Rendered into English by S.H.* London: Mark Pardoe, 1680.
Fielding, Sarah. "Wherein Anna Boleyn relates the History of Her Life". In Henry Fielding, *A Journey from This World to the Next*, edited by Ian A. Bell and Andrew Varney, 102–117. Oxford: Oxford University Press, 1997.
Foxe, John. *The Unabridged Acts and Monuments Online*. HRI Online Publications, Sheffield, 2011. www.johnfoxe.org.
Hays, Mary. *Memoirs of queens, illustrious and celebrated*. London: T & J Allman, 1821.
———. *Female Biography; or, Memoirs of Illustrious and Celebrated Women, of All Ages and Countries. Alphabetically Arranged*. London: Richard Phillips, 1803.
Sander, Nicholas. *The Rise and Growth of the Anglican Schism*, edited by D. Lewis. London: 1877.

SECONDARY SOURCES

Bernard, G.W. "Anne Boleyn's Religion". *The Historical Journal* 36, no. 1 (1993), 1–20.
Bordo, Susan. *The Creation of Anne Boleyn: A New Look at England's Most Notorious Queen*. Boston: Mariner, 2014.
Burrows, F.J. & A.J. Hassall. "*Anna Boleyn* and the Authenticity of Fielding's Feminine Narratives". *Eighteenth-Century Studies* 21 (1988): 429–45.

Chernock, Arianne. "Gender and Politics of Exceptionalism in the Writing of British Women's History". In *Making Women's Histories: Beyond National Perspectives*, edited by Pamela S. Nadell and Kate Haulman, 115–136. New York: NYU Press, 2013.

Crane, Julie. "Whoso list to hunt: The literary fortunes of Anne Boleyn". In *The Female Figure in Contemporary Historical Fiction*, edited by K. Cooper and E. Short, 76–91. Basingstoke: Palgrave Macmillan, 2012.

Goodhue, Elizabeth. "At the Margins of Menippean Dialogue: Sarah Fielding's "History of Anne Boleyn" and the Muted Female Figures of Lucian's Satiric Underworld". *Tulsa Studies in Women's Literature* 29, no. 2 (2010), 263–89.

Ives, Eric. *The Life and Death of Anne Boleyn*. Malden: Blackwell, 2004.

James, Felicity. "Writing *Female Biography*: Mary Hays and the Life Writing of Religious Dissent". In *Women's Life Writing, 1700–1850: Gender, Genre and Authorship*, edited by Daniel Cook and Amy Culley, 117–132. Basingstoke: Palgrave Macmillan, 2012.

Johnson, Christopher D. "History, Fiction, and the Emergence of an Artistic Vision: Sarah Fielding's Anna Boleyn Narrative". *New Perspectives on the Eighteenth Century* 6, no. 1 (2009): 19–33.

Lindsey, Karen. *Divorced, Beheaded, Survived: A Feminist Reinterpretation of the Wives of Henry VIII*. Reading: Addison-Wesley, 1995.

Mackay, Lauren. *Inside the Tudor Court: Henry VIII and his Six Wives Through the Writings of the Spanish Ambassador Eustace Chapuys*. Stroud: Amberley, 2014.

Maitzen, Rohan. "This Feminine Preserve: Historical Biographies by Victorian Women". *Victorian Studies* 38, no. 3 (1995): 371–393.

Mantel, Hilary. "The BBC Reith Lectures: The Day Is For the Living". 13 June 2017. www.bbc.co.uk/programmes/b08tcbrp.

McInnes, Andrew. "Feminism in the Footnotes: Wollstonecraft's Ghost in Mary Hays' *Female Biography*". *Life Writing* 8, no. 3 (2011), 273–85.

Norton, Elizabeth. *Bessie Blount: Mistress to Henry VIII*. Stroud: Amberley Press, 2011.

Palmer, Melvin D. "Madame d'Aulnoy in England". *Comparative Literature* 27, no. 3 (1975): 237–53.

Phillips, Mark Salber. *Society and Sentiment: Genres of Historical Writing in Britain, 1740–1820*. Princeton: Princeton University Press, 2000.

Spongberg, Mary. *Writing Women's History Since the Renaissance*. Basingstoke: Palgrave Macmillan, 2002.

Stone, Lawrence. *The Family, Sex, and Marriage in England, 1500–1800*. London: Weidenfeld & Nicolson, 1977.

Walker, Gina Luria. "The invention of Female Biography". *Enlightenment and Dissent* 29 (2014), 79–136.

————. "Women's voices". In *The Cambridge Companion to British Literature of the French Revolution in the 1790s*, edited by Pamela Clemit, 145–59. Cambridge: Cambridge University Press, 2011.

————. "Pride, Prejudice, Patriarchy: Jane Austen Reads Mary Hays". Fellows' Lecture, Chawton House Library, 2010. www.southampton.ac.uk/english/news/2010/03/11_pride_prejudice_patriarch.page

Walker, Greg. "Rethinking the Fall of Anne Boleyn". *The Historical Journal* 45, no. 1 (2002), 1–29.

Wallace, Miriam L. "Writing Lives and Gendering History in Mary Hays's *Female Biography* (1803)". In *Romantic Autobiography in England*, edited by Eugene Stelzig, 63–78. Farnham: Ashgate, 2009.

Warnicke, Retha. *Elizabeth of York and Her Six Daughters-in-Law: Fashioning Tudor Queenship, 1485–1547*. New York: Palgrave Macmillan, 2017.

————. *Wicked Women of Tudor England: Queens, Aristocrats, Commoners*. Palgrave Macmillan, 2012.

Zipes, Jack. "The Meaning of Fairy Tale Within the Evolution of Culture." *Marvels and Tales* 25, no. 2 (2011), 221–243.

CHAPTER 5

"Of Hopes Great as Himselfe": Tudor and Stuart Legacies of Edward VI

Benjamin M. Guyer

Shortly after his death on July 6, 1553, Edward VI's last prayer and final words were printed for public perusal. This single-page document contained little sustained theological content, but it crystallized important facets of the boy king's legacy. One was his anti-papal conviction. The prayer concluded, "Oh my Lorde God defende this Realme from papistrye, and mayntayne thy true religion, that I and my people may prayse thy holy name."[1] The king's expiration was then related in sparse detail. Turning his head to look at others in the room, Edward had difficulty focusing on those present. He told them that he was praying, and with his

---

Francis Godwin, *Annales of England* (London: A. Islip and W. Stansby, 1630), 258. STC 11947.

[1] Edward VI, *The Prayer of King Edwarde the Syxte* (London: Rychard Iugge, 1553). STC 7509.

B. M. Guyer (✉)
Department of History and Philosophy, The University of Tennessee at Martin, Martin, TN, USA

© The Author(s) 2019
E. Paranque (ed.), *Remembering Queens and Kings of Early Modern England and France*, Queenship and Power,
https://doi.org/10.1007/978-3-030-22344-1_5

last words said, "I am faynte, Lorde haue mercy upon me, and take my sprite [sic]."[2] All of this portrayed Edward VI as pious, even if some English considered the king badly misguided in religious matters. But Edward's legacy was rapidly shaped by other developments as well. On August 22, 1553, John Dudley, the Duke of Northumberland and Lord President of Edward VI's Privy Council, was executed for high treason. Having supported evangelical religious reform during Edward's reign, with his last words Dudley turned his back upon these same convictions and exhorted England to return to the Catholic Church. He repented of the religious developments that took place during his presidency and warned the crowd "to beware of these seditiouse preachers, and teachers of newe doctryne."[3] Northumberland's disavowal gave Edward VI's legacy an additional, permanent feature. Remaining faithful to the end while others did not, he became the pious prince of what might have been, his purity a sharp contrast with the feckless opportunism of those like Northumberland.

This chapter uses the legacy of Edward VI to query two major trends in the recent historiography of the English Reformation. First is the influential "myth" thesis advanced by Diarmaid MacCulloch: "The myth of the English Reformation is that it did not happen, or that it happened by accident rather than design, or that it was half-hearted and sought a middle way between Catholicism and Protestantism."[4] MacCulloch believes that the so-called Laudians of the seventeenth century were the first group to proffer such a myth. However, as we will see, there was no distinctly "Laudian" viewpoint on Edward's reign. Rather, they simply maintained what were, by their time, long-entrenched historical interpretations, many of which originated in the years immediately following Edward's death. The second historiographical trend addressed here is the assumption that iconoclasm was fundamentally ideological. This is most forcefully stated in Eamon Duffy's award-winning study *The Stripping of the Altars*. Writing of the Edwardian reformation, Duffy asserts, "Iconoclasm was the central

---

[2] Edward VI, *The Prayer*.

[3] John Dudley, *The Sayinge of John late Duke of Northumberlande uppon the scaffold, at the tyme of his execution* (London: Iohn Cawood, 1553), no page. STC 7283.

[4] Diarmaid MacCulloch, 'The Myth of the English Reformation', *Journal of British Studies*, Vol. 30, No. 1 (Jan., 1991), 1–19, at 1. The thesis informs much of MacCulloch's other scholarship, such as *The Boy King: Edward VI and the Protestant Reformation* (Berkeley: University of California Press, 1999).

sacrament of the reform."[5] Without denying that animus toward Catholic devotion spurred opposition to, and even the destruction of, traditional religious aesthetics and practices, this chapter notes in detailed fashion that contemporaries frequently named greed a key motivator for desecration as well. According to Tudor contemporaries and their Stuart successors, nearsighted opportunism was at least as iconoclastic as anti-Catholic prejudice. Studying Edward's post mortem reputation can help us reassess current understandings of the English Reformation.

EDWARD AMONG THE TUDORS

A brief overview of Edward's reign will facilitate understanding the fault lines that defined his later reputation. Because Edward inherited the throne in 1547 at the age of nine, a council ruled in his stead. The prince's uncle, Edward Seymour, was appointed Lord Protector of the Realm and Governor of the King's Person. His social policies earned him widespread support,[6] and he governed with much popular approval until the middle of 1549. That summer, the nation was set on edge by a series of uprisings, with some protesting religious changes and others protesting developing economic inequities.[7] While attempting to deal with various rebel groups, a coup was launched against Somerset that scapegoated him as an inept and even greedy enemy of the king. During his brief imprisonment, Seymour was effectively replaced by John Dudley, who first advanced to the position of Lord President of the Privy Council, and later became the duke of Northumberland. Seymour attempted his own coup against Dudley in late 1551 but failed, and was executed on January 22, 1552. Despite this chaotic series of events, Seymour carried with him to the grave something that Dudley could never attain in life: a broad swathe of

---

[5] Eamon Duffy, *The Stripping of the Altars: Traditional Religion in England 1400–1580*, second ed. (New Haven and London: Yale University Press, 2005), 480.

[6] Scott C. Lucas, *A Mirror for Magistrates and the Politics of the English Reformation* (Amherst: University of Massachusetts Press, 2009), 24–28; a dissenting view may be found in Jennifer Loach, *Edward VI* (New Haven and London: Yale University Press, 1999), 39–43. Stephen Alford, *Kingship and Politics in the Reign of Edward VI* (Cambridge: Cambridge University Press, 2002), emphasizes the importance of "commonwealth" ideology throughout.

[7] Helpful contemporary studies include Barrett L. Beer, *Rebellion & Riot: Popular Disorder in England during the Reign of Edward VI*, second ed. (Kent: The Kent State University Press, 2005); Anthony Fletcher and Diarmaid MacCulloch, *Tudor Rebellions*, sixth ed. (London and New York: Routledge, 2016), Chaps. 5 and 6.

supporters. When Edward became unexpectedly sick in 1553, Dudley attempted to divert the succession of the crown away from Mary Tudor by having Jane Grey, his daughter-in-law, crowned. This failed disastrously and brought England to the brink of civil war. Once Mary secured the throne, Dudley and several other members of the Privy Council were executed for treason. For Mary's supporters, Northumberland's actions only revealed the guilt of Edward's entire council. For Edward's supporters, Northumberland's actions wrought an acute need to justify Edward's regime against Marian criticism. The divisions internal to Edward's council played an important role in this; supporters of Seymour penned the earliest defenses of Edward's reign. Two of these authors, John Olde and William Baldwin, were employed by the printer Edward Whitchurch, whose print shop has been described as "a quasi-official government press" tasked with "expressing and advancing the ideals of Seymour's government."[8] Marian censorship prevented the publication of some pro-Edwardian works during her reign, but those that were printed influenced perceptions of the boy king's regime for more than the next 150 years.

In 1555, John Olde published *The acquital or purgation of the moost catholyke Christen Prince, Edwarde the VI*, the earliest printed apologetic for the Edwardian regime. Explicitly opposed to Mary's restoration of Catholicism, the *Acquital* was as effusive in its praise of Edward as it was devoid of specific historical detail about his reign. Directed on its title page "agaynst al suche as blasphemously and traitorously infame hym or the sayd Church, of heresie or sedicion," Olde defended "the Churche of Englande refourmed and gouerned under hym."[9] As one of the English translators of Erasmus' *Paraphrases*, Olde's conception of true Christianity did not fall neatly into the developing confessional allegiances of the mid-1550s. He freely combined support for the study of Biblical Hebrew and Greek with numerous citations of patristic authorities, and he believed that patristic doctrine fully harmonized with the apostles' own teaching. Unusually for an evangelical author, Olde also appealed to the episcopate as a necessary and visible sign of the true church: "Nother is the gospellers churche without continual succession of bishoppes, seyng it hathe her relacion even vnto the Apostles of Christ."[10] Built upon an ancient foundation,

---

[8] Lucas, *A Mirror for Magistrates*, 37.

[9] John Olde, *The acquital or purgation of the moost catholyke Christen Prince, Edwarde the. VI* (Waterford: E. van der Erve, 1555). STC 18797.

[10] Olde, *The acquital*, sig. F2.

Olde's memory of the Edwarian church was a paean to his own distinct vision of orthodoxy. Regrettably, Olde did not outline Edward's reforms. The closest he came to doing so was in the book's introduction, where support for the royal supremacy was united with apocalyptic invective against the papacy. Olde defended Henry VIII for "banyshing the violent usurped power and supremacie of the Romyshe auncient Antichrist."[11] Edward VI, the "most christen catholyke souerayne," followed the same path, leading England's Christians "according to the fotesteppes and examples of Moses, Josua, Dauid, Salomon, Ezechias, Josias, Josaphat and other most godly gouernours & kinges."[12] The *Acquital* was an encomium that credited the late king with the restoration of all that Olde valued. Edward was a saint in all but name, and he fought valiantly if briefly against an apocalyptic foe.

Olde's defense was printed amidst a small amount of commentary on other recent events. Mary's government capitalized upon Northumberland's return to Catholicism by rapidly putting his speech from the scaffold into print; shocked by the sequence of events surrounding Jane Grey, Mary's victory, and Northumberland's own final words, some Edwardian evangelicals returned to Catholicism as well.[13] Evangelicals who maintained their religious convictions but fled England for Europe looked back upon Northumberland in especially negative terms. Writing from Strasbourg in 1556, the former bishop of Winchester John Ponet disavowed Northumberland's attempt at placing Jane on the throne. He alleged that Somerset and Northumberland both sought to "robbe the king, and spoile the Realme,"[14] but that Northumberland went further in his treachery, forging letters "to make the Protectour [Somerset] hated."[15] This early if abbreviated reflection upon the principal members of Edward's council set the two halves of Edward's reign into conflict with one another. By aligning Northumberland with deception and Somerset with victimization, the moral character of each became an explanatory cause for the regime's history and spectacular demise. For many later authors, Somerset's undeserved suffering would effectively

[11] Olde, *The acquital*, sig. A2r-v.
[12] Olde, *The acquital*, sig. A4r.
[13] Eamon Duffy, *Fires of Faith: Catholic England under Mary Tudor* (New Haven and London: Yale University Press, 2009), 88.
[14] John Ponet, *A Shorte Treatise of Politike Pouuer* (Strasbourg: The heirs of W. Köpfel, 1556), 64. STC 20178.
[15] Ponet, *A Shorte Treatise*, 131.

atone for his sins. Regardless of confessional alignment or inclination, Tudor and Stuart Christians read history as a theater of not only divine providence but divine intervention and commendation as well.

Soon after Elizabeth's accession to the throne, several more Edwardian apologetics appeared in print. One result was the dissemination of increasingly effusive rhetoric in praise of the prince. In 1560, William Baldwin published *The Funeralles of King Edward the Syxte*, a collection of three poems. Originally written "before his [Edward VI's] cor[p]se was buryed,"[16] the work was suppressed throughout Mary's reign. Its title page set the tone for what followed. Beneath a woodcut of the king, Baldwin informed his readers, "He pleased God, and was beloved of him, and therefore hath God removed him from sinners among whom he lived."[17] Underneath Edward's portrait, Baldwin also included a reference to the fourth chapter of the [apocryphal] Old Testament book of Wisdom, and he concluded his first poem by citing its sixteenth verse: "Thus the righteous which is dead, condemneth the ungodly which are living, and the youth that is soone brought to an ende, the long life of the unrighteous."[18] The title poem maintained the same thematic tenor, and Baldwin gave Edward's death a moral meaning as well, writing that the king died "In body and soule, a virgin undefilde."[19] As if foreshadowing the virgin queen who had recently ascended the throne, Edward's moral constancy was held up as a model for imitation. The 1563 edition of John Foxe's *Actes and Monuments* was much the same. Foxe described Edward as "a prince in al ornamentes and giftes belonging to a prince incomparable…and yet not so muche beloued as also admirable, by reason of his rare towardnes and hope both of vertue and learning whiche in hym appeared aboue the capacitie of his yeares."[20] Foxe included the full text of the king's last prayer as additional evidence of the same, but like Olde, Foxe's encomiastic tendencies stripped his narrative of specific historical detail. Supporters of Edward, having been largely silenced under Mary, had begun to elevate the king's sanctity to new heights under Elizabeth.

[16] William Baldwin, *The Funeralles of King Edward the Syxte* (London: Thomas Marshe, 1560), sig. A1r. STC 1243.

[17] Baldwin, *The Funeralles*, sig. A1.

[18] Baldwin, *The Funeralles*, sig. B4v.

[19] Baldwin, *The Funeralles*, sig. B4v.

[20] John Foxe, *The Unabridged Acts and Monuments Online* or *TAMO*, 1563 ed., 940. (HRI Online Publications, Sheffield, 2011). Available from: http://www.johnfoxe.org [Accessed: 13.03.18].

Romancing Edward's virtues spurred romancing Edward's reign. In Foxe's words, "he was intierly of his subiectes beloued, so with no lesse good wyll he loued them agayne."[21] Reciprocal love between king and subject was a very old ideal, and narrative details such as this one merely applied to Edward's reign a centuries-old trope about the importance of mutual political fidelity and devotion. But as the early historiography of Edwardian England continued its moral ascent, some of its other features were also developed. Portrayals of Seymour and Dudley were detailed within the broad outlines already penned by those such as Ponet. In the 1570 revision of the *Actes and Monuments*, Foxe included a marginal note to draw attention to "the hartie affection of the people toward the Duke of Somerset,"[22] affirming that Seymour's piety was fully evident at the time of his death because he was "constant in Christes truth."[23] With words that wholly inverted Northumberland's disavowal of evangelical conviction, Seymour is recorded as looking out at the people immediately before his execution and declaring, "Neyther do I repent me of my doinges, but reioyce therein, sith that now the state of Christian religion commeth most neare vnto the forme and order of the primatiue church."[24] Setting divinity within the details, Foxe attested that Seymour's death was accompanied by a sudden peal of thunder. Foxe then went so far as to compare Seymour's death with the crucifixion of Christ: "It happened here, as the Euangelistes write it did vnto Christ, when as the officers of þᵉ high priestes and Phariseis comming with weapons to take hym, being astonyed ranne backwardes & fell to the ground."[25] The popularity of Foxe's work enabled this narrative to blot out earlier memories of Seymour's iniquities. Northumberland received no such narrative grace. With neither fanfare nor detail, Foxe simply noted Dudley's return to Catholicism and subsequent beheading. A bright line of demarcation now defined the reign of Edward VI. Seymour basked not only in the penumbra of Edward's pious radiance but in Christ's own bloody splendor, while Dudley was cast almost silently into the dark depths of personal and religious betrayal.

---

[21] Foxe, *TAMO*, 1563 ed., 940.
[22] Foxe, *TAMO*, 1570 ed., 1587.
[23] Foxe, *TAMO*, 1570 ed., 1590.
[24] Foxe, *TAMO*, 1570 ed., 1588.
[25] Foxe, *TAMO*, 1570 ed., 1588.

EDWARD AMONG THE STUARTS

Early Stuart authors offered more substantive appraisals of Edwardian England, even if their descriptions of Edward remained as hagiographical and two-dimensional as those found in Tudor works. With the exception of Foxe's *Actes and Monuments*, none of the Tudor texts discussed above were popular, but the Stuart authors analyzed here had some purchase upon later generations. The first major author was Bishop Francis Godwin, whose 1616 Latin work *Rerum Anglicarum* contained a lengthy history of Henry VIII's reign and shorter narratives about Edward VI and Mary I. Reprinted in 1628, Godwin's son Morgan translated the work into English in 1630 under the title *Annales of England*; this translation was reprinted in 1675 and again in 1676. The second key study was John Hayward's posthumously published *The Life and Raigne of King Edward the Sixth*. It also appeared in 1630,[26] and a second edition was published in 1636. Although cited often in later seventeenth-century studies of Edward's reign, Hayward's work did not appear again in print until 1706, when it was included in the second volume of White Kennett's *A Complete History of England*, a three-volume compilation of seventeenth-century historical studies that collectively covered English history from the Roman times through the reign of William III. *A Complete History of England* was reprinted five times, including a new edition in 1719.[27] This gave Hayward a prime position in shaping eighteenth- and eventually nineteenth-century Tudor historiography.

Neither Godwin nor Hayward offered lengthy analyses of their ostensible subject. Godwin's most sustained account of Edward's character came in his discussion of the boy king's death. By the time that Edward died, he had "in that tender age given great proofe of his vertue; a Prince of great devotion, constancy of minde, love of the Truth, and incredibly studious; vertues which with Royall Greatnesse seldome concur."[28] Like Foxe, Godwin then cited Edward's last prayer, related the details surrounding Edward's fading vision, and quoted the king's final request for

---

[26] John Hayward, *The Life and Raigne of King Edward the Sixth*, edited by Barrett L. Beer (Kent and London: The Kent State University Press, 1993). The STC entry is 12998, but all citations here come from Beer's edition.
[27] Laird Oakie, 2004 "Kennett, White (1660–1728)." *Oxford Dictionary of National Biography.* 19 Sep. 2018. Oxford University Press.
[28] Godwin, *Annales of England*, 257.

divine clemency.[29] The outlines of the young prince were as clear and devoid of personal detail as those found in earlier accounts. Hayward offered a different perspective. He opened his work by bluntly stating that "What would haue beene either the fortunes or endeavours of King Edward he never attained to yeares of proofe. Assuredly both for the time of his age and raigne, he is rather to bee admired then commended."[30] This was unlike Foxe, who had written that Edward was "not so muche beloued as also admirable."[31] Hayward's dim endorsement was due, at least in part, to his dislike of the young king's council. He described Archbishop Cranmer as "violent both by perswasions and entreaties";[32] unlike most earlier accounts of Somerset, he depicted the Protector as "a man little esteemed either for wisedome or personage," whose impiety was eventually met with divine wrath.[33] Hayward was more conventional in his portrayal of Northumberland as "sometimes almost dissolute," and driven by "a great spirit and highly aspiring, not forebearing to make any mischiefe the meanes for attaining his ambitious endes."[34] Godwin shared this latter perspective, describing Northumberland as "a man of a vast spirit" who "long looked asquint vpon *Somersets* greatnesse."[35] Like their Tudor predecessors, Stuart authors continued to portray Dudley in lurid terms, rendering him the starkest of contrasts with Edward's unrealized but deep piety.

Godwin vividly described the difference between the leadership of Somerset and Northumberland. Again like Foxe, Godwin recounted the appearance of prodigies—preternatural signs of impending divine judgment—immediately after Somerset's execution. The signs and wonders listed, however, were different. Thunder was not mentioned, and Foxe's comparison with Christ was also excised. Godwin instead noted two things. One was the inexplicable appearance of dolphins and whales in English waters. The second prodigy received more extensive comment: "in Oxford-shire was borne a Monster, such as few either Naturalists or Historians write of the like."[36] This was a conjoined twin with "two heads

---

[29] Godwin, *Annales of England*, 258.
[30] Hayward, *Edward VI*, 33.
[31] Foxe, *TAMO*, 1563 ed., 940.
[32] Hayward, *Edward VI*, 37.
[33] Hayward, *Edward VI*, 44, 101.
[34] Hayward, *Edward VI*, 45.
[35] Godwin, *Annales of England*, 234.
[36] Godwin, *Annales of England*, 252.

and two bodies as far as the navill distinct."[37] Godwin included the key detail that "their heads [were] looking alwaies contrary waies."[38] It is difficult to resist the possibility that this feature was rhetorical (even if true), and was included for the sake of indicating that the kingdom under Somerset had gone one way, but that under Northumberland it would go in the opposite direction. In fact, on the very next page, Godwin began his final chapter on Edward VI, writing that because Northumberland

> was more potent than the rest, so did his ambition fly higher. It was somewhat strange, that being not any way able to pretend but a shadow of Right to the Crowne, he should dream of confirming the Succession of it in his Family. But he shall sore so high, that he shall singe his wings, and fall no lesse dangerously than he whome the Poëts feigne to have aspired to a like vnlawfull government.[39]

Godwin's account of Edward's last year thus began by looking forward to the conflict that erupted immediately after the king's death. According to Godwin, Northumberland was positively abusive, and secured loyalty to Jane only "by terrour or promises."[40] This was quite different than Somerset's own character. Despite conspiring against Northumberland, Somerset was "otherwise of a most milde disposition."[41] While Northumberland "pretended" to show affection to the Edwardian church,[42] Somerset died "a pious just man, very zealous in point of Reformation, very sollicitous of the King's safety, every way good, and carefull of the Weale publique."[43] The conjoined twin was an outward sign of England's interior state.[44]

If Edward's personal portrait continued to appear familiar in these works, the same could not be said for their discussions of the reformation of the Church of England. Godwin and Hayward advanced new, and

---

[37] Godwin, *Annales of England*, 252.
[38] Godwin, *Annales of England*, 252.
[39] Godwin, *Annales of England*, 253.
[40] Godwin, *Annales of England*, 264.
[41] Godwin, *Annales of England*, 246.
[42] Godwin, *Annales of England*, 270.
[43] Godwin, *Annales of England*, 252.
[44] Hayward wrote of the same prodigies, including the conjoined twin, but discussed them in the context of Edward's last days rather than Somerset's death. He offers no explanation for this, despite his explicit dislike of Northumberland; perhaps his comparatively low opinion of Somerset blunted the rhetorical force of the image.

sometimes critical, perspectives. Godwin offered a list of key religious changes made under Edward: "our Church was so purged from the dregs of Superstition, that for Purity of Doctrine, and Institution of select Ecclesiasticall Rites, it excelled the most Reformed Churches of Germany."[45] He further highlighted that, among other matters, images had been "pulled downe," priests were allowed to marry, the liturgy was in the vernacular, and that both the bread and the wine of the Eucharist were administered to all.[46] But what began well soon went awry. Godwin expressed surprise that Edward's regime dealt harshly with Cuthbert Tunstall, the bishop of Durham, "a milde man, and of most sweet conditions." During the reign of Henry VIII, Godwin explains, Tunstall was accounted among "the chiefe Lights of our Church,"[47] but once removed from his bishopric, "all kinde of sacriledge" began.[48] Durham's revenues were diverted to the Crown, and although subsequent monarchs (Mary, Elizabeth, and James) all worked to restore church lands, Durham "at this day scarce possesseth the third part of it's antient revenues."[49] Under Northumberland, things went from bad to worse as numerous bishops were deprived of their sees, with some consigned to the Tower of London. At this point, Godwin's narrative simply listed negative events. George Paris was burned for his Arian theology, "seven or eight" villages were afflicted with an earthquake,[50] and finally Somerset was executed. With a narrative move at once prescriptive and descriptive, Godwin praised the early Edwardian reformation by defining and defending it over and against later sacrilege.

Hayward was more critical still. "I will not deny but that some change in religion is often expedient and sometimes necessary," he wrote, but it "must be done with a soft and tender hand."[51] Hayward began his discussion of religion with the king's injunctions: "soone after the beginning of the young kings raigne, certaine injunctions were set forth for remouing images out of Churches which had beene highly, not onely esteemed but honoured before, and for abolishing or altering some other ancient

---

[45] Godwin, *Annales of England*, 217–18.
[46] Godwin, *Annales of England*, 217–18
[47] Godwin, *Annales of England*, 223.
[48] Godwin, *Annales of England*, 224.
[49] Godwin, *Annales of England*, 248.
[50] Godwin, *Annales of England*, 248.
[51] Hayward, *Edward VI*, 67.

observations in the Church."[52] Hayward devoted no space to doctrinal debate, even when he noted contention over the celebration of the mass; he instead detailed the societal effects of these changes. The most important was the sale of ecclesiastical land, which "enriched many, and enobled some, and thereby made them firme in maintaining the change."[53] Greed was the major culprit, and the secularization of land was followed by iconoclasm, which proved just as controversial. It was done "in such vnseasonable and vnseasoned fashion" that "many did expresse a sense of distast,"[54] and soon rebelled against the regime.

For Hayward, the story was not all bad, for he supported the development of the Book of Common Prayer. Borrowing directly from Edward VI's letter to the rebels in Devon,[55] Hayward portrayed liturgical change as minimalistic, which made popular resistance to the new liturgy appear all the more foolish. Hayward took Edward at his word, copying the king's own statement that The Book of Common Prayer was merely an English translation of the Latin mass, excepting "a few things omitted so fond, that it had bin a shame to haue heard them in English…the masse with great judgment and care was reduced to the same manner as Christ left it, as the Apostles vsed it, as the ancient Fathers receaued, practised and left it."[56] One might be tempted to criticize Hayward for proffering a "myth" about Edward's reformation, but as the example of Godwin shows, it was customary well before 1630 to associate the better parts of Edward's reign with Somerset's protectorate. This, in turn, led to a further interpretive development, which became an influential precedent for later authors. Neither Hayward nor Godwin indicated any awareness of ceremonial or theological differences between the 1549 and 1552 Prayer Books. On the eve of the civil wars, operating under the influence of earlier Tudor authors including Edward VI himself, early Stuart historiography developed a homogenizing approach to mid-sixteenth-century religious change. With few exceptions, this interpretive framework long remained the norm in subsequent Anglican perspectives on the English Reformation.

---

[52] Hayward, *Edward VI*, 68.

[53] Hayward, *Edward VI*, 69.

[54] Hayward, *Edward VI*, 70.

[55] Edward VI, *A Message Sent by the Kynges Maiestie, to Certain of His People, Assembled in Devonshire* (London: Richard Grafton, 1549). STC 7506.

[56] Hayward, *Edward VI*, 79.

DIVIDING AND DISSEMINATING THE BOY KING'S LEGACIES

Recent historiography has often drawn a teleological line from Edward's reign to Puritanism,[57] but this perspective developed only haltingly during the civil wars of the 1640s. Not all opponents of the episcopal establishment accepted such a narrative. Some, such as John Milton and Thomas Ford, were among those who roundly criticized the Edwardian church. Milton had his own explanation for why "In *Edward* the 6. Dayes...a compleate *Reform* was not effected."[58] One reason given was the character of Northumberland, "who little minding *Religion*, as his Apostacie well shew'd at his death, bent all his wit how to bring the Right of the *Crowne* into his owne Line."[59] Milton offered another, equally important reason in his description of Edward's bishops as "halting and time-serving *Prelates*."[60] Breaking quite firmly with authors such as Foxe, Milton went so far as to question whether Edward's bishops could be considered evangelical martyrs under Mary. Preaching before Parliament in 1641, Ford argued much same, alleging that under Edward VI, "the generality were but meere Formalists in that reformation, and did but waite for a wind, to carry them to *Rome* againe."[61] While "popery" was a broad brush often used by nonconformists to denigrate the Church of England, it is difficult to ignore the possibility that Ford also thought here of Northumberland's late return to Catholicism. It was only in 1643 that the Westminster Assembly developed a historiography that identified its religious project as the successor to Edward's reformation. The Preface of the Assembly's *Directory for the Public Worship of God* declared, "In the beginning of the blessed Reformation, our wise and pious Ancestors took care to set forth an Order for Redresse of many things, which they, then, by the Word discovered to be Vain, Erroneous, Superstitious, and Idolatrous, in the Publique Worship of God."[62] This led "many Godly and Learned men to rejoyce much in the Book of Common-Prayer at that time set forth,"[63] but

---

[57] Alford, *Kingship and Politics*, Chap. 6; MacCulloch, *The Boy King*, Chap. 4.

[58] John Milton, *Of Reformation Touching Church-Discipline in England* (London: Thomas Underhill, 1641), 9. Wing/M2134.

[59] Milton, *Of Reformation*, 9.

[60] Milton, *Of Reformation*, 10.

[61] Thomas Ford, *Reformation Sure and Stedfast* (London: J.D. for Henry Overton, 1641), 8. Wing/F1515.

[62] Westminster Assembly, *A Directory for the Public Worship of God* (London: Evan Tyler, Alexander Fifield, Ralph Smith, and John Field, 1644), p. 1. Wing/D1544.

[63] Westminster Assembly, *A Directory*, 1.

the Church of England's liturgy was also a limited good. The Assembly noted with approval only that the liturgy and the Scriptures were made available in the vernacular,[64] but they also asserted that if the "first Reformers" were still alive, they "would joyn with us in this work."[65] This bid for the Edwardian past helped define Presbyterian historiography, but opponents of Presbyterianism, whether Congregationalist or Episcopalian, continued to advance their own, equally distinct historical narratives.

Thomas Fuller's *Church-History of Britain* provides a good example of Episcopalian historiography in the mid-1650s. As with other accounts of Edwardian England, John Dudley emerged as the principal villain. Fuller locked Somerset and Northumberland in a duel of opposing character traits; Seymour's virtues were transformed and inverted in Dudley, in whom they reappeared as vices. Somerset was "*free spirited, open hearted, humble, hard to distrust, easie to forgive*," while Northumberland was "*proud, suttle, close, cruell*, and *revengefull*."[66] Slightly later in the narrative, when Fuller wrote that "The Duke of *Somerset* was *religious* himself, a *lover* of all such as were so, and a great *Promoter* of *Reformation*,"[67] the reader was already primed to assume that Dudley was the converse. Fuller then led his readers to see precisely this writing that although Somerset piously restored churches while removing idolatry from the kingdom, Northumberland so ransacked England's parishes for their wealth that parishes struggled to administer the sacraments. Citing Hayward, Fuller explained that the king's commissioners, operating under the oversight of the Privy Council, "left but *one silver Chalice* to every Church, too narrow a proportion to populous Parishes, where they might have left two at the least."[68] This was nothing more than greed, and "All this *Income* rather stayed the stomack, than satisfied the hunger of the Kings Exchequer."[69] When the government turned its sights on the bishopric of Durham and sought to divert its income to the crown, the real culprit was again Northumberland, who "either was, or was to be possessour thereof."[70] In the last half of Edward's reign, the boy king's regime had abandoned its commitment to reformation and simply sought its own

[64] Westminster Assembly, *A Directory*, 1–2.
[65] Westminster Assembly, *A Directory*, 6.
[66] Thomas Fuller, *The Church-History of Britain* (London: Iohn Williams, 1655), Book VII, p. 408. Wing/F2416.
[67] Fuller, *The Church-History*, Book VII, 410.
[68] Fuller, *The Church-History*, Book VII, 419.
[69] Fuller, *The Church-History*, Book VII, 419.
[70] Fuller, *The Church-History*, Book VII, 419.

self-aggrandizement. And yet, even here Edward emerged unscathed. Fuller's account of the king's death closely tracked with earlier accounts. Citing Foxe, Fuller introduced the full text of Edward's final prayer by writing, "We will conclude this Kings most *Pious life* with that His most *devout Prayer* on his Death-Bed, which God heard and graciously answered, for the *good* of the *Church of England*."[71] Edward's constancy remained the perfect antidote to the inconstancy of his regime.

The political sea change of the Restoration in 1660 produced no comparable paradigm shift in later Stuart historiography. This section concludes with two major works. The first came from the "Laudian" theologian Peter Heylyn, who published his mildly popular *Ecclesia Restaurata* in 1661; it saw further editions in 1670 and 1674. Recent scholarship on Heylyn has been largely critical,[72] but placing his work in the context of earlier Stuart historiography enables us to behold a more balanced portrait. Simply stated, Heylyn's narrative of Edward's reign was more detailed than that of his predecessors but quite conventional in its content. He cited Foxe's *Actes and Monuments*,[73] Hayward's *Life and Raigne of King Edward the Sixth*,[74] and Fuller's *Church-History*.[75] Heylyn maintained several of Hayward's arguments, describing the Book of Common Prayer as an English translation of the mass,[76] and he expanded upon but did not deny Somerset's own moral failings.[77] However, in *Ecclesia Restaurata*, the moral division between Somerset and Northumberland was given a confessional gloss not present in earlier studies of the reign. Somerset "had declared himself a Friend to the *Lutheran* Party in the time of King *Henry*,"[78] and this caused him to be "More Moderate in carrying on the Work of *Reformation*, then those who after had the Managing and Conduct of it."[79] The destabilization of Edward's reign thus resulted from theological error as much as moral decline. Far

---

[71] Fuller, *The Church-History*, Book VII, 425.

[72] See, e.g., MacCulloch, 'The Myth of the English Reformation', p. 4; Anthony Milton, *Laudian and royalist polemic in seventeenth-century England: The career and writings of Peter Heylyn* (Manchester and New York: Manchester University Press, 2007); Calvin Lane, *The Laudians and the Elizabethan Church* (London and New York: Routledge, 2013), Chap. 5.

[73] Peter Heylyn, *Ecclesia Restaurata* (London: R.B. for H. Twyford, J. Place, and T. Basset, 1674), e.g., 34, 91, 106, 221, 337. Wing/H1703.

[74] Heylyn, *Ecclesia*, e.g., 2, 7, 9, 43.

[75] Heylyn, *Ecclesia*, e.g., 13, 22.

[76] Heylyn, *Ecclesia*, 42, 58.

[77] Heylyn, *Ecclesia*, 60, 72.

[78] Heylyn, *Ecclesia*, 33.

[79] Heylyn, *Ecclesia*, 118.

more than any earlier writer, Heylyn detailed the influence of foreign theologians upon Edward's court. Heylyn alleged that they inspired disorder and even preached the Arian heresy, which denied the divinity of Christ.[80] Like earlier authors, Heylyn viewed Dudley as wholly sinister, a man guilty of "Hatred" no less than "Malice,"[81] and driven by insatiable greed. Nonetheless, Edward remained undefiled. Heylyn praised "the Bounty and Piety of the king,"[82] and like Foxe, Godwin, and Fuller, Heylyn also gave readers the full text of Edward's final prayer. If anything, *Ecclesia Restaurata* is notable not for a purportedly "Laudian" denigration of the Edwardian reformation, but for its utterly mundane acceptance of a long-standing historiographical consensus.

In 1679, Gilbert Burnet published the first volume of his lengthy *History of the Reformation of the Church of England*. A second volume followed in 1681, and a third in 1714; complete and abridged editions of the work were printed into the middle of the eighteenth century. The great contribution of Burnet's study was his inclusion of extensive primary documentation. In this, he was not unique; Foxe, Fuller, and Heylyn had each incorporated entire primary sources into their narratives, and in 1660, Anthony Sparrow published *A Collection of Articles, Injunctions, Canons, Orders, Ordinances, and Constitutions Ecclesiastical, with other Publick Records of the Church of England*, effectively the first document reader on the English Reformation. Burnet reprinted almost none of the documents in Sparrow's *Collection of Articles*, but directed his readers to Sparrow's compilation when necessary. Burnet published other documents, including Edward VI's journal,[83] but this extensive familiarity with key primary sources did not influence his narrative of Edward's reign, which remained wholly unoriginal.

The Proceedings in King Edward's time were likewise so gentle and Moderate, flowing from the calm temper of Arch-Bishop Cranmer, and the policy of others, who were willing to accept of any thing they could obtain, hoping that time would do the business, if the over-driving it did not precipitate the whole affair...The misgovernment of Affairs under the Duke of

---

[80] Heylyn, *Ecclesia*, 89.
[81] Heylyn, *Ecclesia*, 120.
[82] Heylyn, *Ecclesia*, 129.
[83] Gilbert Burnet, *The History of the Reformation of the Church of England* (London: T.H. for Richard Chiswell, 1681), A Collection of Records...Referred to in the Second Part, 3–67. Wing/B5798.

Somerset, with the restless Ambition of the Duke of Northumberland did alienate the Nation much from them[.][84]

And yet, despite what this might indicate, Burnet described Somerset as "A Person of great Vertues, eminent for Piety, humble and affable in greatness, sincere and candid in all his Transactions."[85] Dudley, however, remained a tyrant. Finally, and true to what had long since become historiographical tradition, Burnet printed for his readers Edward's last prayer, and even proposed that readers refer to him as "*Edward* the Saint."[86] The boy king's moral ascent, which began almost immediately after his death, had now become an unofficial canonization.

CONCLUSION

The reputation of Edward VI is inseparable from posthumous perceptions of his regime, but when taken together, these appear only as conflicting contrasts. Edward's earliest defenders rapidly transformed him into a devout prince, whose simple but sincere piety remained chaste and undefiled, even as his regime slipped further and further into moral and spiritual dissolution. Despite the widespread assumption that a "Laudian" historiography turned against Edward's spiritual legacy, the fact of the matter is that early Stuart writers developed Elizabethan precedent into a historiographical tradition that, even as it further contrasted Somerset with Northumberland, left the boy king a largely abstract but wholly endearing figure. Across multiple works, Edward appeared as a historical actor in but two ways: when he wrote to the Devonshire rebels and described the English liturgy as a purified translation of the Latin mass, and when he offered up his final prayer in the moments before his untimely death. The former text was quoted by Hayward and summarized by Heylyn, but Edward's prayer was printed and reprinted time and again, rendering it not just a popular historical record, but a source of devotional inspiration and even comfort. Prevented from leading in life, the boy king eventually led in death as a saint for the ages. To borrow from Christopher Haigh, "Some Reformation."[87]

---

[84] Burnet, *The History of the Reformation*, Part II, sig. d2r.
[85] Burnet, *The History of the Reformation*, Part II, 185.
[86] Burnet, *The History of the Reformation*, Part II, 226.
[87] Christopher Haigh, *English Reformations: Religion, Politics and Society under the Tudors* (Oxford: Clarendon Press, 1993), 295.

BIBLIOGRAPHY

PRIMARY SOURCES

Baldwin, William. *The Funeralles of King Edward the Syxte*. London: Thomas Marshe, 1560. STC 1243.

Burnet, Gilbert. *The History of the Reformation of the Church of England*. London: T.H. for Richard Chiswell, 1681. Wing/B5798.

Dudley, John. *The Sayinge of John late Duke of Northumberlande uppon the scaffold, at the tyme of his execution*. London: Iohn Cawood, 1553. STC 7283.

Edward VI. *A Message Sent by the Kynges Maiestie, to Certain of His People, Assembled in Devonshire*. London: Richard Grafton, 1549. STC 7506.

———. *The Prayer of King Edwarde the Syxte*. London: Rychard Iugge, 1553. STC 7509.

Foxe, John. *The Unabridged Acts and Monuments Online or TAMO*. 1563 edition. (HRI Online Publications, Sheffield, 2011). Available from: http//www.johnfoxe.org [Accessed: 13.03.18].

Ford, Thomas. *Reformation Sure and Stedfast*. London: J.D. for Henry Overton, 1641. Wing/F1515.

Thomas Fuller, *The Church-History of Britain*. London: Iohn Williams, 1655. Wing/F2416.

Godwin, Francis. *Annales of England*. London: A. Islip and W. Stansby, 1630. STC 11947.

Hayward, John. *The Life and Raigne of King Edward the Sixth*, edited by Barrett L. Beer. Kent and London: The Kent State University Press, 1993.

Heylyn, Peter. *Ecclesia Restuarata*. London: R.B. for H. Twyford, J. Place, and T. Basset, 1674. Wing/H1703.

Milton, John. *Of Reformation Touching Church-Discipline in England*. London: Thomas Underhill, 1641. Wing/M2134.

Olde, John. *The acquital or purgation of the moost catholyke Christen Prince, Edwarde the. VI*. Waterford: E. van der Erve, 1555. STC 18797.

Ponet, John. *A Shorte Treatise of Politike Pouuer*. Strasbourg: The heirs of W. Köpfel, 1556. STC 20178.

Westminster Assembly. *A Directory for the Public Worship of God*. London: Evan Tyler, Alexander Fifield, Ralph Smith, and John Field, 1644. Wing/D1544.

SECONDARY SOURCES

Alford, Stephen. *Kingship and Politics in the Reign of Edward VI*. Cambridge: Cambridge University Press, 2002.

Beer, Barrett L. *Rebellion & Riot: Popular Disorder in England during the Reign of Edward VI*, second ed. Kent: The Kent State University Press, 2005.

Duffy, Eamon. *The Stripping of the Altars: Traditional Religion in England 1400–1580*, second ed. New Haven and London: Yale University Press, 2005.

———. *Fires of Faith: Catholic England under Mary Tudor*. New Haven and London: Yale University Press, 2009.

Fletcher, Anthony and Diarmaid MacCulloch. *Tudor Rebellions*, sixth edition. London and New York: Routledge, 2016.

Haigh, Christopher. *English Reformations: Religion, Politics and Society under the Tudors*. Oxford: Clarendon Press, 1993.

Lane, Calvin. *The Laudians and the Elizabethan Church*. London and New York: Routledge, 2013.

Loach, Jennifer. *Edward VI*. New Haven and London: Yale University Press, 1999.

Lucas, Scott C. *A Mirror for Magistrates and the Politics of the English Reformation*. Amherst: University of Massachusetts Press, 2009.

MacCulloch, Diarmaid. "The Myth of the English Reformation." *Journal of British Studies*, Vol. 30, No. 1 (Jan., 1991): 1–19.

———. *The Boy King: Edward VI and the Protestant Reformation*. Berkeley: University of California Press, 1999.

Milton, Anthony. *Laudian and royalist polemic in seventeenth-century England: The career and writings of Peter Heylyn*. Manchester and New York: Manchester University Press, 2007.

Oakie, Laird. 2004 "Kennett, White (1660–1728)." *Oxford Dictionary of National Biography*. 19 Sep. 2018. Oxford University Press.

CHAPTER 6

Chivalry, Nobility, and Romance: Richard Hurd and the Ideal Elizabethan Past

Jurriaan van Santvoort

In 1762, when Richard Hurd (1720–1808) published a small work of historical-literary criticism, this was for him not the start of a long career in literary endeavor or scholarship. Although a fellow at a Cambridge college, as his good friend Thomas Warton, the future Poet Laureate, was at Oxford, Hurd's own desired future vocation lay in ecclesiastical preferment. Successful in this respect, he became first Bishop of Lichfield and Coventry in 1775, then Bishop of Worcester in 1781, and declined the Archbishopric of Canterbury in 1783, even after George III had personally attempted to persuade him to accept the elevation.[1] A prominent theologian, both his theological and political opinions found favor with the King, who appointed him Preceptor to the Prince of Wales and Prince

---

[1] G. M. Ditchfield and Sarah Brewer, "Richard Hurd (1720–1808), Bishop of Worcester," *Oxford Dictionary of National Biography* http://www.oxforddnb.com/view/10.1093/ref:odnb/9780198614128.001.0001/odnb-9780198614128-e-14249, accessed January 15, 2018.

J. van Santvoort (✉)
Brighton College, Brighton, UK

© The Author(s) 2019
E. Paranque (ed.), *Remembering Queens and Kings of Early Modern England and France*, Queenship and Power, https://doi.org/10.1007/978-3-030-22344-1_6

Frederick.[2] Yet, notwithstanding Hurd's own ambitions for a life and legacy in the Church, historians remember him—if they do so at all—for his two published works of literary and historical criticism: *Moral and Political Dialogues* (1759) and *Letters on Chivalry and Romance* (1762), the latter of which were written specifically to illustrate claims made in the former.

While not seeking a career in literary scholarship, Hurd's two volumes of commentary were hugely successful, going through six editions in just a few years. Thomas Warton (1728–1790) revised his influential *Observations on the Fearie Queene of Spenser* (1754) after reading Hurd's third *Dialogue*, on the Age of Queen Elizabeth. While the 1754 edition had criticized Edmund Spenser for his bad taste in following the style and content of romance poetry, the revised 1762 edition no longer condemned Spenser for "gothic ignorance and barbarity."[3] Instead, as Richard Terry has pointed out, in 1762 he followed Hurd in defending "with [...] express intent and force of elegance the literature of the gothic (or early medieval) era."[4] Like Warton, Thomas Percy, another literary scholar aiming to revive romance literature, credited Hurd with rehabilitating that genre among "our Critics and Poets."[5]

Nevertheless, such close identification of Hurd's works with the revival of gothic and medieval romance literature presents historians with a problem. Hurd declared his intent to restore romance literature as a genre and chivalry as a set of manners to historical prominence, yet in his *Letters on Chivalry and Romance*, Hurd freely admits that he had not read any medieval romances, "these barbarous volumes."[6] Instead he acknowledges the French antiquarian scholar Jean Baptiste de la Curne de Sainte-Palaye as his sole authority for the Middle Ages.[7] This frankness has led scholars to criticize Hurd for his lack of knowledge of medieval manners, literature,

---

[2] Francis Kilvert, *Memoirs of the Life and Writings of the Right Rev. Richard Hurd, D. D., Lord Bishop of Worcester; with a Selection from His Unpublished Correspondence and Other Unpublished Papers* (London, 1860), 120–121.

[3] Thomas Warton, *Observations of the Faerie Queene of Spenser* (London, 1754), 1.

[4] Richard Terry, *Poetry and the Making of the English Literary Past, 1660–1781* (Oxford, 2001), 295.

[5] Thomas Percy to Richard Farmer, September 9, 1762: Cleanth Brooks, ed., *The Percy Letters: Vol. 2, The Correspondence of Thomas Percy and Richard Farmer* (Baton Rouge, 1946), 7.

[6] Richard Hurd, *Letters on Chivalry and Romance* (London, 1762), 24.

[7] Hurd, *Letters*, 24–25.

and general history.[8] Kristine Louise Haugen has countered such criticism by pointing out that when Hurd discusses romance literature, he refers to sixteenth-century, not medieval, romances.[9] Still, even Haugen mistakenly assumed that Hurd was fundamentally commenting on the Middle Ages. To resolve this confusion, it should be noted that, rather than directing his scholarship at the Middle Ages, Hurd was discussing the reign of Queen Elizabeth I, its literature, and its manners. In the process, Hurd made a number of significantly novel claims about the reign of Queen Elizabeth, Elizabethan society, manners, politics, and literature. This chapter examines Hurd's Elizabethan past, in which the monarchy, in the person of Elizabeth, and the nobility were in a balance of political power, while chivalry and romance formed the cultural and literary norms. In this reimagination of Elizabeth's reign, the nobility and landed gentry represented the active participants in society and politics, not the Queen, while its manners were based on an idealized interpretation of chivalry and its literature is a unique blend of romance and classical genres with Edmund Spenser as its archetypal poet. Chivalry was to Hurd the essential system of manners of this ideal Elizabethan society. It held all ranks of a hierarchical society together in a system of mutual esteem and shared obligations of honor and paternalistic duty. In Hurd's eyes, chivalry made Elizabethan England what it was.[10]

Hurd's chivalric revisionism of Elizabeth's reign consists of two parts, each of which will be examined in turn. First, Hurd broke with the established eighteenth-century view of the Virgin Queen's reign, in which she herself was the paragon of both personal and political virtue. Instead, he sought to reduce the active role of Elizabeth by magnifying that of the nobility, turning the Queen into a more passive political figure. Hurd believed a politically over-active monarch to be dangerous to liberty and good governance, and Elizabeth's political power needed to be disarmed to make her fit as a model for eighteenth-century Britons. Second, Hurd

---

[8] David R. Carlson, "Historicism and the In Medium Sordes of Hurd's Letters on Chivalry and Romance," *Exemplaria*, 3 (1991), 95–108; John M. Ganim, "The Myth of Medieval Romance," in eds. R. Howard Bloch and Stephen G. Nichols, *Medievalism and the Modern Temper* (Baltimore, MD, 1996), 148–166, esp. 149–151.

[9] Kristine Louise Haugen, "Chivalry and Romance in the Eighteenth Century: Richard Hurd and the Disenchantment of the Faerie Queene," *Prose Studies: History, Theory, Criticism*, 23 (2000), 45–60, esp. 47.

[10] For modern scholars' views of Elizabethan chivalry and romance: Arthur B. Ferguson, *The Chivalric Tradition in Renaissance England* (Washington D. C., 1986); Richard C. McCoy, *The Rites of Knighthood: The Literature and Politics of Elizabethan Chivalry* (Berkeley, CA, 1986); Alex Davis, *Chivalry and Romance in the English Renaissance* (Cambridge, 2003).

turned to chivalry to describe how a monarch could function within a nobility-dominated polity and culture. Elizabeth became a social fulcrum around which the nobility could express their own prevailing cultural and political ideals. As a set of manners, chivalry united monarch and nobility as the uppermost ranks of a hierarchical society. In this way, Elizabeth's reign, now nobility-centric, could continue to be thought of as the pinnacle of English and British history while avoiding the less advantageous complications of that reign, the reach of the royal prerogative.

A New Elizabethan Past

By emphasizing the primacy of Elizabethan nobility and their manners, and relegating the Virgin Queen herself to that of a passive paragon of chivalric virtue, Hurd's interpretation varies from those of the generations of scholars, poets, and politicians preceding him. During the Restoration, Elizabeth had become an ambivalent symbol of Protestant monarchy,[11] different from the Stuarts in her supposed reliance on Parliament but usable by their supporters as an idealized monarch. After the Glorious Revolution in 1688, Elizabeth was celebrated for her establishment of the Church of England and her resistance to the Catholic powers, while Mary II's reign as joint-monarch brought out comparisons with her female predecessor, although in a de-politicized and domestic setting.[12] The reign of Queen Anne witnessed a flowering of comparisons between her and Elizabeth, this time celebrating the political and martial power of both Queens, as well as their essential Englishness.[13] This was true for the work of both Tories, such as Matthew Prior, who wrote:

> When bright Eliza rul'd Britannia's State,
> Widely distributing her high Commands;
> And boldly Wise and fortunately Great
> Freed the glad Nations from Tyrannick Bands[14]

[11] John Watkins, *Representing Elizabeth in Stuart England: Literature, History, Sovereignty* (Cambridge, 2002), 108–135.

[12] Watkins, *Representing Elizabeth*, 188–206.

[13] Joseph Hone, *Literature and Party Politics at the Accession of Queen Anne* (Oxford, 2017), 72–73.

[14] Matthew Prior, *The Literary Works of Matthew Prior*, eds. H. B. Bunker Wright and Monroe K. Spears, 2 vols. (Oxford, 1959), I, 232.

and Whigs, like John Oldmixon:

> She, for whom Collin touch'd his golden Lyre,
> And Sung her Glorious Acts with equal fire;
> Ev'n She, must now to ANNA'S Reign resign
> The first Bright Page, and in the second shine.
> Eliza's Arms reliev'd an Infant State,
> But Empires are by ANN'S repriev'd from Fate.
> Her Hero's the New World explor'd for Gold,
> But ANN'S for Glory only save the Old.[15]

In poems such as these, and there were many more, written in language and imagery redolent of Edmund Spenser, the martial rule of Elizabeth and Anne as Queens is celebrated, although the Duke of Marlborough features prominently in Oldmixon's poem, making Anne less central by elevating the Duke's warrior role.[16] Nevertheless, Anne is an active queen, defending Britain and bringing peace through her personal power and grace. Such panegyric appeals to Elizabeth as an idealized monarchical model had their apogee in the writings of Henry St. John, Viscount Bolingbroke, and other Patriot writers of the mid-eighteenth century.[17] In their writings, Elizabeth becomes a Patriot Queen *avant-la-lettre*, uniting people and nobility under her benevolent rule, supported by Parliament, casting off the chains of corruption, defeating foreign invasion, and increasing England's mercantile power by the force of her personality alone.[18] Although losing some of its fervency, this type of hagiography continued to be common throughout the eighteenth century.[19] Nevertheless, some eighteenth-century writers resisted this tradition of excessive praise for Elizabeth. David Hume, in his assessment of Elizabeth's reign, concluded

---

[15] John Oldmixon, *A Pastoral Poem on the Victories at Schellenburgh and Blenheim: Obtain'd by the Arms of the Confederates, under the Command of His Grace the Duke of Marlborough* (London, 1704), 4–5.

[16] Watkins, *Representing Elizabeth*, 213.

[17] Christine Gerrard, *The Patriot Opposition to Walpole: Politics, Poetry and National Myth, 1725–1742* (Oxford, 1994), 150–184. For more on how Patriots idealized historical monarchs: Jurriaan M. van Santvoort, "Chivalric Models of Patriot Kingship: Gilbert West, Lord Lyttelton and *The Idea of a Patriot King*," *History of European Ideas*, 44 (2018), 14–34.

[18] Henry St. John, Viscount Bolingbroke, *Historical Writings*, ed. Isaac Kramnick (Chicago, 1972), 238–274.

[19] Julia M. Walker, *The Elizabeth Icon: 1603–2003* (Basingstoke, 2004), 119–120. See also, Jennifer Clement, "Elizabeth I, Patriotism, and the Imagined Nation in Three Eighteenth-Century Plays," *Intellectual History Review*, 22 (2012), 391–410; Jack Lynch, *The Age of Elizabeth in the Age of Johnson* (Cambridge, 2003), 67–69.

"Scarcely any sovereign before Elizabeth, and none after her, carried higher, both in speculation and practice, the authority of the crown."[20] Lord Hervey, a Court Whig supporter of Sir Robert Walpole and political opponent of Bolingbroke's, argued that far from being an ideal monarch reigning in conjunction with Parliament, Elizabeth had been a tyrant, ruling through the royal prerogative and binding the people with the "Yoke of Slavery."[21]

Richard Hurd found himself in the late 1750s stuck between these two positions. On the one hand, he believed fervently that Elizabeth's reign had been the high-point of English history, as well as literature, in particular because of his admiration for Edmund Spenser's *The Faerie Queene*.[22] Therefore, her reign needed defending from claims that it had been that of a tyrant. On the other hand, Hurd's own politically conservative Whig inclinations did not allow him to celebrate Elizabeth as a uniquely patriotic and benevolent monarch. Such a comparison was too critical of the aristocratic Whig system of government in place since the Hanoverian Succession of 1714. Indeed, such a panegyric on the power of monarchy would come close to calling to mind a return to some bastardized version of royal absolutism. For this very reason, Bolingbroke, in his influential but controversial *Idea of a Patriot King* (written 1738, published 1749), had gone out of his way to ensure that his royal patriotism could not be construed with the divine right of kings.[23] At the same time, political radicals were increasingly vocal about the need to drastically reform the, in their eyes, corrupt and oligarchical nature of the Whig-dominated political system in place since the Glorious Revolution and the accession of George I in 1714.[24] Consequently, any full-scale assault on Elizabeth's status as a

---

[20] David Hume, *The History of England: From the Invasion of Julius Caesar to the Revolution of 1688*, 6 vols. (Indianapolis, 1983), iv, 124.

[21] John Hervey, Baron Hervey, *Ancient and Modern Liberty Stated and Compared* (London, 1734), 24. Cited in H. T. Dickinson, *Liberty and Property: Political Ideology in Eighteenth-Century Britain* (London, 1977), 141.

[22] Hurd, *Letters*, 119. For more on the eighteenth-century reception of Spenser: David Hill Radcliffe, *Edmund Spenser: A Reception History* (Columbia, SC., 1996); Richard C. Frushell, *Edmund Spenser in the Early Eighteenth Century: Education, Imitation and the Making of a Literary Model* (Pittsburgh, PA., 1999); Hazel Wilkinson, *Edmund Spenser and the Eighteenth-Century Book* (Cambridge, 2017).

[23] Henry St. John, Viscount Bolingbroke, *Political Writings*, ed. David Armitage (Cambridge: 1997), 228, 231.

[24] For radical politics during the reign of George III: John Brewer, *Party Ideology and Popular Politics at the Accession of George III* (Cambridge, 1976); Brewer, "English Radicalism

symbol of the ideal English monarch would place Hurd dangerously close to the radicals, whom he despised.[25] Hurd stresses that in the reign of Elizabeth, the royal prerogative had reached its zenith, strongly implying that the Virgin Queen had been in a certain sense a tyrannical monarch.[26] Yet, so Hurd stresses equally, like her Tudor father and grandfather, Elizabeth had always ruled with the cooperation of Parliament. While partly a refutation of the traditional eighteenth-century view of Elizabeth as a uniquely and personally virtuous queen, Hurd would not settle for such a simplified balanced opinion. He sought to rehabilitate Elizabeth's reign on different grounds, disarming its politically controversial legacy and emphasizing instead that it was England's Golden Age because of the manners of its nobility.

This nobility-centric argument takes the form of two dialogues between Joseph Addison and Dr. John Arbuthnot, who debate Elizabeth's reign while wandering through the ruins of the Earl of Leicester's great castle at Kenilworth. Arbuthnot defends Elizabeth's reign from the vehement imputations of tyranny made by Addison, whose fictional opinions, Hurd admitted to a friend, were inspired by factious radical politics.[27] The fictional Addison finds no virtue at all in the reign of a Queen who abused her prerogative, the loyalty of her noble subjects, and the pliability of her Parliaments.[28] He does not see her reign as a Golden Age at all[29]; nothing in the ruins of Kenilworth is worthy of praise: "what can these objects call to mind but the memory of barbarous manners and a despotic government?"[30]

in the Age of George III," in ed. J.G.A. Pocock, *Three British Revolutions: 1641, 1688, 1776* (Princeton, NJ, 1980), 323–67; Ian R. Christie, *Wilkes, Wyvill and Reform: The Parliamentary Reform Movement in British Politics 1760–1785* (London, 1962); Dickinson, *Liberty and Property*, 195–231; and Dickinson, *The Politics of the People in Eighteenth-Century Britain* (London, 1995), 221–54.

[25] Hurd to William Mason, May 8, 1770: Ernest Harold Pearce, *The Correspondence of Richard Hurd and William Mason*, ed. Leonard Whibley (Cambridge, 2014), 74–75.

[26] Richard Hurd, *Moral and Political Dialogues; with Letters on Chivalry and Romance*, 3 vols. (London, 1788, sixth edition), II, 21, 263.

[27] Richard Hurd to Thomas Balguy, September 6, 1759: Sarah Brewer, ed., *The Early Letters of Bishop Richard Hurd, 1739–1752* (Woodbridge, 1995), 347. Hurd's views on the prerogative were similar, but not on the implications this had for monarchy. Hurd was a strong supporter of monarchical rule, which he envisioned to be more informal.

[28] Hurd, *Dialogues*, II, 2–82, *passim*.

[29] Hurd, *Dialogues*, I, 155–156.

[30] Hurd, *Dialogues*, I, 158.

Hurd, in a subsequent dialogue, defended the use of the prerogative under the Tudors by pointing out that they ruled with the consent of Parliament but also that these monarchs were always inclined to court the consent and love of their people. "Thus we see that, though the entire reigns of the house of Tudor, that is, the most despotic and arbitrary of our princes, the forms of liberty were still kept up, and the constitution maintained, even amidst the advantages of all sorts which offered for the destruction of both."[31] This courting of the people is key to Hurd's understanding of Elizabethan politics, and it excuses to some extent the size to which the royal prerogative had swelled. Hurd does this by focusing not on the formal politics of the period, but by emphasizing its manners. This change of focus was novel in England, even while in Scotland, the study of manners was the central point of Scottish Enlightenment historiography, already being investigated by William Robertson and Adam Smith and within a few years also by Adam Ferguson and Lord Kames.[32] Like Hurd, the scholars of the Scottish Enlightenment also recognized the historical importance of chivalric manners,[33] although the influence of the Scots on Hurd or vice versa is difficult to assess.

THE CHIVALRY OF THE ELIZABETHANS

What, then, are these manners that Hurd believed ameliorated the rule of Queen Elizabeth and made her reign a Golden Age? Through the voice of Arbuthnot, Hurd argued it was chivalry. Having arisen from the rigors of the feudal constitution, which it served to moderate by binding all noblemen and princes into a system of mutual esteem and honor,[34] chivalry had four essential characteristics. First, being chivalrous meant having a passion for arms, honor, valor, and martial prowess; second, it meant upholding justice and succoring the distressed; third, it meant being courteous, affable, and gallant, in particular with regard to the treatment of women.

---

[31] Hurd, *Dialogues*, II, 269.

[32] David Allan, *Virtue, Learning and the Scottish Enlightenment: Ideas of Scholarship in Early Modern History* (Edinburgh, 1993), 163. The Scottish Enlightenment scholars were profoundly indebted, in ways Hurd was not, to Francis Hutcheson, *An Inquiry into the Original of Our Ideas of Beauty and Virtue in Two Treatises* (Indianapolis, 2004).

[33] David Allen, "'An Institution Quite Misunderstood': Chivalry and Sentimentalism in the Late Scottish Enlightenment," in eds. Katie Stevenson and Barbara Gribling, *Chivalry and the Medieval Past* (Woodbridge, 2016), 15–34.

[34] Hurd, *Letters*, 7–8.

Finally, it meant being a pious Christian.[35] To Hurd, these four character-istics, "PROWESS, GENEROSITY, GALANTRY, and RELIGION," made up "the vaunted characteristics of the purer ages of Chivalry."[36] They continued to dominate Elizabethan England, in his mind, and formed the manners of the Queen's court and of the English nobility. The manners of chivalry determined not simply the interaction of queen and nobility, but also that with the rest of society. To Hurd, chivalry was strongly hierarchical, masculine, and religious, and it in turn shaped the English society as a whole along those lines.

In being chivalrous, the Elizabethan landed nobility, titled or not, exceeded in manners in a certain way those of Hurd's own eighteenth-century noble contemporaries. They lived, metaphorically speaking, "under a brighter sun and [in a] happier climate than we can boast of."[37] Elizabethan noblemen were hospitable, courteous, and frugal, while their pride, martial character, and honor represented a bulwark against the overweening power of the Crown, as represented in the royal preroga-tive.[38] Indeed the heroes of the English past had always been chivalrous: they "as have been most admired for their personal virtues, and have been most concerned in restoring the arts of civility and politeness, have been powerfully addicted to the feats of ancient prowess."[39] This idealization of the Elizabethan nobility could also serve contemporary purposes. Since Elizabethan England was English history's Golden Age and the nobility was the central pillar of its greatness, Hurd's argument had two ramifica-tions. First, it would encourage eighteenth-century noblemen to behave in a better way; and second, it would work to disarm the ideological oppo-nents of the Court Whigs. As Gerald Newman and Bob Harris have noted, the British nobility was by the 1750s increasingly coming under fire for debasing English culture, morals, and society, while its political control of

---

[35] Hurd, *Letters*, 11–23.

[36] Hurd, *Letters*, 22.

[37] Hurd, *Dialogues*, I, 156.

[38] Hurd, *Dialogues*, I, 158–162, 163–164. Philip Connell has hinted that this could be interpreted as a variant of the French *Thèse Nobiliaire*, which aimed to restrain royal power by enlarging the political power of the French nobility: "British Identities and the Politics of Ancient Poetry in Later Eighteenth-Century England," *The Historical Journal*, 49 (2006), 161–192, esp. 187. Hurd's authority for historical chivalry, Sainte-Palaye, wrote his anti-quarian work within the context of the *Thèse Nobiliaire*: Lionel Gossman, *Medievalism and the Ideologies of the Enlightenment: The World and Work of La Curne de Sainte-Palaye* (Baltimore, MD, 1968), 92–93.

[39] Hurd, *Dialogues*, I, 178.

Parliament and government was termed "corruption."[40] By relocating the Elizabethan nobility as the active center of society and politics and praising their manners, Hurd aimed to show that a powerful aristocracy was not as deleterious as its critics pretended, but was in fact the ideal standard. The mixed or balanced constitution, so beloved of the Court Whigs,[41] was retained, but with the aristocratic element as the stabilizing force, supported by an encouraging monarch and in control of a deferential people.

Elizabethan society benefitted immensely from such chivalrous manners. Chivalry spurred noblemen to virtuous behavior:

> The youth, in general, were fired with the love of martial exercises. They were early formed to habits of fatigue and enterprise. And together with this warlike spirit, the profession of chivalry was favorable to every other virtue. Affability, courtesy, generosity, veracity, these were the qualifications most pretended to by men of arms, in the days of pure and uncorrupted chivalry.[42]

Chivalry had been the natural consequence of the feudal constitution. While the nobility had been tied to their sovereign princes by their tenures, they also held a measure of independence, which turned each into a petty tyrant. Given the feudal nobility's penchant for violence, plunder, and injustice, chivalry arose as a system to regulate the behavior of the nobility. Chivalry encouraged "compassion, gentleness, and generous attachment to the unfortunate."[43] These manners reformed the nobility from potential tyrants into the upholders of justice at a time when the state did not yet fulfill this function. And the same was true of princes, who held excessive power, but because of their existence within the chivalric system, did not abuse it. In a way, this allowed Hurd to excuse Elizabeth's use of the royal prerogative, because it was not used for tyrannical actions, but only in accordance with the norms of chivalry, which were always a source of justice and honor.

[40] Gerald Newman, *The Rise of English Nationalism: A Cultural History, 1740–1830* (London, 1987), 63; Bob Harris, *Politics and the Nation: Britain in the Mid-Eighteenth Century* (Oxford, 2002), 85; Philip Harling, *The Waning of 'Old Corruption': The Politics of Economical Reform in Britain, 1779–1846* (Oxford, 1996), 3.

[41] Reed Browning, *Political and Constitutional Ideas of the Court Whigs* (Baton Rouge, LA, 1986), 180–181. For an overview of eighteenth-century defenses of aristocracy and nobility: John Cannon, *Aristocratic Century: The Peerage of Eighteenth-Century England* (Cambridge, 1984), 148–174.

[42] Hurd, Dialogue, I, 176.

[43] Hurd, *Letters*, 36.

Along with a number of his contemporaries, Hurd believed chivalry to have softened the rigors of the feudal system, which according to some other eighteenth-century historians had made virtual slaves of the common people.[44] Rather, so Hurd has it, chivalry gave the nobility a sense of paternalism, an almost symbiotic bond between the upper and lower ranks of society. Through chivalry:

> The pre-eminence of rank and fortune was nobly sustained: the subordination of society preserved: and yet the envy that is so apt to attend the great, happily avoided. Hence the weight and influence of the old nobility, who engaged the love, as well as commanded the veneration, of the people. In the meantime, rural industry flourished: private luxury was discouraged: and in both ways that frugal, simplicity of life, our country's grace and ornament of those days, was preserved and promoted.[45]

The poor and needy would flock to the castles and manor houses of the chivalric nobility in the hopes of finding redress and justice, because they understood that chivalry engendered in the nobility a sort of *noblesse oblige*.[46]

The gallantry and courtesy inherent in chivalry, moreover, gave a softness to the interaction between men and women, and the valor and honor of men and the chastity of women were strengthened by their place within the chivalric system. "[T]his gallantry had no ill influence on morals" when it was custom "for the women to pride themselves in their chastity, as well as the men in their valour."[47] Women were secure because men were chivalric. Chivalry encouraged men to platonically adore women as objects and to protect their chastity and honor against those who would ravage them. This gendered nature of reimagined chivalry was part of what Barbara Taylor has identified as a backlash against perceived reductions in gender differences in the eighteenth century.[48] Indeed, chivalry soon came to form the central part of masculinity itself.[49]

---

[44] Catherine Macaulay, *The History of England from the Accession of James I to That of the Brunswick Line*, 8 vols. (London, 1765); Peter de Rapin-Thoyras, *The History of England, as well Ecclesiastical and Civil*, trans. Nicholas Tindal, 15 vols. (London, 1731).

[45] Hurd, *Dialogues*, I, 162.

[46] Hurd, *Letters*, 62.

[47] Hurd, *Dialogues*, I, 169–171.

[48] Barbara Taylor, "Feminists versus Gallants: Manners and Morals in Enlightenment Britain," in eds. Sarah Knott and Barbara Taylor, *Women, Gender and Enlightenment* (Basingstoke, 2005), 30–52, esp. 40–41.

[49] Michèle Cohen, "'Manners' Make the Man: Politeness, Chivalry, and the Construction of Masculinity," *Journal of British Studies*, vol. 44 (2005), 312–329.

While Hurd was aware that feudalism had lost much of its vigor after the end of the Wars of the Roses, his Elizabethan society still followed the same political and cultural norms.[50] The Queen's function in this idealized, nobility-dominated Elizabethan society was not as a personally ruling monarch, but as the facilitator of chivalrous manners. In an abandonment of classical ideas of political virtue, Elizabeth's personal virtues were to be admired, not her virtues as a political actor. These latter virtues were, as mentioned earlier, those of a ruler relying on the royal prerogative. The social manners the Queen encouraged were those of chivalry.

By disarming Elizabeth as a political actor and assigning her prominent cultural and social power, Hurd was also rendering her into passivity. Whereas the political monarch has an active role to play in society, Hurd assigned Elizabeth a role as a mere encourager of the right and admirable manners of others:

> Every kind of merit was encouraged by her smile, or rewarded by her bounty. Virtue, she knew, would thrive best on its native stock, a generous emulation. This she promoted by all means; by her royal countenance, by a temperate and judicious praise, by the widest distribution of her preferments.[51]

Hurd saw this as a function of monarchs in general, not something confined to past monarchs. He would later in life praise George III for setting an example to be emulated:

> Your Majesty has done your part in the great work [infusing a better spirit into the rising generation], and it is one of the disgraces of our degenerate age, that the effect of it is not everywhere conspicuous. By degrees however this country must feel the influence of the royal countenance and example; and a time will come when your enlarged views for the good of all your subjects, in all parts of your Dominion.[52]

To be sure, a monarch, be it the historical Elizabeth or the reigning George, has a role in politics and a monarch's behavior might coincide with that of their subjects. Like her noble subjects, Elizabeth herself

---

[50] Hurd, *Letters*, 116.

[51] Hurd, *Dialogues*, ii, 21–22.

[52] Richard Hurd to George III, August 17, 1782: Sir John Fortescue, ed., *The Correspondence of King George the Third: From 1760 to December 1783*, 6 vols. (London, 1928), VI, 104.

adored everything chivalric, but in Hurd's *Dialogues* and *Letters* she never appears active: her own inclinations only animated her noble subjects to be ever more chivalrous in their actions.[53] This passivity fits into a growing trend in eighteenth-century historiography, which, for political reasons, sought to disarm the cultural and historical power of queens.[54]

Hurd found the evidence for his idealized chivalric Elizabethan society in the romances written at the time, in particular Spenser's *Faerie Queene*, which he used to fill in the gaps that his limited scholarship had not provided. In Hurd's reading, a Prince or high-ranking nobleman could act like the character of the Faerie Queene, as an encourager of the chivalric actions of the several knights-errant whom she sends on their various quests: "It was usual, in the days of knight-errantry, at the holding of any great feast, for Knights to appear before the Prince, who presided at, and claim the privilege of being sent on any adventure, to which the solemnity might give occasion."[55] He imagined that real-world chivalry in its purest form functioned likewise, with a Prince sending a knight on adventures, and that it symbolically and allegorically continued to be observed into the Elizabethan period: "This was the real practice, in the days of pure and antient chivalry. And an image of this practice was afterwards kept up in the castles of the great, on any extraordinary festival or solemnity."[56] Queen Elizabeth functioned as the Fearie Queene in this reading, as she allows her nobility to act on their chivalry in her honor and at her direction. The nobility of the Elizabethan period, so Hurd would have it, derived their chivalry—the central manners of their social existence—from their Queen. This direct allegorical comparison between the fictional world of Spenser and late sixteenth-century England was not unique to Hurd. John Upton, writing at the same time, identified the Fairy Queen Gloriana's war against the Paynim King as a mirror for Elizabeth's war against the King of Spain: "in one sense you are in Fairy land, yet in another you may be in the British dominions."[57]

---

[53] Hurd, *Letters*, 118.

[54] Karen O'Brien, *Narratives of Enlightenment: Cosmopolitan History from Voltaire to Gibbon* (Cambridge, 1997), 115. See, for example: William Robertson, *The History of Scotland During the Reigns of Queen Mary and King James VI. Till His Accession to the Crown of England*, 2 vols. (London, 1781), I, 430.

[55] Hurd, *Letters*, 62.

[56] Hurd, *Letters*, 63.

[57] John Upton, *Spenser's Faerie Queene: A New Edition with a Glossary, and Notes Explanatory and Critical*, 2 vols. (London, 1758), I, p. xxvii.

In a somewhat circular reasoning, Hurd believed that the Elizabethan period favored romance literature as its genre, and that it was therefore possible to deduce much about the manners of that period by reading those romances. This is why the evidence for Hurd's claims in the *Letters on Chivalry and Romance* is almost exclusively taken from sixteenth-century romance poetry. These romances were, in the end, why Hurd was desperate to defend the Elizabethan period, even against his own view of Elizabeth's use of the royal prerogative, which he mollified by emphasizing the Queen's function as the encourager of chivalric manners.[58] Her reign brought forth the greatest literary product in the English language, and because to eighteenth-century minds, literature, manners, and politics were bound together, the reign of a tyrant could not have produced *Faerie Queene*. Only by turning Elizabeth from a politically powerful Queen into the facilitator of the chivalry of her noble subjects could Spenser's genius be explained. Spenser after all saw chivalry all around him, and naturally turned it into poetry:

> he was [ ] befriended in these fictions, ... by the romantic Spirit of his age; much was brought into fresh credit, by the romantic Elizabeth. Her inclinations for the fancies of Chivalry is well known; and obsequious wits and courtiers would not be wanting to feed and flatter it. In short, tilts and tournaments were in vogue: the Arcadia, and the Faery Queen were written.[59]

Through romance literature and romantic pageants such as that of the Lady of the Lake at Kenilworth, Elizabeth's subjects could celebrate their monarch.[60] The Elizabethan incarnation of romance literature was a mixture of the traditional Gothic romance and revived Classical poetry,[61] avoiding the faults of the ridiculous medieval romances, which Chaucer, Cervantes, and Ben Jonson had mocked. The Elizabethan romances showed the true and pure form of chivalry, and celebrated in lustrous fashion the grandeur of the nobility and the Virgin Queen.

---

[58] Hurd, *Dialogues*, II, 22. Nandini Das has recently emphasized the mutability of Elizabethan court chivalry, showing that it could be used both by the Queen to encourage her noble subjects and by the nobility to assert their own political and cultural power: *Renaissance Romance: The Transformation of English Prose Fiction, 1570–1620* (Farnham, 2011), 35–54.

[59] Hurd, *Letters*, 116–117.

[60] Hurd, *Dialogues*, I, 188.

[61] Hurd, *Letters*, 56.

Conclusion

Hurd was not the only one to use chivalry and romance to celebrate the literature, actions, and behaviors of the English or British past.[62] Thomas Warton and Thomas Percy were engaged in the same projects and took some of their inspiration from Hurd. Like Hurd, Warton viewed this idealized chivalric and romantic past as superior to his own time, associating it with elite institutions such as the nobility, court, and church.[63] By focusing on the Elizabethan period, Hurd was discussing that period most admired by eighteenth-century Britons while arguing against the prevailing wind in the British historical consciousness, which had elevated Elizabeth I into the very model of a virtuous monarch. To Hurd, she was virtuous indeed, but only in a politically passive manner, as the facilitator and encourager of the ideal behavior of her noble subjects. Hurd wanted to describe the Elizabethan Golden Age as the Golden Age of the English nobility, celebrating the "hospitality and bravery of our ancestors" who cultivated among themselves "every flower of humanity, every elegance of art and genius."[64] Their chivalrous manners and the romance literature that they inspired and were inspired by were what made the Elizabethan period a Golden Age, not the actions of Elizabeth I. The nobility stands at the center of this chivalric Elizabethanism, not the Queen; their power enhanced while hers is diminished as the use of the royal prerogative becomes less tyrannical, but also less significant. A chivalrous nobility, after all, would not have permitted such abuses. Elizabeth I, to be sure, had an important role in the society of her time, but for Hurd she plays a subordinate role to the nobility, whose chivalry held her in check, even as they used her to encourage their own chivalry. The Virgin Queen was a passive player; the field being left to those noblemen whose chivalry shone brightest; or at least this was how she was remembered.

---

[62] For this creation of a canonical literary past: Howard D. Weinbrot, *Britannia's Issue: The Rise of British Literature from Dryden to Ossian* (Cambridge, 1993); Jonathan Kramnick, *Making the English Canon: Print-Capitalism and the Cultural Past, 1700–1770* (Cambridge, 1998); Terry, *Poetry and the Making*.

[63] Jonathan Kramnick, "The Cultural Logic of Late Feudalism: Placing Spenser in the Eighteenth-Century," *ELH*, 63 (1996), 871–892, esp. 888.

[64] Hurd, *Dialogues*, I, 186.

BIBLIOGRAPHY

PRIMARY SOURCES

Bolingbroke, H. St. John, Viscount. *Historical Writings*, ed. Isaac Kramnick. Chicago: University of Chicago Press, 1972.

―――. *Political Writings*, ed. David Armitage. Cambridge: Cambridge University Press, 1997.

Brewer, Sarah. ed. *The Early Letters of Bishop Richard Hurd, 1739–1752*. Woodbridge: Boydell and Brewer, 1995.

Brooks, Cleanth. ed. *The Percy Letters: Vol. 2, The Correspondence of Thomas Percy and Richard Farmer*. Baton Rouge: Louisiana University Press, 1946.

Fortescue, Sir J. ed. *The Correspondence of King George the Third: From 1760 to December 1783*, 6 vols. London, 1928.

Hervey, J. Hervey, Baron. *Ancient and Modern Liberty Stated and Compared*. London, 1734.

Hume, David. *The History of England: From the Invasion of Julius Caesar to the Revolution of 1688*, 6 vols. Indianapolis: Online Library of Liberty, 1983.

Hurd, Richard. *Letters on Chivalry and Romance*. London, 1762.

―――. *Moral and Political Dialogues; with Letters on Chivalry and Romance*, 3 vols. London, 1788, sixth edition.

Hutcheson, Francis. *An Inquiry into the Original of Our Ideas of Beauty and Virtue in Two Treatises*. Indianapolis, 2004.

Kilvert, Francis. *Memoirs of the Life and Writings of the Right Rev. Richard Hurd, D. D., Lord Bishop of Worcester; with a Selection from his Unpublished Correspondence and Other Unpublished Papers*. London, 1860.

Macaulay, Catherine. *The History of England from the Accession of James I to That of the Brunswick Line*, 8 vols. London, 1765.

Oldmixon, John. *A Pastoral Poem on the Victories at Schellenburgh and Blenheim: Obtain'd by the Arms of the Confederates, under the Command of His Grace the Duke of Marlborough*. London, 1704.

Pearce, E. H. *The Correspondence of Richard Hurd and William Mason*, ed. Leonard Whibley. Cambridge: Cambridge University Press, 2014.

Prior, Matthew. *The Literary Works of Matthew Prior*, eds. H. B. Bunker Wright and Monroe K. Spears, 2 vols. Oxford: Oxford University Press, 1959.

Rapin-Thoyras, Peter de. *The History of England, as well Ecclesiastical and Civil*, trans. Nicholas Tindal, 15 vols. London, 1731.

Robertson, William. *The History of Scotland During the Reigns of Queen Mary and King James VI. Till His Accession to the Crown of England*, 2 vols. London, 1781.

Upton, John. *Spenser's Faerie Queene: A New Edition with a Glossary, and Notes Explanatory and Critical*, 2 vols. London, 1758.

Warton, Thomas. *Observations of the Faerie Queene of Spenser* London, 1754.

SECONDARY SOURCES

Allan, David W. "'An Institution Quite Misunderstood": Chivalry and Sentimentalism in the Late Scottish Enlightenment', in eds. Katie Stevenson and Barbara Gribling, *Chivalry and the Medieval Past*, 15–34. Woodbridge: Boydell and Brewer, 2016.

———. *Virtue, Learning and the Scottish Enlightenment: Ideas of Scholarship in Early Modern History*. Edinburgh: Edinburg University Press, 1993.

Brewer, John. *Party Ideology and Popular Politics at the Accession of George III*. Cambridge: Cambridge University Press, 1976.

———. 'English Radicalism in the Age of George III', in ed. J.G.A. Pocock, *Three British Revolutions: 1641, 1688, 1776*, 323–67. Princeton, NJ: Princeton Legacy Library, 1980.

Browning, Reed. *Political and Constitutional Ideas of the Court Whigs*. Baton Rouge, LA: Louisiana State University Press, 1986.

Cannon, John. *Aristocratic Century: The Peerage of Eighteenth-Century England*. Cambridge: Cambridge University Press, 1984.

Carlson, David, R. "Historicism and the In Medium Sordes of Hurd's Letters on Chivalry and Romance." *Exemplaria*, 3 (1991): 95–108.

Christie, Ian, R. *Wilkes, Wyvill and Reform: The Parliamentary Reform Movement in British Politics 1760–1785*. London: Macmillan, 1962.

Clement, Jennifer. "Elizabeth I, Patriotism, and the Imagined Nation in Three Eighteenth-Century Plays." *Intellectual History Review*, 22 (2012): 391–410.

Cohen, Michèle. "'Manners' Make the Man: Politeness, Chivalry, and the Construction of Masculinity." *Journal of British Studies*, vol. 44 (2005): 312–329.

Connell, Philip. "British Identities and the Politics of Ancient Poetry in Later Eighteenth-Century England." *The Historical Journal*, 49 (2006): 161–192.

Das, Nandini. *Renaissance Romance: The Transformation of English Prose Fiction, 1570–1620*. Farnham: Routledge, 2011.

Davis, Alex. *Chivalry and Romance in the English Renaissance*. Cambridge: Cambridge University Press, 2003.

Dickinson, H. T. *Liberty and Property: Political Ideology in Eighteenth-Century Britain*. London: Weidenfeld and Nicolson, 1977.

———, *The Politics of the People in Eighteenth-Century Britain*. London: Palgrave Macmillan, 1995.

Ditchfield, G. M. and Sarah Brewer. "Richard Hurd (1720–1808), Bishop of Worcester," *Oxford Dictionary of National Biography* http://www.oxforddnb. com/view/10.1093/ref:odnb/9780198614128.001.0001/odnb-9780198614128-e-14249, accessed January 15, 2018.

Ferguson, Arthur, B. *The Chivalric Tradition in Renaissance England*. Washington D. C.: Folger Books, 1986.

Frushell, Richard, C. *Edmund Spenser in the Early Eighteenth Century: Education, Imitation and the Making of a Literary Model*. Pittsburgh, PA: Dusquene University Press, 1999.

Ganim, John, M. "The Myth of Medieval Romance," in eds. R. Howard Bloch and Stephen G. Nichols, *Medievalism and the Modern Temper*, 148–166. Baltimore, MD, 1996.

Gerrard, Christine. *The Patriot Opposition to Walpole: Politics, Poetry and National Myth, 1725–1742*. Oxford: Oxford University Press, 1994.

Gossman, Lionel. *Medievalism and the Ideologies of the Enlightenment: The World and Work of La Curne de Sainte-Palaye*. Baltimore, MD: John Hopkins Press, 1968.

Harling, Philip. *The Waning of 'Old Corruption': The Politics of Economical Reform in Britain, 1779–1846*. Oxford: Oxford University Press, 1996.

Harris, Robert. *Politics and the Nation: Britain in the Mid-Eighteenth Century*. Oxford: Oxford University Press, 2002.

Haugen, Kristin, L. "Chivalry and Romance in the Eighteenth Century: Richard Hurd and the Disenchantment of the Faerie Queene." *Prose Studies: History, Theory, Criticism*, 23 (2000): 45–60.

Hone, Joseph. *Literature and Party Politics at the Accession of Queen Anne*. Oxford: Oxford University Press, 2017.

Kramnick, Jonathan, B. "The Cultural Logic of Late Feudalism: Placing Spenser in the Eighteenth-Century." *ELH*, 63 (1996): 871–892.

———, *Making the English Canon: Print-Capitalism and the Cultural Past, 1700–1770*. Cambridge: Cambridge University Press, 1998.

Lynch, Jack. *The Age of Elizabeth in the Age of Johnson*. Cambridge: Cambridge University Press, 2003.

McCoy, Richard, C. *The Rites of Knighthood: The Literature and Politics of Elizabethan Chivalry*. Berkeley, CA: University of California Press, 1986.

Newman, Gerald. *The Rise of English Nationalism: A Cultural History, 1740–1830*. London: Palgrave Macmillan, 1987.

O'Brien, Karen. *Narratives of Enlightenment: Cosmopolitan History from Voltaire to Gibbon*. Cambridge: Cambridge University Press, 1997.

Radcliffe, David, H. *Edmund Spenser: A Reception History*. Columbia, SC: Camden House 1996.

Taylor, Barbara. "Feminists versus Gallants: Manners and Morals in Enlightenment Britain," in eds. Sarah Knott and Barbara Taylor, *Women, Gender and Enlightenment*, 30–52. Basingstoke: Palgrave Macmillan, 2005.

Terry, Richard. *Poetry and the Making of the English Literary Past, 1660–1781*. Oxford: Oxford University Press, 2001.

Van Santvoort, Jurriaan, M. "Chivalric Models of Patriot Kingship: Gilbert West, Lord Lyttelton and *The Idea of a Patriot King*." *History of European Ideas*, 44 (2018): 14–34.

Walker, Julia, M. *The Elizabeth Icon: 1603–2003*. Basingstoke: Palgrave Macmillan, 2004.

Watkins, John. *Representing Elizabeth in Stuart England: Literature, History, Sovereignty*. Cambridge: Cambridge University Press, 2002.

Weinbrot, Howard, D., *Britannia's Issue: The Rise of British Literature from Dryden to Ossian*. Cambridge: Cambridge University Press, 1993.

Wilkinson, Hazel. *Edmund Spenser and the Eighteenth-Century Book*. Cambridge: Cambridge University Press, 2017.

PART II

Reinterpretation in Art

Charles IX of France or the Anti-King: His Legacy in Plays and Chronicles in Seventeenth- and Long Eighteenth-Century France

Estelle Paranque

Charles IX of France was born on June 27, 1550, at Saint-Germain-en-Laye. The second son of Henry II of France and Catherine de Medici, he was not raised as *dauphin*; however, following the death of his elder brother Francis II in 1560, he became king of France at the early age of nine.[1] His mother Catherine de Medici acted as regent until his majority

---

All translations are mine. Any errors are mine as well.

[1] Caroline zum Kolk, "'Tout Paix et Amitié.' La maison des enfants d'Henri II et Catherine de Médicis," in *Naissance et petite enfance à la cour de France, Moyen-Age-XIXe siècle*, eds. Pascale Mormiche et Stanis Perez (Villeneuve d'Ascq: Septentrion Presses Universitaire, 2016), 79–96, 88.

E. Paranque (✉)
New College of the Humanities, London, UK

© The Author(s) 2019
E. Paranque (ed.), *Remembering Queens and Kings of Early Modern England and France*, Queenship and Power,
https://doi.org/10.1007/978-3-030-22344-1_7

115

in 1563 but remained an important political figure throughout his reign—
to the point that some historians argue that she was the one ruling France.[2]
Scholarship on the co-rulership of Charles and Catherine has focused on
how Catherine helped her son assert his royal authority over his people
during their royal tours of France and on their respective roles in the wars
of religion.[3]

Despite the queen mother's efforts to present her son as a strong ruler,
Charles's reign is mostly remembered because of the decades of religious
civil wars ravaging the country, climaxing with the horrors of the 1572 St.
Bartholomew's Day Massacre.[4] This devastating event in early modern
French history occurred at the wedding in 1572 of Catherine's daughter,
Marguerite de Valois, and Henri de Navarre, who was next in line to the
throne after the Dukes of Anjou and Alencon. Catherine hoped that the
marriage between her Catholic daughter and the Protestant Navarre
would unite the religious factions and end years of conflict. Instead, a
disastrous bloodbath took place when a French Catholic, possibly under
orders from the Duke of Guise, Phillip II of Spain, or even Catherine herself, attempted to assassinate Gaspard de Coligny, leader of the Protestant
Huguenots. Afraid the Huguenots would retaliate, those in power ordered
mass murder of the unarmed Protestants who had arrived in Paris for the
royal wedding, as well as Huguenots already living in Paris. One contemporary source wrote that "the streets were covered with dead bodies; the

---

[2] See Katherine Crawford, "Catherine de Medicis and the Performance of Political
Motherhood," *The Sixteenth Century Journal*, Vol. 31, No. 3 (Autumn, 2000): 643–673;
Fanny Cosandey, "Puissance Maternelle et pouvoir politique. La régence des reines meres,"
in *Clio. Histoires, femmes et société*, t. 21, (2005): 69–90 and Kathleen Wellman, *Queens and
Mistresses of Renaissance France* (New Haven: Yale University Press, 2013).

[3] See Pierre Champion, *Catherine de Médicis Présente A Charles IX Son Royaume
(1564–1566)* (Paris: B. Grasset, 1937); Linda Briggs, "'Concernant le service de leurs dictes
Majestez et auctorité de leur justice' Perceptions of Royal Power in the Entries of Charles IX
and Catherine de Médicis (1564–1566)," in J. R. Mulryne, Maria Ines Aliverti, and Anna
Maria Testaverde (eds.), *Ceremonial Entries in Early Modern Europe: The Iconography of
Power* (Farnham: Ashgate, 2015), 37–52; Linda Briggs, "Presenting the Most Christian
King: Charles IX's Performance of Catholic Ritual in the Royal Tour of France (1564–1566),"
in *French History*, Vol. 32, 1 (2018): 3–24; Jean Boutier, Alain Dewerpe, Daniel Nordman,
Un tour de France royal: le voyage de Charles IX, (1564–1566) (Paris: Aubier, 1984).

[4] Denis Crouzet, "Charles IX ou le roi sanglant malgré lui?" in *Bulettin de la Société de
l'Histoire du Protestantisme Français (1903–2015)*, Vol. 141 (1995): 323–339, 323. Also
see, Denis Crouzet, *La Nuit de la Saint-Barthélémy: Un Rêve Perdu de la Renaissance* (Paris:
Fayard, 1994) and Arlette Jouanna, *La Saint-Barthélémy. Les mystères d'un crime d'Etat*
(Paris: Gallimard, 1994).

river tinted with blood; and door and entrances to the king's palace painted the same color."[5] The massacre spread beyond Paris, and when it was over, thousands had been killed.

Historians are still debating Charles's involvement in the massacre. For Jean-Louis Bourgon, Charles did not order the massacre but he gave the order to his guards not to oppose the party of the Guises and also expelled from the Louvres the gentlemen that accompanied the king of Navarre.[6] The premeditation of the massacre and Charles's real involvement remain at the heart of a lively debate, but one thing is certain: Charles IX's reputation was stained by the massacre.[7] Scholars, such as Gianmarco Braghi and James Smither, have paid attention to the ways in which Charles IX's contemporary reputation and legacy were affected by the ongoing French Wars of Religion.[8] While it cannot be ignored that benevolent and positive images of the king were also created at the end of his reign, Charles primarily remained an example of an anti-king who murdered his people and was unworthy of the monarchy.[9]

This chapter further examines the legacy of Charles IX's reign and how his rule was represented and reinterpreted in chronicles and plays during the seventeenth- and long eighteenth-century France. I argue that more than simply representing political failure, Charles's reign served a purpose for posterity: it provided his successors an example of how not to rule and helped revolutionary ideas take roots in people's mind. Both in his own century and today, many have argued that Charles IX was one of the

---

[5] From an anonymous pamphlet, "The Wake-up Call for the French and their Neighbors." See Jo Eldridge Carney "'I'll Find a Day to Massacre Them All': Tamora in *Titus Andronicus* and Catherine de Médicis," in *Comparative Drama*, note 4 (Winter 2014): 415–435, 433.

[6] Jean-Louis Bourgon, *Charles IX devant la Saint-Barthélémy* (Genève: Droz, 1995), 31 and 34.

[7] See Arlette Jouanna, *La France du XVIe siècle 1483–1598* (Paris: PUF, 1996), 470–473; Janine Garrisson, *Les Derniers Valois* (Paris: Fayard, 2001) and Janine Garrisson, *Guerre civile et compromis 1559–1598* (Paris: Points, 2016).

[8] Gianmarco Braghi, "The Death of Charles IX Valois: An Assassin's or Martyr's Blood? The Image of Kingship during the French Wars of Religion," in *French History*, Vol. 28, No. 3 (2014): 303–321 and James R. Smither, "The St. Bartholomew's Day Massacre and Images of Kingship in France: 1572–1574," in *Sixteenth Century Journal*, Vol. 22, No. 1 (1991): 27–46. Also see Stuart Carroll, *Blood and Violence in Early Modern France* (Oxford: Oxford University press, 2006) and Penny Robert, *Peace and Authority during the French Religious Wars, c. 1560–1600* (Basingstoke: Palgrave Macmillan, 2013).

[9] Crouzet reassesses Charles's involvement in the St. Barthlomew's Day Massacre, Crouzet, "Charles IX ou le roi sanglant malgré lui?" 323.

weakest kings of France.[10] This image was rooted in portrayals of him following his death that were intended to contrast with allegedly more successful and glorious kings. Even worse, he was often portrayed as an assassin or more bluntly, the butcher of his people. While there have been other unsuccessful kings, Charles is used most often as the example not to follow. One reason why Charles in particular is used to represent failed monarchy may well be not only Charles's own weaknesses, but the strong perception that Charles was the puppet of his mother Catherine de Medici, who was often portrayed as a murderous manipulator who frequently used poison on her enemies. Finally, this chapter draws parallels between the image of an anti-king and the growing desire for liberty.

CHARLES AS AN INCOMPETENT KING OF FRANCE

Early modern monarchs were educated in languages, rhetoric, and military welfare, but they also received books dedicated to them which described their predecessors, allowing the author to draw powerful comparisons between the reigns of various monarchs. In his posthumous work published in 1631, *Histoire de France*, Pierre Matthieu (1563–1621) recalled the reigns of the Valois kings and the first Bourbon king, Henry IV of France, Louis XIII's father. Matthieu was a Catholic Leaguer and a support of the Guises.[11] He was a devout Catholic and was pleased when Henry IV of France chose to convert to Catholicism in 1593.[12]

Matthieu dedicated his *Histoire de France* to Louis warning him that "every reign of kings do not produce great actions as not all lands are

---

[10] On Charles's reign, see: Pierre Champion, *Charles IX, la France et le contrôle de l'Espagne, t. I: Avant la Saint-Barthélemy* (Paris, Bernard Grasset, 1939); Pierre Champion, *Charles IX, la France et le contrôle de l'Espagne, t. II: Après la Saint-Barthélemy* (Paris, Bernard Grasset, 1939); Jean-François Labourdette, *Charles IX et la puissance espagnole: diplomatie et guerres civiles, 1563–1574* (Paris, Honoré Champion, 2013) and Michel Simonin, *Charles IX* (Paris: Fayard, 1995).

[11] Matthieu wrote on the Guises and the death of Henry III of France, see Jean-Claude Ternaux, "La Diabolisation dans *La Guisiade* (1589) de Pierre Matthieu et *Le Guysien* (1592) de Simon Bélyard," *Études Épistémè* [En ligne], 14 | 2008, mis en ligne le 01 octobre 2008, accessed on January 25, 2019. URL: http://journals.openedition.org/episteme/719

[12] See Gilbert Schrenck, "Livres du pouvoir et pouvoirs du livre: l'historiographie royale et la conversion d'Henri IV," *Revue française d'histoire du livre*, 50 (1986): 153–180.

fertile."[13] Matthieu further explained that recalling Louis's predecessors allowed him to compare different reigns and to demonstrate how Henry IV's was "far greater."[14] He legitimized the Bourbon dynasty by portraying incompetent Valois kings and a benevolent Bourbon king whose conversion had brought peace to the kingdom. Matthieu used especially harsh words when it came to describing Charles's reign, claiming that his rule was stained by "days of blood and tears."[15] This strategy of highlighting the failures of a previous monarch in order to praise a current ruler was one that continued in subsequent decades.

For seventeenth-century chroniclers, Charles's reign was the embodiment of ineffective leadership, partly due to the fact that he became king at such an early age and was under the influence of his formidable mother Catherine.[16] The prolific author François de Belleforest, who was a historiographer of King Henry III of France after being "raised by Marguerite of Navarre and studying law at Bordeaux published over fifty literary and historical works."[17] Despite being raised by the reformer Marguerite, Belleforest was a defender of the Catholic faith and he ultimately lost his role as historiographer because his writings did not please the king.[18] In 1572, he contributed to *Les Chroniques et Annales de France*, which would be printed only in 1617. The reasons for his involvement in the project are unknown though one can assume that as a prolific writer, he might have been asked to contribute by someone influential from the court.

In the section of the chronicle he wrote, Belleforest observed Charles's obedience to his mother and weakness even after his majority, when he chose to grant the Huguenots religious freedom and to whom he assured "that they will be conserved, maintained, and safe under our protection with all their goods, honor, and states."[19] For Belleforest, "heretics were triumphant after being such a heavy liberty of conscience" which only

[13] Pierre Matthieu, *Histoire de France soubs les règnes de Fraçois I, Henri II, François II, Charles IX, Henri III, Henri IV, et Louis XIII* (Paris: Pierre Baillet, 1631), 4.

[14] Matthieu, *Histoire de France*, 9.

[15] Matthieu, *Histoire de France*, 9.

[16] Nicole Gille, D. Sauvage, Belleforest, G. Chappuys, *Les Chroniques et Annales de France* (Paris: Sepastien Chappeler, 1617), 607.

[17] Keith Cameron, "François de Belleforest," in *The New Oxford Companion to Literature in French*, Peter France (ed.) (Oxford: Oxford University Press, 1995), 86.

[18] Marie-Nicolas Bouillet and Alexis Chassang (eds.), "François de Belleforest," in *Dictionnaire universel d'histoire et de géographie* (Paris: Librarie Hachette, 1878), 205.

[19] *Les Chroniques et Annales de France*, 620.

reinforced the idea of Charles as a weak and incompetent Catholic king who failed to protect and maintain Catholicism in France.[20] This edict of pacification and attempt at religious toleration did not last and further religious civil wars ravaged France.

Later chronicles also served as a means to compare monarchs' reigns. Antoine Varillas, a writer who was named in 1648 the historiographer of Gaston of Orléans, Louis XIV of France's uncle, a position that he only kept a few months before working for the Library in Paris with Pierre Dupuy, developed an interest in writing historiographical chronicles.[21] In 1680, he wrote *Histoire de Charles IX* and dedicated it to Louis XIV. In his dedication, he explained his choice: "we can see all the breaches made to the French monarchy under the sad reign of this Prince [Charles IX] and your Majesty repair them in such a glorious way."[22] Contrasting Charles's disastrous reign with the current "glorious" one allowed Varillas to further praise Louis XIV's royal authority.

Varillas insisted that "France has never been more peaceful for such a long time than it is under the reign of your Majesty [...] one cannot understand the extent of its happiness without contrasting it to Charles's misfortune."[23] The reference of his Charles's misfortune was a reference to the religious civil wars that occurred during his reign. This contrast made it possible to glorify one reign over another. Furthermore, it gave a strong justification to Varillas to write his book: it was a way to praise Louis's rulership and demonstrate to all readers that the Sun king was a benevolent king who sought the welfare of his people, unlike Charles.

A century later, playwrights also showed a strong interest in highlighting the failures of Charles IX's reign, most notably Marie-Joseph de Chénier's *Charles IX ou la Saint Barthélémi* of 1789, later rewritten as *Charles IX ou L'Ecole des Rois,* and Charles D'Outrepont's *La Saint Barthélémi, Drame en plusieurs scenes* of 1826. In these works, the depiction of a king who was weak and manipulated by his mother dominated the narratives, as did the focus on Charles's role in the St. Bartholomew's Day Massacre.

---

[20] *Les Chroniques et Annales de France,* 621.

[21] Louis-Gabriel Michaud, *Biographie universelle ancienne et moderne: histoire par ordre alphabétique de la vie publique et privée de tous les hommes avec la collaboration de plus de 300 savants et littérateurs français ou étrangers, Tome 42* (Paris: Chez Madame C. Desplaces, 1843–1865), 638–639.

[22] Antoine Varillas, *Histoire de Charles IX* (Paris: Claude Barbin, 1686), 14.

[23] Varillas, *Histoire de Charles IX,* 16–17.

As discussed, the exact causes and implications of this tragic event are still contested, but much of the debate centers on the roles of Catherine and Charles; most scholars argue that throughout the events, the queen mother was as powerful and aggressive as Charles was indecisive and ineffective. This was certainly how later French playwrights portrayed the event. In Chénier's work, Charles is depicted as being overwhelmingly submissive to his mother:

> Catherine: My son, this *coup d'Etat* is so necessary.
> Charles: But on the day of the peace!
> Catherine: Do you think it [peace] is necessary?
> Charles: Sacrificing a whole people!
> Catherine: This is ruling.
> Charles: This horrifying coup can wait.
> Catherine: Let's strike tonight.
> Charles: Ah! My pity prevails.
> Catherine: You agreed.
> Charles: I know.[24]

While in this play, Charles is portrayed as conflicted and uncertain about his decisions regarding the St. Bartholomew's Day Massacre, de Chénier shows him as a king who ultimately had neither power nor political influence:

> Catherine: What trouble is upsetting your heart?
> Charles: I revoke today the order of vengeance before spilling blood in the cities of France.
> Catherine: The orders have been given and will be executed.
> Charles: Who ordered them? Who is the reckless person...
> Catherine: Me. I have ordered everything. Punish your mother. I had to save you.
> Charles: You have betrayed me. I have weakly submitted to your wishes.[25]

De Chénier blamed the queen mother for the St. Bartholomew's Day Massacre and all the bloodshed that happened in all French cities, such as Rouen, but he also represented the king as too weak to stand up to her for the welfare of his country and his people. These depictions, written in 1789, were to have great repercussions in the public sphere.

---

[24] Marie-Joseph de Chénier, *Charles IX ou la Saint Barthélémi, Tragédie* (Paris: Désauges, 1789, second edition, 1826), Acte II, Scène 1, 12.

[25] De Chénier, *Charles IX ou la Saint Barthélémi*, Acte IV, Scène 2, 41.

Charles D'Outrepont's play *La Saint Barthélémi, Drame en plusieurs scenes* similarly illustrates Charles's indecision and lack of power:

Guise: What obstacle could arise?

Catherine de Medici: The king is still uncertain; he wants it and does not want it in the same fifteen minutes.

Guise: There is a solution, Madame, we could blame ourselves for this bloody day, and wake the king up with the screams of the protestants being massacred.[26]

D'Outrepont further represents Charles IX as a king who resisted his role as monarch: "Charles: This crown is a burden. Why did God condemn me to the throne? The least of my subjects is happier than I am."[27] Charles's complaint about being a king reinforced notions of his reluctant and incompetent rule. Eighteenth- and nineteenth-century playwrights depicted a worthless king who did not deserve to be head of his country. But worse than that, Charles's posthumous reputation was stained by the blood he allegedly shed during the religious civil wars.

CHARLES AS THE BUTCHER OF HIS PEOPLE

While the St. Bartholomew's Day Massacre is the most infamous event in the French Wars of Religion, the conflicts had started as early as 1562 and lasted until in 1598. Penny Roberts argues that it was a period "viewed as a time of great monarchical weakness."[28] While Charles IX had endeavored to bring some peace to his people, his posthumous reputation depicts a king who was anything but peaceful: rather, seventeenth- and eighteenth-century chronicles and plays portrayed a king who was cruel enough to be the butcher of his own people.[29]

In Belleforest's chronicle, Charles was depicted as a king who was avenging himself from Coligny's supposedly conspiracy against him and

---

[26] Charles D'Outrepont, *La Saint Barthélémi, Drame en plusieurs scenes* (Paris: Firmin Didot, 1826), Scène 32, 70–71.

[27] D'Outrepont, *La Saint Barthélémi*, Scène 37, 81.

[28] Penny Roberts, "Royal Authority and Justice during the French Religious Wars," in *Past and Present*, No. 184 (2004): 3–32, 3. Also see for more historical context surrounding the religious civil wars: Arlette Jouanna, *La France du XVIe siècle, 1483–1598* (Paris: Puf, 1996) and Denis Crouzet, *Les Guerriers de dieu: La violence au temps des troubles de religion (vers 1525–vers 1610)* (Seyssel: Champ Vallon, 1990).

[29] On the language of peace, see Penny Roberts, "The Languages of Peace during the French Religious Wars," in *Cultural and Social History*, Vol. 4, Issue 3 (2007): 297–315, 300.

his mother: "On Sunday 24th August, the day of St. Bartholomew, on the eve of St. Louis, tamer of all heretics and very loyal servants to God was executed the admiral, leader of all the traitors of this kingdom."[30] The conspiracy mentioned was a way for the royal family to justify the massacre. Coligny's death and Charles's horrific deed was explained in 1631 by Matthieu: "the hatred that the king [Charles] was bearing against those who had forced him at the beginning of his reign to engage with the first civil war, had influenced his mind since his childhood which kept growing with the years and became more dangerous."[31] Being a loving father figure during that period was crucial in order to project a respectful royal authority.[32] By using the word "hatred," Matthieu strongly judged the Valois king and not only did he offer a portrayal of a king unfit to rule over his people, but he also alluded to Charles's tyrannical behavior.

This harsh rhetoric was again reiterated in the eighteenth- and nineteenth-century plays. De Chénier made Charles reflect on his actions: "Charles: remaining virtuous or being guilty! It was time to choose! But what a dreadful choice! Being virtuous means risking my throne and my days. Being guilty for one moment, and I will always be so."[33] He continued, "defending oneself is a right, avenging oneself is vile. No one can make peace holding a dagger and the interest for a man is always to remain human."[34] In De Chénier's play, the Valois king struggled with his own feelings about what was right or wrong. More importantly, De Chénier went even further when he made Charles reflect on his humanity and what such a deed would involve not only for his reputation but also for his conscience.

Despite depicting Charles's conflicting thoughts, the eighteenth-century playwright did not hesitate to portray him as a mere assassin and as a result reinterpreted his reign through the lens of the massacre only:

Charles: I have committed a great crime.
Lorraine: A king has to avenge himself against those who oppress him.
Charles: I am no longer king, I am an assassin.[35]

---

[30] *Les Chroniques et Annales de France*, 633.

[31] Matthieu, *Histoire de France*, 294.

[32] See Estelle Paranque, "Royal Representations Through the Warrior and Father Figures in Early Modern Europe," in *History of Monarchy*, ed. Elena Woodacre (London: Routledge, 2019), 314–329.

[33] De Chénier, *Charles IX ou la Saint Barthélémi*, Acte IV, Scène 1, 39.

[34] De Chénier, *Charles IX ou la Saint Barthélémi*, Acte IV, Scène 1, 40.

[35] De Chénier, *Charles IX ou la Saint Barthélémi*, Acte V, Scène 4, 60.

Centuries later, De Chénier revealed the way in which Charles was remembered: a butcher of his people who sought a personal vendetta against the Huguenots. Yet, the playwright also chose to depict him as a king who had some remorse regarding his choice. He assigns Charles language that recognized he was no longer fit to rule because of his crimes.

In D'Outrepont's play, both Catherine and Charles were responsible for the massacre of the Huguenots, which also was depicted as a personal vendetta:

> Catherine: they have fallen for the trap I have worked on for two years, they will all die. The exterminating angel is waiting for them [...] to avenge the throne and the religion.
>
> Charles: Speak more quietly, Madame, what if someone heard you ... The *coup d'état* that we are planning, others might call it a crime, it requires the greatest secrecy.[36]

While in this scene, the blame is more directed to Catherine, D'Outrepont did not hesitate in portraying the image of an assassin king who was willing to follow his mother's orders even as he showed some hints of remorse:

> Charles: I feel all the strength of your reasons, they persuade me, as king, as enemy of Coligni. But having my hands stained by the blood of my subjects after asking them to come to court. This is a treason unworthy of your son! What will Europe say? What will posterity say?[37]

The reference to the blood of his people on his hands further revealed that in this play, the king had a choice in this massacre and that he eventually chose the path of being an anti-king and a murderer of his people.

This image of a butcher of his people is particularly striking in one of the last scenes of the play where Charles, on a balcony, shoots his people almost for leisure, as if they were his prey:

> (On a balcony)
> Charles: I asked someone to bring me an arquebus to take part in the action. I have already shot a few times.
> Catherine: Did it make you happy?
> Charles: I do not think so. It is easier to write about hunting than to shoot well.[38]

---

[36] D'Outrepont, *La Saint Barthélémi*, Scène 7, 14.

[37] D'Outrepont, *La Saint Barthélémi*, Scène 7, 15.

[38] D'Outrepont, *La Saint Barthélémi*, 143. Also see on Charles IX and hunting, Estelle Paranque, "Royal Representations Through the Warrior and Father Figures."

Charles's love for hunting was well-known; he wrote a book on the subject, *La Chasse Royale*, which was published posthumously in 1625.[39] Here, D'Outrepont depicts a king who hunted his people down for leisure though he even did that ineffectively. The reference to Charles's own book about hunting showed that the playwright based his play on what he believed to be historical facts. As with any historical fiction, he created scenes that conveyed his own opinion of the French royal family and portrayed a king who enjoyed the misery of his people.

For De Chénier, Charles's guilt was undeniable. Yet, the author of the play still conveyed Charles's remorse and distress:

> Charles: What have I done? Cruel, ungrateful, perfidious,
> Perjury to my oath, sacrilege, homicide,
> I have the vilest qualities of tyrants,
> And I am covered with the blood of my subjects.[40]

There is no doubt that Charles was portrayed as an unfit king and a butcher of his people. While some chroniclers and playwrights decided to also touch on Charles being remorseful indicates that to some extent even a bad king or anti-king such as Charles could be repentant and therefore worthy of the French people. Furthermore, that De Chénier wrote this play to be performed in 1789, and which was eventually published in 1790, suggests that the author was well aware of the contemporary relevance of his work in the political landscape.

CHARLES AS AN EXAMPLE NOT TO FOLLOW AND THE EXPRESSION OF LIBERTY

Marie-Joseph de Chénier wrote his play about Charles IX before the French Revolution, which started on July 14, 1789, with the storming of the Bastille. It was written at a time when people's discontent was growing all over the country; he even wrote two versions of it, one called *Charles IX, ou l'Ecole des Rois* and the other *Charles IX ou la Saint Barthélémi*. They are essentially the same play with some minor variations. In his preface of

---

[39] Ingrid De Smet has presented papers on Charles's interest in hunting. Also see, Ingrid De Smet, *La Fauconnerie à la Renaissance: Le Hieracosophion (1582–1584) de Jacques Auguste de Thou* (Genève: Droz, 2013).

[40] Marie-Joseph de Chénier, *Charles IX, ou l'Ecole des Rois, Tragédie* (Paris: Didot Jeune, 1790), Acte V, Scène 4, 143.

Charles IX, ou l'Ecole des Rois, he explained "I have conceived and executed, before the revolution, a tragedy that only the revolution could allow
to be represented."[41] The monarchy was failing the people and poverty due
to poor harvests kept increasing.

De Chénier's play was first performed in the fall of 1789 but it was soon
being harshly criticized by those who viewed the play as an insult to the
monarchy and were threatened by the consequences of the parallels drawn
between the butcher of his people, Charles IX, and the current Louis XVI
of France. In his dedication in the second play, written on December 15,
1789, the author dedicated his play to "the Nation who became free" but
he did not explicitly explain free from what or whom.[42]

The extent of De Chénier's support of the revolution is not entirely
clear. Yet, he stood by his play and was convinced that his tragedy would
inform the current king how to rule effectively. De Chénier attacked his
detractors, declaring that though they criticized the play for claiming that
religious fanaticism still existed in the eighteenth century, he insisted
"What was Voltaire's crime? To have fought against fanaticism for sixty
years. Who avenged itself? Fanaticism. What needs to be destroyed?
Fanaticism. It crawls but it still exists."[43]

In his dedicatory remarks, de Chénier addresses the king himself:

O Louis XVI! King of justice and benevolence, you are worthy to be the
leader of the French. But bad people want to build a wall between your
people and yourself. They aim to persuade you that you are not loved from
your people. Ah! Come to the theatre at Nation when we play Charles IX:
you will hear the French people's plaudit.[44]

He depicted himself as an ally to the king and therefore to the monarchy.
He wanted his play to serve as a counter-example of a good monarch, not
to attack the monarchy itself.

De Chénier was not the only one protesting against the censorship of
his play. Jean-Baptiste-Antoine Suard, a French journalist and translator,
wrote a letter to the gentlemen of Paris. Born in Besançon, he was elected

---

[41] De Chénier, *Charles IX, ou l'Ecole des Rois*, 1.
[42] De Chénier, *Charles IX, ou l'Ecole des Rois*, 166.
[43] De Chénier, *Charles IX, ou l'Ecole des Rois*, 5.
[44] De Chénier, *Charles IX, ou l'Ecole des Rois*, 6.

member of the prestigious *Académie Française* in 1774 and used his reputation to defend De Chénier's play.[45] He started his letter explaining:

> it has been announced, for several days, the tragedy of *Charles IX* by Mr de Chénier, and I dare assuming that all good citizens, who like me, know it, are impatiently waiting for the representation of it. For eight days, it has no longer been announced, to everyone's great surprise.[46]

Suard further described the attacks against the play that he believed to be unfounded.[47] Suard insisted that he had read the play carefully, arguing that "the history has been followed with the most scrupulous exactitude" and that the audience can find "the most flattering and deserved praise given to the French Nation." He maintained that "the tragedy of Charles IX is worth, in all respects, of the applause and enthusiasm of a People who just got rid of slavery so proudly."[48] His defense of the play showed how controversial it was in the public's mind because of its perceived criticism of the monarchy. By insisting on the veracity of the historical facts in the play, Suard aimed to justify the parts which could be seen as antimonarchical. In his opinion, the historical facts could well serve as a lesson for the current king whose monarchical authority was on the brink of being destroyed by the Revolutionaries.

In a discourse that he printed after his play, De Chénier invited the representatives of the *Commune* to reassess their opinion of it. He declared:

> You might have been told that this tragedy would be very dangerous regarding the current political climate. If it is dangerous to make people hate fanaticism and tyranny, if it is dangerous to make people love virtue, laws, liberty, and tolerance, allow me to brag then as there are few works as dangerous as *Charles IX*.[49]

For De Chénier, Charles IX should serve as a useful example for Louis XVI in demonstrating how a king should not act, and by implication, how he should rule instead. But more importantly, the playwright aimed to warn

---

[45] See http://www.e-enlightenment.com/person/suardjeanb003259, accessed on January 10, 2019.

[46] Jean-Baptiste-Antoine Suard, *A Messieurs Les Parisiens, sur la Tragédie de Charles IX*, par M. Suard, l'un des Quarante de l'Académie Française (Paris: s.n., 1789), 1.

[47] Suard, *A Messieurs Les Parisiens*, 2–4.

[48] Suard, *A Messieurs Les Parisiens*, 5.

[49] De Chénier, *Charles IX, ou l'Ecole des Rois*, 165.

the danger that fanaticism could cause to a nation. His portrayal of Charles IX's reign and his alleged involvement in the massacre of the Protestants should be seen as a history lesson for the French people and by extension, for the current king of France.

The most striking sentence in the play that explicitly demonstrates that the work is intended as a cautionary example occurs when Charles, horrified by his deeds, recognizes that he had "betrayed the homeland, honor, and laws, the sky in striking me gives an example to the kings."[50] One can see how controversial and problematic this sentence was, especially given contemporary circumstances. With this declaration, De Chénier makes Charles guilty of betraying his people but more importantly of betraying the honor and legitimacy of his country. He also reminds his audience, and therefore Louis XVI, that "the sky"—a veiled reference to God—was the ultimate authority. Yet, De Chénier makes a deliberate choice not to name "God" to avoid any religious fanaticism that he truly abhorred. In many ways, this play was also seen as problematic given that a mere playwright was implicitly or even directly counseling an absolute ruler who was deeply attached to his divine rights.

For De Chénier, his views were only an expression of his commitment to liberty. But more importantly, he was driven by his desire to contrast Louis XVI from Charles IX and he proudly justified his choice:

> By portraying a perfidious, bloodthirsty, tormenter of his people, it [this play] make the people love, more than ever, the governance of a monarch whose honesty and goodness are known by all, of a monarch, second father to his people, restorer of the French liberty, of a monarch, worthy heir of Henry IV...[51]

He argued that his play, therefore, could only be seen as a means to glorify the current king. His quest for liberty could only be reached under the governance of a good ruler. In De Chénier's eyes, Charles IX's legacy in eighteenth-century France served as a lesson for kings who decided to be tyrannical. The lesson was clearly not learned given Louis's demise but the importance here is how Charles's reign and own mistakes were used to indirectly counsel another king.

---

[50] De Chénier, *Charles IX, ou l'Ecole des Rois*, 165 and De Chénier, *Charles IX, ou la Saint Barthélémi*, 61.

[51] De Chénier, *Charles IX, ou l'Ecole des Rois*, 166.

CONCLUSION

Charles IX remains an obscure figure of sixteenth-century France. Not completely forgotten, he is, however, mostly remembered for his alleged involvement in the St. Bartholomew's Day Massacre. His reign is tarnished by the religious civil wars and he is remembered by many as Catherine de Medici's puppet king. He is the archetype of the anti-king or an exemplar of what a king should not be. Regardless of any successes in his reign, such as securing an alliance with the Holy Roman Empire through his marriage to Elisabeth of Austria, Charles is remembered for failing his people.

In the seventeenth and long eighteenth century, chroniclers, writers, and playwrights continued to paint the horrors of his reign in order to serve political purposes. They highlighted the failures of his reign not only to denounce his injustice and malevolence but also in order to glorify others. During the French Revolution, Charles IX became a lesson and a warning for Louis XVI. Charles was never overthrown and some chroniclers, such as Belleforest who harshly condemned him for all his mistakes and incompetence, admitted that at his death, Charles was actually remembered by some as "a great and benevolent king."[52] Yet, this image of him was reinterpreted and reconstructed to offer a more horrific portrayal of his reign. From an incompetent ruler to a butcher of his people to a cautionary example, Charles's legacy to his successors is clear: he is remembered and reimagined as a king unworthy of his crown because of his inability to save his people from religious fanaticism and division.

BIBLIOGRAPHY

PRIMARY SOURCES

De Chénier, Marie-Joseph. *Charles IX ou la Saint Barthélémi, Tragédie*. Paris: Désauges, 1789, second edition, 1826.
———. *Charles IX, ou l'Ecole des Rois, Tragédie*. Paris: Didot Jeune, 1790.
D'Outrepont, Charles. *La Saint Barthélémi, Drame en plusieurs scenes*. Paris: Firmin Didot, 1826.
Gille, Nicole. Sauvage, D., Belleforest, and Chappuys G. *Les Chroniques et Annales de France*. Paris: Sepastien Chappeler, 1617.

---

[52] *Les Chroniques et Annales de France*, 649.

Matthieu, Pierre. *Histoire de France soubs les règnes de Fraçois I, Henri II, François II, Charles IX, Henri III, Henri IV, et Louis XIII.* Paris: Pierre Baillet, 1631.

Suard, Jean-Baptiste-Antoine. *A Messieurs Les Parisiens, sur la Tragédie de Charles IX,* par M. Suard, l'un des Quarante de l'Académie Française. Paris: s.n., 1789.

Varillas, Antoine. *Histoire de Charles IX.* Paris: Claude Barbin, 1686.

SECONDARY SOURCES

Bouillet, Marie-Nicolas and Chassang, Alexis, eds. *Dictionnaire universel d'histoire et de géographie.* Paris: Librarie Hachette, 1878.

Bourgon, Jean-Louis. *Charles IX devant la Saint-Barthélémy.* Genève: Droz, 1995.

Boutier, Jean, Dewerpe, Alain, Nordman, Daniel. *Un tour de France royal: le voyage de Charles IX, (1564–1566).* Paris: Aubier, 1984.

Braghi, Gianmarco. "The Death of Charles IX Valois: An Assassin's or Martyr's Blood? The Image of Kingship during the French Wars of Religion." *French History,* Vol. 28, No. 3. (2014): 303–321.

Briggs, Linda. "'Concernant le service de leurs dictes Majestez et auctorité de leur justice' Perceptions of Royal Power in the Entries of Charles IX and Catherine de Médicis (1564–1566)." In J. R. Mulryne, Maria Ines Aliverti, and Anna Maria Testaverde eds. *Ceremonial Entries in Early Modern Europe: The Iconography of Power,* 37–52. Farnham: Ashgate, 2015.

———. "Presenting the Most Christian King: Charles IX's Performance of Catholic Ritual in the Royal Tour of France (1564–1566)." in *French History,* Vol. 32, 1. (2018): 3–24.

Cameron, Keith. "François de Belleforest." In *The New Oxford Companion to Literature in French,* edited by Peter France. Oxford: Oxford University Press, 1995.

Carney, Jo Eldridge. "'I'll Find a Day to Massacre Them All': Tamora in *Titus Andronicus* and Catherine de Médicis." In *Comparative Drama,* note 4. (Winter 2014): 415–435.

Carroll, Stuart. *Blood and Violence in Early Modern France.* Oxford: Oxford University press, 2006.

Champion, Pierre. *Catherine de Médicis Présente A Charles IX Son Royaume (1564–1566).* Paris: B. Grasset, 1937.

———. *Charles IX, la France et le contrôle de l'Espagne, t. I: Avant la Saint-Barthélemy.* Paris, Bernard Grasset, 1939.

———. *Charles IX, la France et le contrôle de l'Espagne, t. II: Après la Saint-Barthélemy.* Paris, Bernard Grasset, 1939.

Cosandey, Fanny. "Puissance Maternelle et pouvoir politique. La régence des reines meres." *Clio. Histoires, femmes et société,* t. 21. (2005): 69–90.

Crawford, Katherine. "Catherine de Medicis and the Performance of Political Motherhood." *The Sixteenth Century Journal.* Vol. 31, No. 3 (Autumn, 2000): 643–673.

Crouzet, Denis. "Charles IX ou le roi sanglant malgré lui?" *Bulettin de la Société de l'Histoire du Protestantisme Français (1903–2015).* Vol. 141 (1995): 323–339.

———. *La Nuit de la Saint-Barthélémy: Un Rêve Perdu de la Renaissance.* Paris: Fayard, 1994.

———. *Les Guerriers de dieu: La violence au temps des troubles de religion (vers 1525–vers 1610).* Seyssel: Champ Vallon, 1990.

De Smet, Ingrid. *La Fauconnerie à la Renaissance: Le Hieracosophion (1582–1584) de Jacques Auguste de Thou.* Genève: Droz, 2013.

Garrisson, Janine. *Guerre civile et compromis 1559–1598.* Paris: Points, 2016.

———. *Les Derniers Valois.* Paris: Fayard, 2001.

Jouanna, Arlette. *La France du XVIe siècle, 1483–1598.* Paris: Puf, 1996.

———. *La Saint-Barthélémy. Les mystères d'un crime d'Etat.* Paris: Gallimard, 1994.

Labourdette, Jean-François. *Charles IX et la puissance espagnole: diplomatie et guerres civiles, 1563–1574.* Paris, Honoré Champion, 2013.

Michaud, Louis-Gabriel. *Biographie universelle ancienne et moderne:* histoire par ordre alphabétique de la vie publique et privée de tous les hommes avec la collaboration de plus de 300 savants et littérateurs français ou étrangers, Tome 42. Paris: Chez Madame C. Desplaces, 1843–1865.

Paranque, Estelle. "Royal Representations Through the Warrior and Father Figures in Early Modern Europe." In Elena Woodacre ed. *History of Monarchy,* 314–329. London: Routledge, 2019.

Roberts, Penny. "The Languages of Peace during the French Religious Wars." in *Cultural and Social History,* Vol. 4, Issue 3. (2007): 297–315.

———. *Peace and Authority during the French Religious Wars, c. 1560–1600.* Basingstoke: Palgrave Macmillan, 2013.

———. "Royal Authority and Justice during the French Religious Wars." *Past and Present,* No. 184. (2004): 3–32.

Schrenck, Gilbert. "Livres du pouvoir et pouvoirs du livre: l'historiographie royale et la conversion d'Henri IV." *Revue française d'histoire du livre,* 50. (1986): 153–180.

Simonin, Michel. *Charles IX.* Paris: Fayard, 1995.

Smither, James, R. "The St. Bartholomew's Day Massacre and Images of Kingship in France: 1572–1574." *Sixteenth Century Journal,* Vol. 22, No. 1. (1991): 27–46.

Ternaux, Jean-Claude. « La Diabolisation dans La Guisiade (1589) de Pierre Matthieu et Le Guysien (1592) de Simon Bélyard », *Études Épistémè* [En ligne], 14 | 2008, mis en ligne le 01 octobre 2008, accessed on January 25, 2019. URL: http://journals.openedition.org/episteme/719.

Wellman, Kathleen. *Queens and Mistresses of Renaissance France.* New Havan: Yale University Press, 2013.

zum Kolk, Caroline. "'Tout Paix et Amitié.' La maison des enfants d'Henri II et Catherine de Médicis." In Pascale Mormiche et Stanis Perez eds. *Naissance et petite enfance à la cour de France, Moyen-Age-XIXe siècle,* 79–96. Villeneuve d'Ascq: Septentrion Presses Universitaire, 2016.

ONLINE SOURCE

http://www.e-enlightenment.com/person/suardjeanb003259

Remembering—and Forgetting—Regicide: The Commemoration of the 30th of January, 1649–1660

Imogen Peck

In January 1649, Charles I, King of England, was found guilty of treason against his own people and, on the 30th of that month, executed at Whitehall. Upon the scaffold, he turned to his companion, Dr William Juxon, and uttered the word "Remember."[1] He was not, however, the only figure who perceived the importance of framing the memory of this momentous event. In the precarious political climate of the new republican state, interpretations of the turbulent recent past had a direct bearing on the politics of the present, and, almost as soon as the axe fell, both supporters and opponents of the Commonwealth regime attempted to present the King's death and the bloody events that had preceded it, in a politically favorable light. As the Commonwealth historian Thomas May wrote, it was necessary "to put some Englishmen in minde of what hath

---

[1] Anon, *King Charles his speech made upon the scaffold at Whitehall-Gate, immediately before his execution, on Tuesday the 30th of January 1648* (London, 1649), 13.

I. Peck (✉)
University of Warwick, Coventry, UK

© The Author(s) 2019
E. Paranque (ed.), *Remembering Queens and Kings of Early Modern England and France*, Queenship and Power,
https://doi.org/10.1007/978-3-030-22344-1_8

133

passed heretofore, such Englishmen as in all these time of trouble, have had (to the great mis-fortune of the Common-wealth) very treacherous memories."[2]

In this context, the anniversary of the King's death became not just another date in the calendar, but an opportunity—and a challenge. In seventeenth-century England, the dates of events that were considered to be of particular national importance, such as the gunpowder treason and the accession of the monarch, were commemorated annually, while alma-nac calendars often included "notable events" from previous years that had occurred on a particular day—and the execution of the monarch was nothing if not notable.[3] However, unlike the defeat of the Spanish armada or the foiling of the gunpowder plot, events which broadly conformed to a unifying, Protestant, display of English national identity, the execution of the King was clearly highly divisive. This chapter explores the struggle that occurred in Interregnum England over the commemoration of that most difficult of anniversaries, the 30th of January.

In the year of the 350th anniversary of Charles I's death, Jason Peacey noted that the trial and execution of England's monarch remained an "inexplicably understudied subject."[4] Renewed scholarly interest in the regicide over the last two decades has ensured that this lament was rather less applicable on its 370th anniversary. In recent years, historians have explored—and, in some cases, fiercely debated—topics as diverse as the motivations of the regicides, the staging of the trial, European reactions to the King's execution, and the production of printed material in its imme-diate aftermath.[5] Studies of the commemoration of the regicide, however,

---

[2] [Thomas May], *The changeable Covenant. Shewing in a brief series of relation, how the Scots from time to time have imposed upon England, by their false glosses, and perverse interpretations of the Covenant* (London, 1650), 1.

[3] David Cressy, "The Protestant Calendar and the Voice of Celebration in Early Modern England," *Journal of British Studies*, 29.1 (1990), 31–52.

[4] Jason Peacey, "Introduction," in *The Regicides and the Execution of Charles I*, ed. by Jason Peacey (Basingstoke: Palgrave, 2001), 1–13, 1.

[5] For debates over the motivations of the regicides, and particularly the significance of the Remonstrance, see Clive Holmes, "The Trial and Execution of Charles I," *The Historical Journal*, 53.2 (2002), 289–316; Sean Kelsey, "The Death of Charles I," *The Historical Journal*, 45.4 (2002), 727–754; Philip Baker, "The Regicide", in *The Oxford Handbook of the English Revolution*, ed. by Michael Braddick (Oxford: Oxford University Press, 2015), 154–169; Mark Kishlansky, "Mission Impossible: Charles I, Oliver Cromwell and the Regicide," *English Historical Review*, 125.515 (2010), 844–874. For discussions of staging, European reactions, and print, respectively, see Sean Kelsey, "Staging the Trial of Charles I,"

have generally taken one of two approaches: an exploration of the period after 1660, and particularly the Restoration regime's decision to establish an annual day of fasting and humiliation on the anniversary of the King's death, or a study of the martyrological tradition that dominated pro-Stuart print in the early 1650s and beyond.[6]

While both shed important light on the mental afterlife of this extraordinary event, less attention has been given to the significance and treatment of the date of the execution itself prior to 1660. This chapter seeks to redress this imbalance and, using the 30th of January as a lens, reveals the ways in which the Interregnum governments attempted to control the memory of Charles' death, the extent to which these representations were accepted, subverted, and resisted, and, in so doing, illuminates some of the challenges that the memory of the King's execution and the recent revolution posed for the fledgling state more broadly.

On the day of the King's execution, Bulstrode Whitelocke stayed at home. Though he was one of the 38 committee men who had drawn up the charges against the King, Whitelocke had spoken out against the trial, and, in his diary entry for the 30th of January, he noted that he was "troubled att the death of the King this day, and praying to God to keepe his judgements from us."[7] He was not alone in his distress. Ten days later, the loyalist and future archbishop of Canterbury, William Sancroft, penned a letter to his father in which he reported that "The black act is done, which all the world wonders at, and which an age cannot expiate [...] now we have nothing left."[8] Even the Puritan minister Ralph Josselin, a supporter of both the Parliamentarian cause and the republican state, expressed some unease. He noted in his diary that he was "much troubled with the

---

in *The Regicides*, ed. by Peacey, 71–93; Richard Bonney, "The European Reaction to the Trial and Execution of Charles I," in *The Regicides*, ed. by Peacey, 247–279; Amos Tubb, "Printing the Regicide of Charles I," *History*, 89.296 (2004), 500–524.

[6] Helen W. Randall, "The Rise and Fall of a Martyrology: Sermons on Charles I," *Huntington Library Quarterly*, 10.2 (1947), 135–167; Byron Stewart, "The Cult of the Royal Martyr," *Church History*, 38 (1969), 175–187; Lois Potter, "The Royal Martyr in the Restoration," in *The Royal Image: Representations of Charles I*, ed. by Thomas Corns (Cambridge: Cambridge University Press, 1999), 240–262; Kevin Sharpe, "'So Hard a Text?' Images of Charles I, 1612–1700", *The Historical Journal*, 43.2 (2000), 383–405; Andrew Lacey, *The Cult of King Charles the Martyr* (Woodbridge: Boydell and Brewer, 2012), esp. 129–171.

[7] Ruth Spalding (ed.), *The Diary of Bulstrode Whitelocke, 1605–1675* (Oxford: Oxford University Press, 1990), 229.

[8] George D'Oyly, *The Life of William Sancroft* (London, 1821), vol. i, 43.

blacke providence of putting the King to death," though he went on to articulate the hope that the Lord "in mercy, doe us good by the same."[9]

In addition to these personal reflections, in the days and weeks following the execution there was an outpouring of printed material that sought either to defend or attack the King's fate. The legal case that the High Court of Justice had brought against Charles turned on his having broken a fundamental bond of trust with his people. According to the charges, the King had "a *limited Power*, to Govern by, and according to the Laws of the Land, and not otherwise," a contract that been breached when he had "Trayterously and maliciously levyed War" against the Parliament and the English people.[10] To illustrate this point, the charges went on to enumerate the main transactions of the conflict and Charles' other "*wicked Designs, Wars,* and evill practises," all of which helped to evidence his guilt.[11] This legal framing set the tone for accounts of the recent past produced by the government's supporters more generally, which tended to focus on rehearsing the tyrannous and warlike actions that the late King was purported to have performed during his reign.[12]

However, the King's stoical performance at his trial, and particularly his refusal to acknowledge the court or enter a plea, complicated the Commonwealth's attempts to frame this event. Not only did the King's restraint cast doubt on the legitimacy of the legal process, his patient fortitude at the hands of his captors assisted Royalist attempts to portray the King not as a tyrant, but as a martyr for his church and country, pursued by an aggressive and hostile Parliament.[13] Following the King's conviction and his actual translation from an earthly to a heavenly crown, there was an explosion of printed material that proffered variations on this theme, from epitaphs and elegies to biographies and poetry.

[9] Alan Macfarlane, *The Diary of Ralph Josselin, 1616–1683* (Oxford: Oxford University Press, 1976), 155.

[10] Anon, *The charge of the Commons of England, against Charls Stuart, King of England, of high treason, and other high crimes* (London, 1649), 3–4.

[11] Anon, *The charge of the Commons,* 7.

[12] See, for example, Anon, *A Declaration of the Parliament of England, expressing the grounds of their late proceedings, and of settling the present government in a way of a free state* (London, 1649); Anon, *The none-such Charles his character extracted* (London, 1651); Anon, *The life and reigne of King Charles or, the pseudo-martyr discovered* (London, 1651; Thomason); John Vicars, *A brief review of the most material Parliamentary proceedings of this present Parliament, and their armies* (London, 1652).

[13] Jason Peacey, "Reporting a Revolution: a Failed Propaganda Campaign?," in *The Regicides,* ed. by Peacey, 161–181, 170–173.

In these texts, the date of the King's execution was used to reinforce his martyrology. The second lesson that the book of Common Prayer appointed for this day was the 27th chapter of St Matthew, the passion of the Christ, a concurrence that helped to strengthen the parallels which the King's supporters drew between the martyrdom of Charles I and the death of Jesus. In a sermon printed in the summer of 1649, the bishop of Down, Henry Leslie, highlighted this coincidence, along with a raft of other apparent similarities between Charles I, King of England, and Jesus Christ, King of the Jews.[14] These included the fact that both had been rejected by their own people, apprehended at night, spat upon by soldiers, and had died the same hour. Leslie concluded that Charles was "a most lively image of Christ, so lively an image of him, that amongst all the Martyrs, who followed Christ unto heaven bearing his crosse, never was there any, who expressed so great conformity with our Saviour in his sufferings, as he did."[15] He argued that the date of the regicide was "a day for ever to be noted with a black coale," a reference to the Roman practice of marking lucky days on the calendar with white stone or chalk and "black *and* ominous" days with charcoal.[16] For Leslie, the 30th of January was not only a day that should be eternally remembered; it was a date that possessed ongoing power, when the horrors of the past might reverberate in the present. In the autumn of the same year, the Anglican clergyman Thomas Fuller published a sermon in which he wrestled with the question of why God might allow a righteous man to perish while the wicked continued to prosper. The text did not explicitly mention the late King, but readers would have been in little doubt that he was one possible referent, with Fuller exhorting his readers that "as in the case of *Josiah* his death" they should "let there be an *Anniversarie of Mourning* kept in remembrance thereof."[17]

When the first anniversary of the regicide did come around, and in spite of the strictures of censorship legislation, which had been significantly tightened in the autumn of 1649, the Royalist press made a concerted

---

[14] Henry Leslie, *The martyrdome of King Charles, or His conformity with Christ in his sufferings* (The Hague, 1649), 12.

[15] Leslie, *The martyrdome*, 14.

[16] Leslie, *The martyrdome*, 12; Nathaniel Hardy, *A loud call to great mourning in a sermon preached on the 30th of January 1661* (London, 1662), sig. A2r.

[17] Thomas Fuller, *The just mans funeral* (London, 1649), 23.

effort to mark the occasion.[18] The republication of John Birkenhead's elegy to Charles I, *Loyalties Tears*, first printed in 1649, corresponded with the anniversary of the King's death, and, in this context, the verses' call to "Come, come, *Amazement*, and attend this Day" took on a renewed resonance.[19] The Royalist newsbook *The Man in the Moon* referred to the occasion as, variously, "Saint *Regicides* day," "the *Regicides Holliday*," and "St. *Traytors* Day," and printed imaginary accounts of the ways the government chose to commemorate the date.[20] This apparently included a request that "every 30 of *January* may be printed in red Letters in the Devils Calendar, and observed the highest Holy-Day in the Yeare" and that the authorities had "full power to adjourne, and cease from their *workes of wickednesse* a whole Weeke after, to solemnize that *bloody festivall*, and sing *infernall Dirges* to King *Oliver* [i.e. Oliver Cromwell] the Devils *God Sonne*."[21] The inscribing of red letters in a calendar referred to the practice of printing holy days and other notable dates in almanacs in red ink. Here, however, this tradition took on more sinister connotations, and, along with other established festival practices such as breaks from work and singing, was used to imply that the government had celebrated the anniversary of their wicked deed alongside Satan.

Much was also made of the death of the MP Thomas Hoyle who, rather unfortunately from the point of view of Commonwealth PR, chose the anniversary of the regicide to commit suicide. The coincidence was irresistible, and, according to the pamphlet *The Rebels warning-piece*, Hoyle's actions were a direct result of the guilt he felt at "laying violent hands on upon the sacred Person of my KING."[22] On the night in question, Hoyle had apparently dreamt that Charles, along with his fellow execution victims, the Earl of Strafford and Lord Capel, came by his bed bearing psalms

---

[18] "September 1649: An Act Against Unlicensed and Scandalous Books and Pamphlets," in *Acts and Ordinances of the Interregnum*, ed. by C.H. Firth and R.S. Rait (London, 1911), vol. ii, 245–254. This act aimed to suppress the printed material produced "by the Malignant party at home and abroad." Its provisions included severe fines or jail terms for the authors, printers, and vendors of offending material and orders that all books and pamphlets be licensed by the Stationers' Company.

[19] [John Birkenhead], *Loyalties tears flowing after the bloud of the royall sufferer Charles I* (Unknown, 1650), 1.

[20] *The Man in the Moon*, 30 January–6 February 1650 (London, 1650), 323, 327; *The Man in the Moon*, 6–14 February 1650 (London, 1650), 330.

[21] *The Man in the Moon*, 6–14 February, 330.

[22] Anon, *The rebells warning-piece; being certaine rules and instructions left by Alderman Hoyle* (London, 1650), 3.

in their hands and singing. Hoyle was so alarmed that when he awoke, he used his bed cord to hang himself, though not before he had "given his Sonne twenty shillings to buy Powder to make Crackers to solemnize that Saint *Regicides* day"—another fictitious celebration.[23] In fact, Hoyle had withdrawn from the House at the time of Pride's Purge and he had played no part in the King's trial. Claire Crosse has suggested that his death was more likely to have been motivated by a series of personal tragedies than political despair.[24] Nevertheless, the shared date lent the story significant propaganda potential. The ongoing influence of the Royalist account is reflected in the fact that when, 19 years later, the Yorkshire woman Alice Thornton described Hoyle's death, she did so in strikingly similar terms. According to Thornton, "after that horid murder, he [Hoyle] beeing one of the deepest in his actings and consent [...] was never quiet night or day, but still cried out 'He saw the King follow him without a head' [...] And, as we were credibly informed, did afterwards hang himself, out of consciousnesse of his cryme he was guilty of against that innocent martyer."[25]

In spite of their opponent's colorful characterizations, the Commonwealth government had in fact made no formal effort to mark the first anniversary of the King's execution. Given the widespread unease over the regicide even among the state's supporters, this decision may seem unsurprising. Indeed, it may at first glance appear that our story ends here, and that institutional silence remained the default treatment of this date until the creation of the day of fasting and humiliation after the Restoration: except that, the following year, the Commonwealth state set aside the 30th of January as a day of thanksgiving.[26] The orders for this day, however, were telling. They stated that the 30th of January should be kept as a day of "publique Thanksgiving and holy Rejoycing" for the "wonderful Mercies and signal Salvations" of the previous year, particularly the recent victories at Ayre and Edinburgh, and for the successes enjoyed by General Blake's fleet at sea.[27] In this enumeration, the King's death was conspicuous only by its absence. As with

---

[23] Anon, *The rebells warning-piece*, 3–6; *The Man in the Moon*, 30 January–6 February 1650, 323.

[24] Claire Cross, "A Man of Conscience in Seventeenth Century Urban Politics: Alderman Hoyle of York," in *Public Duty and Private Conscience in Seventeenth-Century England*, ed. by John Morrill, Paul Slack, and Daniel Woolf (Oxford: Clarendon Press, 1993), 205–224.

[25] Charles Jackson (ed.), *The Autobiography of Mrs Alice Thornton, of East Newton, co. York* (Cambridge: Cambridge University Press, 1873), 212.

[26] *House of Commons Journals*, 1648–1651, vol. vi, 516–517.

[27] Anon, *An act for setting apart Thursday the thirtieth day of January, 1650. for a day of publique thanksgiving* (London, 1651), 1272–1273.

other thanksgiving days, citizens were required to mark the occasion by "duly and diligently [...] attending upon the Publique Worship of God solemnly to be performed upon that Day," and ministers were expected to deliver an appropriate sermon.[28]

The desire to give thanks for military victories formed part of a broader providential belief that the army's martial successes were signs of God's favor, and that this posed a corresponding onus on their recipients to remember them. During the Civil Wars, both sides had allocated particular days as special occasions to give thanks to the Lord for His assistance in military engagements, and the Commonwealth state continued this practice after the King's execution.[29] Between 1649 and 1660, the various regimes ordered 25 thanksgivings, including days for the victory over Charles II and the Scots at Worcester, their military successes against the Dutch, and the thwarting of several Royalist plots.[30] The choice of the 30th of January as the date for this particular thanksgiving, however, is intriguing, and seems unlikely to have been entirely coincidental.

The Commonwealth poet George Wither certainly did not think so, and, in the foreword to a series of hymns produced to celebrate the day, he noted that "*The* Supreme Authority *hath enacted a* publique Thanksgiving *throughout this* Common wealth, *on the thirtieth of this* January (*being the last day of the late* Kings *life, as also the first of* Englands *resuming her long lost* Liberty) *a Day, which may by good reason be made an everlasting* Anniversary, *in remembrance of that, and other great* Deliverances."[31] Here, Wither suggested that it was because the anniversary of the regicide was, in effect, also the anniversary of the birth of the republic that it was worthy of memorialization, just as the anniversary of a monarch's ascendance was inevitably—though somewhat less controversially—also the date of their predecessor's death.

---

[28] Anon, *An act for setting [...] apart Thursday the thirtieth day*, 1273.

[29] For further discussion of thanksgiving days during this period see Christopher Durston "'For the Better Humiliation of the People': Public Days of Fasting and Thanksgiving During the English Revolution," *The Seventeenth Century*, 7.2 (1992), 129–149.

[30] This figure has been calculated using data from Lucy-Ann Bates, "Nationwide Fast and Thanksgiving Days in England, 1640–1660" (Unpublished doctoral thesis, Durham University, 2012).

[31] George Wither, *Three grains of spirituall frankincense infused into three hymnes of praise, and humbly offered toward the publike thanksgiving, commanded by authority of Parliament to be celebrated throughout the Commonwealth of England, the 30 of this present January* (London, 1651), sig. A2r.

Wither expressed similar sentiments in his commemorative poem, *The British Appeals*, which had also been composed to mark the 30th of January thanksgiving. In the verse's opening dedication, Wither stated that his purpose was to "offer, here, a brief commem'rative / Of those things, for which, *Thanks*, this day we give."[32] However, in the text that followed, Wither went far beyond the narrow remit prescribed by the government orders for the day, providing a narrative of the recent past that spanned from the reign of Charles I right through to the present. Along the way, Wither offered a lengthy recital of the King's mismanagement of the kingdom, relating the "multitude of wayes" that England had been oppressed and concluding that the nation had cause

> to sing Gods *Praise*, this day,
> For taking of our *Slaveries* away:
> And in the *first place*, for removing *Him*,
> Who, wore, *unworthily*, the *Diadem*,
> Of *Supreme Government*. But, least, some, yet,
> May our *fore-past-condition* so forget,
> As to believe, we might have been secur'd,
> From that, which under *Kingship* we endur'd,
> By regulating it (which, I once thought,
> Till, I by *Providence*, was better taught).[33]

That is, this should be a day to recall the mercy that God had shown to the English people by removing their tyrannous King, and to remind citizens of the hardships that they had endured prior to this fortunate providence. The 30th of January was, Wither concluded, worthy of keeping as "an *Everlasting Holyday*," for "this is the *Day*, whereon our *Yoke* / Of *Norman Bondage*, first was broke / And, *England* from her chains made free."[34] Though England had not, technically, been declared a Commonwealth until May 1649, for Wither the date of the regicide represented the moment when the tyranny of the line of Norman king's descended from William I had been lifted and England had become a free state.[35] As such,

---

[32] George Wither, *The British appeals, with Gods mercifull replies on behalf of the Commonwealth of England contained in a brief commemorative poem* (London, 1651), sig. A3r.

[33] George Wither, *The British appeals*, 20, 27.

[34] George Wither, *The British appeals*, 38, 49.

[35] "May 1649: An Act Declaring and Constituting the People of England to be a Commonwealth and Free-State," in *Acts and Ordinances*, ed. Firth and Rait, vol. ii, 122.

it was the ideal time to remember the King's evil deeds, the mercy of his death, and all the other favors that God had granted to the Parliament and Commonwealth. In his verses, Wither had co-opted the 30th of January thanksgiving far beyond its original purpose—though the fact the House of Commons Speaker, William Lenthall, ordered that *The British Appeals* should be printed suggests that the Parliament did not disapprove of his interpretation.

From the point of view of the government, the choice of date was probably less an attempt to establish the notion of a "republic day" than it was an effort to eclipse the imagined, devilish celebrations that had been pedaled in the Royalist press the previous year with a genuine occasion: one that was appropriate, Godly, and which dwelt on the victories of the entire English Commonwealth over their foreign foes. By focusing on recent successes against external enemies, the orders attempted to transform a day of potential domestic division into a show of unity, perhaps in the hope that nationalistic sentiment might unite all Englishmen together in celebrating the defeat of their long-standing rivals, the Scots.

In some places, at least, the occasion appears to have been enthusiastically observed. At Trinity College, Cambridge, a "thanksgiving fire" was lit, and Corpus Christi College also held a day of thanksgiving on this date.[36] The wardens' accounts of the London guilds show that several associations recorded expenses for the occasion. Both the carpenters and the masons noted that their companies had attended St Paul's, and the curriers spent £1 9s 5d, it "being thancks gyveinge day As by Bill."[37] The cordwainers paid £7 11s 8d for a "dynner on the 30th of Januarie 1650 [i.e. 1651] being a day of thankgiving and Livery present allowed", while the vintners held a dinner at The Three Tons in Newgate Market, which, at a cost of £5 1s, was among their most lavish of the year.[38] The founders, meanwhile, paid £5 9s for "a Thansgaiveinge day at the Cardinals Cap," an area of London known for its pubs and brothels.[39] Both bonfires and

---

[36] John Twigg, *The University of Cambridge and the English Revolution* (Woodbridge: Boydell and Brewer, 1990), 163.

[37] London, Guildhall Library, CLC/L/CC/D/002/MS4326/10, f. 81v; CLC/L/MB/D/001/MS05303/001, f. 190v; CLC/L/CK/D/001/MS14346/002, unfoliated.

[38] London, Guildhall Library, CLC/L/CJ/D/001/MS07351/002, f. 164v; CLC/L/VA/D/002/MS15333/004, unfoliated.

[39] London, Guildhall, CLC/L/FG/D/001/MS06330/002, f. 263r. Other companies that recorded expenditure on this date included the blacksmiths and the plumbers. See

feasting were part of the vocabulary of celebration, and their use suggests that reflective sermons were accompanied by a degree of joyous revelling—though it is also possible to read the Company of Founders' trip to the less salubrious parts of a London as an affront to the religious tone of the day.[40]

Overt subversion was certainly in evidence elsewhere in the country. George Holdroyd, the minister for Foston in Derbyshire, was reported to the authorities by several different members of his congregation for having said, variously, that: "it [the 30th of January] was rather a day of mourninge"; that "there was nothinge now, but cuttinge of throates"; and that the "slaughteringe and killinge one another of our [bre]thren [...] was no cause of rejoycinge, alledginge some chapters and verses to prove the same as [...] how David mourned and fasted for Saul, Jonathan and Abner when they were slayne."[41] By reminding his audience of the story of David and Saul, Holdroyd drew uncomfortable parallels between the biblical King's distress at the death of his enemies, and the present authorities' apparent "rejoycinge" on the day that they had killed their King.[42] Similarly, in February 1651, one William Farthing gave evidence against his local minister, Mr Loullurd, claiming that he had made the 30th of January "A day of unthankfulnes or of disorder [...] by Goeing about to make it Apeare by [...] Expressions That there was noe such Ackaysion [...] as was pretended."[43] Loullard had also apparently said that the current government

Exersisse nothing but Opression and Tiarranny [...] and order [...] nothing but disorder nothing but Butchering and routing [...] continuing raging for the space of A our [i.e. an hour] and upwards In Thesse and such like Expressions to the disonner of our Government And to the dishartining of those that did desire to be thankful And to the Incourraging of there Ennemis.[44]

London, Guildhall Library, CLC/L/BD/D/001/MS02883/005, f. 80v; CLC/L/PH/D/002/MS02210/001, f. 245v.

[40] David Cressy, *Bonfires and Bells: National Memory and the Protestant Calendar in Elizabethan and Stuart England* (London: Weidenfeld and Nicholson, 1989), 83–84.

[41] London, The National Archives ASSI 45/4/1/96; ASSI 45/4/1/94; ASSI 45/4/1/97.

[42] 2 Samuel 1, v. 1–27.

[43] London, The National Archives ASSI 45/4/1/92.

[44] London, The National Archives ASSI 45/4/1/92.

In these cases, ministers directly contested the official meaning of the day, using it as an opportunity to express their disapprobation for the present government, rather than give thanks for its recent success.

Ultimately, Wither's suggestion that the 30th of January should be made an "*everlasting* Anniversary" was not heeded, and the 1651 thanksgiving was both the first and the last official commemorative event to be held on this day until after the Restoration. When, in September 1651, a motion was brought before Parliament to establish a permanent memorial day celebrating the outcome of the wars, the date that was posited was the 3rd of September, the anniversary of the Commonwealth's victories over the Scots at Dunbar and Worcester, though even this proposal was eventually abandoned.[45] Both John Morrill and Kevin Sharpe have criticized the Commonwealth regime for this decision.[46] Sharpe, in particular, has argued that the government's reluctance formed part of their wider failure to overthrow the symbols of monarchy and create a distinct, republican culture. However, when viewed in light of the rather mixed response to the 30th of January thanksgiving held earlier that year, such reticence seems entirely explicable. To create an annual day of commemoration—whether on the anniversary of the regicide, or any other significant date—would have been to establish an occasion that was fraught with the potential for subversion and provide the state's opponents with a clear locus for resistance. Nor would it have conformed to the government's professed desire, that, following their victory over Charles II and the Scots, all "Rancour and Evill Will occasioned by the late Differences may be buried in perpetual Oblivion."[47] Constrained by these twin pressures of resistance and reconciliation, the Commonwealth and Protectorate governments shied away from establishing an annual day that marked the execution of the King, the establishment of the

---

[45] *House of Commons Journals*, 1651–1660, vol. vii, 13.

[46] John Morrill, "The Church in England," in *Reactions to the English Civil War, 1642–1649*, ed. by John Morrill (New York: St Martin's Press, 1982), 89–114, 113–114; Kevin Sharpe, *Remapping Early Modern England: The Culture of Seventeenth Century Politics* (Cambridge: Cambridge University Press, 2000), 234; Kevin Sharpe, *Image Wars: Kings and Commonwealths in England, 1603–1660* (Yale: Yale University Press, 2010), 417. For a more upbeat account of the Commonwealth's efforts to enshrine a distinct political culture see Sean Kelsey, *Inventing a Republic: The Political Culture of the English Commonwealth, 1649–1653* (Manchester: Manchester University Press, 1997).

[47] "February 1652: An Act of General Pardon and Oblivion," in *Acts and Ordinances*, ed. by Firth and Rait, vol. ii, 565–577, 565.

republic, or their God-given victory in the Civil Wars for the duration of the 1650s. The only exception was Cromwell's order, in August 1657, that the 3rd of September be kept as a day of thanksgiving for the victories at Dunbar and Worcester—and, even then, this was a one-off attempt to harness nationalist sentiment in support of the Protectorate by celebrating the successes that the English had enjoyed over the Scots.[48]

Of course, official public acts of commemoration were not the only form of memorialization available, and the absence of an "Everlasting Holyday" on the 30th of January did not mean that the significance of this date was simply forgotten. Almanac compilers added the regicide to the lists of notable dates printed in their calendars, and, in so doing, they provided their readers with a yearly reminder of the importance of the day. While some of these records were purely factual—"K. C. beheaded 1648," "K. Ch. beheaded at White-hall, 1648"—other writers gave their references a more partisan gloss.[49] The Royalist George Wharton recorded that on this day "*he* [Charles I] *had Sentence of Death pronounced against Him, by that bold Traytour* Bradshaw," while Richard Fitzsmith borrowed a phrase from Lamentations: "The *breath* of our *Nostrils*, the *anointed* of the *Lord* was taken."[50] In 1653, the anonymous author of a satirical pamphlet, *Bibliotheca Parliamenti*, asked their readers to consider "Whether we ought not to lament on the 30 of *January*, as well as to give thanks on the 5 of *November*."[51] According to the Church of England divine William Lloyd, "many devout People of the Church of *England*" had done exactly that, keeping a "true Fast on this day, for many Years before there was any Law to Authorize it."[52] William Juxon, William Sanderson, and other Royalist Anglicans were alleged to have "met privately every 30th January" throughout the 1650s, even going so far as to compile their own "private

---

[48] *An Order by the Protector appointing 3 Sept as a Day of Public Thanksgiving for the victories at Dunbar and Worcester* (London, 1657).

[49] Schardanus Rider, *Merlinus, Cambro-Britannus. Or the Brittish Merlin* (London, 1654), sig. B1r; Francis Pigot, *The countrey-mans kalendar, or, an almanack for the year of our Lord God, 1655* (London, 1655), sig. A2r.

[50] George Wharton, *Hemeroscopeion; the loyall almanack, for the year of Christ, 1650* (London, 1650), sig. B1v; Richard Fitzsmith, *Syzygiasticon instauratum: or, An almanack & ephemeris for the year of our Lord God, 1654* (London, 1654), sig. C4r; Lamentations 4, v. 20.

[51] Anon, *Bibliotheca Parliamenti, libri theologici, politici, historici, qui prostant voenales in vico vulgò vocato Little-Britain* (London, 1653), 6.

[52] William Lloyd, *A sermon preach'd before the House of Lords at the Abbey-Church of St. Peter's-Westminster, on Saturday the 30th of January, 1696/7 being the anniversary of the death of King Charles I of Glorious Memory* (London, 1697), 23.

form of service for the day."[53] Similarly, Nathaniel Hardy claimed that prior to the Restoration he had "adventured *to become a* remembrancer" to the people of that "bloudy fact" of regicide—an event which, *"though it is not to be* mentioned *without* abhorrency, *yet cannot be* forgotten without stupidity."[54] While some of these reports may have been subject to the embellishment of hindsight—all were recorded after 1660—contemporaneous sources also suggest that the anniversary of the regicide inspired both personal reflection and private commemoration.

In 1659, a book of prayers written by the committed Royalist and Anglican, John Hewitt, were printed posthumously.[55] Aimed at those *"who Mourn in Secret for the Publick Calamities of this Nation,"* it included *"A proper Prayer for the Thirtieth of* January, *the Anniversary of* England's *Captivity,* and *Tyrants Liberty."*[56] In the text that followed, Hewitt reminded his readers of the "amazing Judgment, which as this Day befel us, in thy permitting cruel Men, Sons of *Belial* [i.e. the devil] to execute their fury of their Rebellions upon Our late Gracious Soveraign."[57] He called on the people of England to offer repentance for their own part in this tragedy, in the hope that God might "forgive our great and manifold Transgressions" and "deliver this Nation from Bloodguiltiness, that of this Day especially."[58] For Hewitt, the regicide was a punishment from God, one for which all England bore a degree of responsibility, and the anniversary offered the ideal occasion on which to remember this offence, seek forgiveness, and implore the Lord to show mercy on the English people by thwarting the current authorities. While it is impossible to know how many people actually used Hewitt's prayer, that this devotion was expected to be of sufficient popularity as to warrant a spot on the collection's title page suggests that there was a perceived consumer demand for such material. The Surrey gentleman John Evelyn did not explicitly mention prayer, but he recorded in his diary that news of the King's death had struck him "with such horror that I kept the day of his

---

[53] Edward Ward, *The Secret History of the Calves-Head Club: or, the Republican Unmask'd* (London, 1709), 17.

[54] Hardy, *A loud call to great mourning,* sig. A2v.

[55] Hewitt had been executed the previous year on suspicion of fomenting a plot against the state; like the King before him, he steadfastly refused to enter a plea.

[56] Jo[hn] Huit [i.e. Hewitt], *Prayers of intercession for their use who mourn in secret for the publick calamities of this nation,* (London, 1659), 3, 51.

[57] Huit [i.e. Hewitt], *Prayers,* 51.

[58] Huit [i.e. Hewitt], *Prayers,* 52.

martyrdom a fast."[59] Rather more idiosyncratic was the response of the doctor Robert Ashton, who claimed to be able to heal the king's evil (scrofula) and memorialized the day of the King's death not just every year but every month "in a long white garment, with other ceremonies."[60] Devotional jewelry produced to commemorate the royal martyr often featured an inscription that denoted the date of his death, tying the memory of the King to a particular day in the calendar. A mourning ring made in or around 1649 featured an image of a skull, flanked by two crowns and the initials "C.R.," while the border bore the words "IA: the 30/1648."[61] Commemoration was not solely a top-down process, and, even in the absence of a formal occasion, some people lent significance to, and continued to mark, the date itself.

After the Restoration, the authorities made a concerted attempt to harness the anniversary of the regicide in support of the new regime. On the 30th of January 1661, Oliver Cromwell and his fellow regicides, John Bradshaw and Henry Ireton, were exhumed and posthumously executed, their heads displayed on a spike at Westminster Hall.[62] The same year, a royal proclamation established the 30th of January as an annual day of fasting and humiliation that would serve as "a lasting Monument" to the "villainous and abominable Fact" of regicide.[63] By creating a day of national humiliation, the Restoration state attempted to control the public memory of the recent past—but, in so doing, they also created a potential flashpoint for dissent. In 1664, the newsbook the *Intelligencer* complained that those who had supported the regicide "Usher'd [in] and Enterteyn'd [the day] with seditious Practices against his most Sacred and Merciful Majesty."[64] In Weymouth, there were reports that local residents refused to observe the occasion and "in derision kept open there shoppes and would not goe to church."[65] A party of horse was dispatched to assist the

[59] Austin Dobson, (ed.), *The Diary of John Evelyn* (London: Macmillan, 1906), vol. ii, 8.

[60] James Raine (ed.), *Depositions from the Castle of York, Relating to Offences Committed in the Northern Counties in the Seventeenth Century*, vol. xl (Durham: Surtees Society, 1861), 37.

[61] London, Victoria and Albert Museum, Mourning Ring, c. 1649, engraved and enamelled gold, ref. M 274–1962.

[62] *Kingdomes Intelligencer*, 4 February–11 February 1661 (London, 1661), n. p.

[63] Anon, *A proclamation for observation of the thirtieth day of January as a day of Fast and Humiliation according to the late Act for that purpose* (London, 1661).

[64] *Intelligencer Published for the Satisfaction and Information of the People*, 1 February 1664 (London, 1664), n. p.

[65] London, The National Archives, SP 29/111, f. 163.

mayor in enforcing conformity, but, even then, four men—a mercer, a shoemaker, a glover, and a wool draper who had "bin formerly a Rump [Parliament] Officer"—refused to comply.[66] Meanwhile, the Somerset man Francis Griffin chose to spend the day, not in church, but in an alehouse where he sang Parliamentarian songs and declared that Oliver Cromwell was as "Good a man as the King."[67]

As the years wore on, the day became increasingly politicized even among those who did observe it. During the exclusion crisis, 30th of January sermons were co-opted both by those who sought to remove James, Duke of York, from the royal succession and his defenders.[68] In 1681, Samuel Crossman used the occasion as an opportunity to remind his Bristol congregation, that, to atone for their actions against Charles I, they should "take all faithful care" to "repay a double Loyalty" and the "utmost Allegiance and Duty" to Charles II.[69] For the exclusionist Gilbert Burnet, by contrast, the main lesson to be learned from the regicide was the threat posed by popery, from whose doctrines the rebels had "borrowed," and, by implication, the young James Stuart.[70] In this climate of adversarial preaching, it is perhaps understandable that the Presbyterian minister Philip Henry should conclude that, though he abhorred the act of regicide, he "like[d] not ye annual commemoration of it."[71]

However, as this chapter has sought to emphasize, debates over the appropriate commemoration of the regicide had a lengthy pedigree even

[66] London, The National Archives, SP 29/111, f. 163.

[67] Taunton, Somerset Record Office, Q/SR/105/35.

[68] Stewart, "The Cult of the Royal Martyr," 175–187; Lacey, *The Cult of King Charles the Martyr*, 129–171, 179–211; Tony Claydon, "The Sermon Culture of the Glorious Revolution: Williamite Preaching and Jacobite Anti-Preaching, 1685–1702," in *The Oxford Handbook of the Early Modern Sermon*, ed. by Peter McCullough, Hugh Adlinton, and Emma Rhatigan (Oxford: Oxford University Press, 2011), 480–496, 483–486. For a similar discussion of the changing use and meaning of sermons delivered on the 29th of May, the anniversary of Charles II's Restoration, see Matthew Neufeld, *The Civil Wars After 1660: Public Remembering in Late Stuart England* (Woodbridge: Boydell and Brewer, 2013), 203–241.

[69] Samuel Crossman, *Two sermons preached in the cathedral-church of Bristol, January the 30th 1679/80 and January the 31th 1680/81 being the days of publick humiliation for the execrable murder of King Charles the first* (London, 1681), 39.

[70] Gilbert Burnet, *A sermon preached before the Aldermen of the city of London, at St. Lawrence-church, Jan 30. 1680* (London, 1681), 15. For further discussion of both Crossman and Burnet's sermons see Sharpe, "So Hard a Text?", 396–397.

[71] Matthew Henry Lee (ed.), *Diaries and Letters of Philip Henry of Broad Oak, Flintshire, 1631–1696* (London, 1882), 284.

prior to the creation of a formal annual occasion in 1661. The "Anniversary of England's Captivity," the "Regicides Holliday," an "everlasting Holyday": throughout the 1650s, the 30th of January was subject to diverse interpretations that reflected deeper divisions over the political settlement and the formation of a republican state. Though, ultimately, successive Interregnum regimes chose not to memorialize the date, this decision was less the result of institutional incompetence than it was a conscious response to the twin pressures of resistance and reconciliation. As the experience of the 1651 thanksgiving had shown, national commemorative occasions were easily misappropriated both by the state's supporters and their opponents, re-inflaming tensions over the meaning of the recent past. In light of this formal forgetting, the fact that some English citizens continued to mark the 30th of January shows that early modern commemoration was not necessarily the product of top-down forces. People were aware of the importance of this date, and many chose to imbue it with ongoing significance, whether as the day of England's freedom, her captivity, or the heinous sin of regicide.

BIBLIOGRAPHY

PRIMARY

MANUSCRIPTS

Guildhall Library, London

CLC/L/BD/D/001/MS02883/005	Blacksmiths' Company, Wardens' Account Book, 1646–1680
CLC/L/CC/D/002/MS4326/10	Carpenters' Company, Wardens' Account Book, 1647–1670
CLC/L/CJ/D/001/MS07351/002	Cordwainers' Company, Warden's Annual Accounts, 1636–1678
CLC/L/CK/D/001/MS14346/002	Curriers' Company, Annual Accounts of Master and Warden, 1627/8–1673/4
CLC/L/FG/D/001/MS06330/002	Founders' Company, Wardens' Account Book, 1577–1681
CLC/L/MB/D/001/MS05303/001	Masons' Company, Renter Wardens' Account Book, 1620–1706
CLC/L/PH/D/002/MS02210/001	Plumbers' Company, Accounts of Master and Warden, 1593–1661
CLC/L/VA/D/002/MS15333/004	Vintners' Company, Wardens' Accounts, 1636–1658

Somerset Record Office, Taunton

Q/SR/105   Somerset quarter sessions: sessions roll for 1664

The National Archives, London

SP 29   Secretaries of State: State Papers Domestic, Charles II
ASSI 45/4   Assizes: Northern and North-eastern Circuits: criminal depositions
             and case papers, 1651–1653

Victoria and Albert Museum, London

M 274-1962   Mourning Ring, c. 1649, engraved and enamelled gold, 1.9 cm ×
             2.2 cm

Newsbooks

Intelligencer Published for the Satisfaction and Information of the People. 1 February
     1664. London, 1664.
Kingdomes Intelligencer. 4 February–11 February 1661. London, 1661.
The Man in the Moon. 30 January–6 February 1650. London, 1650.
The Man in the Moon. 6–14 February 1650. London, 1650.

Pamphlets and Books

Anon. *A Declaration of the Parliament of England, expressing the grounds of their
     late proceedings, and of settling the present government in a way of a free state.*
     London, 1649.
———. *A proclamation for observation of the thirtieth day of January as a day of
     Fast and Humiliation according to the late Act for that purpose.* London, 1661.
———. *An act for setting apart Thursday the thirtieth day of January, 1650. for a
     day of publique thanksgiving.* London, 1651.
———. *An Order by the Protector appointing 3 Sept as a Day of Public Thanksgiving
     for the victories at Dunbar and Worcester.* London, 1657.
———. *Bibliotheca Parliamenti, libri theologici, politici, historici, qui prostant voe-
     nales in vico vulgò vocato Little-Britain.* London, 1653.
———. *King Charles his speech made upon the scaffold at Whitehall-Gate, immedi-
     ately before his execution, on Tuesday the 30 of Jan. 1648.* London, 1649.
———. *The charge of the Commons of England, against Charls Stuart, King of
     England, of high treason, and other high crimes.* London, 1649.
———. *The life and reigne of King Charles or, the pseudo-martyr discovered.*
     London, 1651.

———. *The none-such Charles his character extracted.* London, 1651.

———. *The rebells warning-piece; being certaine rules and instructions left by Alderman Hoyle.* London, 1650.

[Birkenhead, John]. *Loyalties tears flowing after the bloud of the royall sufferer Charles I.* Unknown, 1650.

Fitzsmith, Richard. *Syzygiasticon instauratum: or, An almanack & ephemeris for the year of our Lord God, 1654.* London, 1654.

Fuller, Thomas. *The just mans funeral.* London, 1649.

Hardy, Nathaniel. *A loud call to great mourning in a sermon preached on the 30th of January 1661/*London, 1662.

Huit [Hewitt], Jo[hn]. *Prayers of intercession for their use who mourn in secret for the publick calamities of this nation/*London, 1659.

Leslie, Henry. *The martyrdome of King Charles, or His conformity with Christ in his sufferings.* The Hague, 1649.

Lloyd, William. *A sermon preach'd before the House of Lords at the Abbey-Church of St. Peter's-Westminster, on Saturday the 30th of January, 1696/7 being the anniversary of the death of King Charles I of Glorious Memory.* London, 1697.

[May, Thomas]. *The changeable Covenant. Shewing in a brief series of relation, how the Scots from time to time have imposed upon England, by their false glosses, and perverse interpretations of the Covenant.* London, 1650.

Pigot, Francis. *The countrey-mans kalendar, or, an almanack for the year of our Lord God, 1655.* London, 1655.

Rider, Schardanus. *Merlinus, Cambro-Britannus. Or the Brittish Merlin.* London, 1654.

Vicars, John. *A brief review of the most material Parliamentary proceedings of this present Parliament, and their armies.* London, 1652.

Ward, Edward. *The Secret History of the Calves-Head Club: or, the Republican Unmask'd.* London, 1709.

Wharton, George. *Hemeroscopeion; the loyall almanack, for the year of Christ, 1650.* London, 1650.

Wither, George. *The British appeals, with Gods mercifull replies on behalf of the Commonwealth of England contained in a brief commemorative poem.* London, 1651.

———. *Three grains of spirituall frankincense infused into three hymns of praise, and humbly offered toward the publike thanksgiving, commanded by authority of Parliament to be celebrated throughout the Commonwealth of England, the 30 of this present January.* London, 1651.

PRINTED EDITIONS

House of Commons Journals: Volume 6, 1648–1651. London, 1802.

House of Commons Journals: Volume 7, 1651–1660. London, 1802.

D'Oyly, George. *The Life of William Sancroft*, 2 vols. London, 1821.

Dobson, Austin, ed. *The Diary of John Evelyn*, 3 vols. London: Macmillan, 1906.

Firth, C. H. and Rait, R. S. eds. *Acts and Ordinances of the Interregnum*, 2 vols. London, 1911.

Jackson, Charles, ed. *The Autobiography of Mrs Alice Thornton, of East Newton, co. York.* Cambridge: Cambridge University Press, 1873.

Lee, Matthew Henry, ed. *Diaries and Letters of Philip Henry of Broad Oak, Flintshire, 1631–1696*. London, 1882.

Macfarlane, Alan. *The Diary of Ralph Josselin, 1616–1683*. Oxford: Oxford University Press, 1976.

Raine, James, ed. *Depositions from the Castle of York, Relating to Offences Committed in the Northern Counties in the Seventeenth Century*, vol. xl. Durham: Surtees Society, 1861.

Spalding, Ruth, ed. *The Diary of Bulstrode Whitelocke, 1605–1675*. Oxford: Oxford University Press, 1990.

SECONDARY

PUBLISHED

Baker, Philip. "The Regicide." in *The Oxford Handbook of the English Revolution*, ed. by Michael Braddick, 154–169. Oxford: Oxford University Press, 2015.

Bonney, Richard. "The European Reaction to the Trial and Execution of Charles I." in *The Regicides and the Execution of Charles I*, ed. by Jason Peacey, 247–279. Basingstoke: Palgrave, 2001.

Claydon, Tony. "The Sermon Culture of the Glorious Revolution: Williamite Preaching and Jacobite Anti-Preaching, 1685–1702." in *The Oxford Handbook of the Early Modern Sermon*, ed. by Peter McCullough, Hugh Adlinton, and Emma Rhatigan, 480–496. Oxford: Oxford University Press, 2011.

Cressy, David. "The Protestant Calendar and the Voice of Celebration in Early Modern England." *Journal of British Studies*, 29.1 (1990): 31–52.

———. *Bonfires and Bells: National Memory and the Protestant Calendar in Elizabethan and Stuart England*. London: Weidenfeld and Nicholson, 1989.

Cross, Claire. "A Man of Conscience in Seventeenth Century Urban Politics: Alderman Hoyle of York." in *Public Duty and Private Conscience in Seventeenth-Century England*, ed. by John Morrill, Paul Slack, and Daniel Woolf, 205–224. Oxford: Clarendon Press, 1993.

Durston, Christopher. "'For the Better Humiliation of the People': Public Days of Fasting and Thanksgiving During the English Revolution." *The Seventeenth Century*, 7.2 (1992): 129–149.

Holmes, Clive. "The Trial and Execution of Charles I." *The Historical Journal*, 53.2 (2002): 289–316.

Kelsey, Sean. "Staging the Trial of Charles I." in *The Regicides and the Execution of Charles I*, ed. by Jason Peacey, 71–93. Basingstoke: Palgrave, 2001.

———. "The Death of Charles I." *The Historical Journal*, 45.4 (2002): 727–754.

———. *Inventing a Republic: The Political Culture of the English Commonwealth, 1649–1653*. Manchester: Manchester University Press, 1997.

Kishlansky, Mark. "Mission Impossible: Charles I, Oliver Cromwell and the Regicide." *English Historical Review*, 125.515 (2010): 844–874.

Lacey, Andrew. *The Cult of King Charles the Martyr*. Woodbridge: Boydell and Brewer, 2012.

Morrill, John. "The Church in England." in *Reactions to the English Civil War, 1642–1649*, ed. by John Morrill, 89–114. New York: St Martin's Press, 1982.

Neufeld, Matthew. *The Civil Wars After 1660: Public Remembering in Late Stuart England*. Woodbridge: Boydell and Brewer, 2013.

Peacey, Jason. "Introduction." in *The Regicides and the Execution of Charles I*, ed. by Jason Peacey, 1–13. Basingstoke: Palgrave, 2001.

———. "Reporting a Revolution: a Failed Propaganda Campaign?" in *The Regicides and the Execution of Charles I*, ed. by Jason Peacey, 161–181. Basingstoke: Palgrave, 2001.

Potter, Lois. "The Royal Martyr in the Restoration." in *The Royal Image: Representations of Charles I*, ed. by Thomas Corns, 240–262. Cambridge: Cambridge University Press, 1999.

Randall, Helen W. "The Rise and Fall of a Martyrology: Sermons on Charles I." *Huntington Library Quarterly*, 10.2 (1947): 135–167.

Sharpe, Kevin. *Image Wars: Kings and Commonwealths in England, 1603–1660*. Yale: Yale University Press, 2010.

———. *Rebranding Rule: The Restoration and Revolution Monarchy, 1660–1714*. New Haven: Yale University Press, 2013.

———. *Remapping Early Modern England: The Culture of Seventeenth Century Politics*. Cambridge: Cambridge University Press, 2000.

———. "'So Hard a Text?' Images of Charles I, 1612–1700." *The Historical Journal*, 43.2 (2000): 383–405.

Stewart, Byron. "The Cult of the Royal Martyr." *Church History*, 38 (1969): 175–187.

Tubb, Amos. "Printing the Regicide of Charles I." *History*, 89.296 (2004): 500–524.

Twigg, John. *The University of Cambridge and the English Revolution*. Woodbridge: Boydell and Brewer, 1990.

UNPUBLISHED

Bates, Lucy-Ann. *Nationwide Fast and Thanksgiving Days in England, 1640–1660*. Unpublished doctoral thesis, Durham University, 2012.

CHAPTER 9

Henrietta Maria, "Queen of Tears"?: Picturing and Performing the Cavalier Queen

Sarah Betts

he saw with her eyes, and determined by her judgment; and did not only pay her this adoration, but desired that all men should know that he was swayed by her: which was not good for either of them.[1]

Thus wrote Edward Hyde, Earl of Clarendon, of Charles I, and his wife, Henrietta Maria of France. The nature and extent of what C.V. Wedgwood described as Henrietta's "mental ascendancy" over her husband has occupied historians of Charles's troubled reign across the centuries since the restoration of the monarchy in 1660.[2] Her portrayal in these histories has varied by degrees and combination between frivolous distraction, personal martyr, misguided advisor, and *femme fatale*, but, although Michelle White, Carolyn Harris, and Susan Dunn-Hensley have comprehensively demonstrated that the reputation and representations of the Queen (as much as her actual influence) played a fundamental role in the propaganda

[1] Edward Hyde, *Life of Edward, Earl of Clarendon,* (Oxford: Clarendon Printing House, 1759), 79.
[2] C. V. Wedgwood, *The King's Peace 1637–1641,* (London: Folio Society, 2001), 70.

S. Betts (✉)
University of York, York, UK

© The Author(s) 2019
E. Paranque (ed.), *Remembering Queens and Kings of Early Modern England and France*, Queenship and Power,
https://doi.org/10.1007/978-3-030-22344-1_9

155

wars and eventual outcome of the civil wars, surprisingly little attention has been paid to her longer-term image outside of traditional historiography.[3] In recent years, literary scholars have begun to unpick representations and memories of her public persona (in both deed and reputation) in drama and poetry of the immediately post-civil war period.[4] Created in a time when English culture was attempting to make sense of a moment of profound tumult, in these texts have been identified images of a past (though still living) Henrietta that later pervade historical studies of the period. Critical, apologist, and celebratory figures of uxorious Kings and militarized Queens took to the stage, whilst Anna-Marie Linnell has argued that Restoration panegyrists "purposefully engaged" with the reconfiguring of her controversial civil war legacy through "craft[ing]an aesthetic of affliction which praises Henrietta Maria by reminding readers about her suffering."[5] From another angle, scholars of the Stuart monarchy, Laura Lunger Knoppers and Catriona Murray have noted the reverberation of the "politicised domesticity" of Charles and Henrietta's public image through Victorian idealizations of monarchy.[6] In doing so they contribute to a longer scholarship on the memory of the English Civil Wars in nineteenth-century English *and* French culture, but, although Cromwell, Charles I, and a few other key "revolutionary" figures have garnered individual attention in this vein, Henrietta's personal image seldom gets more than a passing mention.[7] In spite of recognition that esthetic and political

---

[3] Michelle Anne White, *Henrietta Maria and the English Civil Wars,* Aldershot: Ashgate, 2006. Carolyn Harris, *Queenship and Revolution in Early Modern Europe: Henrietta Maria and Marie Antoinette,* (London: Springer, 2016). Susan Dunn-Hensley, *Anna of Denmark and Henrietta Maria: Virgins, Witches and Catholic Queens,* Basingstoke: Palgrave Macmillan, 2017, p. 227.

[4] See, for example, Kamille Stone Stanton, "An Amazonian Heroickess": The Military Leadership of Queen Henrietta Maria in Margaret Cavendish's *Bell in Campo* (1662)', *Early Theatre,* 10:2, (2007): 71–86; Rachel Willie, *Staging the Revolution: Drama, Reinvention and History 1647–72,* Manchester: Manchester University Press, 2015; Anna-Marie Linnell, *Writing the Royal Consort in Stuart England,* PhD Thesis, University of Exeter, 2016.

[5] Linnell, *Writing the Royal Consort,* 135.

[6] Laura Lunger Knoppers, *"Politicizing Domesticity from Henrietta Maria to Milton's Eve,"* (Cambridge: Cambridge University Press, 2011); Laura Lunger Knoppers, "Cultural Legacies: The English Revolution in Nineteenth-Century British and French Literature and Art" in Michael J. Braddick [ed.], *The Oxford Handbook of the English Revolution,* (Oxford: Oxford University Press, 2015), 536; Catriona Murray, *Imagining Stuart Family Politics: Dynastic Crisis and Continuity,* (London: Routledge, 2017).

[7] Roy Strong, *And when did you last see your father? The Victorian Painter and British History,* (London: Thames and Hudson, 1978); Edward Morris and Frank Milner, *"And*

connections and correlations between English and French history were a key component of cultural and historiographical conceptions of seventeenth-century English history on both sides of The Channel in this period, shared and contrasting images of the French-born Queen of England have been relatively neglected. Likewise, the crucial interplay between art, fiction, historical scholarship, and public education has been largely ignored in the case of Henrietta's legacy. This chapter seeks to examine some of the many different contexts in which Henrietta has been visualized in the modern public arena through image, text, and performance in Britain and abroad particularly in the nineteenth and twentieth centuries. Identifying three key themes in portrayals of the Queen's life story, it will demonstrate the indivisibility of the visual and emotional esthetic of character-driven anecdote, from culturally and politically charged presentations and interpretations of local, national, and even international history.

MALIGNANT INFLUENCE

"It is only too easy," wrote one DVD reviewer of Ken Hughes's epic *Cromwell* (1970), "to think that the English Civil War was fought because Cromwell didn't get on with the King's wife."[8] Certainly this Henrietta, painstakingly dressed to imitate the glorious Van Dyck portraits and animated by the considerable presence of Dorothy Tutin, is autocratic, scheming and obsessed with Catholicism and French politics, to the detriment of the English King and Country. Although this openly partisan film

---

When Did You Last See Your Father?": *The Painting, Its Background, and Fame,* (Liverpool: National Museums and Galleries on Merseyside, 1992); and Helen Bennett, *Van Dyck in Check Trousers: Fancy Dress in Art and Life 1700–1900,* (Edinburgh: Scottish National Portrait Gallery, 1978); Laura Lunger Knoppers, "Cultural Legacies: The English Revolution in Nineteenth-Century British and French Literature and Art," in Michael J. Braddick [ed.], *The Oxford Handbook of the English Revolution,* (Oxford: Oxford University Press, 2015); "Revolutions Compared: The English Civil War as Political Touchstone in Romantic Literature," in Hanley, Keith, and Selden, Raman [eds.], *Revolution and English Romanticism: Politics and Rhetoric,* (New York: St Martin's Press, 1990); Kenneth Johnston and Joseph Nicholes, "Transitory Actions, Men Betrayed: The French Revolution in Romantic Drama" in Hoagwood, Terence Allan and Watkins, Daniel P., *British Romantic Drama: Historical and Critical Essays,* (London: Associated Press, 1998).

[8] Anon., Amazon Review of *Cromwell* DVD, https://www.amazon.co.uk/Cromwell-DVD-Richard-Harris/product-reviews/B0000BV1K5/ref=cm_cr_getr_d_paging_btm_17?ie=UTF8&reviewerType=all_reviews&pageNumber=17 accessed April 14 2018.

portrays Charles I as a deeply flawed character, Alex Guiness's portrayal is still moving and at times sympathetic. Henrietta meanwhile is irredeemably and inherently villainous. Both Cromwell and Charles blame her for the disintegration of Crown-Parliament relations, and when Cromwell visits the King at Whitehall with a deputation from Parliament, even before the onset of fighting, he is instantly distracted and disturbed by Henrietta's very being, her imagery and idolatry. Emphasized by promotional images depicting her standing imperiously over her enthralled and troubled husband, Tutin's Henrietta embodies the "evil counsellor" that dominates traditional historiography. John Hawkesworth's 1983 BBC drama serial, *By The Sword Divided*, also references this image. Henrietta appears only briefly however, as war approached, Charles's willingness to allow her to "rule both head and heart" was bemoaned even by a devoted Cavalier, an interpretation very much in the spirit of Clarendon, and one very similar to passages in earlier dramatizations of the couple, such as Maurice Colbourne's 1937, *Charles the King*.[9]

Clarendon's work was widely read and considered authoritative throughout the eighteenth and nineteenth centuries.[10] Publication and circulation of other seventeenth-century texts also consolidated this interpretation. Memoirs of Parliamentarian, Edmund Ludlow repeatedly refer to Henrietta as "instrumental" in Charles's misguided, "illegal" actions, and in the "contriving and formenting the long and bloody Civil War."[11] In the 1640s, reputations of both King and Queen were fatally undermined through publication of their private correspondence, and collection and publication of Henrietta's letters in 1857 renewed perceptions of her as the power behind the throne.[12] One reviewer wrote that the letters revealed that Charles followed "her dictates" unquestioningly, pursuing absolutism at her "prompting" and "thoroughly...under the influence of her ambitious spirit and resolute will." She is interpreted as the chief architect and prolonger of the wars, "in cabinet what Rupert was in the field"

[9] Maurice Colborne, *Charles the King: A Chronicle Play*, (London: Samuel French, 1937), 13, 28.

[10] Francis P. Wilson, *"That Memorable Scene": The Image of King Charles the First in Seventeenth and Eighteenth-Century Literature*, PhD Thesis, University of York (1993), 300–302.

[11] Edmund Ludlow, *Memoirs of Edmund Ludlow*, Volume III, (London: Publisher Unknown, 1720), 96, 224.

[12] Mary Anne Everett Green [ed.], *Letters of Queen Henrietta Maria*, (London: Richard Bentley, 1857).

and even essentially, "the real regicide."[13] The image of Charles as Henrietta's puppet was also found in fictional representations of the Queen's character, one example portraying Charles with "faraway glance and abstracted smile" listening and indulging every whim of his forceful wife whose irreparable faults included "restless meddling in affairs out of her province,[and] incorrigible plotting and scheming to attain her ends."[14] A 1935 novel by Elinor M. Brent-Dyer, also portrays Henrietta as overwhelmingly and knowingly charismatic, satisfied to "enthrall...many hearts" and be "adored" with her beauty and charm and confident in the use of her consequent influence.[15]

As Susan Dunn-Hensley observes in Chap. 15 of this volume, the decreasing cultural resonance of anti-Catholicism has diminished the significance of Henrietta's faith in itself. However, her clear agenda for promoting Catholicism, "repugnant to the creed of the [British] nation" has been viewed as misguided at best, and her French-ness has been much highlighted, from observations that ignorance of English language, history, and culture rendered her unsuitable for queenship, to adoption of French accents in performing her.[16] This was particularly important in the presentation of the Queen in the 1934 *Pageant of Parliament*. Organized by (particularly Conservative) politicians, the highly acclaimed show celebrated the institution's past and present, particularly emphasizing the exemplary nature of Westminster democracy and the English-ness of its virtues.[17] Henrietta, represented almost as a foil to English democracy, was played to acclaim by French star, Yvonne Arnaud.[18] Actively and openly

[13] *Newcastle Journal*, "Charles I and his Queen Henrietta Maria," Saturday 24 January 1857.

[14] Sarah Tytler, "A Young Oxford Maid: (In the Days of the King and the Parliament)," Girl's Own Paper, 13th April 1889, 460.

[15] Elinor M. Brent-Dyer, *Elizabeth the Gallant*, (Modern Edition, Bath: Girls Gone By, 2006), 5.

[16] Tytler, "Young Oxford Maid," p. 460. Agnes Strickland, *Lives of the Queens of England*, (Philadelphia: Blanchard and Lea, 1852), 10; Frances Copeland Stickles, *A Crown for Henrietta Maria: Maryland's Namesake Queen*, (Lanham, Maryland: Maryland Historical Press, 1988), 23; Jean Plaidy, *Loyal in Love: Henrietta Maria, Wife of Charles I*, New York: Three Rivers Press, 1983; Austin Brereton, *The Lyceum and Henry Irving*, (London: Lawrence and Bullen, 1903), 182; "The New Play at the Lyceum Theatre," The Spectator, October 12 1872; Colbourne, *Charles the King*, 24.

[17] Angela Bartie, Paul Caton, Linda Fleming, Mark Freeman, Tom Hulme, Alex Hutton and Paul Readman, *The Redress of the Past*, http://www.historicalpageants.ac.uk/pageants/

[18] *Aberdeen Press and Journal*, "Stirring Pageant of Parliament," Saturday 30 June 1934, 7.

leading Charles into conflict with Parliament and People, she also attempts to educate her eldest son to disregard the institution in an exchange with her husband on its significance where Charles explicitly highlights her alien cultural compass; "Parlement you call it – that is your mistake…Your French Parlements are nothing, but our English Parliament is the High Council of the Realm."[19]

Ultimately, Henrietta has been portrayed as alienated from the English people, alienating Charles from them in turn. This alienation was not always deliberate and sinister, but sometimes brought about by the self-absorption and frivolity of a woman who despite loving "intentions became…[Charles's] evil genius."[20] Brent-Dyer's Henrietta appears as "gaily dressed as ever" even in the midst of war, whilst on the very brink of war, Hawkesworth's Henrietta in *By the Sword Divided* sits for Van Dyck whilst Edmund Waller recites sycophantic poetical compliments to her, apparently oblivious to the concurrent political turmoil.[21] Even the choice of painting here is significant as it is clearly the piece known as "*The Great Peece*," painted several years earlier than this fictional setting at the height of personal rule, and often remarked upon for being symbolic of the remote and insulated monarchy projecting domestic harmony and ignoring the gathering storm in the background. As one reviewer of Jane Oliver's 1940 biography of the Queen summarized, Charles "might have [been] saved" by a "wiser" wife, "but if there was bad advice to be given she gave it; if there were fatal intrigues to be indulged in she went into them."[22]

Royal Love Story

Imagining Henrietta as Charles's driving influence hinges upon impressions of his "over-indulgent" affection for her and a particularly passionate and loving relationship between them.[23] The disastrous implications of the role of weak, emasculated and uxorious King, assigned to Charles in seventeenth-century politics and propaganda has been well documented, whilst recent scholarship has demonstrated that some of this anti-royalist

---

[19] Walter Creighton, *Pageant of Parliament*, (London: Fleetway Press, 1934), 23–24.
[20] *The Sphere*, "The World of Books," Saturday 23 November 1940, 254.
[21] Brent-Dyer, *Elizabeth the Gallant*, 62.
[22] *The Sphere*, "The World of Books," 254.
[23] Tytler, "A Young Oxford Maid," 460. Katie Whitaker, *A Royal Passion: The Turbulent Marriage of Charles I and Henrietta Maria*, (London: Weidenfeld and Nicholson, 2010), xviii–xix.

propaganda was forged as an unfortunate by-product of a concerted projection of idyllic chivalric and married love of and by the couple themselves, particularly during the 1630s.[24] In nineteenth-century Britain, the confluence of a new vogue for "history painting" (where great events were reimagined as personal, private moments), an increase in interest in the Civil War Period as socio-political progenitor of their own era of Parliamentary democracy, and the increasing "domestication" of the contemporary Royal image reinvigorated familiarity with, and to some extent reinterpreted perceptions of, the Stuart Royal Family. These images were not just on display at the Royal Academy, but pervaded through a multimedia, cross-contextualized milieu of dialogue between painting, literature, drama, popular and "professional" historical writing and educational texts.[25] The re-emphasis on Charles I as model husband and father in contrast to his political and military failings has endured throughout the generations since, a common feature of art and drama featuring the King, and as such has received some scholarly attention.[26] Henrietta's role in this image is more complex. Partly this is undoubtedly because of the controversy over her political and military role. Whilst Victorians might identify in the couple a model for the idyllic image of their own Victoria and Albert, a wife dominating her husband was hardly more conducive to nineteenth-century notions of domestic order and propriety than it had been to seventeenth-century ones. Dwelling upon the influence of a foreign consort also had contentious potential. However, it must also be noted that Henrietta and Charles were apart for most of the wars. Henrietta was not at Charles's side in battle or even in the country for most of the 1640s. She was not present at his trial or execution, and, unlike Marie Antoinette, did not share her husband's gruesome fate. Thus, she was not necessarily a go-to subject for the vignettes of great events favored by history painters or illustrators of popular or educational history texts. However, images of Henrietta as beloved and loving wife do feature in reflections back on to the pre-war years, images which would become ingrained in perceptions of both King and Queen and used to create a new more emotional, esthetic, and sympathetic image of the Queen and her

---

[24] White, *Queenship and Revolution*, Knoppers, "Cultural Legacies."

[25] Strong, *And When Did You Last See Your Father?*, 154; Martin Meisel, *Realizations: Narrative, Pictorial and Theatrical Arts in Nineteenth-Century England*, Princeton University Press, Princeton, New Jersey, 1983.

[26] Knoppers, "*Politicizing Domesticity from Henrietta Maria to Milton's Eve*," Cambridge: Cambridge University Press, 2011, 1–16.

place in seventeenth-century history as the heroine of a picturesque yet relatable romance. In a modern age increasingly valuing romantic affection, passion, and companionship over diplomatic convenience in royal marriages, the idea of a genuine, growing and lifelong affection between Charles and Henrietta has endured throughout the twentieth century from references to it in newspapers and biographies to grounding the novels by Jean Plaidy and Fiona Mountain which Dunn-Hensley discusses in Chap. 15.[27]

Whilst civil war novels and histories have focused upon the dramatic and even catastrophic element of Charles and Henrietta's love, international contexts reinterpret this royal romance to present other aspects of seventeenth-century English history and its place within a grand march of history toward the modern world. In America, the small anecdotal fact of the naming of Maryland in tribute to the wife that the state's charter-granting King had loved, created a small but significant role for her within a foundation mythos across the Atlantic. It is largely an esthetic role, and one largely removed from the controversies of the civil war, though Charles's tolerance (and even sympathy with) his beloved's Catholicism can still be found cited as contributing to Maryland's place as a catholic refuge and its early passing of religious toleration laws.[28] Citing her religious exclusion from coronational consecration as Queen, a children's history book published by the Maryland Historical Society (MdHS) in 1988 concluded that "For Henrietta Maria…an English queen without a crown, her legacy endures in the name of the state of Maryland. It is a crown of another sort, and one which marks her place in history."[29]

This (largely visual) legacy, heavily supported by the MdHS, grafts an almost dioramic figure of Henrietta onto a quasi-mural of a romantic local past. The MdHS and the State Archives Art Collection contain multiple images of the Queen, presumably collected and commissioned on account of this "namesake" foundation connection. In 1934 at the time of the State's tercentenary a "large" 1630s portrait of Henrietta from the Studio of Van Dyck could be seen and visited hanging around the mantel in the Governor's Reception Room of the State House displayed alongside those of Charles I and George Calvert, first Lord

---

[27] Jean Plaidy, *Loyal in Love*; Fiona Mountain, *Cavalier Queen*, (London: Arrow Books, 2012).

[28] Carl Schoettler, "A Royal State of Affairs," *The Baltimore Sun*, 25th March 1998.

[29] Frances Copeland Stickles, *A Crown for Henrietta Maria: Maryland's Namesake Queen*, Lanham, Maryland: Maryland Historical Press, 1988, 73.

Baltimore, (seeker of Maryland's founding charter), marking her as a key character in the State's formation and identity.[30]

This role is still more pronounced in her inclusion in James Carroll Mansfield's 1943 "Cavalcade of Colonial Maryland" exhibition at the MdHS, and the large-scale 1944 oil paintings of muralists John and Mabel Georgi. Mansfield's exhibition identified key moments in Maryland's colonial history, providing for each both titles and brief explanatory descriptions. Moments ranged from Lord Baltimore "plann[ing] his Colonial undertakings in America" from his home in Yorkshire, to the outbreak of the American Revolution.[31] Amongst them, *Lord Baltimore Receiving the Grant of Maryland from King Charles I, 1632*, specifically notes the colony's name derivation through "compliment to Queen Henrietta Maria."[32] Henrietta herself plays a clearly active role in this interpretation. This important state business intrudes upon a domestic scene of a relaxed King. Whilst the attitudes of Baltimore and the other attendants present direct respect almost exclusively toward him, Charles himself, almost deferentially, transfers attention to his business-like wife sitting behind the desk actively considering Baltimore's proposals. Thus Henrietta, like Baltimore (who died shortly afterward), is interpreted as an active, rather than merely nominal, part of the history of colonial Maryland despite never having set foot there. The Georgi portrait was clearly created as part of a triptych, this time with Balitmore and his son, Cecil (who actually founded and settled Maryland, and whose colonial exploits are referenced in the background of the Georgis's painting), and was displayed as part of this storyboard of Maryland history in the lobby of Annapolis's Treasury House into the twenty-first century.[33]

Finally, in addition to the original from Van Dyck's studio, the State collection also owns and displays two early twentieth-century copies. The first, by an unknown artist, can be found hanging today in the entrance

---

[30] Adelyn Dohme Breeskin, *Catalogue of the Paintings in the State House at Annapolis Maryland,* 1934. Available Online at http://msa.maryland.gov/megafile/msa/stagsere/se1/se14/000027/html/hesitant_revolut/msa/speccol/sc1500/sc1545/e_catalog_2002/1934catalog.html, accessed March 1 2018.

[31] I am grateful for all information about the "Cavalcade" series and exhibition, including Mansfield's painting descriptions, to the archives of the MdHS and particularly for the assistance and research of MdHS volunteer, Elizabeth Nilson.

[32] Ibid.

[33] Breeskin, *Catalogue of the Paintings.*

hall of the Governor's Reception Room.[34] The second, more high-profile piece was commissioned by the Board of Public Works of Maryland from Marylander, Florence Mackubin, a prominent "society" portraitist, sent to Warwick Castle, England, to copy Van Dyck's original.[35] Purposefully including Henrietta as a prominent local dignitary in this way denotes her a significant figure in Maryland history, and the portrait has hung for years in the entrance lobby of the State's Government House.

Respect for the Queen that Charles loved served largely as an anecdotal backdrop for her image in Maryland. In Britain, memory of the couple's love could be reinterpreted as a more direct exposition of the place of current concerns within the pageant of history. Early twentieth-century Britain witnessed an explosion of enthusiasm for historical pageants promoting local legends and events within wider national or even international histories. These displays usually took the form of either a procession of historical figures or tableaux vivant, and or longer play-like performances made up of several "episodes" in the local timeline in advancing chronological order.

The civil war was a recurring theme in many of these recitals, and Henrietta featured in a handful, but obviously tended to be absent from episodes concentrating upon actual warfare. The Dover Pageant (1908), however, represented the couple's first meeting in 1625, already married by proxy before Henrietta left France. Although the idea of the young bride of an arranged marriage arriving in a strange land is obviously alluded to throughout the text, the notion that this was a stepping stone to a great romantic love is a central tenet.[36] Charles is obviously taken with his bride, and she is reassured and comforted by him in her homesickness so that by the end she is not only willing but eager to "love" the newly anglicized version of her name as her husband's personal gift and allow him to teach her to be "a thorough Englishwoman."[37] The stark political convenience of the marriage is diluted through reference to Charles having actually previously developed feelings for her when visiting the Louvre en route to

---

[34] The Annapolis Collection: A Wealth of Maryland History. http://msa.maryland.gov/megafile/msa/stagsere/se1/se14/000027/html/hesitant_revolut/msa/speccol/sc1500/sc1545/e_catalog_2002/georgi.html, accessed March 2 2018.

[35] H.L. Motter [ed.], *The International Who's Who: Who's Who in the World 1912*, New York: William G. Hewitt Press, 1912, 727.

[36] Louis Napoleon Parker, *The Dover Pageant July 27, 28, 29, 30, 31, August 1, 1908*, Dover: Grigg and Son, 1908, 50–67.

[37] Parker, *The Dover Pagent*, 67.

court the Spanish Infanta and noted a young Henrietta to be a "Queen of Beauty," "eclipsing" even the famous beauty of the Queen of France "hundredfold."[38] This built upon an old legend originating as a face-saving myth at the time of the actual marriage itself and often speculated upon in popular and fictional discussions of the couple's relationship.[39]

Even more than *Pageant of Parliament*, Dover's Pageant emphasized Henrietta's foreignness, from employing well-known French poet, Louis Tiercelin, to write the episode (much of which was also performed in French), to using French performers, to textual reference to local mispronunciation of her alien Christian name as "Hungry-hetter."[40] On this occasion though, the references are positive and/or good-natured. Cultural misunderstandings are laughed off or overcome by warm intentions and friendship, "l'entente des coeurs"/"heart-sympathy" as Tiercelin's Charles proclaims.[41] In wake of *entente cordiale* (1904), the 1625 episode was the culmination of a celebration of Dover as a nexus-point of Anglo-French relations. Former dangers and hostilities dissolved in the burgeoning love between King and Queen, a romantic resolution to the historic which championed the promised peace and prosperity of contemporary foreign politics, a reinterpretation easily perceived and reported in press coverage of the pageant.[42]

As Britain moved away from "Splendid Isolation" and began to look toward European alliances, the image of Henrietta combining her strong European identity with her powerful attachment and romantic entanglement with an English King could be reimagined as a symbol of international cooperation. This was demonstrated again in the (albeit rather bizarre) interpretation which British magazine, *The Sphere*, placed upon her role in a Student pageant at Leiden University in 1910 which featured the Queen, dressed in classic Van Dyck inspired costume "riding through the streets of [Leiden] in a beautiful coach of the period" recalling her visit there in the 1640s.[43] It was, The Sphere told its readers, a "most pictur-

---

[38] Parker, The Dover Pagent, 63.

[39] Strickland, *Lives of the Queens*, 11–15; Plaidy, *Loyal in Love*, 45–46.

[40] *Whitstable Times and Hearne Bay Herald*, "The Dover Pageant," Saturday 25 July 1908. 7; Parker, *The Dover Pageant*, 64–67.

[41] Parker, *The Dover Pageant*, 64–67.

[42] *The Times*, "The Coming Dover Pageant," Thursday 9 July 1908; *Yorkshire Post and Leeds Intelligencer*, "The Dover Pageant," Tuesday 28 July 1908, 9.

[43] *The Sphere*, "In the Old Days When We Fought the Dons," Saturday 09 July 1910, 33.

esque revival of [a] history" of international cooperation between Britain and "our continental friends against a common foe."[44]

Once more, the centrality of Van Dyck's work to Henrietta's posthumous image must be noted. Portrayals of the couple at the height of their domestic peace and prosperity heavily reference his portraiture and, in pursuing little, backstage stories of great historical moments, painters, dramatists, theatrical and pageant costumiers, and fancy dress ball-goers, found in Charles I's family in his studio both inspiration and, occasionally, subject.[45] As noted above, Hawkesworth portrayed Henrietta sitting for *The Great Peece*, and he was not the first. Colbourne's *Charles the King*, also features Van Dyck painting her in picturesque romantic harmony of marital happiness. The directions in the actors' edition relate that she is confident in her position and impervious to her unpopularity "because for ten years she has been in love with Charles," the supremacy and security of her love for Charles is viewed as a central element in the writing and performance of her character, and is clearly rooted in the legacy of Van Dyck's renowned portraiture.[46]

This legacy has been profoundly mediated through Frederick Goodall's 1853, *An Episode in the Happier Days of Charles I*. Familiar with it from school textbooks, Roy Strong famously wrote that the sight of "the tragic King[and] his beautiful Queen...sail[ing] down-river on a summer's day" evoked such a response in him as it "fused" romance with history that it "made [him, innately] a Cavalier for life," and he has not been the only art-historian to attribute this interpretation of history to schoolroom familiarity with Goodall's painting.[47] Goodall's royal bodies and costumes, particularly Charles and Henrietta clearly echo Van Dyck originals which he spent considerable time studying at Windsor Castle.[48] The piece, which fused the easy familiarity of "Van Dyck" royal figures with an apparently

---

[44] *The Sphere*, "In the Old Days," 33.

[45] Diane Russcol, "Images of Charles I and Henrietta-Maria in French art, ca. 1815–1855," *Arts Magazine*, 62 (1988), 46–47.

[46] Maurice Colborne, *Charles the King: A Chronicle Play*, (London: Samuel French, 1937), 24.

[47] Strong, *And When Did You Last See Your Father*, 11; Christopher Wood, "Realist or Romantic – Narrative Choices in Victorian Art," in Carolyn Hill [ed.], *Artist as Narrator: Nineteenth Century Narrative Art in England and France*, Oklahoma City: Oklahoma City Museum, 9–10.

[48] Frederick Goodall, *The Reminiscences of Frederick Goodall, R.A.* (London: The Walter Scott Publishing Co. Ltd., 1902), 34, 330.

effortless though actually meticulously studied harmonious river scene of water, swans, and lillies, was much copied and well known, not only through textbooks, but as a "popular adornment for drawing rooms" in the mid-late nineteenth century.[49] A moment of purely imagined interpretation, it became a canonical image. It directly inspired playwright, W.G. Wills and actor, Henry Irving's *Charles the First* (1872), the first act of which culminated in a living recreation of Goodall's painting as the royal family depart to "holiday" aboard a barge.[50] Irving's Charles voiced the very essence of the painting, "thirst[ing] for peace" and dictating,

> So now the gentle sail shall be our wing;
> The air we rise upon shall be sweet music;
> Breathe music softly till the wave shall seem
> To move in silent glamour, and the banks
> Be rimmed with rainbow...
> ...like the heaven we are sailing for.[51]

The scene was then fulfilled as the music played and the curtain fell upon the departing barge.[52] Irving's visual representation as well as performance as the King was much-admired, but as much as he may have looked "as if he had stepped from the [Van Dyck] canvases," it was a multi-layered image, which drew upon Goodall's study as much as the originals.[53] The play was a huge success, and the Victorian public was able to absorb this interpretation of Goodall's vision not only in the theater, but in the text (published the following year), and also in theatrical illustrations (prints or paintings published in papers and periodicals, or sold as domestic decorative art). An image of the barge scene by William Henry Margetson, demonstrates once again the layering of images, inspired by Wills's scene, it is

[49] Frederick Goodall, *The Reminiscences of Frederick Goodall, R.A.*, 34–35, 330–331, 381; Madeleine Bingham, *Henry Irving and the Victorian Theatre* (London: George Allen and Unwin, 1978), 93.

[50] Bingham, *Henry Irving*, 1978, 93; Jeffrey Richards, *Sir Henry Irving: A Victorian Actor and His World*, Hambledon and London, London and New York, 2005, 331; Martin Meisel, Realizations: Narrative, *Pictorial and Theatrical Arts in Nineteenth-Century England*, Princeton University Press, Princeton, New Jersey, 1983, 240. W. G. Wills, *Charles the First: An Historical Tragedy in Four Acts*, (William Blackwood and Sons, Edinburgh and London, 1873), 28–29.

[51] Wills, *Charles the First*, 28–29.

[52] Wills, *Charles the First*, 29.

[53] Bingham, *Henry Irving*, p. 94; Helen Walter, "Van Dyck in Action": Dressing Charles I for the Victorian Stage', *Costume*, 47:2, (2013): 161–179.

situated not on the stage but in the scene's natural environmental setting. This environment is clearly lifted from Goodall, and Irving's Charles, from appearance to posture, is clearly imagined as an almost carbon copy of *Happier Days*. Margetson's Henrietta, however, is more clearly a portrait of actress, Ellen Terry, drawing upon the more contemporary-stylized images of Henrietta in circulation of Terry in the role, inserting the current fame of the actress and the play into an historical scene in fact based upon Goodall's interpretation.

As historical pageants proliferated, the pervasiveness of *Happier Days* in contemporary conceptualizations of the historical Queen became clear. The Dover Pageant episode was of course set too early in the marriage for a direct portrayal, but the echoes of the picture are pronounced in the image of the beautiful Henrietta "waft[ing]" across the sea to her new husband, and more explicitly in the choice, *and re-lyricizing*, of Orlando Gibbons's madrigal, *The Silver Swan*.[54] As well as both directly and indirectly associating her with swans (a feature so prominent in Goodall's work), the new lyrics specifically lay out the "enchanting" portrait of the "beauteous Queen" "glid[ing]" to England across a very unrealistically imagined "lake"-like Channel powered by "gentle breezes."[55] Other pageants referenced the painting more directly. An 1896 pageant Ripon featured Charles "on horseback" after Van Dyck but Henrietta aboard a "Royal Barge," showing the particular predominance of this image in relation to her personal image.[56] Almost ten years later, a scene of Charles I "in the days of his greatness, in his barge, with his Queen" on the Thames was imagined as a classic, likely, and appropriate scene for a proposed London Pageant.[57] Most prominently the scene was brought to life in the Oxford Pageant (1907) which featured three scenes from the period, the first of which was actually entitled "The Happy Days, A.D. 1636" and featured Charles, Henrietta and their children floating down river on a barge, accompanied by madrigal music.[58] This living representation of Goodall's image enjoyed a wider circulation and longer shelf-life than the mere performance-time of the pageant. Oxford was upheld as a particu-

---

[54] Parker, *The Dover Pageant*, 50.

[55] Parker, *The Dover Pageant*, 54.

[56] *Belfast Newsletter*, "Historic Pageant at Fountains Abbey," Thursday 20 August 1908, 7; *Yorkshire Gazette*, "Historic Pageant at Ripon," Saturday 22 August 1908, 5.

[57] *The Stage*, "London's Pageant," Thursday 9 January 1908, 15.

[58] Lawrence Housman et al., *The Oxford Historical Pageant June 27–July 3 1907 Book of Words* (Oxford: Oxford University Press, 1907), 105.

larly successful exemplar for other similar events and was certainly in the foreground when the similar vignette was posited for London.[59] *The Sphere* printed a full page photograph of the "Charming Scene" as a highlight of the festivities, and souvenir postcards of the scene were available to buy, in photographic form, but also as oilette impressions, clearly based more on the original painting than on the actual performative moment.[60]

TRAGIC HEROINE

The Oxford Pageant juxtaposed this careless romance with incidents from the 1640s, ultimately crowning its representation of Charles's reign with the city's surrender to Parliament in 1646, a moment when the King's position became "desperate" and ultimately led him downhill toward execution.[61] The barge scene imagined for London was also envisioned as being offset by a scene of Whitehall in 1649.[62] The episode's "nostalgic" element, contrasting with the retrospectively well-known and oft-depicted ultimate destiny of the Stuart king, was noted at the first exhibition of Goodall's painting in 1853 and was clearly essential in its subsequent cultural resonance.[63] The inherent melodrama of jarring reversal of fortune held natural appeal for writers and artists and has allowed the politically controversial Queen to be interpreted as a tragic heroine, mixing to varying degrees steadfast valor and pathetic misery. In historiographically surveying Henrietta's reputation, White relegates Oliver's biography, *Queen of Tears*, to the footnotes because of its primary focus on "historical personality" over analysis, but this interpretation and its alluring lexical marketing was a product both of and for contemporary sympathies of taste and familiarities of reference.[64] In the 1870s, Wills was pressured into reworking the ending of *Charles the First* to focus on domestic tragedy over political commentary, creating a "lachrymose conclusion" by ahistorically including Henrietta in Charles's pre-execution finale.[65] Opposite

[59] *The Sphere*, "London's Pageant," 15.

[60] *The Sphere*, "A Charming Scene From the Oxford Pageant," Saturday 29 June 1907, 289.

[61] Housman et al., *The Oxford Historical Pageant*, 109.

[62] *The Sphere*, "London's Pageant," 15.

[63] Edward Morris, "Catalogue of paintings drawings and photographs" in Morris, Edward, and Milner, Frank, *"And When Did You Last See Your Father?": The Painting, Its Background, and Fame* (Liverpool: National Museums and Galleries on Merseyside, 1992), 49.

[64] White, *Henrietta Maria and the English Civil Wars*, 2–3.

[65] Bingham, *Henry Irving*, 93–94.

Irving, first Isabel Bateman, and then Terry played Henrietta. Both were renowned tragic actresses and the part both cemented their reputations as such and became itself identified as such a role, listed in summaries of Terry's illustrious career alongside the great Shakespearean parts.[66] Both actresses compared their own performances to their respective "Ophelia," Bateman emphasizing her efforts and success in "wringing tears" from the audience, and Terry describing the "wan lily" effect that Oscar Wilde saw in her Henrietta as "perfectly what I had tried to convey, not only in this part but in Ophelia."[67] Adding to the role's tragic profile, both were photographed in the role, and Kimberly Rhodes has convincingly argued that one image of Bateman in particular appears to have been particularly widely circulated. Julia Cameron's image of Henrietta with her children awaiting Charles's execution, Rhodes argues, "capitalizes on pathos, audience recognition of an actress in a familiar role and more commercial practices" to profit from and consolidate a particular view of the character in the public mind.[68]

Terry's critical appraisal of her own performances is preoccupied with whether she "cried too much" so as to render Henrietta ridiculous, whilst also acknowledging the dramatic need and commercial value of her emotional and emotive performance, of which it was written she "was so infinitely pathetic that she reached absolute greatness."[69] However, tragic renditions of the Queen have not been wholly passively piteous and pathetic. Twenty-first century titles in popular history marketing Henrietta as "intrepid" or "indomitable" demonstrate the lasting allure of melodramatic misery, but simultaneously emphasize a more stoical and pro-active response to suffering to cater to modern sensibilities of gendered representation.[70] Nevertheless, elements of this courageous and enduring Henrietta can be found going right back into the nineteenth century.

---

[66] *Nottingham Evening Post*, "Dame Ellen Terry: Passing of a Famous Actress," Saturday 21 July 1928, 6.

[67] Kimberly Rhodes, *Ophelia and Victorian Visual Culture: Representing Body Politics in the Nineteenth Century*, Aldershot: Ashgate, 2008, 143; Ellen Terry, *The Story of My Life: Recollections and Reflections* (New York: Doubleday, 1908), 181.

[68] Rhodes, *Ophelia and Victorian Visual Culture*, 144–145.

[69] Terry, *The Story of My Life*, 234, 258; Charles Hiatt, *Ellen Terry and her impersonations: An Appreciation* (London: G. Bell, 1899), 126–127.

[70] Rosalind K. Marshall, *Henrietta Maria, The Intrepid Queen* (Owings Mills, Maryland: Stemmer House Publishers, 1991); *Henrietta Maria: Charles I's Indomitable Queen* (London: Sutton, 2001).

Audiences viewed Terry's portrayal as a mix of sorry victim and passionate resilience, "exquisitely feminine...[yet]every inch a queen...tender...[,] exhibit[ing imperious regality] side by side with a magnificent graciousness and a gentleness which won all hearts."[71]

In a cross-channel exchange of artistic and historical culture Henrietta's wartime travels and travails, combined with her French heritage fed the image of the suffering but brave and adventurous wronged princess. Both British and French painters composed scenes of Henrietta's perilous journeys as a hunted prize in the 1640s, and in France, depictions of her arrival and life in exile there portrayed her as a tragic daughter of France, mistreated by, and/or vulnerably isolated from, her English subjects.[72] Cross-national cross-referencing of anecdote and texts, created ever-more familiar and perpetuating circles of imagery of her character.[73] Several scholars have observed that cultural and esthetic familiarity and engagement with the English "revolutionary" period in nineteenth-century France was a useful means of processing the cultural shock, whilst negotiating the political sensitivities of their own very recent past.[74] Others have identified in Romantic-era France, a "virtual cult of Henri IV," national hero, icon of the French Monarchy as an institution, and father of the Bourbon dynasty, so it is worth noting that, almost universally, French *and* English nineteenth-century texts painstakingly associate Henrietta with her illustrious father.[75] She is often referred to as his namesake child and similar to him in strength of personality.[76] She is also frequently, specifically, and even *primarily* introduced in literary and dramatic works as his daughter, most strikingly in Jacques-Arsène-François-Polycarpe Ancelot and Joseph-Xavier-Boniface Saintine's 1833 play, *Têtes rondes et cavaliers*, where, in Cromwellian England, a suspected Stuart-sympathizer turns for help to the

---

[71] Terry, *The Story of My Life*, 179–181; Hiatt, *Ellen Terry*, 126.

[72] Strong, *And When Did You Last See Your Father?*, 136–151; Wright, *Painting and History*, 99–103.

[73] Geoffrey Cubitt, "The Political Uses of Seventeenth-Century English History in Bourbon Restoration France," *The Historical Journal*, 50:1, (2007), 76.

[74] Cubitt, "The Political Uses of Seventeenth-Century English History"; Ruscol "Images of Charles I and Henrietta-Maria"; Wright, *Painting and History*, 77–120.

[75] David A. Bell, *The Cult of the Nation in France: Inventing Nationalism, 1680–1800*, Cambridge, Massachusetts, USA: Harvard University Press, 2001, 30; Nadia Tscherny and Guy Stair Sainty, *Romance and Chivalry: History and Literature Reflected in Early Nineteenth-Century French Painting* (New York: Matthiesen Gallery and Stair Sainty Matthiesen, 1996).

[76] Strickland, *Lives of the Queens*, 5–60; Francois Chateaubriand, *Les Quatre Stuarts*, Paris: Gabriel Roux, 1857, 94–5.

play's cavalier hero, Arthur, revealing her secret identity by identifying herself as "Henriette de France, fille de Henri IV et veuve de Charles Ier," her natal identity trumping marital and maternal ones in establishing her true character.[77] When the play was adapted into Bellini's hugely successful opera, *I Puritani*, Carlo Pepoli's libretto borrowed this manner of self-identification for "Enrichetta," "*Figlia a Enrico e a Carlo Sposo.*"[78]

Entwining Henrietta's image with Henri IV's enhanced her characterization as a symbol of monarchical heroism, braving and surviving the trials of war secure in her self-identification as a member of a divinely chosen elite, the natural rulers of the known world. It also deepened her story's tragic undertones. From apparently declaring herself "the happiest woman in the world," adored by her husband, two decades later she was a widow dependent upon her nephew, Louis XIV, with little hope of Restoration.[79] Just as the contrast with Goodall's image of domestic bliss intensified the pathos of the knowledge of the King's execution, so the identification of Henrietta as somehow entitled to automatic respect and assistance, rendered her all the more pathetic and/or wronged when these dues were not paid. Such ideas of the almost hagiographed family of Henri IV can be found in both French and English literature. In England, Wills's Henrietta, for example, dwells upon what constitutes "fit treatment for King Henri's child."[80] In France, Dumas's famous Musketeers in *Twenty Years After* cannot "hide [their] indignation" at discovering the neglect and ill-treatment of "the daughter of Henry IV" and are spurred into her service.[81] In the set up for his characters' involvement in the English Civil War in this novel, Dumas repeatedly reminds his readers of her status as a "daughter of France" and specifically of Henri, "that sublime King."[82] Dumas's Henrietta's idyllic earlier life is recalled through references to the love and love tokens exchanged between herself and her husband, and also to her former "beauty" in contrast to her appearance now ravaged by "sorrow," and ultimately "mute" horror upon learning of Charles's execution.[83]

[77] Jacques-Arsene-Francois Polcarpe Ancelot, *Tête Rondes et Cavaliers: Drame Historique en Trois Actes,* (Paris, 1833), 20. For another example of this, see also Alexandre Dumas, *Twenty Years After,* London: Wordsworth, Wordsworth Classics Edition, 2009, 285, 287, 295.

[78] Herbert Weinstock, *Vincenzo Bellini: His Life and His Operas* (London: Weidenfeld and Nicolson, 1964), 163–164, 311–327.

[79] Strickland, *Lives of the Queen of England,* 6–33.

[80] Will, *Charles the First,* 17.

[81] Dumas, *Twenty Years After,* 319.

[82] Dumas, *Twenty Years After,* 285, 287, 292, 295–6, 298.

[83] Dumas, *Twenty Years After,* 284, 587.

CONCLUSION

Dumas's invocation of a nationalistic duty of the French to acknowledge ownership of their native Princess reinforces his reader's investment into an internationalized historical setting. As in many of the examples discussed above, representations and memories of Henrietta have often taken the form of artistic, textual, or performative vignettes, of esthetic moments in her career, both real and imaginary, but certainly reinterpreted as part of wider cultural understandings of local, national, and international history. In Britain's era of historical pageantry she was a familiar figure, whether representative of a bygone but picturesque time, or of the personal tragedy of great events (such as her appearance in pageants around Exeter, the site of her ultimate departure for exile from the besieged city in 1644, within days of the birth of her youngest child).[84] Interestingly, on the other side of the channel, the other part of her flight has recently been chosen as the theme for the annual 13–14th July history festival in Vannes, where the Queen stopped in 1644 (already commemorated through a plaque affixed to the building where she was received), a modern celebration and reinterpretation of a shared history between England and France.[85]

As tastes and practices of historical research and teaching have changed, Henrietta's image, like that of the civil war more generally, has become less prominent in popular culture.[86] When she is mentioned in public engagements with seventeenth-century history however, the core themes of the images discussed in this chapter resurface, demonstrating how ingrained these central vignettes, perpetuated by their constant echoing through and between different media, are in public, artistic, and even scholarly understandings of the period.[87] These understandings are not merely a familiarity with historical fact, but an emotional and imaginative response (judgmental and/or sentimental) to imagery in text, picture, or performance which facilitates interpretation, or reinterpretation, of, and engagement with, the past.

---

[84] Joy Thompson, "The Watery Maze: A Pageant for Exeter," paper given at *History in the Limelight: Performing the Past c.1850 to Present*, at UCL Institute of Education. *Exeter and Plymouth Gazette*, "Exeter Pageant," Friday 24 June 1932, 7.

[85] Ouest France website, https://www.ouest-france.fr/bretagne/vannes-56000/henriette-de-france-reine-des-fetes-historiques-5532291, Accessed 2nd March 2018.

[86] Sarah Betts, "Power and Passion: Seventeenth-Century Masculinities Dramatized on the BBC in the Twenty-First Century," in Katherine Byrne, Julie Anne Taddeo and James Leggott [eds.], *Conflicting Masculinities: Men in Television Period Drama*, (London: I.B. Taurus, 2018), 72–73.

[87] See, for example, Whitaker, *A Royal Passion*, xviii–xix.

BIBLIOGRAPHY

PRIMARY

Aberdeen Press and Journal. "Stirring Pageant of Parliament." Saturday 30 June 1934.

Ancelot, Jacques-Arsene-Francois Polcarpe. *Tête Rondes et Cavaliers: Drame Historique en Trois Actes.* Paris, 1833.

Anon. Amazon Review of *Cromwell* DVD, https://www.amazon.co.uk/Cromwell-DVD-Richard-Harris/product-reviews/B0000BV1K5/ref=cm_cr_getr_d_pag-ing_btm_17?ie=UTF8&reviewerType=all_reviews&pageNumber=17 accessed April 14 2018.

Breeskin, Adelyn Dohme. *Catalogue of the Paintings in the State House at Annapolis Maryland,* 1934. Available Online at http://msa.maryland.gov/megafile/msa/stagsere/se1/se14/000027/html/hesitant_revolut/msa/speccol/sc1500/sc1545/e_catalog_2002/1934catalog.html, accessed March 1, 2018.

Brent-Dyer, Elinor M. *Elizabeth the Gallant.* Modern Edition, Bath: Girls Gone By, 2006.

Chateaubriand, Francois. *Les Quatre Stuarts.* Paris: Gabriel Roux, 1857.

Colbourne, Maurice. *Charles the King: A Chronicle Play.* London: Samuel French, 1937.

Creighton, Walter. *Pageant of Parliament.* London: Fleetway Press, 1934.

Belfast Newsletter. "Historic Pageant at Fountains Abbey." Thursday 20 August 1908.

Dumas, Alexandre. *Twenty Years After.* London: Wordsworth, Wordsworth Classics Edition, 2009.

Exeter and Plymouth Gazette. "Exeter Pageant." Friday 24 June 1932.

Goodall, Frederick. *The Reminiscences of Frederick Goodall, R.A.* London: The Walter Scott Publishing Co. Ltd, 1902.

Green, Mary Anne Everett, ed. *Letters of Queen Henrietta Maria.* London: Richard Bentley, 1857.

Hiatt, Charles. *Ellen Terry and her impersonations: An Appreciation.* London: G. Bell, 1899.

Housman, Lawrence. et al. *The Oxford Historical Pageant June 27–July 3 1907 Book of Words,* Oxford: Oxford University Press, 1907.

Hyde, Edward. *Life of Edward, Earl of Clarendon.* Oxford: Clarendon Printing House, 1759.

Ludlow, Edmund. *Memoirs of Edmund Ludlow.* Volume III. London: Publisher Unknown, 1720.

Motter, H.L., ed. *The International Who's Who: Who's Who in the World 1912.* New York: William G. Hewitt Press, 1912.

Mountain, Fiona. *Cavalier Queen.* London: Arrow Books, 2012.

Newcastle Journal. "Charles I and his Queen Henrietta Maria." Saturday 24 January 1857.

Nottingham Evening Post. "Dame Ellen Terry: Passing of a Famous Actress." Saturday 21 July 1928.

Ouest France website. https://www.ouest-france.fr/bretagne/vannes-56000/henriette-de-france-reine-des-fetes-historiques-5532291, Accessed 2nd March 2018.

Parker, Louis Napoleon. *The Dover Pageant July 27, 28, 29, 30, 31, August 1, 1908.* Dover: Grigg and Son, 1908.

Plaidy, Jean. *Loyal in Love: Henrietta Maria, Wife of Charles I.* New York: Three Rivers Press, 1983.

Stickles, Frances Copeland. *A Crown for Henrietta Maria: Maryland's Namesake Queen.* Lanham, Maryland: Maryland Historical Press, 1988.

Terry, Ellen. *The Story of My Life: Recollections and Reflections.* New York: Doubleday, 1908.

The Annapolis Collection: A Wealth of Maryland History. http://msa.maryland.gov/megafile/msa/stagsere/se1/se14/000027/html/hesitant_revolut/msa/speccol/sc1500/sc1545/e_catalog_2002/georgi.html, accessed March 2 2018.

The Spectator. "The New Play at the Lyceum Theatre." October 12, 1872.

The Sphere. "A Charming Scene From the Oxford Pageant." Saturday 29 June 1907.

The Sphere. "In the Old Days When We Fought the Dons." Saturday 09 July 1910.

The Sphere. "The World of Books." Saturday 23 November 1940.

The Stage. "London's Pageant." Thursday 9 January 1908.

The Times. "The Coming Dover Pageant." Thursday 9 July 1908.

Tytler, Sarah. "A Young Oxford Maid: (In the Days of the King and the Parliament)." *Girl's Own Paper.* 13th April 1889.

Wills, W.G. *Charles the First: An Historical Tragedy in Four Acts.* William Blackwood and Sons, Edinburgh and London, 1873.

Yorkshire Gazette. "Historic Pageant at Ripon." Saturday 22 August 1908.

Yorkshire Post and Leeds Intelligencer. "The Dover Pageant." Tuesday 28 July 1908.

SECONDARY

Bartie, Angela, Paul Caton, Linda Fleming, Mark Freeman, Tom Hulme, Alex Hutton and Paul Readman. *The Redress of the Past*, http://www.historicalpageants.ac.uk/pageants/

Bell, David A. *The Cult of the Nation in France: Inventing Nationalism, 1680–1800.* Cambridge, Massachusetts, USA: Harvard University Press, 2001.

Betts, Sarah. "Power and Passion: Seventeenth-Century Masculinities Dramatized on the BBC in the Twenty-First Century." In Katherine Byrne, Julie Anne Taddeo and James Leggott (eds.), *Conflicting Masculinities: Men in Television Period Drama*. London: I.B. Taurus, 2018.

Bingham, Madeleine. *Henry Irving and the Victorian Theatre*. London: George Allen and Unwin, 1978.

Cubitt, Geoffrey. "The Political Uses of Seventeenth-Century English History in Bourbon Restoration France." *The Historical Journal*. 50:1, 2007.

Dunn-Hensley, Susan. *Anna of Denmark and Henrietta Maria: Virgins, Witches and Catholic Queens*. Palgrave Macmillan: Basingstoke, 2017.

Harris, Carolyn. *Queenship and Revolution in Early Modern Europe: Henrietta Maria and Marie Antoinette*. London: Springer, 2016.

Johnston, Kenneth R. and Nicholes, Joseph. "Transitory Actions, Men Betrayed: The French Revolution in Romantic Drama." In Hoagwood, Terence Allan and Watkins, Daniel P. (eds.), *British Romantic Drama: Historical and Critical Essays*. London: Associated Press, 1998.

Knoppers, Laura Lunger. "Cultural Legacies: The English Revolution in Nineteenth-Century British and French Literature and Art." In Michael J. Braddick (eds.), *The Oxford Handbook of the English Revolution*. Oxford: Oxford University Press, 2015.

———. *Politicizing Domesticity from Henrietta Maria to Milton's Eve*. Cambridge: Cambridge University Press, 2011.

Linnell, Anna-Marie. *Writing the Royal Consort in Stuart England*. PhD Thesis, University of Exeter, 2016.

Marshall, Rosalind Kay. *Henrietta Maria, The Intrepid Queen*. Owings Mills, Maryland: Stemmer House Publishers, 1991.

Meisel, Martin. *Realizations: Narrative, Pictorial and Theatrical Arts in Nineteenth-Century England*. Princeton University Press, Princeton, New Jersey, 1983.

Morris, Edward. "Catalogue of paintings drawings and photographs." In Morris, Edward, and Milner, Frank (eds.), *'And When Did You Last See Your Father?': The Painting, Its Background, and Fame*. Liverpool: National Museums and Galleries on Merseyside, 1992.

Morris, Edward, and Milner, Frank. *'And When Did You Last See Your Father?': The Painting, Its Background, and Fame*. Liverpool: National Museums and Galleries on Merseyside, 1992.

Murray, Catriona. *Imagining Stuart Family Politics: Dynastic Crisis and Continuity*. London: Routledge, 2017.

Nicholes, Joseph. "Revolutions Compared: The English Civil War as Political Touchstone in Romantic Literature." In Hanley, Keith, and Selden, Raman [eds.], *Revolution and English Romanticism: Politics and Rhetoric*. New York: St Martin's Press, 1990.

Plowden, Alison. *Henrietta Maria: Charles I's Indomitable Queen.* London: Sutton, 2001.

Rhodes, Kimberley. *Ophelia and Victorian Visual Culture: Representing Body Politics in the Nineteenth Century.* Aldershot: Ashgate, 2008.

Richards, Jeffrey. *Sir Henry Irving: A Victorian Actor and His World.* Hambledon and London, London and New York, 2005.

Russcol, Diane. "Images of Charles I and Henrietta-Maria in French art, ca. 1815–1855." *Arts Magazine,* 62 (1988).

Schoettler, Carl. "A Royal State of Affairs." *The Baltimore Sun,* 25th March 1998.

Stanton, Kamille Stone. "'An Amazonian Heroickess': The Military Leadership of Queen Henrietta Maria in Margaret Cavendish's *Bell in Campo* (1662)." *Early Theatre,* 10:2 (2007): 71–86.

Stevenson, Sara, and Helen Bennett. *Van Dyck in Check Trousers: Fancy Dress in Art and Life 1700–1900.* Edinburgh: Scottish National Portrait Gallery, 1978.

Strong, Roy. *And when did you last see your father? The Victorian Painter and British History.* London: Thames and Hudson, 1978.

Tscherny, Nadia, and Guy Stair Sainty. *Romance and Chivalry: History and Literature Reflected in Early Nineteenth-Century French Painting.* New York: Matthiesen Gallery and Stair Sainty Matthiesen, 1996.

Walter, Helen. "'Van Dyck in Action': Dressing Charles I for the Victorian Stage." *Costume.* 47:2 (2013).

Wedgewood, C.V. *The King's Peace 1637–1641.* London: Folio Society, 2001.

White, Michelle Anne. *Henrietta Maria and the English Civil Wars.* Aldershot: Ashgate, 2006.

Whitaker, Katie. *A Royal Passion: The Turbulent Marriage of Charles I and Henrietta Maria.* London: Weidenfeld and Nicholson, 2010.

Willie, Rachel. *Staging the Revolution: Drama, Reinvention and History 1647–72.* Manchester: Manchester University Press, 2015.

Wilson, Francis. *'That Memorable Scene': The Image of King Charles the First in Seventeenth and Eighteenth-Century Literature.* PhD Thesis. University of York, 1993.

Wood, Christopher. "Realist or Romantic – Narrative Choices in Victorian Art." in Carolyn Hill [ed.], *Artist as Narrator: Nineteenth Century Narrative Art in England and France.* Oklahoma City: Oklahoma City Museum of Art, 2005.

Worden, Blair. *Roundhead Reputations: The English Civil Wars and the Passions of Posterity.* London: Allen Lane, 2001.

Wright, Beth S. *Painting and History during the French Restoration: Abandoned by the Past.* Cambridge: Cambridge University Press, 1997.

Thompson, Joy. 'The Watery Maze: A Pageant for Exeter." Paper given at History in the Limelight: Performing the Past c.1850 to Present, at UCL Institute of Education, September 2016.

CHAPTER 10

Romantic Recreations: Remembering Stuart Monarchy in Nineteenth-Century Fancy Dress Entertainments

Benjamin L. Wild

Reverie for Britain's Stuart dynasty in the nineteenth century reveals much about contemporary insecurities and the malleability of memory. At a time when people were grappling with life-changing developments in nearly every aspect of their lives, chiefly because of industrialization, the past provided a captivating opportunity to forge new, public identities, especially when it was recreated through fancy dress costume. In an age of invented traditions and chivalric reimagining, when fancy dress frequently drew inspiration from larger-than-life characters of the near and distant past, the period of Stuart rule between 1603 and 1714, which had been variously reinterpreted since the seventeenth century, was a crucible in which personal stories and national traditions could be fashioned. The lives of Mary Queen of Scots and Charles I, in particular, were frequently

I am grateful to Kate Strasdin for reading and commenting on a draft of this chapter.

B. L. Wild (✉)
London, UK

© The Author(s) 2019
E. Paranque (ed.), *Remembering Queens and Kings of Early Modern England and France*, Queenship and Power,
https://doi.org/10.1007/978-3-030-22344-1_10

179

recast to convey messages of romance, resolve, and personal integrity. Britain's monarchy fueled this interest. George IV wore Elizabethan- and Stuart-inspired garments at his coronation in 1821.[1] Queen Victoria hosted a Restoration Ball at Buckingham Palace in 1851. More prosaically, specific interest in Mary Queen of Scots reveals much about the changing aspirations and roles of nineteenth-century British women, who were becoming more literate and economically active.

In this chapter, I argue that people in Britain, between the eighteenth and twentieth centuries, and across all social levels, dressed as members of the Stuart dynasty at costumed entertainments as a means to reflect upon, and to reconfigure, their place within society. The Stuarts were compelling subjects to imitate because of a superficial affiliation, gained through contemporary literature, historical writing, and art, that impressed upon people the dramatic narratives of their lives, which made them appear relatable and relevant at a time of profound social change. Fancy dress entertainments were an efficacious medium to consider the relationship between self and society. They were liminal events, to borrow the terminology of Victor Turner, that temporarily effaced social and political hierarchies and enabled people to give fuller expression to their characters, perhaps unlike anywhere else in their public lives.[2] Changing attitudes toward sexual and gendered identities during the nineteenth century meant that women were particularly keen to explore the possibilities that fancy dress, and the Stuarts, provided for self-reflection and refashioning, but men were no less involved. In short, the Stuart dynasty was remembered romantically rather than realistically. Memories of it, made malleable through time, were shaped creatively, carefully, always consciously, to serve the needs of people in the present.

The Absolutist tendencies and Catholic sympathies of Britain's Stuart dynasty would seem to make them unconventional, even uncomfortable, subjects for remembrance. Many of the family were maligned, by contemporaries and later commentators, for their political and religious judgment. Mary, Queen of Scots (r. 1542–1567), Queen-Consort of France (r. 1559–1560), and mother of Britain's first Stuart ruler, James I (r. 1603–1625), was executed in 1587 for conspiring against Elizabeth I of

---

[1] E.A. Smith, *George IV* (New Haven and London: Yale University Press, 1999), 88–92, 186.

[2] Victor Turner, *The Anthropology of Performance* (New York: PAJ Publications, 1987), 34–35, 74–75.

England (r. 1558–1603). Charles I (r. 1625–1649) was proclaimed a tyrant by his subjects and beheaded; an unprecedented act that led to the dissolution of Britain's monarchy between 1649 and 1660. Charles II's reign (1660–1685) was beset by natural and political calamities. His brother, James II (r. 1685–1688), was deposed after three years in the Glorious Revolution. Consequently, within three decades of its Restoration, the British monarchy needed the support of William of Orange and his wife, James' daughter Mary, to survive. Memories of these rulers were consequently painful, controversial, and much debated. However, during the late-eighteenth and nineteenth century, the Stuarts became the subject of renewed interest, and sympathy, through academic inquiry and artistic endeavor. Much of this interest focused on the life of Mary Queen of Scots and, to a lesser extent, her grandson Charles I.

Mary's appeal stemmed from her tumultuous life.[3] A great-granddaughter of Henry VII of England (r. 1485–1509), she became Queen of Scotland within six days of her birth. Educated in France at the court of Henry II (r. 1547–1559), she was Queen-Consort of the kingdom between 1559 and 1560, when her husband ruled as Francis II. Raised as a Catholic, Mary was not easily accepted by her Protestant nobility when she returned to Scotland after Francis' death. Through marriage, she attempted to control court factions, but this exacerbated tensions. In 1566, Mary's second husband, English Catholic Henry Stuart, the Lord Darnley, murdered her personal secretary David Rizzio in cold blood. Eleven months later, Darnley was murdered. Suspicion fell on Scottish noble James Hepburn, the Lord Bothwell, whom Mary married in 1567; a union that cast doubt on her claim to have been ignorant of Darnley's death. In 1568, Mary was dethroned by her Protestant lords in favor of her 13-month-old son, James. She fled to England where she spent the remainder of her life, ostensibly under house arrest. Implicated in plots to kill and usurp Elizabeth I, she was beheaded in 1587. Apparently preparing for her final act, Mary appeared on the scaffold wearing a black satin gown with slashed sleeves, a crimson velvet bodice, and a white linen veil, an outfit that would feature in many subsequent portraits.[4]

---

[3] There are many biographies of Mary. One of the more recent, and academic, contributions is John Guy, *My Heart Is My Own: The Life of Mary Queen of Scots* (London: Harper Perennial, 2004).

[4] Guy, *My Heart Is My Own* 2–3.

The political and personal trials of Mary's grandson Charles I were hardly less turbulent.[5] Charles had a steadfast belief in his singular prerogatives as monarch, which he celebrated through painting, masques, and architecture.[6] His sympathy for Catholicism, which he made manifest by marrying Henrietta Maria of Spain in 1625 and promoting anti-Calvinist clerics, increased tensions with his avowedly Protestant Church and parliament. Questioning the loyalty of his legislative assembly, and his ability to control it, Charles withdrew from London and raised the royal standard on August 22, 1642, signaling the start of the English Civil War. The first phase of the conflict lasted until 1646, by which time the royal armies had been defeated in battle and the King was under house arrest. Fighting resumed between 1647 and 1648 after Charles escaped captivity, but the royal armies were quickly, and decisively, beaten by Oliver Cromwell's New Model Army. Accused of tyranny, Charles mounted his own defense when tried by parliament. The legal proceedings and subsequent execution of the King were carefully staged. The Lord President of the High Court of Justice sat on a cushion of crimson velvet; the jurors sat on cloths of scarlet, to "legitimize the new regime and [to] abolish the mystique of kingship."[7] The King's appearance on the scaffold in a simple blue-green vest, and his statement, "I am the Martyr of the People," may suggest that he, too, was acting a part to convey the gravity of this undertaking, as much as to create a psychological salve.[8] For Mary and Charles, the boundary between reality and recreation had often blurred, particularly in dress. Both monarchs enjoyed the masque and, at decisive moments in their reigns, they wore disguises to escape harm.[9] It was these vignettes, as much as the broader themes of their lives, that enabled them to maintain the interest, and capture the imagination, of later generations.

As dynastic matriarch, national mother, hapless victim, or deserving miscreant, Mary's "libidinous glow" and "charisma of distress" were sufficiently compelling, and challenging, to capture the zeitgeist of successive

---

[5] There are a similarly large number of biographies on Charles I. An accessible and comprehensive introduction is Richard Cust, *Charles I: A Political Life* (Harlow: Pearson, 2005).

[6] See *Charles I: King and Collector*, ed. Per Rumberg and Desmond Shawe-Taylor (London: Royal Academy of Arts, 2018).

[7] Nancy Klein Maguire, "The Theatrical Mask/Masque of Politics: The Case of Charles I," *Journal of British Studies* 28, no. 1 (1989), 18.

[8] Maguire, "The Theatrical Mask/Masque of Politics," 17.

[9] Guy, *My Heart Is My Own*, 152, 254, 342, 367.

generations who believed her life, however distorted its narrative retelling had become, could provide solace and solutions in the present.[10] Jayne Elizabeth Lewis has shown how Mary's posthumous reputation was variously (re)interpreted. In the seventeenth century, following the Restoration, her plight satisfied a "squeamish sentimentality" as Stuart rulers and their subjects reflected on the tenacity and traumas of her dynasty.[11] In the eighteenth century, Georgian Britain's "culture of sensibility" provoked a wave of sorrow for the Queen, who was admired for her "exemplary femininity."[12] Reflecting contemporary gender inequalities, historian William Robertson opined that Mary had been "formed with the qualities which we love, not with the talents that we admire."[13] In the nineteenth century, Mary was more broadly a figure of "fascination" and the events of her life were increasingly used as a conduit through which people tried to make sense of their present.[14] Interest in Mary's life, the details of which had frequently focused on her marital affairs, may have also elided with what has been termed the "sexual anarchy" of the late-nineteenth century. Long-standing notions about sexual behavior were questioned, if not entirely overturned, and studies of sexuality argued that gender identity was socially constructed.[15] The relevance of Mary's story to contemporaries is evidenced by her depiction in paintings, novels, and fancy dress costume. Between 1820 and 1892, Lewis notes the Royal Academy displayed 56 new scenes from her life; in 1887, the tercentenary of Mary's death, exhibitions were organized between London and Glasgow.[16]

There are many examples of women dressing as Mary Queen of Scots during the nineteenth century. Several contemporary descriptions and images of Marian costumes were acquired by Queen Victoria (r. 1837–1901) and now form part of Britain's Royal Collection Trust. One photograph

---

[10] Jayne Elizabeth Lewis, *Mary Queen of Scots: Romance and Nation* (London: Routledge, 1998), 38.

[11] Lewis, *Mary Queen of Scots*, 96.

[12] Lewis, Mary Queen of Scots, 130.

[13] Quoted by Lewis, Lewis, Mary Queen of Scots, 130.

[14] Lewis, Mary Queen of Scots, 180.

[15] Colleen McQuillen, *The Modernist Masquerade: Stylizing Life, Literature, and Costumes in Russia* (Wisconsin, The University of Wisconsin Press, 2013), 88.

[16] Lewis, *Mary Queen of Scots*, 173; Stephen Bann and Linda Whiteley, *Painting History: Delaroche & Lady Jane Grey* (London: National Gallery Company, 2010), 50–51, 59, 104, 130.

shows Lady Harriet Hamilton dressed as Mary at the Walewska Ball of May 12, 1854. Standing three-quarters left and facing the camera, she wears a long white gown decorated with bands of pearls. A white train is attached to the rear of her dress at the shoulders.[17] A watercolor and lithograph depict Princess Alexandra, Victoria's daughter-in-law, who dressed as Mary for the Waverley Ball of July 6, 1871, a fancy dress entertainment that honored author Sir Walter Scott.[18] Alexandra's costume, which survives in the Royal Collection, is a floor-length gown of deep red velvet.[19] The costume was apposite because Mary had featured as a character in Scott's novel, *The Abbot*, of 1820. In 1876, Britain's governor-general in Canada hosted a fancy dress ball in Ottawa. The Governor-General and his wife dressed as the parents of Mary Queen of Scots, James V of Scotland and Mary of Guise. The couple's children appeared in complementary costumes of blue and orange satin as Mary Queen of Scots and Lord Darnley. Three other guests attended the ball as Mary Queen of Scots.[20] In New York, Cornelia Bradley dressed as Mary Queen of Scots at a ball she hosted in February 1897.[21] In London, the Devonshire House Ball of July 1897, organized to celebrate Victoria's diamond jubilee, provided another occasion for guests to dress as characters associated with the Scottish Queen. Photographs from the Lafayette archive in the National Portrait Gallery show Lady Katherine Scott as the Queen in an elaborate white gown decorated with bands of pearls and costume jewelry. The Dowager Duchess of Hamilton wore a white satin and gold embroidered robe as Mary Hamilton, one of Mary's lady-in-waiting.[22] In a similar gown, Lady Lister Kaye attended as the Duchesse de Guise Antoinette de Bourbon, Mary's maternal grandmother. Queen Victoria collected artifacts associated with Mary, including a lock of her hair, but she is not known to have dressed in Marian costume.[23] Victoria's description of the

---

[17] Royal Collection, RCIN 2906577.

[18] Royal Collection, RCIN 981599; RCIN 2108791.

[19] Kate Strasdin, *Inside the Royal Wardrobe: A Dress History of Queen Alexandra* (London: Bloomsbury Academic, 2017), 82–84.

[20] Cynthia Cooper, *Magnificent Entertainments: Fancy Dress Balls of Canada's Governors General 1876–1898* (Fredericton: Goose Lane Editions, 1997), 44–46.

[21] Emilia Müller, "Fashion & Fancy in New York: The American Monarchs." Paper presented at Fashion: Exploring Critical Issues, Oxford, September 2011. www.inter-disciplinary.net/wp-content/uploads/2011/08/muellerfapaper.pdf. Accessed: December 2017, 5.

[22] *The Echo*, July 3, 1897, 2.

[23] Royal Collection, RCIN 43826.

gown she wore to her Restoration Ball of 1851, which celebrated the reign of Mary's great-great-grandson Charles II, imitated period fashions rather than a specific historical figure:

> My costume was of grey moiré antique, ornamented with gold lace, – a very long waist and sleeves trimmed with old lace. The petticoat showing under the dress which was all open in front, was of rich gold and silver brocade (Indian manufacture) richly trimmed with silver lace ... In my hair I wore an arrangement of pearls.[24]

Detailed evidence of women dressing as Mary at costumed entertainments, or those associated with her, is greater for aristocratic and royal subjects, but Ardern Holt's guide to costuming, *Fancy Dresses Described; Or What to Wear at Fancy Balls*, which was reprinted several times during the nineteenth century by London department store Debenham & Freebody, indicates her appeal was not confined to members of the social elite. A cartoon of 1885 from the satirical journal *Punch* by George Du Marnier pokes fun at the popularity of Marian costumes by suggesting her dress was a common sight at fancy dress events. In the cartoon, a lady dressed as Mary appears in conversation with a man, who wears an eighteenth-century style suit. Under the caption, "Who'd have thought it?", the lady remarks, "I'm Mary, Queen of Scots, as you can see, Dr. Squills!' And who are you?" "I'm Horace Walpole" is his response. The cartoon mocks the prevalence of Marian costumes at nineteenth-century fancy dress entertainments by suggesting the lady's explanation of her costume is unnecessary.[25] It is appropriate that the lady's companion is depicted as Horace Walpole. An avid participant in eighteenth-century fancy dress balls, Walpole complained of the "dozens of ugly Queens of Scots" at costumed entertainments in 1742.[26] Perhaps aware of Walpole's stinging critique, Du Marnier seems to imply that some women's decision to dress as Mary was ill-advised by depicting the lady in the cartoon as stout and middle-aged. The suggestion might be that she, like the many other women were appeared as the Queen, put sensibility before sense and overlooked the fact that she was too old to represent somebody renowned for her beauty. It is possible that Du Marnier intended another meaning,

[24] RA VIC/MAIN/QVJ(W), July 13, 1851 (Princess Beatrice's copies).
[25] Sara Stevenson and Helen Bennett, *Van Dyck in Check Trousers: Fancy Dress in Art and Life 1700–1900* (Edinburgh: Scottish National Portrait Gallery, 1978), 5–6.
[26] Stevenson and Bennett, *Van Dyck*.

now unfathomable a century later. Nonetheless, his drawing clearly shows how people's remembrance of Mary, and their use of this, was informed by contemporary concerns.

Costumes for Charles I and Charles II were equally appealing according to the evidence of Holt's fancy dress guides. Whilst her guidance focuses on women's dress, Holt observes that a major source of inspiration for Carolingian fancy dress, worn by men and women, were the portraits of Sir Anthony Van Dyke.[27] At the Devonshire House Ball, the costume of Lord Charles William Augustus Montagu, who appeared as Charles I wearing a white satin coat, red velvet breeches and a blue garter ribbon, was based on the Van Dyke portrait *Le Roi à Chasse* of 1637.[28] Sir John Leslie attended the ball as Earl Darnley. The appeal of Stuart males as a subject for fancy dress costume was shared by people of different social levels and continued into the early twentieth century, along with interest in Mary Queen of Scots. A catalog published for London-based fancy dress supplier Weldon's Ltd in the mid- to late-1920s contains specific listings for "Charles I," "Lord Darnley," and "Mary Queen of Scots," along with "Charles I, period lady."[29] The widespread interest in dressing as members of the Stuart dynasty at costumed entertainments between the eighteenth and twentieth centuries shows that there was a general familiarity and interest in remembering these rulers. However, the frequency and nature of their depiction through fancy dress costume suggests people were not concerned with faithful re-enactment but sought to use these figures and what they knew of them through contemporary retellings of their lives to convey messages about themselves. It may have been that some people felt, or wanted to feel, an affinity between their lives and the supposedly dramatic lives of the Stuarts. In other cases, people may have chosen to dress as Stuart royals simply to appear *au courant* with contemporary tastes.

Whatever the specific motivation, nineteenth-century people's fascination with the Stuart dynasty was part of a much broader interest in the past. This wider historical appeal needs to be acknowledged if the appearance and meaning of Stuart royals in fancy dress are to be understood. An

[27] Ardern Holt, *Fancy Dresses Described; Or, What to Wear at Fancy Balls*, Fifth Edition (London: Debenham & Freebody, 1887), 52–54.

[28] *The Daily Telegraph* (July 3, 1897), 9.

[29] Anon., *Weldon's Fancy Dress for Ladies and Gentleman* (London: Weldons Ltd., date unknown), 3.

explanation of the myriad factors that made the Stuart dynasty and fancy dress entertainments popular between the eighteenth and twentieth centuries is therefore necessary.

Eric Hobsbawm and David Cannadine have shown how civic traditions on both sides of the Atlantic were (re)created during the 1800s to reify public institutions.[30] Concurrently, Ronald Hutton has argued that ardent folklorists were responsible for recording and reviving many of Britain's rural festivities that were celebrated as pre-Christian rites at the change of season.[31] Similar recreations occurred across continental Europe where the desire to reconnect with national and regional traditions "lost" in the clamor for social and commercial progress was at least as strong. In Germany, for example, the concept of *Heimat* ("homeland") became a powerful means of attaining civic and political cohesion during the eighteenth and nineteenth centuries.[32] Interest in the past was not confined to policymakers and academics. Literacy rates in Britain were probably the highest in Europe and Paul Readman has calculated that Britons' engagement with the past, as evidenced by history book publications between 1870 and 1914, increased steadily; the past, he concludes, "sold well."[33] People's inclination to demonstrate a connection with historical events and figures, and to make centuries-old ideas purposeful in the present—in this instance, through fancy dress costume—suggests their interest in history during the nineteenth century was a change of both degree and kind.

Determining the extent of people's historical fascination is more straightforward than defining its causes. In Britain, the Act of Union of 1704 sparked interest in the countries that comprised the United Kingdom.[34] The expansion of the country's empire, combined with the ascendancy of its parliament following the Glorious Revolution of 1688, cultivated confident, if not triumphalist, histories of Britain's development that sought to explain its economic and political pre-eminence. More generally, the Enlightenment provided a spur for people to improve themselves by reflecting on who they

[30] *The Invention of Tradition*, ed. Eric Hobsbawm and Terence Ranger (Cambridge: Cambridge University Press, [1983] 2016).

[31] Ronald Hutton, *The Stations of the Sun: A History of the Ritual year in Britain* (Oxford: Oxford History Press, 1996), 37–41, 43, 75, 126–127, 262–263.

[32] Celia Applegate, *A Nation of Provincials: The German Idea of Heimat* (Berkeley: University of California Press, 1990).

[33] G.J. Barker-Benfield, *The Culture of Sensibility: Sex and Society in Eighteenth-Century Britain* (Chicago: The University of Chicago Press, 1992), 162; Paul Readman, "The Place of the Past in English Culture, c.1890–1914," *Past & Present*, no. 186 (2005), 159.

[34] Lewis, *Mary Queen of Scots*, 103.

were; an inquiry that encouraged historical reflection on the communities and country they inhabited. Perhaps a more pressing motivation for remembrance and nostalgia, albeit harder to define, were the feelings of alienation that followed in the wake of industrialization. Richard Sennett has argued that industrialization fundamentally changed how people regarded themselves and others. As northern European cities—he focuses on London and Paris—were gradually remodeled to provide new spaces for construction and commerce, and the economic migrants who fueled both, the nature of people's interactions changed. Sennett suggests the city formalized human relationships, which became pragmatic and less personal. The unease that people may have experienced in public was exacerbated by wider social and political grievances that were expressed most fulsomely in the European revolutions of 1848. There were at least three, more personal, consequences of the changes noted by Sennett that are germane to this chapter and which help to explain people's active interest in the past. First, social and political ennui compounded a belief that economic progress could be harmful and, potentially, the cause of greater problems than those which it appeared to solve. Second, there was an enhanced distinction between the public and private spheres of people's lives, although Sennett argues this was never satisfactorily articulated. Third, people were encouraged in their attempts to develop relief strategies in public, chiefly through the creation of what Terry Eagleton terms "discursive spaces" that enabled them to act more freely.[35]

Various methods were employed to cope with the challenges of industrial and social change, but a pervading belief that contemporary society lacked moral vitality because of its focus on progress, led people, particularly artists and scholars, to look to the past as model for self-improvement. Between 1848 and 1853, the Pre-Raphaelite Brotherhood sought to replicate the "honesty and simplicity [of] primitive Christian artists" in their paintings, which typically featured allegorical scenes.[36] One of the nineteenth century's most popular authors, Walter Scott, captured the imagination of many people on both sides of the Atlantic with chivalric epics that appeared to provide an alternative, and more robust, set of values to live by.[37] The criticisms of contemporary life and

---

[35] Discussed in Peter Stallybrass and Allon White, *The Politics and Poetics of Transgression* (Ithaca, New York: Cornell University Press, 1986), 82–86.

[36] Christopher Wood, *The Pre-Raphaelites* (London: Weidenfeld and Nicolson, 1981), 10.

[37] Mark Girouard, *The Return to Camelot: Chivalry and the English Gentleman* (New Haven and London: Yale University Press, 1981), 30–54.

the strategies employed to cope with it frequently coalesced in fancy dress entertainments, which were regularly held in northwest Europe, America, and Canada during the nineteenth century.[38] One of the main attractions of fancy dress was its (at least) dual ability to reflect the zeitgeist and provide a form of escapism. Fancy dress costume was frequently used to praise and pour scorn on contemporary fashions. Topical events and political scandals also inspired the outfits people wore.[39] The use of clothing to explore new identities was especially appealing when many strictures appeared to govern a person's public appearance. Sennett observes that an increasing solemnity and use of hierarchical registers in clothing was one of the main strategies that people adopted to situate themselves within an urban environment that was at once crowded and isolating.[40] Lord Dunraven, who attended the Devonshire House Ball of 1897 as Cardinal Mazarin, remarked that fancy dress costume provided a rare opportunity to give imagination full rein.[41] His point was that the wearing of costume, which temporarily effaced conventional social and political hierarchies, created an environment in which people felt they could express their characters perhaps as nowhere else in public.

Paradoxically, the more fancy dress was conceived to counter contemporary ills, the more the opportunity to dress freely at costumed entertainments declined. During the nineteenth century, costumed events increasingly developed a broader social purpose, perhaps in response to the social ennui, and were organized to raise awareness or funds for political and social causes. In this context, where people were encouraged to appear as historical characters, to acknowledge the perceived achievements of ancestors and periods from a community's past, dressing up was as much about edification as it was entertainment. Colleen McQuillen argues that character costumes were particularly important in "preserving cultural memory."[42] Referring to costumed entertainments that drew upon "cultural patrimony" as "philological masquerades," she suggests that such events performed "a museum-like function of evaluating cultural

---

[38] On the history of fancy dress entertainments, see Benjamin L. Wild, *Carnival to Catwalk: Global Perspectives on Fancy Dress Costume* (London: Bloomsbury Academic, forthcoming).

[39] Celina Fox and Aileen Ribeiro, *Masquerade* (London: Museum of London, 1983), 2–4.

[40] Richard Sennett, *The Fall of Public Man* (London: Penguin, [1977] 2002), 48, 54.

[41] Sophia Topley, "The Devonshire House Ball," *House Style: Five Centuries of Fashion at Chatsworth*, ed. Laura Burlington and Hamish Bowles (New York: Skira Rizzoli, 2017), 128; Sophia Murphy, *The Duchess of Devonshire's Ball* (London: Sidgwick & Jackson, 1984), 158.

[42] McQuillen, *The Modernist Masquerade*, 144.

artifacts through careful curation and, like the art museum that perpetuates exclusivity by housing works by and for the elite, [they are] a public exhibition space for erudition and refined taste."[43] The effect of people dressing as historic figures was akin to an art museum because the choice of who to mimic was analogous to selecting objects to display. Through their chosen costume, and among peers who were similarly arrayed, guests constructed a loaded narrative that legitimated the positions they occupied within contemporary society.

Ostensibly, the act of dressing up remained enjoyable, but people's inclination to dress as important descendants and leading political figures tended to reduce personal inventiveness and to galvanize social hierarchies in the present.[44] Among the social elite, the inclination to use costume to exert social position was marked. For example, Mrs Bradley, who dressed as Mary Queen of Scots in 1897, "covered herself in jewels that had once belonged to the Empresses Marie Louise, Josephine, and Queen Marie Antoinette" in order to "capture the splendour of her regal essence," according to Emilia Müller.[45] This sartorial strategy was not limited to the very wealthy. Fancy dress catalogs published by Liberty & Co. argued explicitly that faux-historic costume elevated dressing up to an art form. For each outfit available for purchase, Liberty provided several fabric options, including many accessories, to make historical appearances more accurate and to make social status in the present unambiguous.[46]

The overt connection that existed between people's roles in and out of costume deepened the appeal of fancy dress, which could seem relevant rather than merely enjoyable. There are various contemporary examples of the crossover that existed between the clothing worn for day-wear and dress-up, but one stands out. In January 1821, eight knights on horseback, clad in armor and accompanied by squires, rode through London, ostensibly to protest the treatment of Queen Caroline by George IV. These knights in shining armor, who were followed by approximately 1,800 people, hoped their intercession would induce the King to behave in a more chivalric,

---

[43] McQuillen, The Modernist Masquerade.

[44] Anthea Jarvis and Patricia Raine, *Fancy Dress* (Haverfordwest: Shire Publications Ltd., 1984) 13–17.

[45] Müller, "Fashion & Fancy in New York," 5.

[46] Anon., *Fancy Dress: A Short Chronological Series of Costumes* (London & Edinburgh, Ballantyne & Hanson, 1898).

certainly gentlemanly, way toward his estranged wife.[47] Lewis has suggested that the King's conduct toward his wife may have encouraged comparison with Mary Queen of Scots; apparently, the women were of a similar height—although the extent to which Georgians appreciated this point is unclear—and the marital difficulties faced by both appeared to raise "the question of how far a kingdom which wishes to be united can tolerate the authority ... of a woman who wants something for herself, and who arouses a mixed and often untoward measure of longing in return."[48] However, accurate this assessment, the blurring of past and present indicates that history was often a dynamic element within nineteenth-century people's lives. Fancy dress costume facilitated this connection; McQuillen suggests the philological masquerade was uniquely able to "unify life and art."[49] During the nineteenth century, the role of fancy dress costume at the interstices between past and present, fact and fiction, was possibly amplified in a historical context because early historians and biographers had, in Lewis' view, been "prone to see themselves less as faithful transcribers of a firmly distanced past than as mediators between competing desires and instincts of belief."[50] Lewis' observation is chiefly made of seventeenth-century authors, but the continual reinterpretation of Mary Queen of Scots' life suggests historical fluidity was not absent in the nineteenth century.

In *The Culture of Sensibility*, G.J. Barker-Benfield suggests the boundary between fiction and fact was particularly elastic for women, chiefly because of their ability and inclination to read (non-)fiction. If literacy rates in eighteenth- and nineteenth-century Britain were the highest in Europe, it was among women that the growth in reading and writing was most notable. An ability to read was important in changing women's aspirations and gendered roles because "the very privacy of reading opens up possibilities for independence of mind, freedom of thought, and deviance from the norm."[51] Mary Wollstonecraft, a contemporary and vocal critic of the socialized concepts and behaviors that curtailed women's public roles, balked at the proliferation of literature that targeted female audiences. She argued that women's "overstretched sensibility" relaxed

---

[47] Girouard suggests the stunt was more specifically conceived to express dissatisfaction with George IV's rule, *The Return to Camelot*, 68–76.

[48] Lewis, *Mary Queen of Scots*, 148.

[49] McQuillen, *The Modernist Masquerade*, 144.

[50] McQuillen, *The Modernist Masquerade*, 78.

[51] William Stafford, quoted in Barker-Benfield, *The Culture of Sensibility*, 162.

"other parts of [their] minds" and prevented "intellect from attaining the sovereignty which it ought."[52] By contrast, Barker-Benfield avers that women's reading, along with their participation in Britain's "commercialist culture," enabled them to attain a greater independence through "deep play," the pursuit of engaging and challenging activities, usually enjoyed with other women, that enabled them to explore greater freedoms; he provides examples of women participating in public lotteries and gambling, attending tea parties and dinners.[53]

"Deep play" is analogous to Beverly Gordon's concept of "saturated experience" in which nineteenth- and twentieth-century (American) women created occasions, often "self-contained, enchanted worlds, that provided heightened sensory awareness to increase the emotional, intellectual, and social satisfaction they derived from undertaking routine domestic tasks."[54] Gordon argues that esthetic sensitivity was greater among women than men because of the more insular lives they led, which typically involved repetitive and, on the face of it, more menial tasks that offered limited scope for interaction with adults. Wollstonecraft regarded this behavior as harmful to women's development, but this was not necessarily the case. Albeit with reference to the twentieth century, studies have shown that "world making" was instrumental in galvanizing incipient feminist and AIDS reform movements.[55] The creation of what might be termed safe places could insulate activists from detractors and distractions by bolstering and emboldening them. The act of imagining was therefore purposeful rather than frivolous, as Wollstonecraft thought. It is possible that nineteenth-century women were doing something similar without the theoretical terms of reference: their "deep play" or "saturated experience" was not solely about coping with the present but seeking, however imperceptibly, to advance their public roles within it. McQuillen's philological masquerade was a particularly useful conduit in which women could explore these issues further. She explains that "[t]he syncretism of the philological masquerade positions it as a productive metaphor for memory and a tool for inscribing historical experience into personal biography, or writing oneself into cultural tradition."[56]

[52] Quoted in Barker-Benfield, *The Culture of Sensibility*, 208.

[53] Barker-Benfield, *The Culture of Sensibility*, 198–199.

[54] Beverly Gordon, *The Saturated World: Aesthetic Meaning, Intimate Objects, Women's Lives, 1840–1940* (Knoxville: The University of Tennessee Press, 2006), 1.

[55] Deborah B. Gould, *Moving Politics: Emotion and ACT UP's Fight Against AIDS* (Chicago and London: The University of Chicago Press, 2009), 178–179.

[56] Quillen, *The Modernist Masquerade*, 160.

In this context, a woman's decision to dress as Mary Queen of Scots in the nineteenth century may assume more significance. The point can be explored with reference to the costume Princess Alexandra wore to the Waverley Ball in 1871. According to Kate Strasdin, the Princess' motivation is not easily explained. On the one hand, she may have sought to channel one of two dominant contemporary interpretations of Mary, which saw her as either diminutive or demanding. Strasdin suggests that Alexandra may have purposely sought a "duality in dress," which is evident in some of her other clothing.[57] Contemporaries certainly used elements of Mary's character to convey personal meanings in the present. Schiller's five-act tragedy *Maria Stuart*, which debuted in Weimar in 1800, is one example of how Mary's history was used to achieve specific aims; in this case, pursuit of the dramatic form. In letters exchanged with Goethe in 1799, Schiller asserted, "Meine Maria wird keine weiche Stimmung erregen ... Sie empfindet und erreget keine Zärtlichkeit, ihr Schicksal ist nur heftige Passionen zu erfahren und zu entzünden."[58] On the other hand, Strasdin suggests Alexandra may have attended the Ball "as an image of Mary and not as the historical figure."[59] Emilia Müller has also questioned the motivations of American women who dressed as Mary and incorporated valuable and historic jewelry into their costumes. For example, to acquire Marie-Antoinette's jewelry for her Marian costume in 1897, Mrs Bradley sent agents from Tiffany to a Parisian auction. Müller suggests,

> the adoption of real precious stones of the European monarchy not only confused ideas about authenticity and falsity in the fantastically clad body, but conceptions of time and history. By donning the jewels of various queens of different time periods simultaneously, the wearers were embodying a general conception of a female aristocracy with no chronological delimitations.[60]

Whilst it is impossible to ascertain people's motivations with certainty, the prevalence of Stuart costume during the nineteenth century, and that of Mary Queen of Scots in particular, suggests women, cognizant of the

[57] Strasdin, *Inside the Royal Wardrobe*, 85.

[58] "My Mary will not arouse a soft mood ... She does not feel and provoke tenderness, her fate is only to experience violent passions" (my translation). Freidrich Schiller, *Maria Stuart*, ed. Dietrich Bode (Stuttgart: Philip Reclam jun., 1990), 156.

[59] Strasdin, *Inside the Royal Wardrobe*, 84.

[60] Müller, "Fashion & Fancy in New York," 6.

challenges and opportunities created by social and economic change, harnessed long-standing and malleable memories of the dynasty to explore new identities through the popular and flexible medium of fancy dress, in particular, the philological masquerade in which costumed revelers dressed as specific historic characters. Terry Castle asserts that people in costume are "often unreflective and unanalytical about what they are doing," but it is reasonable to assume the choice of costume and the accessories this warranted, which nineteenth-century people were encouraged to think carefully about, was deliberate and planned, even if they were not always part of a wider sartorial strategy.[61] Furthermore, persistent, if less widespread, interest in male members of the Stuart dynasty as subjects of fancy dress may suggest that notions of "deep play" and "saturated experience," are not solely applicable to women. The societal changes that followed in the wake of industrialization affected both sexes and their gendered roles. If women could utilize the powerful memories of Mary Queen of Scots to explore new identities and public roles in the present, there is no reason why men could not do the same by harnessing the shifting interpretations of Charles I.

BIBLIOGRAPHY

PRIMARY SOURCES

Anon. *Fancy Dress: A Short Chronological Series of Costumes.* London & Edinburgh, Ballantyne & Hanson, 1898.
———. *Weldon's Fancy Dress for Ladies and Gentleman.* London: Weldons Ltd., date unknown.
Holt, Ardern. *Fancy Dresses Described; Or, What to Wear at Fancy Balls,* Fifth Edition. London: Debenham & Freebody, 1887.

SECONDARY SOURCES

Applegate, Celia. *A Nation of Provincials: The German Idea of Heimat.* Berkeley: University of California Press, 1990.
Bann, Stephen and Whiteley, Linda. *Painting History: Delaroche & Lady Jane Grey.* London: National Gallery Company, 2010.
Barker-Benfield, G.J. *The Culture of Sensibility: Sex and Society in Eighteenth-Century Britain.* Chicago: The University of Chicago Press, 1992.

---

[61] Terry Castle, *Masquerade and Civilization: The Carnivalesque in Eighteenth-Century English Culture and Fiction* (Stanford: Stanford University Press, 1986), 27.

Castle, Terry. *Masquerade and Civilization: The Carnivalesque in Eighteenth-Century English Culture and Fiction*. Stanford: Stanford University Press, 1986.

Cooper, Cynthia. *Magnificent Entertainments: Fancy Dress Balls of Canada's Governors General 1876–1898*. Fredericton: Goose Lane Editions, 1997.

Cust, Richard. *Charles I: A Political Life*. Harlow: Pearson, 2005.

Fox, Celina and Ribeiro, Aileen. *Masquerade*. London: Museum of London, 1983.

Girouard, Mark. *The Return to Camelot: Chivalry and the English Gentleman*. New Haven and London: Yale University Press, 1981.

Gordon, Beverly. *The Saturated World: Aesthetic Meaning, Intimate Objects, Women's Lives, 1840–1940*. Knoxville: The University of Tennessee Press, 2006.

Gould, Deborah B. *Moving Politics: Emotion and ACT UP's Fight Against AIDS*. Chicago and London: The University of Chicago Press, 2009.

Guy, John. *My Heart Is My Own: The Life of Mary Queen of Scots*. London: Harper Perennial, 2004.

Hobsbawm, Eric and Ranger, Terence ed. *The Invention of Tradition*. Cambridge: Cambridge University Press, [1983] 2016.

Hutton, Ronald. *The Stations of the Sun: A History of the Ritual year in Britain*. Oxford: Oxford History Press, 1996.

Jarvis, Anthea and Raine, Patricia. *Fancy Dress*. Haverfordwest: Shire Publications Ltd., 1984.

Lewis, Jayne Elizabeth, *Mary Queen of Scots: Romance and Nation*. London: Routledge, 1998.

Maguire, Nancy Klein. "The Theatrical Mask/Masque of Politics: The Case of Charles I." *Journal of British Studies* 28, no. 1 (1989): 1–22.

McQuillen, Colleen. *The Modernist Masquerade: Stylizing Life, Literature, and Costumes in Russia*. Wisconsin, The University of Wisconsin Press, 2013.

Müller, Emilia. "Fashion & Fancy in New York: The American Monarchs." Paper presented at Fashion: Exploring Critical Issues, Oxford, September 2011. www.inter-disciplinary.net/wp-content/uploads/2011/08/muellerfapaper.pdf.

Murphy, Sophia. *The Duchess of Devonshire's Ball*. London: Sidgwick & Jackson, 1984.

Readman, Paul. "The Place of the Past in English Culture, *c.*1890–1914," *Past & Present*, no. 186 (2005): 147–199.

Rumberg, Per and Shawe-Taylor, Desmond, ed. *Charles I: King and Collector*. London: Royal Academy of Arts, 2018.

Schiller, Freidrich. *Maria Stuart*, ed. Dietrich Bode. Stuttgart: Philip Reclam jun., 1990.

Sennett, Richard. *The Fall of Public Man*. London: Penguin, [1977] 2002.

Smith, E.A. *George IV*. New Haven and London: Yale University Press, 1999.

Stallybrass, Peter and White, Allon. *The Politics and Poetics of Transgression.* Ithaca, New York: Cornell University Press, 1986.

Stevenson, Sara and Bennett, Helen. *Van Dyck in Check Trousers: Fancy Dress in Art and Life 1700–1900.* Edinburgh: Scottish National Portrait Gallery, 1978.

Strasdin, Kate. *Inside the Royal Wardrobe: A Dress History of Queen Alexandra.* London: Bloomsbury Academic, 2017.

Topley, Sophia. "The Devonshire House Ball." *House Style: Five Centuries of Fashion at Chatsworth,* ed. Laura Burlington and Hamish Bowles, 122–139. New York: Skira Rizzoli, 2017.

Turner, Victor, *The Anthropology of Performance.* New York: PAJ Publications, 1987.

Wild, Benjamin L. *Carnival to Catwalk: Global Reflections on Fancy Dress Costume.* London: Bloomsbury Academic, forthcoming.

Wood, Christopher. *The Pre-Raphaelites.* London: Weidenfeld and Nicolson, 1981.

PART III

Reincarnation in Popular Culture

She-Wolf or Feminist Heroine? Representations of Margaret of Anjou in Modern History and Literature

Imogene Dudley

INTRODUCTION

Margaret of Anjou (1430–1482) led an eventful life even by the standards of the fifteenth century. She spent her childhood in the circles of the French court until, aged fifteen, she was married to Henry VI of England as part of a peace treaty. A set of related issues such as court infighting, mismanagement of government and foreign policy, a failing economy, and the increasing severity of Henry's mental illness led to a contest of succession now known as the Wars of the Roses. Henry's cousin, Richard duke of York, challenged him for the crown and Henry and Margaret's forces were defeated at the Battle of Towton on March 29, 1461. York's early death led his heir, Edward IV, to take the throne. Defeated, the Lancastrians separated, with Margaret taking their only child, Edward, into French exile. With Henry's capture and imprisonment in 1465, the Lancastrian cause was seemingly lost.

I. Dudley (✉)
University of Exeter, Exeter, UK

© The Author(s) 2019
E. Paranque (ed.), *Remembering Queens and Kings of Early Modern England and France,* Queenship and Power,
https://doi.org/10.1007/978-3-030-22344-1_11

199

However, in 1471, the former Yorkist Earl of Warwick broke with Edward IV and fled. Warwick and Margaret formed an alliance sealed with the marriage of her son Edward to Warwick's daughter Anne. Warwick succeeded in restoring Henry VI but was killed by Edward IV at the Battle of Barnet on April 14, 1471. Upon landing in England, Margaret and Edward learnt of the death of Warwick and the return of Edward IV from exile. For both Lancaster and York, what happened next would be the final throw of the dice. The two forces clashed at the Battle of Tewkesbury on May 4, 1471; Margaret's army was routed, her son slain, and she was captured. Henry was murdered in his bed. Margaret spent four years in imprisonment before being eventually ransomed, and lived her last seven years in France before dying on August 25, 1482.

Margaret has been harshly treated by both early modern and modern historians; her reputation has suffered due to her association with Henry, a failed monarch, and the propaganda produced during a decade of civil strife and the change of dynasty from Lancaster to York in 1461.[1] Historian Patricia-Ann Lee has traced the beginning of the downfall of her reputation to 1459, where "under the pressure of factional strife, the full picture of the ambitious woman, the virago with the spirit of a man, the adulterous queen, began to appear."[2] This picture was recognized in the political poems, notices, and chronicles written by Yorkist propagandists, "who sought to make political capital out of their interpretation of the past as they struggled to find ways to justify the deposition of Henry VI."[3] In the early sixteenth century, Polydore Vergil judged Margaret to be a second Eve for beginning the Wars of the Roses, explaining that "by meane of a woman, sprange up a newe mischief that sett all out of order," whilst Shakespeare's portrayal of Margaret as a she-wolf, with a "tiger's heart wrapped in a woman's hide," cemented her reputation for centuries.[4]

---

[1] Diana Dunn, "Margaret of Anjou: Monster-Queen or Dutiful Wife?" *Medieval History*, 4 (1994), 200; Diana Dunn, "Margaret of Anjou, Queen Consort of Henry VI: A Reassessment of her Role, 1445–53" in *Crown, Government and People in the Fifteenth Century* ed. by Rowena E. Archer (Stroud: Alan Sutton Publishing Ltd., 1995), 107–108.

[2] Patricia-Ann Lee, "Reflections of Power: Margaret of Anjou and the Dark Side of Queenship," *Renaissance Quarterly*, 39.2 (1986): 193.

[3] Dunn, "Margaret of Anjou: Monster-Queen or Dutiful Wife," 201.

[4] Polydore Vergil and Henry Ellis (ed.), *Three Books of Polydore Vergil's English History, comprising the reigns of Henry VI, Edward IV and Richard III* (London: Camden Society, 1844), 70; William Shakespeare, "The Third Part of Henry the Sixth, with the Death of the Duke of York," in *The RSC Shakespeare: William Shakespeare's Complete Works*, ed. Jonathan Bate and Eric Rasmussen (Basingstoke: Macmillan Publishers Ltd., 2007), 1247–1248.

Helen Castor has described the insinuations of the "she-wolf" epithet given to strong queens such as Margaret who transgressed the gender boundaries set by society; it implies that the queen in question is "a feral creature driven by instinct rather than reason, a sexual predator whose savagery matched that of her mate – or exceeded it, even, in the ferocity in which she defended her young."[5] Margaret had been judged by male commentators, and found wanting. This viewpoint then influenced historians, who have acknowledged her bravery and devoted motherhood, but ultimately presented a negative view of Margaret.[6] In the twentieth century, Ralph Griffiths characterized Margaret as severe in her vendetta against the Yorkists, whilst John Gillingham presented her as scheming for ultimate control of government.[7] Regarding the fall of the Lancastrian dynasty, R. L. Storey placed a large amount of the blame onto Margaret due to her desire for power and promotion of faction over country.[8] There have been exceptions where Margaret has been romanticized as a tragic heroine and her actions justified by her motherhood. Examples are Agnes Strickland's nineteenth-century *Lives of the Queens of England* and a biography of Margaret by Jock Haswell in 1976, who himself stated that he wrote in an attempt to overthrow Margaret's negative representation, but these were few and far between.[9] The majority viewpoint is summarized by Anne Crawford: "as an object lesson in how not to behave as a queen consort, [Margaret] could hardly be bettered."[10]

The advent of women's history saw Margaret's rehabilitation. Helen Maurer and Diana Dunn utilized feminist and gender theory to present an alternative picture of Margaret as a woman forced by circumstances to act

[5] Helen Castor, *She-Wolves: The Women Who Ruled England Before Elizabeth* (London: Faber and Faber Ltd., 2010), 31.

[6] Helen E. Maurer, *Margaret of Anjou: Queenship and Power in Late Medieval England* (Woodbridge: The Boydell Press, 2003), 3.

[7] R. A. Griffiths, *The Reign of King Henry VI (Second Edition)* (Stroud: Sutton Publishing Ltd., 2004), 804; John Gillingham, *The Wars of the Roses: Peace and Conflict in Fifteenth Century England* (London: Phoenix Press, 2001).

[8] R. L. Storey, *The End of the House of Lancaster* (London: Barrie and Rockliff, 1966), 177, 192.

[9] Agnes Strickland, *Lives of the Queens of England, Volume III* (London: Lea and Blanchard, 1852); Jock Haswell, *The Ardent Queen: Margaret of Anjou and the Lancastrian Heritage* (London: Peter Davies Ltd., 1976), 11.

[10] Anne Crawford, "The Kings Burden?: The Consequences of Royal Marriage in Fifteenth-Century England," in *Patronage, the Crown and the Provinces in Later Medieval England*, ed. Ralph A. Griffiths (Gloucester: Alan Sutton Publishing Ltd., 1981), 53.

outside gender expectations, while J. L. Laynesmith evaluated Margaret's actions within the confines of medieval queenship.[11] This has led to a more nuanced and three-dimensional reincarnation of Margaret, fueled by the sympathy and interest of new generations toward such, as she was called by her contemporary John Boking, a "stronge labourid woman."[12]

Margaret of Anjou's extraordinary life, marked by the perennial turning of fortune's wheel, alternating between privilege and penury, falling from luxurious queenship to an ignominious end, has indelibly cemented her presence in popular culture. The influence of surviving Yorkist propaganda in the forms of poetry and chronicles, coupled with the fact that little documentary evidence of Margaret's thoughts remain, has complicated her portrayals even further and it is difficult to find the real Margaret under such layers of misinformation.[13] These circumstances have allowed two opposing reincarnations of Margaret to take hold in the popular imagination: she is either a vicious, vengeful virago, or a proto-feminist figure constrained by circumstance.

Historical fiction is a thriving industry and both the popularity of the Wars of the Roses and the preference for strong female characters mean that Margaret is often reincarnated among the pages of such novels. This chapter explores in depth five authors who feature Margaret as a primary character in their novels, while also referring to other authors to illustrate relevant points. The five primary authors are Jean Plaidy (*The Red Rose of Anjou*, 1982), Christopher Nicole writing as Alan Savage (*Queen of Lions*, 1994), Susan Higginbotham (*The Queen of Last Hopes*, 2011), Philippa Gregory (*The Lady of the Rivers*, 2011 and *The Kingmaker's Daughter*, 2012), and Conn Iggulden (the *Wars of the Roses* series, 2013–2016).[14]

[11] Maurer, *Margaret of Anjou*; Dunn, "Margaret of Anjou: Monster-Queen or Dutiful Wife?"; Dunn, "Margaret of Anjou, Queen Consort of Henry VI"; J. L. Laynesmith, *The Last Medieval Queens: English Queenship 1445–1503* (Oxford: Oxford University Press, 2004).

[12] "A.D. 1456, 9 Feb, John Boking to Sir John Falstof" in *The Paston Letters I: Henry VI, 1422–1461 A.D.* ed. James Gairdner (London: Edward Arber, 1872), 378.

[13] Maurer, *Margaret of Anjou*, 3; Dunn, "Margaret of Anjou, Queen Consort to Henry VI," 109; Castor, 339.

[14] Jean Plaidy. *The Red Rose of Anjou* (London: Arrow Books, 2009); Alan Savage, *Queen of Lions* (London: Warner Books, 1994); Susan Higginbotham, *The Queen of Last Hopes* (Naperville, Illinois: Sourcebooks Landmark, 2011); Philippa Gregory, *The Lady of the Rivers* (London: Simon and Schuster, 2011); Philippa Gregory, *The Kingmaker's Daughter* (London: Simon and Schuster, 2013); Conn Iggulden, *Wars of the Roses: Stormbird* (London: Penguin, 2014); Conn Iggulden, *Wars of the Roses: Trinity* (London: Penguin, 2015); Conn Iggulden, *Wars of the Roses: Bloodline* (London: Penguin, 2016); Conn Iggulden, *Wars of the Roses: Ravenspur, Rise of the Tudors* (London: Penguin, 2017).

These novels differ in the depiction of Margaret as a character, and in the extent to which the author succeeds in making the reader empathize with her. Savage's Margaret, for example, is more manipulative and prouder than the other four portrayals. Plaidy's incarnation of Margaret is slightly less antagonistic, but they are both in keeping with the "she-wolf" tradition. In contrast, Higginbotham's interpretation of Margaret is much more sympathetic, and, in her author's notes, she stated that "had Margaret won her dogged fight... she might well be remembered as a heroine."[15] Gregory and Iggulden's portrayals lie somewhere in the middle of the spectrum. Each novel in Gregory's series is told by a different woman of the period, meaning that her Margaret alters with the viewpoint of each narrator: the Margaret of *The Lady of the Rivers*, narrated by Jacquetta of Luxembourg, one of Margaret's ladies-in-waiting, is more sympathetic than the Margaret of *The Kingmaker's Daughter*, narrated by Anne Neville, whose viewpoint is Yorkist despite her father's change of allegiance. In Iggulden's series, Margaret is given four novels to develop from a hopeful, vibrant teenager to a hardened, cynical, middle-aged woman; this and the fact that Iggulden writes from different angles within each book makes for a nuanced reincarnation, neither wholly "she-wolf" nor feminist ideal.

Using these fictional works, this chapter will explore whether modern fiction continues to perpetuate these two opposing reincarnations of Margaret in popular culture, or whether decades of historical research have succeeded in creating a more nuanced, balanced portrayal. By comparing these novels to primary sources and the resulting historiography, their historical accuracy will be assessed and weighed against the three aspects of Margaret that have generated the most debate: her personality, her sexuality, and her desire for power. Unsurprisingly, these elements of Margaret have been the ones to grip the public imagination and are all vital influences in deciding how Margaret is reincarnated in any work of popular culture.

Margaret's Personality

Margaret's personality is a key part of her portrayal in popular culture, and historically she has been censured for it. Shakespeare infamously illustrated Margaret's vengefulness by depicting her murdering the Duke of York and

---

[15] Higginbotham, 332.

crowning his severed head with paper. This is fictitious; Margaret was still in Scotland and had entrusted leadership to the Duke of Somerset at this time.[16] However, the temptation to echo Shakespeare's dramatic moment can be irresistible. Sharon Penman demonstrates this, with her Margaret being a mirror of Shakespeare's "she-wolf" in keeping with the heavily Yorkist perspective of her novel, *The Sunne in Splendour* (1982).[17] Conn Iggulden's Margaret also personally orders York's death and posthumous crowning, which seems at odds with her previously sympathetic depiction. However, she offers her justification: "so many fathers and sons have died and all because [York] would not accept Henry on the throne... there are good men avenged... make a paper crown for [York] who wished to wear a real one. Let the people of York know the price of his ambition."[18] These sentences explain her motivations and actions from her viewpoint and allow the reader to make a judgment in accordance with their own morality.

There is primary evidence extant for Margaret's tempestuous personality. Regarding her alliance with Warwick, it was recorded by John Vale, a fifteenth-century chronicler, how "the seide quene was right dificyle," keeping Warwick on his knees for 15 minutes before pardoning him.[19] Again, this makes for a dramatic episode in a novel. Joanna Hickson (*First of the Tudors*, 2016) ensures that her lead character Jasper Tudor can witness this event and exaggerates it by having Margaret make Warwick crawl across the room and kiss her feet.[20] On first glance, the occasion does Margaret no credit. However, at this time Margaret was in much need of support and she had to justify to loyal Lancastrians her alliance with their former enemy. By publicizing her reluctance to the alliance, she was acknowledging their concerns. This example of fifteenth-century political maneuvering does not translate easily into modern culture though, and the nuance is often lost, with Margaret coming across simply as bitter and vindictive.

Many positive personality traits can be glimpsed through Margaret's personal letters, often written to people of influence on behalf of her tenants. Not only do they demonstrate a capable woman in command of

---

[16] Dunn, "Margaret of Anjou: Monster-Queen or Dutiful Wife?": 200.

[17] Sharon Penman, *The Sunne in Splendour* (London: Penman, 1984), especially 19–21 and 43–45.

[18] Iggulden, *Trinity*, 459.

[19] "The Reconciliation of Queen Margaret and her son with Warwick and Clarence, Angers, 1470" in Margaret Lucille Kekevich, Colin Richmond et al., *The Politics of Fifteenth-Century England: John Vale's Book* (Stroud: Alan Sutton Publishing Ltd., 1995), 216.

[20] Joanna Hickson, *First of the Tudors* (London: Harper, 2016), 403–406.

her own affairs but also a compassionate one, with a desire to help the less fortunate and a strong sense of interpersonal relationships.[21] Her letter to Nicholas Straunge, which asked him to permit the forbidden marriage of his daughter Katherine, revealed a romantic side of Margaret that wished happiness for young lovers; while her letter to the Lord Chancellor requesting his favor toward a "late clerk and familiar servant of ours" showed a desire to help former servants in their future endeavors.[22] This side of Margaret is emphasized by Susan Higginbotham, notably in a fictitious episode where Margaret sends money to Somerset's mistress during his imprisonment.[23] Unfortunately, many novels reject this evidence and show Margaret as unpleasant to those beneath her. Margaret's arrogance in Jean Plaidy's novel results in her servants having no qualms about robbing her, and Sharon Penman's Margaret is cruel to her servant Veronique.[24]

Margaret's love and loyalty to her friends was manifest through her generosity and her attempts to protect them from danger. When the Commons called for the Duke of Suffolk's execution in 1450, Henry and Margaret sought to protect him by sending him into exile; unfortunately, this did not prevent his murder. Historian Jock Haswell deemed it ironic that Margaret "reviled by many historians as the symbol of unrelenting hatred and cruelty...was in fact motivated by that most Christian of emotions, love."[25] Jean Plaidy writes of how "she never sought to hide the love she bore her friends... [for them] she would do a great deal," while Philippa Gregory's Margaret says of Suffolk and Somerset: "these men are everything to me... they both deserve the highest of honours and we will give honours where they are due."[26] It is interesting that this side of Margaret is permitted even by those novelists most firmly in the Yorkist camp, who all depict her loyal friendships. It is a facet of her personality which lends itself to the two opposing interpretations of her character. In a negative reincarnation, it is presented as Margaret being unfair, favoring

---

[21] Dunn, "Margaret of Anjou, Queen Consort of Henry VI: A Reassessment of her Role, 1445–53," 118.

[22] "A Letter from the Queen to Nicholas Straunge of Iseldon, respecting the marriage of his daughter Katherine" and "A Letter from the Queen to the Lord Chancellor" in *Letters of Margaret of Anjou and Bishop Beckington and Others Written in the Reigns of Henry V and Henry VI* ed. Cecil Monro (London: The Camden Society, 1863), 125, 132.

[23] Higginbotham, 125.

[24] Plaidy, 328; Penman, 397.

[25] Jock Haswell, *The Ardent Queen: Margaret of Anjou and the Lancastrian Heritage* (London: Peter Davies Ltd., 1976), 103.

[26] Plaidy, 204, 206; Gregory, *The Lady of the Rivers*, 178.

her friends over other nobles, promoting faction, and seeking revenge against those who slander her favorites; in a more sympathetic reincarnation she is simply a loyal and faithful friend.

It is Margaret's feelings toward Henry which provoke more variance in literary portrayals. Higginbotham is the only author studied who writes of a romantic and sexual love between them. After her capture in 1471, Margaret longs to see Henry, saying that "we would grow old and die here, no doubt, but at least we would spend our last days together," and his death is a tragic blow, "the moment when [she] lost everything"; she demands to view Henry's body and clips a lock of his hair.[27] The interpretation preferred by Jean Plaidy, Conn Iggulden, and Philippa Gregory is that Margaret's affection for Henry was real, but more maternal than romantic.[28] Nevertheless, they show that Margaret's tenderness faded over time, as Henry's weakness endangered their family and throne.[29] Only Alan Savage's Margaret, out of all those with a narrative voice, fails to display love or affection for Henry. She revels in the title and power he gives her, but is aware of his weakness from the outset, and his disinterest in sex only compounds this. By the end, she despises Henry and confesses that "our marriage was long over... as far as I was concerned the sooner he went off to join his famous forebears the better; I had at my side and in my care a far more positive prospect as King of England... I know I did not miss [Henry]."[30] This reveals that Henry's only value to Margaret in this novel is his royalty, and signals Margaret's total ambition, materialism, and lack of humanity—another indication that this incarnation of Margaret is unsympathetic and more in line with Shakespeare's "she-wolf" than any historical reality.

As the novels of Conn Iggulden and Philippa Gregory span a whole series and are told by those on both sides of the conflict, Margaret's character can develop over time and in response to events, with more breathing space than in a single novel. At the beginning of both series, Margaret is reincarnated into a bright and hopeful young girl. She is not without her faults—Gregory's Margaret especially is spoilt and self-centered, although this is tempered by her winning charm—but in both novels she is still a sympathetic and promising teenager. By Iggulden's third novel, *Bloodline*, Margaret is no longer "a young girl ... she had been tempered

---

[27] Higginbotham, 307, 311–313.
[28] Plaidy, 242; King, 63; Iggulden, *Trinity*, 258; Gregory, *The Lady of the Rivers*, 375.
[29] Plaidy, 331, 384, Iggulden, *Bloodline*, 142.
[30] Savage, 363.

in plots and battles and negotiations into a subtle and vengeful woman."[31] Betrayal and warfare have altered Margaret into a reincarnation not unrecognizable from that of Shakespeare, although her sympathetically rendered back-story prevents this wholly, and ensures that the reader still understands and sympathizes with her. Philippa Gregory goes even further in the transformation of her Margaret, who in *The Kingmaker's Daughter* is shown from the perspective of Anne Neville. Anne has been schooled to hate Margaret "the bad queen, a she-wolf worse than the wolves of France."[32] This is a deliberate echoing of Shakespeare and signals that, here too, Margaret has been reincarnated as an unsympathetic antagonist. Anne later hears Margaret's story first-hand as a lesson: "I was just a girl... when I first came to England and I learned quickly enough that to hold the throne of England you have to cleave to your husband and fight for his throne, night and day... I was hammered into a blade... [if] you want to keep your crown, you will be ready to do anything... kill innocents if need be."[33] Here, Margaret is attempting to justify her actions, undertaken to preserve her husband's throne and life. However, the final reference to killing innocents is a signal from Gregory that she is not meant to be a sympathetic character, unlike her earlier reincarnation in *The Lady of the Rivers*; the slaughter of innocent people for a greater good is not a moral principle which tends to be applauded in modern popular culture.

The depiction of Margaret as forged and hardened through travail is shared by all the novelists in this chapter to some degree. Disentangled from the fictional and poetic license, it also rings true enough to be recognized, however slightly, by historians of the period. It takes the two opposing reincarnations of Margaret and moulds them to show the development of her personality in response to events in her life; a much more humane and three-dimensional portrayal for twenty-first century consumers of popular culture.

MARGARET'S SEXUALITY

During Margaret's lifetime rumors about her sex life were rife, chiefly that she was an adulteress and her son a bastard. It is no surprise that many fictitious portrayals of her feature this in one way or another, and that this

---

[31] Iggulden, *Bloodline*, 22.
[32] Gregory, *The Kingmaker's Daughter*, 9.
[33] Gregory, *The Kingmaker's Daughter*, 100–101.

is a key component of most reincarnations of Margaret in popular culture. When novelists write of Margaret, there is one vital decision they need to make: was Edward the son of Henry, or the result of adultery? Historically, Henry's initial inability to recognize Edward as his son was understandable due to his mental incapacitation, but it spawned rumors that Edward's real father was Somerset.[34] These rumors gained momentum as the Yorkist opposition became more active. The English Chronicle was written under the Yorkist regime and claimed that "he that was called Prince... [was] a bastard goten in avoutry [adultery]," while the Milanese ambassador reported in 1461 that Henry thought Edward was the son of the Holy Spirit.[35] The aim of this was threefold: to delegitimize Edward, emphasize Henry's inability to rule and to lessen popular support for Lancaster.[36] Indeed, his disinheritance in the Act of Accord in November 1460 was not widely resisted, even before the Yorkists took the throne.[37]

These allegations have little basis in fact. The story related by the Milanese ambassador was no more than that, as Henry never publicly doubted Edward's paternity and all sources written immediately following his birth assumed that he was the legitimate heir—it is no coincidence that the first sources questioning Edward's paternity herald from the mid-1450s, when the Yorkist faction was beginning to agitate.[38] The eight-year gap between marriage and pregnancy is often given as proof that Henry and Margaret could not conceive and Margaret had looked elsewhere, but this is not necessarily the case. A contemporaneous example is that of Cecily, the wife of Richard of York. Like Margaret, she became a wife in her mid-teens and she also did not conceive immediately; it took her ten years to give birth to her first child. Despite the drama that bastardy would lend a novel, some novelists stick closer to historical fact, although Susan Higginbotham is the only author who writes of Henry and Margaret desiring each other and having a healthy sex life. Margaret relates that

---

[34] Dunn, "Margaret of Anjou: Monster-Queen or Dutiful Wife?": 202.

[35] John Silvester Davies (ed.), *An English Chronicle of the Reigns of Richard II, Henry IV, Henry V and Henry VI written before the year 1471* (New York: Johnson Reprint Corporation, 1968), 79; Laynesmith, 138.

[36] Laynesmith, 136.

[37] Helen Maurer, "Delegitimizing Lancaster: The Yorkist Use of Gendered Propaganda During the Wars of the Roses" in *Reputation and Representation in Fifteenth-Century Europe*, ed. Douglas L. Biggs, Sharon D. Michalove and A. Compton Reeves (Leiden: Brill, 2004), 182.

[38] Maurer, *Margaret of Anjou*, 45.

"Henry came to my bed that evening and loved me... I myself responded in a manner that I hadn't before, which far from shocking Henry had emboldened him."[39] It is on such a night that Edward is conceived.[40] Only from 1455 onward does Margaret confess that "Henry no longer had sexual relations with me."[41] Conn Iggulden and Jean Plaidy also confirm that Edward is Henry's son and Joanna Hickson heavily implies it; although in their versions Henry is not as eager to have sex with Margaret.[42] This is inspired by a description made by Henry's confessor, John Blacman, of a young Henry sending away bare-breasted dancers sent by one of his lords to please him and exclaiming "fy, fy, for shame!"[43] Plaidy is unusual in making Margaret equally as disinterested in intercourse, explaining that "it was to them both a necessary duty," and it is in this spirit that Edward's conception takes place.[44] In Iggulden, Margaret takes advantage of Henry's illness to consummate the marriage; in Hickson, Henry is plied with alcohol to make him more willing.[45]

Edward's legitimacy aside, Margaret's adultery was a key proponent in contemporary Yorkist propaganda, with the Duke of Suffolk and both the elder and younger Dukes of Somerset among her accused lovers.[46] It is difficult to ground these accusations in historical reality, as the nature of any such affair would ensure that it left no traces. Men accused of adultery with Margaret were certainly much in her company, as her advisors and military commanders, but this is not evidence of infidelity. However, it must be questioned *why* the Yorkists were propagating this slander. The primary purpose was to discredit Margaret, there being no surer a way to slander a powerful woman than by casting aspersions on her sexual morality. As Margaret's most recent biographer Helen Maurer elucidated, accusations of adultery implied that the rest of Margaret's activities were also disorderly, and this was extended to the wider realm. It also cast aspersions

[39] Higginbotham, 18.

[40] Higginbotham, 85.

[41] Higginbotham, 125.

[42] Plaidy, 224–225; Hickson, 51, 59, 93, 489; Iggulden, *Stormbird*, 172; Iggulden, *Trinity*, 104.

[43] "John Blacman" in *Henry VI, Margaret of Anjou and the Wars of the Roses: From Contemporary Chronicles, Letters and Records* ed. Keith Dockray (Stroud: Fonthill Media, 2016), 66.

[44] Plaidy, 224–225.

[45] Iggulden, *Stormbird*, 272–273; Hickson, 60–61.

[46] Lee, 191.

on Henry's ability to control his wife and, if he could not do that, how could he rule effectively?[47] It was more convenient for the Yorkists to spread such rumors than it was for Margaret to engage in such behavior. However, whether true or not, these rumors often serve as a springboard for novelists to portray Margaret as an adulteress. Without access to the original sources, and an explanation of these nuances, Margaret's lasciviousness has permeated its way into popular culture.

This is most visibly seen in Alan Savage's incarnation of Margaret, whose sex life verges on caricature. She states her lax position on adultery from the outset: "I was in a great haste [for intercourse], while understanding that in the first instance, at least it must necessarily be done with a husband or one's reputation would be irretrievably ruined."[48] Margaret tempts Suffolk with her naked body as a teenager and she later ends up in bed with him, although she sends him away before the relationship is consummated.[49] Over the course of the book, she has intercourse with Henry at her urging, with the elder Somerset who is Edward's father, with his son the younger Somerset, with Pierre de Brézé, with an outlaw in the woods, with a squire named John Combe and with the Duke of Burgundy.[50] This is in addition to having lesbian relations with Elizabeth Woodville and Mary of Guise, and threesomes with Mary of Guise and the younger Somerset in what is described as "one long orgy."[51] This is obviously exaggerated and is in line with her overblown portrayal in the rest of the work as a highly sexual, adulterous, and immoral "she-wolf." Fifteenth century Yorkist propaganda and the overreaching influence of Shakespeare's immoral Margaret can partly explain this reincarnation, in addition to the fact that Savage wrote in the 1990s, before the academic work of Maurer rehabilitating Margaret had been published. However, more sympathetic and romantic views of Margaret already existed. It seems that Savage's motivation in writing Margaret this way was a personal choice, perhaps to add more drama and spice to his work.

Other authors who reincarnate Margaret as an adulteress choose to portray her actions in a more sympathetic and understanding light. Betty King (*Margaret of Anjou*, 1974) has Margaret sleeping with the elder

---

[47] Maurer, "Delegitimizing Lancaster," 180–181.
[48] Savage, 24.
[49] Savage, 11, 133.
[50] Savage, 75, 165, 271, 337, 358, 366–7, 198, 282.
[51] Savage, 284.

Somerset in a moment of weakness and therefore conceiving Edward, although her honor prevents her from continuing the affair.[52] Later, in France, she succumbs to the French soldier Pierre de Brézé; the pair has loved each other chastely from afar since her teenage years.[53] Even Susan Higginbotham's more virtuous Margaret engages in an affair with the younger Somerset during their exile, although this is a tryst of love as well as passion, a fact which does not prevent Margaret from feeling guilty: "I love you… it is wrong of us. I am wracked with guilt when I leave you."[54] In Philippa Gregory's series, Margaret is passionately in love with the elder Somerset, who is Edward's real father, and her all-encompassing feelings coupled with a lack of judgment spur her to commit adultery and are a justification for the audience. Gregory chooses to make this a key part of her representation, as the sight of Margaret and Somerset in bed together is a trigger which hastens Henry's descent into madness.

However, the lack of concrete evidence for Margaret's adultery can also support a reincarnation of her as a faithful wife to Henry. In the works of Conn Iggulden, Joanna Hickson, and Sharon Penman, Margaret is a visible object of male lust and rumors abound as to her sexual continency, but her adultery is not confirmed. This allows the authors to present her as a sensual being, open to temptation, without conclusively casting her as lascivious. By treading this line carefully, they acknowledge any preconceptions their audience may have from other popular depictions of Margaret, without addressing the issue. Plaidy's Margaret does not commit adultery, in keeping with her complete disinterest in the procreative act. This portrayal is rare in that it does not involve any sexualization of Margaret or her motives, and as such makes for a completely different reincarnation. This is interesting, especially as Plaidy's Margaret is closer to the Margaret of Shakespeare and Savage in terms of her character and ambition than any other incarnation in this chapter. This device does serve to attribute Margaret's motivations and actions firmly to her personality and desire for power, however, while at the same time making Margaret, with her lack of romantic love and lust, less sympathetic and human to the reader.

The negative version of Margaret, epitomized by Yorkist propaganda, is an immoral temptress who commits adultery and attempts to place the illegitimate result on the throne. This version lends itself to fiction due to

---

[52] Betty King, *Margaret of Anjou* (London: Robert Hale Limited, 2004), 180, 186, 193.
[53] King, 279.
[54] Higginbotham, 202.

its irresistible dramatic potential and can primarily be seen in Savage. Only one novel in the selection, Plaidy, adheres to the opposite view: that Edward was legitimate, and that Margaret never committed adultery. The rest, especially Higginbotham and King, depicts a more nuanced account of Margaret's sexuality, her actions often excused by love, with herself aware of the potential ramifications. It seems that this nuance, rather than the simple black-and-white, is more interesting to novelists. It also speaks more successfully to modern opinions concerning sex. The well-worn trope depicting female characters as either a Madonna or a whore has been widely criticized, and modern audiences prefer more nuanced and realistic portrayals of women as sexual beings. This can also extend to reincarnations and representations of historical women, with Anne Boleyn being a prime example of a female historical figure who has been rehabilitated in recent decades, especially with regard to her sexuality.[55]

MARGARET'S DESIRE FOR POWER

The extent to which Margaret sought, gained, and controlled power is debatable. The traditional view, proliferated by Yorkist propaganda, is that Margaret was hungry for power and had gained effective control over Henry and the government. This was an aberration as women were "so thoroughly identified with the point of separation from God, with chaos, with man's tendency to evil, that the intimations of a woman's access to power... were deeply threatening to the misogynistic philosophy of patriarchy."[56] Thanks largely to Shakespeare, this portrayal has caught hold in the public imagination. Fabyan's Chronicle claimed that shortly after the marriage "all was ruled by the quene and her counsayll to the great disprofite of the kynge and his realme."[57] This Margaret is most fully visualized by Alan Savage. At the novel's outset, Margaret revels in her new state as queen: "I arrived at the summit of my ambitions and with [Henry] I had no doubt I would rise higher yet, as together we scaled the paths of fame

---

[55] See Susan Bordo, *The Creation of Anne Boleyn: In Search of the Tudors' Most Notorious Queen* (London: OneWorld Publications, 2014), for a reconstruction and explanation of Anne Boleyn's reputation, using both historiography and popular culture.

[56] Joanna L. Chamberlayne, "Crowns and Virgins: Queenmaking During the Wars of the Roses" in *Young Medieval Women* ed. by Katherine J. Lewis, Noël James Menuge and Kim M. Phillips (Stroud: Sutton Publishing Ltd., 1999), 54.

[57] Robert Fabyan and Henry Ellis (ed.), *The New Chronicles of England and France in Two Parts* (London: F.C. and J. Rivington, 1811), 618.

and glory."[58] From the beginning it is she who rules, proudly stating that "it was clear to everyone that Suffolk and his Queen were the *de facto* rulers of England. To go against us would have been to go against the King."[59] By 1456, "I [Margaret] was in control, and I was determined that it was going to remain that way."[60] Jean Plaidy's Margaret declared on her marriage that "she had a country of her own. She had a husband who was already beginning to adore her, to respect her, to talk to her and listen to her opinions. The King ruled the country and the Queen would rule the King."[61] These portrayals are in keeping with Shakespeare's "she-wolf" and the image of Margaret who took power and used it for her own ends. However, Plaidy is different from Shakespeare and Savage, in that her Margaret lusted after power but did not show the same desire for sexual activity. Both Shakespeare and Savage portray Margaret's sexual immorality as inseparable from her ambition and desire. Whether or not this was a conscious reflection on their part, it mirrored the attitude of the male commentators of Margaret's time, who deliberately connected Margaret's ambition and sexuality to portray her as an unnatural woman who strayed outside the accepted bounds of queenship and wifehood to bring her husband and her country to ruin with her actions.[62] Plaidy's separation of Margaret's sexuality and ambition runs in opposition to this tradition.

Historian Diana Dunn, however, proved that before 1453 there is little evidence of Margaret being involved in any political activity. Instead, she acted like a conventional medieval queen, administering her estates and distributing patronage, a view supported by her letters.[63] Susan Higginbotham conformed to the evidence presented by Dunn, and her Margaret states that "as a woman, I had no place in the negotiations and wanted none" and watches "from a queenly distance as Somerset and York struggled for control of the kingdom – limiting [her] own role to the occasional well-chosen word."[64] This portrayal of Margaret adheres not only to the historical record but also the traditional ideals of the queen being above faction and direct political involvement. It also goes directly

[58] Savage, 61.

[59] Savage, 61, 123.

[60] Savage, 220.

[61] Plaidy, 121–122.

[62] Maurer, "Delegitimising Lancaster," 170, 180–1, 183.

[63] Dunn, "Margaret of Anjou, Queen Consort of Henry VI: A Reassessment of her Role, 1445–53," 109–110.

[64] Higginbotham, 19, 79.

against the view that an audience schooled on Shakespeare would have of Margaret of Anjou, limiting her ambition and lust for power, and adhering to a more traditional female role.

Helen Maurer's historical account shows that Margaret always commanded authority in the name of her husband and son, even when Henry was captured and Edward only a child.[65] This was demonstrated in 1459 when Margaret toured Cheshire gathering support: the badges which she distributed bore Edward's swan insignia, showing that she was raising an army in his name, not her own.[66] It could be argued that she was manipulating the contemporary political structure which meant that, as a woman, she could only access power through her male relatives. However, after 1471 her actions seem to defy her "lust for power," showing that her ambition was solely for Edward, for whom she was determined to secure the crown: after his death that year, she fades into obscurity, with no more attempts for fame and power. However, not all authors attempt to portray her like this. In Gregory's *The Kingmaker's Daughter*, when the future Richard III captures Margaret after Tewkesbury, after attempting to intimidate him she offers to make him her heir if he supports her for the throne, with seemingly no thought for her recently deceased son. This vignette shows Margaret desiring power at any cost, irrespective of familial love and loyalty: not a trait that endears her to the reader. This is an extreme portrayal, even for those authors who cast Margaret as a woman who enjoys and seeks power; in every other novel studied, she is a broken woman post-Tewkesbury, resigned to her fate and deeply mourning the loss of her only child.[67] This incarnation of Margaret's final years as a failed political actor and a devoted mourning mother invites the reader's sympathy if not their affection.

Another interpretation is that Margaret took advantage of Henry's varying degrees of incapacity from 1453 onward to seize the reins of power. In 1454, John Stodely wrote that Margaret "desireth to have the hole reule of this land."[68] This source refers to her bid for the regency during Henry's incapacitation and it cannot be entirely trusted, as Stodely admitted that he was not sufficiently well informed, and he may have just

---

[65] Maurer, *Margaret of Anjou*, 127.

[66] Maurer, *Margaret of Anjou*, 165–166.

[67] Plaidy, 452, 458; Iggulden, *Ravenspur*, 238–239; Savage, 414; King, 313; Penman, 363.

[68] "A.D. 1454, 19 Jan: News Letter of John Stodeley" in Gairdner, 265.

been reporting rumors. The Margaret of Philippa Gregory's novels is eager for the regency, and encouraged by Somerset to pursue this goal, but retains good intentions: "Edmund says the lords will support me...I will do my duty as Queen of England. If they make me regent, I will bring peace to England."[69] In contrast, historian Michael Hicks asserted that government initiative was always with Henry as bills bore his signature with no mention of Margaret. However, this opens another debate about Henry's signature and whether its presence automatically indicated his reasoned authority.[70] Savage and Iggulden both exploit this gray area and depict Margaret as being behind such bills. The motive of Savage's Margaret is purely power and a desire to govern, although she sincerely believes that she is better at it than Henry. She even relates how "it was necessary for me to hold his hand and guide the pen."[71] Iggulden's Margaret is less power-hungry: she wishes to prevent the trusting Henry from being taken advantage of, saying that Henry "does not read the petitions or the laws he must sign... he *trusts*."[72] In 1460, she still refuses to forge Henry's signature as she "would not be found out in a lie" but she admits that "I would only do what Henry would do – if he were able."[73] This Margaret is both capable and willing to take the reins of power but is too morally upright to do so: a modern reinterpretation of the proto-feminist heroine more palatable to modern audiences, as opposed to Savage's and Plaidy's power-hungry representation.

Conclusion

The turbulent life of Margaret of Anjou is proof that reality can sometimes be stranger than fiction and it is of no surprise that many authors of historical novels have found, in her, their inspiration. The lack of sources in her own words describing her feelings and motivations, and the fact that so many of her actions have only reached us through the means of biased accounts, have created a historical lacuna, a gift to novelists. It would be impossible for this chapter to pass absolute judgment on the veracity of all aspects of these novels due to the paucity of historical evidence. It is unsur-

[69] Gregory, *The Lady of the Rivers*, 326, 328.
[70] Michael Hicks, *The Wars of the Roses* (London: Yale University Press, 2010), 127–128.
[71] Savage, 200–201.
[72] Iggulden, *Stormbird*, 189–191.
[73] Iggulden, *Bloodline*, 128.

prising that on the areas where there is the least information, such as Margaret's emotions and sexuality, authors take the most dramatic license. On matters such as Edward's parentage and Margaret's adulterous lovers, many novelists take their inspiration from the surviving Yorkist propaganda, cherry-picking that which suits their version of Margaret. It is to be expected that later pro-Margaret novels, such as *The Queen of Last Hopes* by Susan Higginbotham, consider recent research on her political power, such as that by Helen Maurer, whose study of queenship was influenced by gender theory.

The nature of the primary sources and the developing historiography has culminated in the creation of two opposing Margarets in popular culture: a proud, cold, power-hungry, and sexually immoral she-wolf on one hand, and a softer, courageous proto-feminist heroine on the other. Authors have naturally picked the parts of Margaret that have suited their narrative and the interpretation of her character depends mainly upon whether the novel is told from a Lancastrian or Yorkist standpoint. Pro-Yorkist novels, such Sharon Penman's, still present a Margaret similar to Shakespeare, written five hundred years ago. Savage is the sole author writing from Margaret's perspective who entirely retains Shakespeare's "she-wolf" version of her character, although Plaidy's incarnation also demonstrates certain elements. However, the remainder of the novelists manage to portray Margaret with both positive and negative sides to her personality and the authors which change narrator and emphasis, such as Iggulden and Gregory, are the most obvious examples of this.

The historiography of Margaret has shifted in more recent times, with her character becoming rehabilitated and recognized as a strong woman in an unsympathetic world, and this has been reflected in some modern reincarnations, such as that of Susan Higginbotham. Popular culture is highly receptive to such depictions of strong historical heroines and Higginbotham fits this trend. However, reviewing the novels as a whole, Margaret in modern historical fiction still seems bound by the same prejudices and propaganda that have surrounded her and done her discredit throughout the hundreds of years since her death. In the end, it seems, Margaret of Anjou is a figure who can still inspire love and fear, disgust and admiration. Perhaps it is fitting that popular culture continues to reincarnate her to suit the preferences of authors and audiences, relying on historical sources to suit a narrative; to entertain rather than to enlighten. In this sense, the modern portrayals of Margaret are not so different those written by her peers.

BIBLIOGRAPHY

PRIMARY SOURCES

Davies, John Silvester, ed. *An English Chronicle of the Reigns of Richard II, Henry IV, Henry V and Henry VI written before the year 1471.* New York: Johnson Reprint Corporation, 1968.

Dockray, Keith, ed. *Henry VI, Margaret of Anjou and the Wars of the Roses: From Contemporary Chronicles, Letters and Records.* Stroud: Fonthill Media, 2016.

Fabyan, Robert and Henry Ellis, ed. *The New Chronicles of England and France in Two Parts.* London: F.C. and J. Rivington, 1811.

Gairdner, James, ed. *The Paston Letters I: Henry VI, 1422–1461 A.D.* London: Edward Arber, 1872.

Kekevich, Margaret Lucille, Colin Richmond et al. *The Politics of Fifteenth-Century England: John Vale's Book.* Stroud: Alan Sutton Publishing Ltd, 1995.

Monro, Cecil, ed. *Letters of Margaret of Anjou and Bishop Beckington and Others Written in the Reigns of Henry V and Henry VI.* London: The Camden Society, 1863.

Shakespeare, William. "The Third Part of Henry the Sixth, with the Death of the Duke of York." In *The RSC Shakespeare: William Shakespeare's Complete Works,* edited by Jonathan Bate and Eric Rasmussen. Basingstoke: Macmillan Publishers Ltd, 2007.

Vergil, Polydore and Henry Ellis, ed. *Three Books of Polydore Vergil's English History, comprising the reigns of Henry VI, Edward IV and Richard III.* London: Camden Society.

SECONDARY SOURCES

Bordo, Susan. *The Creation of Anne Boleyn: In Search of the Tudors' Most Notorious Queen.* London: OneWorld Publications, 2014.

Castor, Helen. *She-Wolves: The Women Who Ruled England Before Elizabeth.* London: Faber and Faber Ltd, 2010.

Chamberlayne, Joanna L. "Crowns and Virgins: Queenmaking During the Wars of the Roses." In *Young Medieval Women* ed. by Katherine J. Lewis, Noël James Menuge and Kim M. Phillips. Stroud: Sutton Publishing Ltd, 1999.

Crawford, Anne. "The Kings Burden?: The Consequences of Royal Marriage in Fifteenth-Century England." In *Patronage, the Crown and the Provinces in Later Medieval England,* edited by Ralph A. Griffiths, 33–57. Gloucester: Alan Sutton Publishing Ltd, 1981.

Dunn, Diana. "Margaret of Anjou: Monster-Queen or Dutiful Wife?" *Medieval History,* 4 (1994): 199–212.

———. "Margaret of Anjou, Queen Consort of Henry VI: A Reassessment of her Role, 1445–53." In *Crown, Government and People in the Fifteenth Century*, edited by Rowena E. Archer, 107–143. Stroud: Alan Sutton Publishing Ltd, 1995.

Gillingham, John. *The Wars of the Roses: Peace and Conflict in Fifteenth Century England*. London: Phoenix Press, 2001.

Gregory, Philippa. *The Lady of the Rivers*. London: Simon and Schuster, 2012.

———. *The Kingmaker's Daughter*. London: Simon and Schuster, 2013.

Griffiths, R. A. *The Reign of King Henry VI (Second Edition)*. Stroud: Sutton Publishing Ltd, 2004.

Haswell, Jock. *The Ardent Queen: Margaret of Anjou and the Lancastrian Heritage*. London: Peter Davies Ltd, 1976.

Hicks, Michael. *The Wars of the Roses*. London: Yale University Press, 2010.

Hickson, Joanna. *First of the Tudors*. London: Harper, 2016.

Higginbotham, Susan. *The Queen of Last Hopes*. Naperville, Illinois: Sourcebooks Landmark, 2011.

Iggulden, Conn. *Wars of the Roses: Bloodline*. London: Penguin, 2016.

———. *Wars of the Roses: Ravenspur, Rise of the Tudors*. London: Penguin, 2017.

———. *Wars of the Roses: Stormbird*. London: Penguin, 2014.

———. *Wars of the Roses: Trinity*. London: Penguin, 2015.

King, Betty. *Margaret of Anjou*. London: Robert Hale Limited, 2000.

Laynesmith, J. L. *The Last Medieval Queens: English Queenship 1445–1503*. Oxford: Oxford University Press, 2004.

Lee, Patricia-Ann. "Reflections of Power: Margaret of Anjou and the Dark Side of Queenship." *Renaissance Quarterly*, 39.2 (1986): 183–217.

Maurer, Helen E. *Margaret of Anjou: Queenship and Power in Late Medieval England*. Woodbridge: The Boydell Press, 2003.

———. "Delegitimizing Lancaster: The Yorkist Use of Gendered Propaganda During the Wars of the Roses." In *Reputation and Representation in Fifteenth-Century Europe*, edited by Douglas L. Biggs, Sharon D. Michalove and A. Compton Reeves, 169–187. Leiden: Brill, 2004.

Penman, Sharon. *The Sunne in Splendour*. London: Penguin, 1984.

Plaidy, Jean. *The Red Rose of Anjou*. London: Arrow Books, 2009.

Savage, Alan. *Queen of Lions*. London: Warner Books, 1994.

Storey, R. L. *The End of the House of Lancaster*. London: Barrie and Rockliff, 1966.

Strickland, Agnes. *Lives of the Queens of England, Volume III*. London: Lea and Blanchard, 1852.

Reincarnating the Forgotten Francis II: From Puerile Pubescent to Heroic Heartthrob

Kelly D. Peebles

In a 2011 article in a French popular history magazine, a perplexed reader poses the question: "Why has so much ink been spilled about King Francis I? Wasn't there a Francis II? If so, why doesn't anyone talk about him?"[1] Comic columnist Alain Rémond humorously confirms the existence of the other, often-forgotten Francis, remarking that, sadly, not a single French monument has been named for this "roi aux oubliettes," the king lost in obscurity.[2] Though he was decidedly better known in his own century, contemporary court chronicler Pierre de Bourdeille, the abbot of Brantôme, subtly casts judgment on Francis II (1544–60) by comparing him to his grandfather, Francis I (1494–1547). On numerous occasions in his unwieldy and outrageous chronicle of the sixteenth-century French court, Brantôme refers to the reign of Francis II in diminutive terms: his

---

[1] Alain Rémond, "Un roi aux oubliettes," *Historia* 772 (April 2011): 98. Translation mine.
[2] Rémond, "Un roi aux oubliettes," 98.

K. D. Peebles (✉)
Clemson University, Clemson, SC, USA

© The Author(s) 2019
E. Paranque (ed.), *Remembering Queens and Kings of Early Modern England and France*, Queenship and Power,
https://doi.org/10.1007/978-3-030-22344-1_12

rule was "le temps du petit Françoys," that is, the time of the little, or perhaps lesser, or less accomplished, Francis. In stark contrast, the author refers to Francis I with praise: he was "le grand Roy François," that is, the great King Francis.[3] Francis I unquestionably brought tremendous cultural and political innovation to France, but the length of his rule—32 years—offered ample time for his achievements. Francis II did not have that opportunity. Not only was his reign brief, barely 17 months, but to many of his contemporaries, his physical presence was also diminutive. For sixteenth-century historian Louis Régnier de la Planche, Francis is a puerile pubescent, "a prince of ill health, who showed signs of great indisposition from infancy [...]."[4] The same author also believed him incapable of fathering children, declaring that "his genital organs were undescended and blocked, unable to function at all."[5] And due to his myriad health problems, he would surely not live long after his accession. Régnier de la Planche laments: "he could live yet another two or three years, if no new illness or accident befell him, which they tried to avoid [...]."[6]

Since neither retrospective nor contemporary analysis has done Francis II any favors, it is rather surprising that for a significant number of Millennials and Generation Xers, adults within the 18–49 year-old age bracket, Francis II is better known than his gallant grandfather and likely better known than most other French kings.[7] In the wake of several popular series depicting the lives of late-medieval- and Renaissance-era personalities, the CW Network proposed its own brand of historical fantasy in 2013 with *Reign*, a dramatization of the courtship, marriage, and rule of

[3] For example, Brantôme describes the influence of Francis I on his daughter-in-law, Catherine de Medicis: "ceste Reyne faicte de la main de ce grand Roy François." [This Queen, formed by the hand of this great King Francis.] *Recueil des Dames, poésies et tombeaux,* ed. Étienne Vaucheret (Paris: Gallimard), 68.

[4] See Louis Régnier de la Planche, where the original French reads: "[...] ce Prince malsain, & qui des son enfance avoit monstré de grandes indispositions [...]." *Histoire de l'Estat de France, tant de la République que de la Religion: sous le règne de François II* (S.l.: s.n., 1576), 105.

[5] Régnier de la Planche, *Histoire*: "[...] il avoit les parties generatives du tout constipees & empeschees, sans faires auncune action [...]," 106.

[6] Régnier de la Planche, *Histoire*: "[...] toutesfois ils pensoyent qu'il pourroit bien vivre encor deux ou trois ans, s'il ne luy survenoit autre nouvel accident, lequel on empescheroit par le moyen des preservatifs [...]," 106.

[7] According to "*Reign:* Season Four Ratings," 752 million viewers tuned in for the series finale of 16 June 2017. The third season averaged 950,000 viewers. All four seasons are now available on the video streaming service Netflix.

Francis II and Mary Stuart, Queen of Scots. Created by Stephanie SenGupta and Laurie McCarthy, four seasons, each with over 20 episodes, aired through June 2017. There is nothing diminutive about the Francis portrayed in *Reign*. On the contrary, he is a veritable heroic heart throb, and the show writers work quickly to dispel any prior conception the viewer may have had of Francis's historical appearance. In an early episode, he attributes rumors of his slight appearance to a poorly executed painting, complaining to Mary: "that half-blind portrait artist didn't realize I was sitting in a chair while my sister was standing, and now, half of Europe thinks I'm a dwarf."[8]

The goal of this chapter is not to challenge the historical accuracy of portrayals such as that in *Reign*, but rather to consider both historic and fictional reincarnations of Francis II. How do the target audience's expectations influence how the author represents his physical health, character, and role as a ruler? I first focus on the fantasy television series *Reign*, in which actor Toby Regbo interprets the young king as vibrant and virile, and we witness him navigating the throes of adolescent hormones, pagan blood rituals, and political power plays as a worthy—though equally ill-fated—counterpart to his notorious wife, Mary, Queen of Scots, portrayed by Adelaide Kane and cunningly foiled by Megan Follows's Catherine de Medici. I then consider a dramatic interpretation of Francis's reign, Charles-Jean-François Hénault's 1747 play, *François II, roi de France*. Curiously, in this experimental work inspired by Shakespeare's historical tragedies, the title character is entirely absent, and the author dwells instead on a political power struggle at his court. Finally, I turn to two pamphlets printed shortly after Francis's death: a narrative account of his final illness and a series of poems intended to console the French public over the loss of their king.

One is hard-pressed to find scholarly literature about Francis II. A handful of modern studies retrospectively examine the cause of his death, likely due to chronic ear infections and upper respiratory difficulties that plagued him from birth.[9] Biographies of his infamous wife, Mary Stuart, include only brief and superficial mentions of her first husband. Among

---

[8] *Reign* episode 1.4, "Hearts and Minds."

[9] See, for example, Albert Potiquet, *La Maladie et la mort de François II Roi de France* (Paris: Rueff et Cie, 1893) and J. F. Gouteyron, E. Salf, and J. M. Faugère, "La mort de François II. Conséquence de l'évolution d'une otite moyenne chronique," in *Histoire des sciences médicales* (1990): 49–54.

the best-selling biographies, that of Antonia Fraser offers a derogatory portrait of the young king's physique and intelligence, and while John Guy's contribution is more measured, he depicts Francis as delicate, sickly, and uncomfortable speaking in public due to a stutter.[10] Although Guy devotes roughly 15 percent of his 500-page biography to Mary's and Francis's relationship and marriage, in the 2018 feature-film adaptation of his book, *Mary Queen of Scots*, director Josie Rourke chooses not to dramatize this 12-year timespan. Modern scholarship on the origins of the French Wars of Religion, which ignited in early 1562, thus slightly over a year after Francis's death, focuses on the power struggle between the catholic Guise faction, led by Mary's maternal uncles, and the reform-inclined Bourbon princes of the blood.[11] Primary sources related to Francis II include his tomb in the Basilica of Saint Denis, portraits and miniatures located at the Bibliothèque nationale de France and the Louvre, and a suit of armor displayed at the Musée de l'Armée in Paris. Manuscript and print sources include ordonnances promulgated during his reign, correspondence, and pamphlets commemorating his baptism, marriage, royal entries, and death, that is, the essential events of a royal life.[12]

Born in January of 1544, Francis II was the first of a large brood of royal children born to Henry II (1519–59) and Catherine de Medici (1519–89). His birth was a celebrated occasion, as it occurred ten years into his parents' marriage and finally disproved rumors of his mother's infertility and fears of her repudiation. Though he became *dauphin* at the age of three,[13] his accession to the throne at the age of 15 in July 1559,

---

[10] See chapter six, "The White Lily of France," in Antonia Fraser's *Mary Queen of Scots* (New York: Delta, 1993). See chapters six, "A Dynastic Marriage" and eight, "The Return to Scotland," in John Guy, *Queen of Scots. The True Life of Mary Stuart* (Boston: Houghton Mifflin, 2004).

[11] See, for example, Hugues Daussy, *Le Parti Huguenot: Chronique d'une désillusion (1557–1572)* (Geneva: Droz, 2014), in particular chapter two, "La Genèse d'une conscience politique."

[12] Many of these sources have been digitized by the Bibliothèque nationale de France and are available on http://gallica.bnf.fr. Print sources can be searched on the Universal Short Title Catalog, where available digitized records are linked.

[13] According to Bernard Barbiche, from the fourteenth century on, the heir presumptive to the French throne was given the dynastic title of *Dauphin de France,* so named after his seigneurie of the *Dauphiné* in southeastern France. Until his accession to the throne, his coat of arms depicted both a dolphin and the fleur-de-lys of French royalty. This terminology applies only to direct male descendants and not to collateral branches. Thus, Louis XII, Francis I, and Henry IV were not known as *dauphin. Les Institutions de la monarchie française à l'époque moderne* (Paris: Presses universitaires de France, 1999), 27–28.

was unexpected. His father was in the prime of his life, enjoying the public celebrations of the Treaty of Cateau-Cambrésis, a peace accord among Spain, England, Scotland, and France that also resulted in the marriage between his daughter Elisabeth and King Phillip II of Spain, when he was mortally wounded in a jousting tournament.[14] Just over a year before, in April 1558, the court had celebrated Francis's marriage to Mary Stuart (1542–87), Queen of Scots, to whom he had been engaged since childhood.

At some point between the couple's marriage and Henry II's death, when Francis was addressed as the King Dauphin—he was simultaneously king consort of Scotland and *dauphin* of France—Brantôme dedicated the below poem to him, writing with hope for the future and respect for the past:

> *For the King Dauphin*
> To the young King – born of a King so great,
> Who gave him the name of his father, the first of that name –
> Our bountiful heaven bestowed you with many a gift,
> Worthy of your high and royal nature.
> France is fortunate in its fate,
> Having a firm sense of security in its current welfare,
> And retaining for its future joy
> A secure alliance between father and son.[15]

Through rhyme and alliteration in the original French, pointing to "ferme asseurance" (a firm sense of security) and "seure alliance" (a secure alliance) in the sixth and eighth lines, the poet underscores with a heavy hand the nation's current welfare and the potential for continuity between father and son.[16] Francis is judged to be worthy of his future office and

---

[14] On French public opinion of the peace treaty, primarily in printed pamphlets, as well as on Mary's claims to the English throne, see Alexander Wilkinson, *Mary Queen of Scots and French Public Opinion, 1542–1600* (New York: Palgrave Macmillan, 2004), 48–52.

[15] All translations are my own, unless otherwise indicated. For poetry, I have not attempted to reproduce rhyme or meter, but simply to give an approximation of the message. The original French reads as follows: "*Pour le Roy Dauphin* / Au jeune Roy du grand Roy geniture, / Qui nom premier du pere luy donna, / Le Ciel bening maint present ordonna, / Digne de haute et royalle nature. / Heureuse France est de son adventure, / Du bien present ayant ferme asseurance, / Et recevant pour sa joye future / Du pere et filz une seure alliance" in *Recueil des Dames, poésies et tombeaux*, 806–807.

[16] On the publishing history of Brantôme's *Recueil de poésies*, see Étienne Vaucheret's explanatory "notice," in *Recueil des Dames, poésies et tombeaux*, 1467–78.

capable of maintaining France's prosperity. Their "alliance" implies an affinity between the two, a consistency in their ideas and pursuits.[17] In other words, the *dauphin* supports his ruling father by physically embodying the Valois blood line, and his eventual accession will reincarnate, in a sense, his predecessors' rule. France never was, at least until its Revolution, without a king. In fact, Henry II's premature death and Francis II's equally premature accession were decried in immediate succession in the great hall of the Palais de la Cité and before Parlement in Paris.[18] But as *dauphin,* Francis also supports his ruling father by morally embodying Valois values and valor, and his eventual reign will revitalize his father's and grandfather's prior examples of leadership, thereby preserving the conditions for France's future well-being. In reality, Francis II had little preparation for his short-lived rule and little time to demonstrate any personal or political qualities or faults. For Brantôme, the weight of his heritage offered sufficient promise for his praise. And for twenty-first-century screenwriters, the paucity of archival evidence offered ample room for fantasy television.

FRANCIS II AS HEROIC HEARTTHROB

The 2013 pilot for the television series *Reign* opens with Mary's arrival in France.[19] Though queen since her infancy, she is depicted as determined and plucky, but also uninitiated to court intrigues and highly susceptible to teenaged flights of fancy, such as jewels, clothing, and talk of first love. Her blond and dashing prince charming, Francis, greets her before a medieval stone castle, alongside numerous other dazzlingly dressed courtiers,

---

[17] For sixteenth-century definitions of the French "alliance," see the online *Dictionnaire du moyen français*, http://atilf.fr/dmf. Of interest here is the definition describing "alliance" as a personal relationship: "Entente entre deux ou plusieurs personnes, rapprochées par une communauté de sentiments, d'idées, d'intérêts" [two or more people in harmony with one another, brought together due to commonly shared feelings, ideas, interests].

[18] On the public announcement in Paris of Henry II's death and Francis II's accession, see Nicole Gilles, *Le Second Volume des Annales et Croniques de France, augmentees, en la fin dudict volume, d'aucuns faictz dignes de memoire, des feuz Roys Henry, deuxiesme, Francoys, deuxiesme, & Charles, IX. du nom, jusques en l'an mil cinq cens soixante & deux* (Paris: Gabriel Buon, 1562), 173. Barbiche specifies that the office of the king existed independently of the person of the king, resulting in a "physical" body and a "political" body, the latter of which could never die, thus ensuring the continuity of royal functions. *Les Institutions,* 28.

[19] Episode 1.1, "Pilot," depicts Mary arriving in France not long before her marriage. In reality, she arrived in France at the age of 5, in 1548, and was raised at the court of France alongside Francis and the other royal children.

though he soon hurries off for a tryst between the bedsheets with another young woman. The show's pilot is clearly designed to draw in the target audience of 18- to 34-year-old women, in particular the devoted fan base of the CW network's popular *Vampire Diaries*, airing in the time slot immediately prior to *Reign*. The viewers confront numerous dramatic intrigues within and without the French court in rapid succession: romantic tension among adults and teenagers of all social levels, pagan death rituals in nearby woods and villages, ghost hauntings in the castle's secret passageways, and prophecies pronounced by court seer Nostradamus proclaiming that Mary's presence at French court will lead to Francis's death. The lavish costume designs aim not to harken the spectator back 500 years, but rather to evoke the underlying nature—hippie, conservative, romantic, and nouveau riche—of each of Mary's ladies-in-waiting, known then as "the four Maries," as they all shared the name, but known here as Kenna, Aylee, Lola, and Greer, respectively.[20] The show's creator, Laurie McCarthy, pitched the series idea as "*Game of Thrones* meets Marie Antoinette," and professed to reimagining the Queen of Scots as a "warrior queen" with a "girl posse."[21] Indeed, perennial young women's issues are preponderant themes in *Reign*. As a result, the viewer witnesses Mary's ladies-in-waiting acting independently and claiming their right to love, despite social strictures requiring young women of marrying age to remain obedient and pure: Aylee occasionally steals Mary's jewelry for her own gratification, Kenna becomes mistress to Henry II, Lola gives birth to Francis's love child, and Greer becomes a financially independent brothel owner. On the other hand, each young woman also finds herself manipulated by others with greater political or social power: Aylee is to convey secrets to Catherine in exchange for concealing her kleptomania, Kenna is forced to marry Henry's bastard, Lola is disowned by her family back in Scotland, and Greer is dismissed from court and stripped of her wealth due to her husband's Protestant sympathies.[22]

[20] For a description of the show's costumes, see Tierney Bricker, "All Hail *Reign's* Fashion! The CW Hit's Costume Designer Breaks Down Mary and Her Ladies-in-Waiting's Looks," *E! News.* 22 November 2013.

[21] *Broadway World,* "The CW to Develop Mary Queen of Scots Teen Drama *Reign*," 24 October 2012. https://www.broadwayworld.com/bwwtv/article/The-CW-to-Develop-Mary-Queen-of-Scots-Teen-Drama-REIGN-20121024

[22] Aylee is murdered early in the series by Clarissa, initially believed to be the castle ghost, but later revealed to be Catherine de Medici's illegitimate daughter. *Reign,* episode 1.8, "Fated." The other three women continue to have principle roles throughout the series.

What the series writers do seem to understand about early modern rulers (or perhaps arrived at by dumb luck) is signaled with a rousing and dramatic theme song, sung by American folk rock band The Lumineers: "They all need something to hold onto / they all mean well [...]. You could never feel my story / it's all you know."[23] The lyrics suggest that the reigning monarchs in the show represent a strong, unifying ideal to their subjects, and by extension to the show's viewers. In other words, they give us "something to hold on to."[24] However, neither their subjects, nor the television spectators, can fully understand what it means to live the life of a monarch. *Reign* ostensibly treats us to a behind-the-scenes glimpse of that life in all its decadent splendor (and occasional filth), and its actors, sets, and storylines are thus contrived so that we may "feel" their stories, notably the turbulence of Mary's and Francis's courtship and marriage due to competing personal and political agendas at court and increasing tension between Catholics and Protestants, the former being the predominant faith within the royal family and the latter, the faith espoused by rival political factions. A compounding factor in Mary's and Francis's marital strife, and among the more far-fetched of *Reign*'s storylines, is how the show's writers imagine the French court and royal family coping with the death of Henry II.

As season 1 reaches its climax, Francis is increasingly troubled by King Henry's erratic behavior. The entire French court suffers from a progression of irrational actions. Henry attempts to seduce Mary in order to increase his power; he murders two women during kinky sexual games and forces his wife to cover his tracks, and he plots wildly unrealistic imperial conquests that Francis tries to preempt before they are launched. The twenty-first-century television viewer would recognize nothing in Brantôme's sixteenth-century poetic imagining of Henry's and Francis's shared political and moral traits. In stark contrast to that profoundly laudatory and optimistic portrayal of a *dauphin* poised to carry on his father's legacy is an overwhelmingly gloomy and pessimistic dramatization of an heir apparent determined to reject everything that his father represents. As apparently the sole responsible adult at court, *Reign*'s Francis resolves to eliminate the threat that his father poses to the stability of France, and indeed, the show writers frame Henry's murder as an inevitable and

---

[23] The Lumineers, "Scotland." *Genius.* Accessed March 15, 2018. https://genius.com/The-lumineers-scotland-lyrics
[24] The Lumineers, "Scotland."

ethically justified decision. Francis is shown carefully considering alternatives before concluding: "I was wrong. He is lost. [...] It's too late for assassination. We'd never get near him. He must be removed from the throne by a superior force."[25] A jousting tournament takes place not long after this declaration, an event obviously modeled after the Cateau-Cambrésis celebrations, though Elisabeth's wedding is displaced in an earlier episode and Marguerite appears nowhere in the entire series. Clad in head-to-toe armor, Francis conceals his true identity from the spectators, switches places with his father's intended opponent, and mortally wounds him, piercing Henry through the eye with a lance.[26] Francis is visibly shaken for several episodes following this supposed accident, though most of the court, including Mary, believes that the predicted intervening superior force was the hand of God. Francis's brooding, his head shaking, and his foul moods are all attributed to grief rather than guilt, and Francis is proclaimed king in the season 1 finale.

Season 2 presents the ruling couple as coming fully into their power and attempting to make morally just decisions. However, the desire to rule in concert and to do so in a fair and just manner is complicated when the ruler is also a murderer. Knowledge of Francis's regicide proves to be considerable leverage for a coercive, self-important French noble aptly named Stéphane Narcisse. And blackmail proves to be fierce motivation for a compassionate king devoted to his wife. Francis bends to Narcisse's will in order to protect Mary, for knowledge of her husband's crime would make her equally culpable. As Protestant factions grow increasingly restless, Francis promulgates unethical edicts that punish religious dissidence but favor Narcisse's Catholic preferences, which are merely thinly veiled self-serving interests aimed at preserving and expanding his personal wealth. When Mary scolds him with incredulous defiance, Francis retorts: "There are limits to what I can do. Even as king. When the nobles are united, I am boxed in. [...] I need to handle this on my own, and I need to do it my way. What I need from you is to be patient and to believe in me."[27] Although Mary remained a staunch Catholic, the series creators' aim of casting her as an enlightened and independent woman warrior require that she question her husband's motives, urge him to change course, and reject his attempts at affection and détente when he disappoints her.

---

[25] Episode 1.22, "Slaughter of Innocence."
[26] Episode 1.22, "Slaughter of Innocence."
[27] *Reign* episode 2.7, "The Prince of the Blood."

Reign's season 2 does a formidable job at catering to its fan base. Its writers deftly garner sympathy for a murderous king by displaying the inner turmoil that results as Francis weighs his determined devotion for Mary and the misery that his dishonesty provokes. Though *Reign* excels in its particular brand of speculative fiction—the realm of emotional manipulation and maddening misunderstandings—what its season 2 puzzlingly does not show its viewers is the power struggle that ensues immediately on Francis's accession. Indeed, the real-life situation was sufficiently fascinating to warrant dramatic interpretation. Mary's mother, Marie of Guise (dowager queen and regent of Scotland while Mary resided in France), had several ambitious younger brothers, among them Francis (1519–63), Duke of Guise and Charles (1524–74), Cardinal of Lorraine and archbishop of Reims. Both men were powerful personalities at the French court, looked after their niece's affairs in France, and were keenly aware of their potential to influence the young ruling couple. They almost immediately began jockeying for power, seeking to diminish the influence of their highest-ranking rivals, the princes of the blood, Antoine of Bourbon (1518–62), the King of Navarre, and Louis of Bourbon (1530–69), the Prince of Condé. By effectively removing the Guise faction from the scene, *Reign* attributes a measure of that family's intrigues to Narcisse, while it assigns several of its accomplishments to Francis, namely the victory over the English at Calais and the preempting of a Bourbon coup against the throne (very loosely based on the Amboise Conspiracy).[28]

In this type of television show, there is no room for a weak king. Tormented by Narcisse's hold over him, Francis steals away to eliminate his rival, but during his absence a restless Protestant mob, angered by the recent edict, storms the castle. Unable to find the king, the Protestants force their way into the royal bedchamber, and one of them forces himself onto Mary. Francis's failure to protect his wife and his failure to please his subjects underscores the difficulties resulting from a solitary reign: the secret of his regicide allowed his manipulation by Narcisse, which led to social revolt among his subjects and sexual assault of his wife. Shared decisions and mutual support are the hallmark of this show; a reign is a partnership, and preferably a romantic one.

[28] In *Reign*, the taking of Calais plays out in episodes 1.20, "Higher Ground" and 1.21, "Love Live the King." Francis leads the charge and returns to court victorious, where he finds his father growing increasingly mad. In reality, the Duke of Guise captured Calais from the English in January 1558.

In order to repair this damage and redeem his reign in his subjects' and his wife's eyes, Francis sincerely desires for his wife to heal emotionally and sexually after her assault, which both he and Mary attribute to his poor decisions and failure to govern effectively. But within the often outlandish economy of *Reign,* Francis's perceived weaknesses transform into a strength. With magnanimous acquiescence, Francis condones a love affair between Mary and Louis, Prince of Condé, who in the real, historical record was her uncle Francis of Guise's arch rival! Though Louis gains sympathy in her eyes for his compassion for the Protestant cause, his assistance in assuaging their uprising, and his complicity in executing her rapist, Mary's eyes are gradually opened to the dangers that she has posed to France by cavorting with her husband's rival. Louis and his brother Antoine, King of Navarre, had been secretly negotiating with Elizabeth I of England and planning a coup to overthrow Francis. Feigning pregnancy—ostensibly resulting from her affair with Condé—and claiming her intent to abandon Francis and flee to Scotland with her lover, Mary stabs an unsuspecting Condé in the gut, giving her husband and his troops the opportunity to quash their rival's rebel forces. Though acting independently in this instance, through Mary's unilateral action, she and Francis are able to come full circle, reuniting emotionally, physically, and politically. And again, the union of their love and their mutual dependence strengthens their shared reign, for *Reign* seeks to demonstrate that political weaknesses are surmountable when emotional ties are strong.

The same may be said for physical weaknesses, for in season 3, Francis begins to suffer from ill health. He progressively weakens, collapses, and faints due to the severe pain of an ear infection and brain fever, and after consulting Nostradamus for medical advice, he begins to prepare for his imminent death, cherishing time with his wife and securing his brother's succession. It is important to note that it is not physical illness that ultimately takes Francis's life, but a Scottish assassin, who had attempted to kill his wife.[29] Francis dies fighting, all the while protecting his wife and her own reign. His dying words express his love for Mary, his desire for her to find love again, and his request for her to remain in France until the regency of his brother Charles's rule is assured. The Francis in *Reign* is resolved to be different from his father, Henry. He strives to be a compassionate, forward-thinking, and morally just ruler, one who is also genuinely in love with his wife and supportive of her career goals as Queen of Scotland. In other words, Francis is represented as a perfect, twenty-first century heroic heart throb.

---

[29] *Reign* episode 3.5, "In a Clearing."

THE ABSENT KING IN HÉNAULT'S *FRANCIS II, KING OF FRANCE*

In the eighteenth century, during the reign of Louis XV and barely three decades after the absolute rule of Louis XIV, Francis II is presented in an entirely different light. In the preface to his experimental historical play, Charles-Jean-François Hénault presents himself as favoring Classical literary principles, professing admiration of Shakespeare's ability to give life to history, but criticizing his ignorance of the Three Unities: the unity of time (a play's action should take place over not more than 24 hours), the unity of place (the stage should represent a single physical place), and the unity of action (the play should interpret a single action, with minimal subplots). Hénault's esteem for English historical plays stems from his belief that details are not easily grasped in a narrative, are remembered only with great difficulty, and are made evermore captivating through action and dialogue.[30] What makes Francis II's reign a suitable subject is the brevity of his rule and the machinations of the Guise faction, which closely, yet imperfectly, approximate the unities of time and action.[31]

The play opens with a set representing the Tournelles palace in Paris, the site of the abruptly ended jousting tournament celebrating the peace of Cateau-Cambrésis. Festival decorations are draped in mourning cloths, and Henry II's coffin dominates the scene. The spectator first confronts a conversation between two men who enjoyed significant power at the late king's court: the marshal of Saint André and the constable Montmorency, both of whom had been deeply involved in the Cateau-Cambrésis peace negotiations. Saint André sees Francis as little more than an impressionable child, pulled in every direction by a "whirlwind of storms."[32] The rule of the old and the new are uncomfortably juxtaposed, as Montmorency guards King Henry's body and the Guise faction protects "the person of the young king."[33] Henry's immobile presence on stage represents the static past, while Francis should embody the dynamic, evolving future of France. However, we learn only of his shortcomings, and it becomes increasingly apparent that he is at the fulcrum of a complicated balancing act, with each side—the Guise faction and the Bourbon faction—struggling for influence.

---

[30] See Charles-Jean-François Hénault, *François II, roi de France,* ed. Thomas Wynn (London: Modern Humanities Research Association, 2006), 32.

[31] Hénault, *François II*, 35–36.

[32] Hénault, *François II*, 42–43.

[33] Hénault, *François II*: "la personne du jeune Roi," 45.

The Queen Mother occupies a unique position in this power struggle, and as the play unfolds, she becomes, in effect, its true hero. As a mother, she displays unfailing devotion to her son, insisting that "the king my son is of age, and it is up to him to choose his ministers and up to me to obey him."[34] However, she also subtly asserts her power, stating to Montmorency that she speaks "on behalf of the king."[35] Catherine must walk a fine line: while she prefers the legitimacy of the Bourbons, the Prince de Condé is their only strength, giving that side little chance of success when faced with the formidable and numerous personalities of the Guise faction. Further complicating the issue is the matter of religion, for the Bourbons and their allies are "infected" by the "new religion," and "its popular nature threatens to overturn the foundations of authority. [...] An anarchical religion leads to indocile subjects."[36] Indocile subjects are the real nemesis of the Guise faction, and Francis of Guise realizes that in order to solidify their still tenuous power, they must "draw the people onto our side" and preempt any attempt on power from the Bourbons.[37] Indeed, the Cardinal of Lorraine declares: "I want from him [Condé] some sort of clear revolt, a coup that will make him a criminal in the king's eyes and authorize us to deal with him severely so that the people will withdraw any credence they gave him for being a prince of the blood."[38]

These rival brothers confront one another in Act II, scene II on a set that eerily echoes the play's opening in its structural setting, yet the dialogue places it in stark contrast. The Guise and Bourbon brothers have gathered with the Queen Mother to discuss religious dissidence. The late king, though his coffin has now been removed from the scene, still looms large, and the new king is markedly absent. His armchair is placed at center stage, but stands empty. The Queen Mother speaks in his stead: "I will explain these opinions to the king, but I do fear, after hearing what has been said, that he will find a severe response [to religious uprisings] neces-

---

[34] Hénault, *François II*: "The Roi mon fils est majeur, c'est à lui à choisir ses Ministres, & à moi d'obéir," 55.

[35] Hénault, *François II*: "[...] je vous parle au nom du Roi," 55.

[36] Hénault, *François II*: "[...] la Religion nouvelle, dont le Roi de Navarre est infecté. [...] c'est une Religion dont le génie populaire tend à renverser tous les fondemens de l'autorité," 61–62.

[37] Hénault, *François II*: "[...] mettre le peuple de notre parti," 67.

[38] Hénault, *François II*: "[...] je veux de lui quelque révolte bien marquée, quelque action d'éclat qui puisse le rendre criminel auprès du Roi, & qui nous autorise à le traiter avec tant de rigueur, que le peuple soit détrompé du crédit qu'il suppose à un Prince du Sang," 69.

sary because the late king set that example and in the early stages of a reign, it would be a sign of weakness to stray from that path."[39] Catherine effectively serves as a placeholder for her son, tilting the balance of power in her favor by relying on her late husband's authority. It is she, not Francis, who in practice reincarnates Henry II, as she sets herself up as a formidable defender of the French throne.

In Act III, the Amboise Conspiracy unfolds. The Guise brothers learn of a plot aimed at Catherine and the king and opportunistically posture themselves as saviors. Hénault then juxtaposes their cunning with the moral principles of the Bourbons in a conversation between the admiral Coligny and the Prince of Condé. While the two share religious and political views, they disagree in approach. Coligny counsels acquiescence, stating "no one can deny that the Guise brothers have taken the place that you, by rights, deserved; but this has happened at other times, and kings may choose their ministers as they see fit [...]."[40] As for the Guise's persecution of religious dissenters, he counsels patience, stating: "I am persuaded that they only pursue reformers for hatred of their leaders, whose ambition they fear; and if they were truly convinced that the leaders wanted to live in peace, they would leave us alone." Condé, however, believes that "one may take arms against an authority that is illegitimate, such as that of the Guise faction."[41] By the beginning of Act IV, the court is preparing for a revival of the Estates General, where the people may air their complaints. After being lured there, Condé is arrested, tried, and nearly condemned to death. However, soon after arriving in Orléans, the king falls gravely ill, and we witness the internal monologue of Catherine de Medici as she grapples with the situation and weighs her decisions:

[39] Hénault, *François II*: "Je rendrai compte au Roi des opinion; mais je crains bien, sur ce qui vient d'être dit, qu'il ne croye la sévérité d'autant plus nécessaire, que le feu Roi en a donné l'exemple, & qu'en effet sous un Régne naissant ce ne fût marquer de la foiblesse, que de s'écarter de la route qui lui a été tracée," 76.

[40] Hénault, *François II*: "On ne peut nier que Messieurs de Guise occupent une place où vous aviez droit de prétendre; mais cela est arrivé de tous les tems, & les Rois prennent leurs Ministres où il leur plaît," 96–97.

[41] Hénault, *François II*: "L'Amiral: 'Je suis persuadé que l'on ne poursuit les Réformés qu'en haine de leurs chefs, dont on craint l'ambition; & que si l'on étoit bien convaincu que les chefs voulussent demeurer en paix, on nous y laisseroit.' Le P. de Condé: '[...] l'on pouvoit prendre les armes contre une autorité qui n'étoit pas légitime, telle que celle de Messieurs de Guise,'" 96–97.

Wake up, Medici! The state is your family, and if Francis II dies, heaven will have allowed it in order to save France from this divisiveness that is about to rip it apart. [...] Once they realize what is truly in their interest, our people will understand that a true minority is worth more than an imaginary majority.[42]

As the last act unfolds, we witness Catherine's internal turmoil as she decides for herself, by speaking to each faction, how to protect her son Charles's rule after her son Francis's death. Ultimately, she elects to stand with the princes of the blood, those with blood ties to the crown. The play ends with the King of Navarre informing his brother that he is free thanks to Catherine, and he must now dedicate his life to serving her.[43] Hénault's final act reveals that his play is not about its title character, but rather, it is about the Queen Mother's devotion to her children. She will do better to diminish the influence of the Guise brothers and to rely on the Bourbon brothers' participation in Charles's council, for now they are in her debt. Catherine de Medici is Hénault's response to Racine's Phèdre. She is a tragic heroine from French history, motivated by love, but unlike Phèdre, hers is a well-meaning love of family and France.

FRANCIS II'S DEATH IN SIXTEENTH-CENTURY PAMPHLET LITERATURE

Francis's last days in Orléans are narrated in a four-page pamphlet, a single quarto quire printed by the Lyonnais workshop of Benoist Rigaud in 1561, the text of which was decried in public in order to inform the French of their king's illness and death.[44] Francis and Mary arrived in Orléans on

---

[42] Hénault, *François II*: "Réveille-toi, Médicis; l'État est ta famille, & si François II. meurt, le Ciel l'aura permis pour sauver la France des divisions qui sont prêtes à la déchirer. [...] ce peuple, quand il aura senti ses véritables intérêts reconnoîtra qu'un minorité véritable vaut mieux qu'une majorité imaginaire," 139.

[43] Hénault, *François II*, 148.

[44] A quick search of the Universal Short Title Catalog using the terms "François II" and "Rigaud" indicates that seven pamphlets were printed in this workshop in 1560 and 1561, among them edicts, letters patent, and this narrative recounting his death. Similar pamphlets announcing political and economic policies were printed routinely in Paris, often by the same printing workshops (Vincent Sertenas and Guillaume Nyverd, among others) and in Tours (by Jean Rousset and Guillaume Bougeat). In late 1560, during the king's stay in Orléans, a series of pamphlets was printed there by Eloi Gibier.

18 October 1560, on what would be their last journey together.[45] According to the pamphlet, "on the sixteenth of November, 1560, [...] after dinner [Francis] had a spell of shivering and a headache behind his left ear, on the side where there had long been a fistula. He went to bed with a fever and some sort of fluid continued to drain for the next several days."[46]

As the narrative unfolds, we learn that Francis never rose from his sickbed, where he was continuously bled and purged. Twelve days after the initial attack, "his fever rose, and along with the pain came great bouts of panic and delirium."[47] From that time on, a small group of intimates kept vigil over him, including his wife and mother, the King of Navarre, and the Guise brothers. Although the royal surgeons and apothecaries were forbidden from speaking of the king's illness, the mood in the town must have been tense: "couriers were not allowed to carry out their post without an official attestation; everyone was speaking of the change in rulers, as if it had already occurred."[48] Measures were also taken in anticipation of civic unrest. The Queen Mother had isolated herself with her other children and commanded the city officials to provide her with "a list of foreigners lodged in each quarter of the town, along with an inventory of their arms," and she required "all noblemen following the court to present a list of their domestic servants and others in their entourage."[49] Rumors were spreading that numerous soldiers had entered the town in order to supervise prisoners taken captive after the king's *entrée* and held in local homes. Two weeks after taking to his bed in mid-November, Francis succumbed to his illness,

---

[45] For a full description of the entry, including preparations and participants, see *L'Entrée du Roy et de la Royne en la ville d'Orléans, faicte le dixhuictiesme jour d'Octobre. Lan mil cinq cens soixante* (Orléans: Eloy Gibier, 1560).

[46] *Discours contenant toutes les choses notables, qui sont advenues en France, depuis le commencement de la maladie du feu Roy Francoys second, jusques au Roy Charles qui regne à présent* (Lyon: Benoist Rigaud, 1561): "Le seiziesme de Novembre, Mil cinq cens soixante, [...]. Apres disner il eust frisson, & sentoit douleur à la teste au dernier de l'oreille senestre, du costé ou il avoit des-long temps une fistule. Se myt au lict avec une fievre & par quelques jours suyvans distilla de ceste partie quelque humeur," A1v.

[47] "[...] lors augmenta la fievre avec les douleurs, & grandes inquietudes & resveries," A1v.

[48] "L'on ne permettoit à aucun corrier aller poste sans bulletin, chascun faisoit le discours de mutation de regne, comme s'il fust ja advenu," A2r.

[49] "La Royne mere fit faire commandement aux quaterniers à chascun quartier de ville apporter dans le lendemain le nom & surnom de tous les estrangiers logez ausdictz quartiers, & denombrement de leurs armes. Fut aussi cryé que tous Seigneurs estans à la suite de la court, eussent aussi à rendre au Prevost de l'hostel, le rolle de leurs domestiques & autres qui sont à leur suite [...]," A2v-A3r.

likely a complication of a chronic ear infection.[50] The following morning, the king's body was displayed in its coffin, attended by the Dukes of Guise and Nemours, the Marshal of Saint André, the King of Navarre and his brother, the Cardinal of Bourbon (their other brother, the Prince of Condé was held among the prisoners in Orléans), as well as the Prince of la Roche-sur-Yon, who was governor of Orléans. By that time, "one took it as agreed upon by a common accord that the Queen Mother would remain regent, and in her absence, illness, or indisposition, the King of Navarre, and that all decisions would be made by a full council."[51] By the eighth, the official pageantry of the successive reign began with Charles IX attending mass, fully decked out in mourning apparel, with an entourage of the princes, noblemen, and knights, all of whom showed him reverence and paid him homage. That evening at vespers, the late king's heart was interred at the church of Sainte Croix, with the bishop of Orléans presiding and all the gentlemen and officers of the king's household attending. The final sentence of the pamphlet deals not with Francis's death, but with the first act of the newly formed council: "it had been decided in the council that all those who had come to make their case before the Estates would be forbidden from speaking about Religion, and those who wished to speak about it would be silenced."[52]

Just three weeks after Francis II's death, court poet François Habert published *La Consolation du peuple Gauloys, griefvement desolé, pour le trespas du Roy François II*, a commemorative pamphlet containing a four-page poem addressed to the king's subjects, followed by five shorter poems, epitaphs aimed at assuaging their grief, inspiring hope for the future, and reminding the reader that none can escape death. This work clearly was modeled after two previously published poems. The first, a pastoral eclogue written in celebration of the marriage between Phillip II of Spain and Princess Elisabeth of France, consists of a 14-page dialogue between two shepherds, Janot and Herbat (a thinly veiled anagram of the

---

[50] For a retrospective account of the evolution of Francis's illness and death, see Gouteyron, Salf, and Faugère, "La mort de François II. Conséquence de l'évolution d'une otite moyenne chronique," *Histoire des sciences médicales* (1990): 49–54.

[51] "On tient pour resolu que par accord faict la mere Royne demeure regente, & en son absence, maladie, ou occupation, le Roy de Navarre: & que aucune chose ne delibera sinon en plein conseil," A3v.

[52] "L'on à arresté au conseil qu'on fera deffence à ceulx qui sont venuz pour faire remonstrance aux Estatz, de ne parler du faict de la Religion, & ou ilz en voudroyent parler on leur imposera silence," A4v.

author's last name Habert), who rejoice in the marriage and peace accord. The second, a poem commemorating Henry II's death, is also written in the form of a dialogue, this time between the author and the French people. The author observes the French people's sadness, a marked change in light of their recent joy after the peace accord and marriage, and reminds his readers of two factors that should assuage their grief: first, the promise of eternal life through Christ, and second, the promise of continuity through his son, Francis (B2v). Habert's *Consolation of the Gallic People* was likely a hasty composition, designed using the same bibliographic *mise en page* as the two printed in 1559: two quarto quires (A-B⁴) with poems and dedications of varying lengths that fill up the available space. Compared to the first two pamphlets, in which the poet praises Henry II for pages at a time, here, only the first ten lines speak directly about Francis:

> I am rather certain, oh miserable people,
> That you justly and lamentably grieve
> For Francis the second, whose reign over Gaul
> Should have lasted another thirty years,
> But seeing that cruel and inhuman Atropos
> Deprived him of his human life
> In the flower of his youth, and during the Peace
> With which he tamed that significant discord,
> Which had subsumed both Spain and France,
> And caused so many people great suffering.[53]

Apart from these generic lines, which in fact praise Henry II's Peace of Cateau-Cambrésis, rather than anything Francis achieved himself, the remainder of the poem reminds the French people that the king's death was God's will. Fortunately, however, the French never remain without a king, for "Of the defunct King Henry, his lineage was such that / Despite death he will be immortal."[54] It is thus in Charles that the people should place their hope and find their happiness. These pamphlets effectively

[53] See Habert's *La Consolation du people Gauloys...* for the original French: "Je suis assez certain, ô peuple miserable, / Qu'à juste occasion tu fais dueil lamentable / Pour François le second, qui au regne Gauloys / Encor' plus de trente ans devoit imposer loix, / Veu que par Atropos cruelle & inhumaine / Il a esté prive de ceste vie humaine / En sa fleur de jeunesse, & au cours de la Paix / Qui avoit subjugué tous les discords espais / Qui souloient émouvoir & l'Espagne & la France, / Et tant de peuple humain tenir en grand souffrance," A3r.

[54] "Du Roy deffunct Henry le lignage est bien tel / Qu'en despit de la Mort il sera immortel," A4r.

accomplish a goal identified over 450 years later in the theme song of the *Reign* television show. In other words, these contemporary pamphlets offer Francis's aggrieved subjects "something to hold on to." By recounting Francis's final days and calling attention to the diverging interests of the king's body physical—the narrative of his illness and death—and the king's body political—the sequence of decisions made to protect the office of the king—the readers are able to "feel" the story of this transitional moment. While the king's physical presence is human and ephemeral, successively reiterated by each man who held the office, his political presence is sacred and eternal, its continuity reinforced by rites and traditions applied to each successor. Habert's poetic eulogy accomplishes much the same goal as does Hénault's play. Despite the thematic content that their titles announce, neither work reincarnates the particular narrative of Francis II. Rather, both works point to the brevity of his reign, to his potential cut short, and most of all, to the importance of ensuring the royal succession. These works remind their readers that France is never without a king and that hope may be found in the permanence of the office. Toby Regbo's dramatic reincarnation of Francis II allows today's viewers to imagine his unfulfilled potential, albeit by rewriting and distorting much of the historical record. The actor and his storylines flesh out the king's physical body and remind us that he was a living, breathing person, a teenager who married an infamous beauty and certainly experienced some measure of the emotional turmoil alluded to in the CW television show. Perhaps this most recent reincarnation will draw renewed interest to the study of Francis II, to his birth, youth, education, succession, and brief reign. In the meantime, we do have more to remember Francis II than Alain Rémond suggests. In the basilica cathedral of Saint Denis, just north of Paris, a single marble column has been placed in an out-of-the-way corner, behind a ticket booth and roped off to render access difficult. On the base of this column reads a Latin inscription:

> To God, the most good and most great, and to the eternal memory of Francis II, King of the Franks, Charles the Ninth, successor to his kingdom, through the urging of our mother, the Queen Catherine, we took care to have this column erected, in the year of our salvation, 1562.[55]

[55] Thanks to my colleague, Kenneth Widgren, for translating the original Latin inscription, which reads: "Deo. Opt. Max. et perenni memoriae Francisci II Franc regis, carolus nonus eius in regno successor suadente regina matre Catarina hanc columnam erigi curavit anno salvatis M.D.LXII."

Originally intended as a tomb to Francis II's heart, an urn at the pinnacle of this monument was destroyed following the French Revolution. But nonetheless, with this single, unobtrusive marble column, his mother and brother left us with a tangible reminder of Francis's life and reign.

BIBLIOGRAPHY

PRIMARY SOURCES

Discours contenant toutes les choses notables, qui sont adfvenues en France, dpeuis le commencement de la maladie du feu Roy Francoys second, jusques au Roy Charles qui regne à present. Lyon: Benoist Rigaud, 1561. Available at http://reader. digitale-sammlungen.de/resolve/display/bsb10178171.html

L'Entrée du Roy et de la Royne en la ville d'Orléans, faicte le dixhuictiesme jour d'Octobre. Lan mil cinq cens soixante. Orléans: Eloy Gibier, 1560. Bibliothèque nationale de France réserve: 8-LB32-22.

Gilles, Nicole. *Le Second Volume des Annales et Croniques de France, augmentees, en la fin dudict volume, d'aucuns faictz dignes de memoire, des feuz Roys Henry, deuxiesme, Francoys, deuxiesme, & Charles, IX. du nom, jusques en l'an mil cinq cens soixante & deux*. Paris: Gabriel Buon, 1562.

Habert, François, de Berry. *Egloque Pastorale sur l'union nuptialle de treshault, & trespuissant Seigneur, Philippes, Roy d'Hespagne, & de tresexcellente, & tresvertueuse Princesse, ma dame Elisabeth, premiere fille du Roy Henry II*. Paris: Pour Jean Moreau, chez la veufve Nicolas Buffet, 1559.

———. *Les Regrets et tristes lamentations sur le trespas du Treschrestien Roy Henry II, composé en forme de Dialogue, par François Habert, de Berry*. Paris: Pour Jean Moreau, chez la veufve N. Buffet, 1559.

———. *La Consolation du peuple Gauloys, griefvement desolé, pour le trespas du Roy Francois II. Avec les Epitaphes dudict Seigneur*. Paris: Pour Jean Moreau, chez la veufve Nicolas Buffet, 1561.

Hénault, Charles-Jean-François. *François II, roi de France. En cinq actes*. S.l.: s.n., 1747.

———. *Nouvel abrégé chronologique de l'histoire de France*. Paris: Prault père, 1744.

Régnier de la Planche, Louis. *Histoire de l'Estat de France, tant de la Republique que de la Religion: sous le regne de François II*. S.l.: s.n., 1576.

SECONDARY SOURCES

Barbiche, Bernard. *Les Institutions de la monarchie française à l'époque moderne*. Paris: Presses universitaires de France, 1999.

Benedict, Philip. *Graphic History. The Wars, Massacres and Troubles of Tortorel and Perrissin*. Geneva: Droz, 2007.

Bourdeille, Pierre de, abbé de Brantôme. *Recueil des Dames, poésies et tombeaux.* Edited by Étienne Vaucheret. Paris: Gallimard, 1991.

Bricker, Tierney. "All Hail *Reign's* Fashion! The CW Hit's Costume Designer Breaks Down Mary and Her Ladies-in-Waiting's Looks." *E! News.* 22 November 2013. Available at https://www.eonline.com/uk/news/484037/all-hail-reign-s-fashion-the-cw-hit-s-costume-designer-breaks-down-mary-and-her-ladies-in-waiting-s-looks

"The CW to Develop Mary Queen of Scots Teen Drama *Reign*." *Broadway World.* 24 October 2012. Available at https://www.broadwayworld.com/bwwtv/article/The-CW-to-Develop-Mary-Queen-of-Scots-Teen-Drama-REIGN-20121024

Daussy, Hugues. *Le Parti Huguenot: Chronique d'une désillusion (1557–1572).* Geneva: Droz, 2014.

Dictionnaire du Moyen Français, version 2015 (DMF 2015). ATILF – CNRS & Université de Lorraine. Available at http://www.atilf.fr/dmf

Fraser, Antonia. *Mary Queen of Scots.* New York: Delta, 1993.

Gouteyron, J.F., E. Salf, and J. M. Faugère. "La mort de François II. Conséquence de l'évolution d'une otite moyenne chronique." *Histoire des sciences médicales* (1990): 49–54.

Guy, John. *Queen of Scots. The True Life of Mary Stuart.* Boston: Houghton Mifflin, 2004.

Hénault, Charles-Jean-François. *François II, roi de France.* Edited by Thomas Wynn. London: Modern Humanities Research Association, 2004.

Kingdon, Robert. *Geneva and the Coming of the Wars of Religion in France, 1555–1563.* Geneva: Droz, 1956.

The Lumineers. "Scotland." *Genuis.* Accessed March 15, 2018. https://genius.com/The-lumineers-scotland-lyrics

Mentzer, Raymond A. and Andrew Spicer, ed. *Society and Culture in the Huguenot World 1559–1685.* New York: Cambridge University Press, 2002.

Potiquet, Albert. *La Maladie et la mort de François II Roi de France.* Paris: Rueff et Cie, 1893.

Reign. Seasons 1–3. Created by Stephanie SenGupta and Laurie McCarthy. CW Network, 2013–2016.

"*Reign*: Season Four Ratings," *TV Series Finale.* 12 June 2017. Available at https://tvseriesfinale.com/tv-show/reign-season-four-ratings/

Rémond, Alain. "Un roi aux oubliettes." *Historia* 772 (April 2011): 98.

Rourke, Josie. *Mary Queen of Scots.* 2018; Los Angeles: Focus Features, 2019. DVD.

Universal Short Title Catalog, version 2018. University of Saint Andrews. Available at http://ustc.ac.uk/index.php

Wilkinson, Alexander S. *Mary Queen of Scots and French Public Opinion.* New York: Palgrave Macmillan, 2004.

CHAPTER 13

Daenerys Targaryen as Queen Elizabeth I's Spiritual Daughter

Estelle Paranque

Emilia Clarke, the actress who plays the role of Daenerys Targaryen, explained in an interview she gave to Vanity Fair in 2015 that "Cate Blanchett in *Elizabeth*, that was something I watched a lot while preparing for Season 1 [of Game of Thrones]."[1] This is not surprising that Clarke would seek inspiration from Blanchett's Elizabeth as the two women, Daenerys and Elizabeth I of England, have so much in common. As a powerful queen who refused to marry and yet enjoyed a long and successful reign, Elizabeth I has been a source of fascination for centuries. From Camden's chronicles and Edmund Spenser's *Faerie Queene* in the early modern period to Carole Levin's *The Heart and Stomach of a King* and Shekhar Kapur's movies in recent decades, historians, scholars, poets,

---

[1] https://www.vanityfair.com/hollywood/2015/10/game-of-thrones-cate-blanchett-inspired-emilia-clarke. Last Accessed on December 9, 2018. Also see on the two women: http://history-behind-game-of-thrones.com/tudors/daenerys-as-elizabeth-i. Last accessed on November 7, 2018. And http://www.themarysue.com/daenerys-targaryen/. Last accessed on November 7, 2018.

E. Paranque (✉)
New College of the Humanities, London, UK

© The Author(s) 2019   241
E. Paranque (ed.), *Remembering Queens and Kings of Early Modern England and France*, Queenship and Power,
https://doi.org/10.1007/978-3-030-22344-1_13

dramatists, modern screenwriters, and producers have scrutinized Elizabeth's actions, portraits, prayers, and rhetoric.[2]

For scholars, students, and a more general audience, Elizabeth continues to live in our imagination today, as evidenced in her continuing representations in popular culture.[3] Ultimately, she is remembered through Camden's claim that she said: "To conclude, I am already bound unto an husband, which is the kingdom of England, and that may suffice you."[4] In the centuries following Elizabeth's death, novels, plays, films, and television shows have revisited the life and reign of the last Tudor queen.[5] Reminding us of the influence of popular culture on our understanding of history, Patrick Collinson points out:

> we should not confine our attention to the verdicts of professional historians. Many Victorian and post-Victorian readers learned their Elizabethan history not from James Anthony Froude, nor dare I say it on this occasion, Mandell Creighton, but from that dark Gothic novel by Walter Scott, *Kenilworth*.[6]

Even today, both academic and popular histories continue to contribute to our understanding of Elizabeth's legacy and reputation. But there is more to Elizabeth than her mere reputation—notably, how the last Tudor

---

[2] Camden, *Annales*; Michael Dobson and Nicola J. Watson, *England's Elizabeth: an Afterlife in Fame and Fantasy* (Oxford: Oxford University Press, 2002); Thomas Betteridge, "A queen for all seasons: Elizabeth I on film," in *The Myth of Elizabeth*, ed. Susan Doran and Thomas S. Freeman (Basingstoke: Palgrave Macmillan, 2003), 242–259. See also Jo Eldridge Carney, *Fairy Tale Queens: Representations of Early Modern Queenship* (New York: Palgrave Macmillan, 2012).

[3] See Sue Parrill and William B. Robison, *The Tudors on Film and Television* (Jefferson, North Carolina and London: McFarland & Company, Inc., Publishers, 2013); William B. Robison (ed.), *History, Fiction, and the Tudors: Sex, Politics, Power, and Artistic License in the Showtime Television Series* (New York: Palgrave Macmillan, 2016) and Aidan Norrie, "A Man? A woman? A lesbian? A whore?: Queen Elizabeth I and the Cinematic Subversion of Gender," in *Premodern Rulers and Postmodern Viewers: Gender, Sex, and Power in Popular Culture*, ed. Janice North, Karl C. Alvestad, and Elena Woodacre (New York: Palgrave Macmillan, 2018), 319–340.

[4] Elizabeth's speech on February 10, 1559, William Camden, *Annales: The True and Royal History of the Famous Empress Elizabeth* (London: B. Fisher, 1625), STC 4497, 27.

[5] See Elizabeth H. Hageman and Katherine Conway (eds.), *Resurrecting Elizabeth I in Seventeenth-Century England* (Cranbury: Rosemont Publishing & Printing Corp, 2007).

[6] Patrick Collinson, "Elizabeth I and the verdicts of history," *Historical Research*, 76, 194 (2003): 469–491, 470.

monarch has influenced our modern conception of female rule, particularly regarding the complex ways in which a woman can wield political power in a largely patriarchal world.

In popular culture, fascination with female rule has been evident most recently in the widely beloved *Game of Thrones*, a television show created by American producers and writers that to date is entering its eighth and final season. *Game of Thrones*, adapted from the best-selling fantasy novels by George R.R. Martin, has scored a massive audience and garnered the interest of scholars as well as the devoted enthusiasm of a general audience. More and more historians working on Royal Studies continue to pay attention to this television phenomenon.[7] It is not surprising, then, to find some correlations between one of the show's central characters and Elizabeth, given how deeply the Tudor queen is engrained in American memory and history.

As Michael Dobson and Nicola Watson explain there is "evidence of familiar-looking claims to Elizabethan cultural roots."[8] Drawing parallels between such a well-known historical figure as Gloriana and a fictional character in a popular television show reveals the cultural fascination with Elizabeth in particular and female rule in general. In *Game of Thrones*, several central female characters have increasingly gained power as the series has progressed. Despite some criticism regarding the roles of women in the TV show, many of them are resilient, independent, politically active, and influential in spite of considerable resistance to their power.[9] These qualities are shared with the last Tudor queen who faced—and overcame—tumultuous obstacles before and during her reign.

This chapter argues that in many ways, Daenerys can be seen as Elizabeth's spiritual daughter. This is not just a matter of comparing any two strong female rulers, for indeed, they share several remarkable similarities: in their speeches given to their troops, in their relations to their councilors, in their attitudes toward their subjects, in their views on marriage, and in the way they were treated as princesses and as queens. I am not claiming that Daenerys is intended to be seen as a direct counterpart

---

[7] Brian A. Palvac (ed.), *Game of Thrones versus History* (Hoboken: Wiley Blackwell, 2017) and Lisa Benz and Zita Rohr (eds.), *Tales of Ice and Fire: Queenship, Female Agency, and the Role of Advice in Game of Thrones* (forthcoming).

[8] Dobson and Watson, *England's Elizabeth*, 268.

[9] On the discussion regarding feminism and misogyny in *Game of Thrones*, see Sonam Rai, *Women With(out) Dragons: A Critical Analysis of the Representation of Women in Game of Thrones* (Unpublished MA Dissertation, St Joseph College, 2017).

to Elizabeth, but rather, that she reflects the spirit and example of the last Tudor queen in her actual rule. Finally, I examine how this particular representation of female power engages with our own modern perception of female rule and its intersection with female sexuality. More than four centuries later we are still learning from a queen who continues to embody female queenship and power.

DAENERYS IN THE FOOTSTEPS OF ELIZABETH: LAST OF THEIR DYNASTY, FIGHT FOR LEGITIMACY, AND SIBLINGS RELATIONSHIPS

Both Daenerys and Elizabeth are last of their dynasty. Daenerys has two elder brothers, Raegen and Viserys. Raegen died before their father. At the death of their father, who was named the Mad King, Daenerys and her brother had to flee and the throne was taken over by the Barratheon Dynasty, but Viserys and Daenerys never forgot their birth rights and claim to the throne. Daenerys is therefore like Elizabeth: third in line.

However, the only reason Elizabeth was third in line was because male rulers were legally preferred to female ones.[10] Her younger brother Edward VI of England reigned from 1547 to 1553, followed by their eldest sister Mary I of England who reigned until her death in 1558. Elizabeth then accessed the throne. Prior to her accession, Elizabeth did not have to flee as Daenerys did, but she was declared a bastard by her father Henry VIII at the age of three and then put in line of succession but not legitimate. When Edward accessed the throne, he did try to remove his sisters from the succession and for nine days Lady Jane Grey was crowned Queen of England.[11] Mary I of England then marched to London as John Dudley, Duke of Northumberland's army drifted away and reconquered the throne. Elizabeth joined her half-sister in London after Mary was declared queen of England.

This parallel leads to the more striking and crucial obstacle for both queens: challenges to their legitimacy. Catholics inside and outside the borders of England did not recognize Elizabeth's rights to the English throne as they did not recognize the marriage between Henry VIII and

---

[10] Legal rule that was changed in 2012.

[11] An explanation on how Edward proceeded can be found in Thomas Fuller, *The Church History of Britain, from the birth of Jesus Christ until the year M.DC.XLVIII*, ed. J. S. Brewer, vol. 4 (Oxford: Oxford University Press, 1845), 138–140.

Anne Boleyn. Similarly, although Daenerys has supporters, she also has many enemies in Westeros who do not recognize her as the legitimate ruler of Westeros.

The fight for legitimacy and recognition marked Elizabeth's reign and is echoed in Daenerys's pursuit to claim the Iron Throne. In series one, episode seven, Daenerys is almost poisoned and further assassination attempts occur in series two, episode ten, and in series three episodes one and eight—strong echoes of the many Catholic plots that Elizabeth had to face during her reign, including the Northern Rebellion in 1569, the Ridolfi Plot in 1571, and the Babington plot in 1586. Elizabeth too feared to be poisoned as the conspirators discussed the ways in which they should kill the English queen.[12] These plots and the fear of being poisoned emphasize even further the two queens' struggle to obtain power and to maintain it.

Furthermore, both queens suffered difficult relationships with their surviving siblings. Daenerys refers to her oldest brother, Raegan, as a good brother in series one—which reminds us of Elizabeth's rather benevolent relationship that she had had growing up with her younger brother Edward, especially as they shared a common education.[13] But both women experienced contentious relationships with their other siblings that complicated their assumption of power.

At one point, Daenerys's brother Viserys compares his sister to cattle and in series one, episode one, he warns his sister: "We go home with an army. With Khal Drogo's army. I would let his whole tribe fuck you – all forty thousand men – and their horses too if that's what it took." There are obviously no such appalling statements recorded between Mary and Elizabeth. However, we cannot overlook the fact that Mary's relationship with her younger sister was often marked by jealousy and by frustration over Elizabeth's refusal to conform to Catholicism. In 1554, Mary sent her younger sister to the Tower of London and in fact, Elizabeth "was often in peril in her sister's reign."[14]

---

[12] Carolly Erickson, *The First Elizabeth* (New York: St. Martin's Griffin, 1983), 362–363. Also see Carole Levin, *The Reign of Elizabeth I* (New York: Palgrave, 2002) and Jo Eldridge Carney, "Poisoning Queens in Early Modern Fact and Fiction," in *Scholars and Poets Talk About Queens*, eds. Carole Levin and associate editor Christine Stewart-Nunez (New York: Palgrave Macmillan, 2015), 269–284.

[13] See Levin, *The Reign of Elizabeth I*, 8 and on Elizabeth's years as a princess see: David Starkey, *Elizabeth: Apprenticeship* (London: Chatto and Windus, 2000).

[14] Carole Levin, *The Heart and Stomach of a King: Elizabeth I and the Politics of Sex and Power* (Philadelphia: Pennsylvania University Press, 1998, second edition 2013), 8.

A day before being sent to the Tower of London, Elizabeth wrote to Mary. Instead of beginning her letter with a common opening such as "Your good Majesty" or "Madam my good sister," she began with an interesting sentence: "If any ever did try this old saying that a king's word was more than another man's oath, I most humbly beseech your Majesty to verify it in me."[15] This opening allowed the princess to flatter the queen as well as demonstrating her humility and respect toward her. She did not put herself at the same level of the queen and instead showed her vulnerability. Elizabeth signed her letter, submitting to the queen: "Your Highness' most faithful subject that hath been from the beginning and will be to my end."[16]

Daenerys also first submitted to her brother's will and accepted all his requests and demands. But in spite of their allegiance to their older siblings, both queens were ultimately betrayed by them, and were eventually made aware that they could not rely on their blood relatives to be protected and loved.

Loved Queens

This notion of love is one that has dominated Elizabeth's reign. Ilona Bell argues "the rhetoric of love was also traditional political discourse, regularly used by male monarchs to win the support of their subjects."[17] The emphasis on love was also used by Elizabeth I of England to represent herself as both mother and father of her country.[18] On November 30, 1601, Elizabeth declared in her Golden Speech:

> I do assure you there is no prince that loveth his subjects better, or whose love can countervail our love. There is no jewel, be it of never so rich a price, which I set before this jewel—I mean your loves. [...] this I count the glory of my crown: that I have reigned with your loves.[19]

[15] Elizabeth to Queen Mary I, March, 17, 1554, TNA, PRO SP 11/4/3.

[16] Elizabeth to Queen Mary I, March, 17, 1554.

[17] Ilona Bell, *Elizabeth I: The Voice of a Monarch* (New York: Palgrave Macmillan, 2010), xiii.

[18] Estelle Paranque, "Royal Representations Through the Father and the Warrior Figures," in *History of Monarchy*, eds. Elena Woodacre et al. (London: Routledge, 2019), 314–329.

[19] Elizabeth's Golden Speech, November 30, 1601, versions 1, in Leah Marcus, Janel Mueller, and Mary Beth Rose (eds.), *Elizabeth I: Collected Works* (Chicago: Chicago University Press, 2000), 337.

Both Elizabeth and Daenerys repeatedly fashion themselves as queens who base their rule on love of their people, and they deliberately equate the care of their subjects with maternal love.

In *Game of Thrones*, Daenerys frees slaves from their masters in the city of Yunkai and in series three, episode ten, the liberated people praise her and call her "mhysa" which means "mother" in their native language. She is beloved by her people that she has freed from slavery and they swear loyalty to her. While there is no such direct parallel with Elizabeth, she too was known as mother of her country.[20] In 1625, William Camden, one of Elizabeth's contemporaries, printed his own version of Elizabeth's 1559 speech that she gave in front of the Commons. In his version, Elizabeth supposedly asserted, "that I have no children: for every one of you, and as many as are English, are my children and kinsfolks."[21]

In emphasizing her self-representation as a mother figure in *Game of Thrones*, Daenerys is a direct embodiment of Elizabeth. In series one, one of Daenerys's advisers, Jorah Mormont, tells her that she will be a great queen because her people will not fear her but will love her. In series one, episode six, in a scene where Daenerys is forced to eat a horse's heart according to the customs of the Dothrakis, her brother fears that "they love her."

Elizabeth also learned from experience that being a loving queen was paramount in order to rule a country. Throughout her reign, she made sure to show important bonds with her people. In 1593, while given her speech at the closing parliament, Elizabeth insisted:

> This kingdom hath had many noble and victorious princes. I will not compare with any of them in wisdom, fortitude, and other virtues; but (saving the duty of a child that is not to compare with her father) in love, care, sincerity, and justice, I will compare with any prince that ever you had or ever shall have.[22]

---

[20] See Helen Hackett, *Virgin Mother, Maiden Queen: Elizabeth I and the Cult of the Virgin Mary* (London: Palgrave, 1994) and Christine Coch, "'Mother of my Contreye': Elizabeth I and Tudor Constructions of Motherhood," *English Literary Renaissance* 26/3 (1996): 423–50.

[21] Camden, *Annales*, 27.

[22] Elizabeth's Speech at the closing of parliament, April 10, 1593, in *Elizabeth I: Collected Works*, 329.

Love and justice were two ruling pillars for Elizabeth and this is echoed repeatedly in how Daenerys rules over her people. Similarly, both queens understood the importance of surrounding themselves with advisors who were trustworthy and loyal.

QUEENS AND MARRIAGE: COUNSEL AND DECISION

Elizabeth and Daenerys are successful monarchs in large part because of the devotion that they inspire. Both queens have major political advisers who have much in common. This chapter does not claim that the fictional characters of the TV show and the historical characters are the same but rather that some parallels can be drawn. For once, both Daenerys and Elizabeth have four advisers each.

From series one, Daenerys is supported by Jorah Mormont, who is at first a spy plotting against her and who then changes his mind and allegiance; he decides to devote his life to her and to ensure her safety. Mormont has a network of spies in Westeros and knows well Daenerys's enemies. In many ways, he has some common points with Elizabeth's Francis Walsingham. One striking major difference that cannot be overlooked is the fact that Mormont is madly in love with Daenerys whereas there is no record of such romantic feelings regarding Walsingham and the Tudor queen. However, both men are deeply committed to the queen's welfare and security.

Daenerys is also surrounded by Barristan Selmy and Dario Naharis from series two to six. Selmy is a well-known warrior figure in Westeros and knew Daenerys's father. He swore to protect him but during the war he turned his back on him because of his madness and instead joined the king's enemies. Once he realized that the new king of Westeros, Joffrey Baratheon, was a cruel and vindictive king, he decided to leave Westeros to serve Daenerys. In many ways, his steady counsel reminds us of William Cecil, Lord Burghley. While Selmy is more of a warrior than Cecil, both men are completely devoted to their queens and become close and wise counselors.

Daario is in no doubt a cheekier version of Elizabeth's Robert Dudley, Earl of Leicester. Daario becomes Daenerys's lover but ultimately fails to marry her (series six, episode ten)—echoing greatly Elizabeth's complicated and tumultuous relationship with Dudley.[23] In the end, Daenerys

---

[23] On Elizabeth's relationship with Leicester, see Susan Doran, *Monarchy and Matrimony: The Courtship of Elizabeth* (London and New York: Routledge, 1996), 40–72; Elizabeth

renounces to her love and attraction for Daario in order to rule on her own—reminding the audience of a similar choice that Elizabeth made concerning Dudley. The last adviser, Robert Cecil, reminds us of Tyrion Lannister, Daenerys's hand of the queen; Tyrion insists on the importance of the succession, as Robert Cecil did with Elizabeth toward the end of her reign.[24]

During her lifetime, Elizabeth was pressured to marry in order to ensure the succession. This pressure is perhaps less intense with Daenerys but interesting parallels can be drawn between the situations of the two women. In series seven, episode six, Tyrion and Daenerys discuss her succession and she tells him, "You have been talking about my death quite a bit haven't you? Is this one of the items you discuss with your brothers and kings?" She then leaves the room without giving a firm answer about her marital intentions. This discussion with her adviser echoes Elizabeth's speech to the parliament in 1563 where she declared: "the two petitions that you presented me, expressed in many words, contained in sum as of your cares the greatest: my marriage and my successor, of which two I think best the last be touched, and of the other a silent thought may serve."[25]

Elizabeth never married. However, many marriage negotiations took place when she was a princess and a queen.[26] From Swedish kings to their French counterparts, Elizabeth was the most famous single woman in Europe.[27] But both Elizabeth and Daenerys resist marriage; they both experienced traumatic events that perhaps contributed to their reluctance, and they both were unwilling to compromise their political power by sharing it with a consort.

During series one, Daenerys's brother Vyserys sells her to the Dothrakis. She is forced to marry Khal Drogo with whom she ultimately falls in love. However, in the beginning the relationship is violent; there is even a scene where she is raped by Drogo. At the end of series one, Drogo is poisoned by a witch and dies. Daenerys leaves the Dothrakis with her adviser Jorah Mormont and they meet Barristan Selmy. Later on, after many perils, she and her advisers arrive in a city called Meereen. There, she is advised to

Jenkins, *Elizabeth and Leicester* (London: Phoenix Press, 2003) and Sarah Gristwood, *Elizabeth and Leicester* (London: Bantam, 2017).

[24] See John Guy, *Elizabeth: The Forgotten Years* (New York: Penguin, 2016).

[25] Elizabeth's answer to the Lords' petition that she marry, April 10, 1563, delivered by Lord Keeper Nicholas Bacon, *Elizabeth I: Collected Works*, 79.

[26] See Doran, *Monarchy and Matrimony*.

[27] On the French and Elizabeth, see Paranque, *Elizabeth I of England Through Valois Eyes*.

marry an important noble of the city in order to bring peace to the people. She eventually agrees and weds Hizdahr zo Loraq. Their union remains a political one and we do not see them engage in any form of intimacy. He dies shortly after their union during a riot.

After his death, Daenerys seems more confident and decides to be completely in charge of her people and of her private life; she insists that she alone should be the one to choose any future husband. When in series six episode ten Daario asks to marry her, she refuses, explaining that she needs "to be a queen before being a woman." While Elizabeth never expressed this so bluntly, she asserted "I did send them answer by my Council I would marry, although of mine own disposition I was not inclined thereunto. But that as not accepted nor credited, although spoken by their prince."[28] Ultimately, Elizabeth also determined that her role as queen should supersede all other roles.

FEMALE KINGS: DEMONSTRATION OF POWER

By series six, Daenerys is no longer married and appears as a strong female ruler. While many studies and portrayals of Elizabeth have been focused on her gender, many historians, especially Carole Levin, agree that in remaining single, she was both queen and king of England.[29] Both queens are aware of the symbolic representation of their queenship. At the end of series one, when Khal Drogo dies, Daenerys buries him in fire and puts herself with three dragon eggs in the fire. When the fire burns out, she is left with three baby dragons and becomes known as the Mother of Dragons. Similarly, one of Elizabeth's emblems is the phoenix. In Greek mythology, the phoenix is a long-lived bird that is cyclically regenerated or reborn. It is associated with the sun and a phoenix obtains a new life by arising from the ashes of its predecessor.[30] In this scene with Daenerys and the birth of her dragons, we have a reminder of Elizabeth's Phoenix. Furthermore, Elizabeth's coat of arms includes both a lion and a dragon, further emphasizing the parallels between the two women.

[28] Elizabeth's Speech to a joint delegation of Lords and Commons, November 5, 1566, in *Elizabeth I: Collected Works*, 95.

[29] Levin, *The Heart and Stomach of a King*, 121–148.

[30] More on this portrait can be found on the National Portrait Gallery's website: https://www.npg.org.uk/research/programmes/making-art-in-tudor-britain/the-phoenix-and-the-pelican-two-portraits-of-elizabeth-i-c.1575.php. Last accessed on November 9, 2018.

Both queens are repeatedly called upon to demonstrate their resolution and to act as powerful monarch regardless of gender. The Tudor queen is known for claiming "I will have but one mistress here, and no master"—in series three episode four, Daenerys buys an army of unsullied soldiers in exchange for her strongest dragon.[31] When the master experiences difficulty in taming the dragon, and asks the queen why her dragon does not come down, she answers "a dragon is a not a slave" and orders the soldiers to slay any masters and to free slaves. The master screams "I am your Master" and she answers "Drakarys"—which orders her dragon to exterminate him. Her dragon is an extension of herself and as such, this scene could be considered as a modern version of Elizabeth's well-known claim.

Perhaps more strikingly, series six of *Game of Thrones* depicts different scenes that recall England's victory over the Spanish Armada. In 1588, England faced the most serious crisis of the reign with the Spanish Armada and Elizabeth is known for asserting her royal authority in front of her army with the now-famous words: "I know I have the body but of a weak and feeble woman but I have the heart and stomach of a king, and of a king of England too."[32] In series six, episode six, Daenerys gives a speech in front of the Dothrakis that she has just reconquered. She asks them to follow her to Westeros—a land that no Dothraki has ever visited. She claims that it is the conquest of a lifetime and that no Khal, which means leader in Dothrakis language, has ever achieved such a great endeavor. She ends her speech with "But I am no Khal," implying that being a Queen was much more powerful than being a male ruler and embodying as well her female kingship. In addition, in episode nine of the same season, there is a scene that reproduces and modernizes the victory of England over the Armada.

Meereen, the land conquered by Daenerys in season five, is besieged by the masters who aim to reconquer the city to enslave the people Daenerys has freed. When they discuss Daenerys's surrender, the masters, who want to regain control of Meereen, become arrogant and insult her, to which she replies: "You have misunderstood. We are discussing your surrender." At this moment, her largest and strongest dragon sits next to her. She insists "my reign has just begun." She and her dragon both fly away, joining the two other dragons and burning the masters' fleets. This powerful

---

[31] Levin explains the context in which Elizabeth uttered those words and how cautious we have to be regarding the source that claims the queen said that, see Levin, *Heart and Stomach of a King*, 47.

[32] Elizabeth's Armada Speech to the Troops at Tilbury, August, 9, 1588, in *Elizabeth I: Collected Works*, 326.

scene demonstrates Daenerys' strength and directly reminding the audience of Elizabeth I and her victory over the Spanish Armada in 1588.

Both women frequently have to overcome misogynistic preconceptions. Elizabeth's authority was challenged by her male counterparts, including Philip II of Spain and ambassadors who told Henry III of France that Elizabeth "was only a woman."[33] Her royal authority was also challenged by pamphleteers, by Catholic missionaries and even by her cousin, Mary Stuart who wrote to Philip II of Spain in 1565 referring to England and asking for help to protect the "pretentions we may have elsewhere."[34] Mary had been using the English royal coat of arms since she was a princess—emphasizing her rights to the English crown.

Daenerys's authority is also undermined and questioned. In series six, episode nine, Daenerys receives at her court another female ruler from the Iron Lands. They discuss the difficulties they have to face as women and how men constantly challenge their legitimacy. At times, even Daenerys's counsel\ors overstep. In series three, episode three, during the negotiations between the queen and a slave master over a powerful army, The Unsullied, Selmy and Mormont question Daenerys's decision when she agrees to trade the army for her biggest dragon. With anger, she takes them apart and warns them: "You are both here to advise me, I value your advice but if you ever question me in front of strangers again you will be advising someone else." Yet, this does not prevent people trying to undermine her authority, often through sexualizing the female body.

WOMEN AND SEXUALITY: BREASTS, FEMININITY, AND CONTROL OF THE FEMALE BODY

From the 1580s, Elizabeth was portrayed as the Virgin Queen.[35] Daenerys, who married Drogo and gave birth to a still born child, was not a virgin. The white dresses she frequently wears echo ideals of

[33] Henry III to Mauvissière, December 12, 1580, BNF MS. Fr. 3307, fol. 28r°, "que la dicte dame royne n'étoist juste une femme." Quoted in Estelle Paranque, *Elizabeth I of England Through Valois Eyes: Power, Representation, and Diplomacy in the Reign of the Queen 1558–1588* (New York: Palgrave Macmillan, 2019), page.

[34] Queen of Scots to Philip II of Spain, September 10, 1565 in *Letters of Mary, Queen of Scots, and documents connected with her personal history*, Agnes Strickland (ed.), vol. 1, (London: Henry Colburn Publisher, 1842), 16.

[35] Susan Doran, "Why Did Elizabeth Not Marry?," in *Dissing Elizabeth: Negative Representations of Gloriana*, ed. Julia M. Walker (Durham and London: Duke University Press, 1998), 37.

purity, and yet, any suggestions of virginal chasteness are overshadowed by the sexualization of her female body. Moreover, black and white were the colors of Elizabeth I so in many ways Daenerys's white dresses remind the audience of Elizabeth.

There is no portrait of Elizabeth with bare breasts.[36] However, in *The Secret History of the most renowned Queen Elizabeth and the Earl of Essex* Elizabeth is depicted as half-naked in the frontispiece.[37] This sexualization of the female body diminishes women's roles as effective rulers by emphasizing their presumed primary function: to attract men and bear children. The dramatic objectification of her female body detracts from the queen's political authority and reminds us of the limited roles that have defined women: a virgin or a whore.

What does such sexualized representation of female power tell us about how modern audiences perceive female rule? Are we so advanced that the sexualization of the female body for powerful women is now behind us? The representation of Daenerys's character reminds us that female authority is often still subverted by a male gaze that seeks to undermine female power. Indeed, for Daenerys Targaryen, the sexualization of her body is repeatedly used in *Game of Thrones* to appeal to popular audiences. In 2015, Emilia Clarke herself expressed that she no longer wanted to have act in naked scenes if it was not totally necessary to the plot.[38]

In series one, Daenerys is represented almost entirely as an objectified female body with no rights of her own. Her first husband rapes her and her brother threatens her with rape by hundreds of men and horses. Up to series four, there are many gratuitous scenes in which Daenerys is naked and in which seduction and attraction factor enormously into her character's development—notably with Daario Naharis who will betray his close friends because of her beautiful body. In series three, episode eight, Daenerys is taking a bath with her servant. Daario arrives and reveals that he has killed his friends and partners who wanted to kill Daenerys. When she asks why he did not agree to be part of the plot organized against her,

---

[36] On Elizabeth's sexuality, see Levin, *Heart and Stomach of a King*, 65–90.

[37] *The Secret History of the Most Renowned Queen Elizabeth and the Earl of Essex*, by a Person of Quality (Cologne: Printed for Will with the Wisp, at the Sign of the Moon in the Ecliptick, 1680), Wing S2342A.

[38] http://www.digitalspy.com/tv/game-of-thrones/feature/a668633/game-of-thrones-nudity-crisis-emilia-clarke-is-saying-no-to-nudes-but-who-else-in-the-cast-wants-to-cover-up/. Last accessed on November 9, 2018.

he replies "Your beauty, it meant more to me than it did to them." She replies, "Why would I trust a man who murder his comrades?" and he answers "They ordered me to murder you." She then stands up, completely naked and vulnerable in front of him and asks him to swear his loyalty to her. He accepts. The only reason Daario Naharis gives for agreeing to serve and protect the queen is based on her physical appearance: if she had not been attractive, he presumably would not sacrifice so much to defend her.[39]

In our modern conception of queenship or female rulership, to be able to rule a woman's imperative to be beautiful comes before the need to be strong, just, intelligent, and dedicated to her people. For male rulers, the question of beauty is less sexualized. They are less judged on how attractive they are and they do not elicit supporters based upon their physical appearance. To some extent, this demonstrates how unfairly we consider female authority in our society and in our cultural expectations of women. To be successful as a ruler, a woman's power is linked to her appearance.

Will women's abilities to occupy positions of leadership ever be sufficient or will the specters of beauty, attraction, and sexualization always undermine their authority? Can women be considered as powerful rulers without concerns over their physical appearance or their ability to bear children being raised? These questions are important as they greatly determine our relation to the equitable exercise of power. More problematically, the sexualization of the female body weakens our perception of women's power and reveals our inability to respect female rulers as equal to male rulers. As Mary Beard argues "the point is simple but important: as far back as we can see in Western history there is a radical separation – real, cultural, and imaginary – between women and power."[40] Yet, women have ruled over the centuries and in our popular imagination and in one of the most successful contemporary television shows, a woman is arguably the most powerful character and ruler.

[39] On Elizabeth's relation to beauty, see Jo Eldridge Carney, *Fairy Tale Queens: Representations of Early Modern Queenship* (New York: Palgrave Macmillan, 2012), 87–116 and Anna Riehl Bertolet, *The Face of Queenship: Early Modern Representations of Elizabeth I* (New York: Palgrave Macmillan, 2010).

[40] Mary Beard, *Women and Power: A Manifesto* (London: Profile Books, 2017), 70.

CONCLUSION: "ALL MEN MUST DIE, BUT WE ARE NOT MEN"

Elizabeth's authority was not only challenged and contested because she was a Protestant monarch, but also because she was a woman ruling alone and in her own rights. *Game of Thrones'* Daenerys portrays a young queen who becomes increasingly powerful as the story unfolds. In many ways, *Game of Thrones* demonstrates a profound interest in women's power and ability to rule. In series three, episode three, Daenerys frees a slave and asks her if she will follow her into battles. She replies yes and continues, "all men must die." Daenerys answers "yes, all men must die, but we are not men." As we approach the end of the series, we can see that the women of the show are depicted as resilient, powerful, and to some extent invincible—characteristics that we can relate to Elizabeth I who had to face multiple dangers to be able to rule and who finally ruled over England for more than 44 years.

Daenerys is a modernized and romanticized version of Elizabeth I or her spiritual daughter (at least up to series seven), and while Elizabeth never left England and did not have to conquer half of the world before being able to sit on her throne, she also inspired people and represented hope and peace for many Protestants in England and in other European countries. Yet, even with the vivid historical example of the successful reign of Elizabeth I and fictional attempts to celebrate women in power, we still struggle with our complex conception of female rulers. It is time to move beyond romanticized and sexualized representations of powerful women and consider them on their merits as potential successful rulers.

BIBLIOGRAPHY

PRIMARY SOURCES

MANUSCRIPTS

BNF MS. Fr. 3307.
TNA, PRO SP 11/4/3.

PRINTED SOURCES

Baker, Richard. *The Chronicle of the Kings of England*, EX DA30.B168 1653q. Princeton University, Firestone Library.
Camden, William. *Annales: The True and Royal History of the Famous Empress Elizabeth*. London: B. Fisher, 1625.

Elizabeth I: Collected Works. Leah Marcus, Janel Mueller, and Mary Beth Rose, eds. Chicago: Chicago University Press, 2000.

Fuller, Thomas. *The Church History of Britain, from the birth of Jesus Christ until the year M.DC.XLVIII*, edited by J. S. Brewer, vol. 4. Oxford: Oxford University Press, 1845.

Letters of Mary, Queen of Scots, and documents connected with her personal history, edited by Agnes Strickland, vol. 1. London: Henry Colburn Publisher, 1842.

The Secret History of the Most Renowned Queen Elizabeth and the Earl of Essex, by a Person of Quality. Cologne: Printed for Will with the Wisp, at the Sign of the Moon in the Ecliptick, 1680). Wing S2342A.

SECONDARY SOURCES

Beard, Mary. *Women and Power: A Manifesto.* London: Profile Books, 2017.

Bell, Ilona. *Elizabeth I: The Voice of a Monarch.* New York: Palgrave Macmillan, 2010.

Benz, Lisa, and Rohr, Zita, eds. *Tales of Ice and Fire: Queenship, Female Agency, and the Role of Advice in Game of Thrones.* Forthcoming.

Betteridge, Thomas. "A queen for all seasons: Elizabeth I on film." In *The Myth of Elizabeth,* edited by Susan Doran and Thomas S. Freeman, 242–259. Basingstoke: Palgrave Macmillan, 2003.

Coch, Christine. "'Mother of my Contreye': Elizabeth I and Tudor Constructions of Motherhood." *English Literary Renaissance* 26/3 (1996): 423–50.

Collinson, Patrick. "Elizabeth I and the verdicts of history." *Historical Research,* 76, 194 (2003): 469–491.

Dobson, Michael and Watson, Nicola, J. *England's Elizabeth: an Afterlife in Fame and Fantasy.* Oxford: Oxford University Press, 2002.

Doran, Susan. *Monarchy and Matrimony: The Courtship of Elizabeth.* London and New York: Routledge, 1996.

———. "Why Did Elizabeth Not Marry?" in Julia M. Walker ed. *Dissing Elizabeth: Negative Representations of Gloriana,* 30–59. Durham and London: Duke University Press, 1998.

Eldridge Carney, Jo. *Fairy Tale Queens: Representations of Early Modern Queenship.* New York: Palgrave Macmillan, 2012.

———. "Poisoning Queens in Early Modern Fact and Fiction." In *Scholars and Poets Talk About Queens.* Edited by Carole Levin and associate editor Christine Stewart-Nunez, 269–284. New York: Palgrave Macmillan, 2015.

Erickson, Carolly. *The First Elizabeth.* New York: St. Martin's Griffin, 1983.

Gristwood, Sarah. *Elizabeth and Leicester.* London: Bantam, 2017.

Guy, John. *Elizabeth: The Forgotten Years.* New York: Penguin, 2016.

Hackett, Helen. *Virgin Mother, Maiden Queen: Elizabeth I and the Cult of the Virgin Mary.* London: Palgrave, 1994.

Hageman, Elizabeth, and Conway, Katherine, eds. *Resurrecting Elizabeth I in Seventeenth-Century England*. Cranbury: Rosemont Publishing & Printing Corp, 2007.

Jenkins, Elizabeth. *Elizabeth and Leicester*. London: Phoenix Press, 2003.

Levin, Carole. *The Heart and Stomach of a King: Elizabeth I and the Politics of Sex and Power*. Philadelphia: Pennsylvania University Press, 1998, second edition 2013.

———. *The Reign of Elizabeth I*. New York: Palgrave Macmillan, 2002.

Norrie, Aidan. "A Man? A woman? A lesbian? A whore?: Queen Elizabeth I and the Cinematic Subversion of Gender." In *Premodern Rulers and Postmodern Viewers: Gender, Sex, and Power in Popular Culture*, ed. Janice North, Karl C. Alvestad, and Elena Woodacre, 319–340. New York: Palgrave Macmillan, 2018.

Palvac, Brian, A. ed. *Game of Thrones versus History*. Hoboken: Wiley Blackwell, 2017.

Paranque, Estelle. *Elizabeth I of England Through Valois Eyes: Power, Representation and Diplomacy in the Reign of the Queen, 1558–1588*. New York: Palgrave Macmillan, 2019.

———. "Royal Representations Through the Father and the Warrior Figures." In *History of Monarchy*, edited by Elena Woodacre et al., 314–329. London: Routledge, 2019.

Parrill, Sue and Robison, William B. *The Tudors on Film and Television*. Jefferson, North Carolina and London: McFarland & Company, Inc., Publishers, 2013.

Rai, Sonam. *Women With(out) Dragons: A Critical Analysis of the Representation of Women in Game of Thrones*. Unpublished MA Dissertation, St Joseph College, 2017.

Riehl Bertolet, Anna. *The Face of Queenship: Early Modern Representations of Elizabeth I*. New York: Palgrave Macmillan, 2010.

Robison, William, ed. *History, Fiction, and the Tudors: Sex, Politics, Power, and Artistic License in the Showtime Television Series*. New York: Palgrave Macmillan, 2016.

Starkey, David. *Elizabeth: Apprenticeship*. London: Chatto and Windus, 2000.

ONLINE SOURCES

http://history-behind-game-of-thrones.com/tudors/daenerys-as-elizabeth-i

http://www.digitalspy.com/tv/game-of-thrones/feature/a668633/game-of-thrones-nudity-crisis-emilia-clarke-is-saying-no-to-nudes-but-who-else-in-the-cast-wants-to-cover-up/

https://www.npg.org.uk/research/programmes/making-art-in-tudor-britain/the-phoenix-and-the-pelican-two-portraits-of-elizabeth-i-c.1575.php

http://www.themarysue.com/daenerys-targaryen/

CHAPTER 14

50 Shades of Elizabeth; or, "Doing History" in Pop Fiction

Elizabeth Ann Mackay

In the academic world, it's a commonplace that history and fiction make strange bedfellows. Or do they? In *50 Shades of Grey*, Christian Grey says that pleasure and pain are "two sides of the same coin, one not existing without the other," and perhaps the same can be said of history and fiction.[1] In *British Women Writers and the Writing of History*, Devoney Looser argues this very point, writing that "to investigate history without considering fiction (or vice versa) prevents our achieving a more complete understanding of either."[2] In the sixteenth and seventeenth centuries, history and fiction, and especially the *writing of* history and fiction, were not mutually exclusive enterprises, but rather mirrored and mirroring activities. Writers like George Puttenham, Philip Sidney, Edmund Spenser, and William Shakespeare consistently demonstrate that history and "poesy," taken together, were necessary to elucidate readers on "things authentic,"

---

[1] E. L. James, *Fifty Shades of Grey* (New York: Vintage Books, 2011), 221.
[2] Devoney Looser, *British Women Writers and the Writing of History, 1670–1820* (Baltimore: The Johns Hopkins University Press, 2000), 22.

E. A. Mackay (✉)
English Department, University of Dayton, Dayton, OH, USA

© The Author(s) 2019   259
E. Paranque (ed.), *Remembering Queens and Kings of Early Modern England and France*, Queenship and Power,
https://doi.org/10.1007/978-3-030-22344-1_14

things like "old memories and like successes happened in times past."[3] And early modern historians and chroniclers, such as Raphael Holinshed, John Speed, William Camden, and Richard Brathwaite, also employed imaginative writing techniques; Brathwaite, for one, emphasizes the importance of blending both styles, as he indicates on his *Survey*'s title page, noting that his history is "Contrived and Comprised in an Intermixt Discourse upon Historicall and Poetical Relations" for the reader's "profit and modest Delight."[4]

Nowhere is the complicated relationship between history and fiction more apparent than in contemporary women writers' historical fictional novels and popular romance novels about the life and legacy of Elizabeth I. Indeed, like our academic culture, our popular culture is fascinated with Elizabeth, her myth, and its various mysteries. Like scholars, women novelists explore crucial questions about Elizabeth's life and her legacy, while also making arguments about who can and is allowed to untangle her mysteries. Such novels, depicting Elizabeth I as a protagonist and/or as a romance heroine, include *Legacy* (2010), *The Virgin's Lover* (2004), *The Queen's Bastard* (1999), *I, Elizabeth* (1994), among others.[5] In this chapter, I investigate the language moves women writers use to answer their readers' questions about Elizabeth I's life, and more specifically, about her sex life. My investigation of the novels emphasizes several ways women writers claim to "do" history in their fictional portraits of Elizabeth. Such "doing" of history can mean many things: performing a certain action;

---

[3] George Puttenham, *The Art of English Poesy: A Critical Edition*, eds. Frank Whighan and Wayne A. Rebhorn (Ithaca: Cornell University Press, 2007), 129, 128.

[4] Richard Brathwaite, *A Survey of History: Or, a Nursery for Gentry* (London: J. Okes, 1638).

[5] There is quite a long list of contemporary historical and/or romance novels featuring Elizabeth I as a protagonist. For this chapter, I focused on the following texts: Philippa Gregory, *The Virgin's Lover* (New York: Touchstone, 2004); Susan Kay, *Legacy* (Naperville: Sourcebooks Landmark, 2010); Robin Maxwell, *The Secret Diary of Anne Boleyn* (New York: Scribner Paperback Fiction, 1997); Maxwell, *The Queen's Bastard* (New York: Scribner Paperback Fiction, 1999); Maxwell, *Virgin* (New York: Scribner Paperback Fiction, 2001); Rosalind Miles, *I, Elizabeth* (New York: Three Rivers Press, 1994); Alison Weir, *The Lady Elizabeth* (New York: Ballantine Books, 2008); and Weir, *The Marriage Game* (New York: Ballantine Books, 2014). Additionally, I also consulted the following novels: Anne Clinard Barnhill, *Queen Elizabeth's Daughter* (New York: St. Martin's Griffin, 2014); Karen Harper, *The Thorne Maze* (New York: St. Martin's Paperbacks, 2003); Harper, *The Poyson Garden* (New York: Dell Publishing, 1999); and Harper, *The Queen's Governess* (New York: New American Library, 2010).

carrying out the duties and responsibilities of one's profession; the collo-quial, LL Cool J sense of "doing someone" or "doing it;"[6] and, in another colloquial sense, "screwing" or swindling readers. Exploring the variety of ways that women "do" Elizabeth I's history, I interrogate explicit claims made by contemporary fiction writers, who argue that their novels are historically accurate, are accurate interpretations of historical records, and are *histories* of Elizabeth.

An important caveat: my study of these novels is not concerned with their content; that is, this chapter does not attempt to put these novels' histories to rights. As a literary critic and a rhetorical scholar, I make no claims to a historian's credentials, training, or knowledge to offer substan-tive challenges to or critiques of women's narratives about Elizabeth, her history, or her legends. Nor will I analyze or assess these novels' literary merits, although, spoiler alert: most of these novels are bad, very, *very* bad. Instead, I am intrigued by and therefore investigate the language moves and rhetorical strategies women novelists use to influence and thereby convince readers to accept as "fact" their historical claims about Elizabeth; I also think about the consequences of such rhetorical moves. To trace the writers' strategies, then, I closely read the novels' paratexts—authors' notes, appendices, bibliographies, book jacket blurbs, and the like that frame novels in ways similar to the acknowledgment pages, bibliographies, indexes, and book jackets that frame scholarly monographs. It is in these sites, I argue, where women writers make explicit claims to "do" history," that is, to do the work of historians and to participate in the writing of Elizabeth I's history and its various reincarnations in these novels.

History = Poesy = Romance

The book jacket blurb for Philippa Gregory's romance novel, *The Virgin's Lover* (2004), claims the novel "answers the question about an unsolved crime that has fascinated … historians for centuries."[7] The crime is the mysterious 1560 death of Amy Robsart, Robert Dudley's wife. In *The Virgin's Lover*, Amy is Elizabeth I's foil; Elizabeth, of course, is the hero-ine of this romance novel who finds herself involved in an extramarital love affair with Dudley. Gregory's Elizabeth is an utterly unappealing and dis-tasteful character; she is ultragirly, giggly, immature, a newly crowned

---

[6] James Todd Smith, *Mr. Smith*, LL Cool J. Def Jam Recordings, 1996, CD.
[7] Philippa Gregory, *The Virgin's Lover* (New York: Touchstone, 2005), no page.

monarch who is a nail-biter and -picker, and is, by turns, petulant, flirtatious, easily frightened, prone to temper tantrums, a conventionally wimpy
yet oversexed heroine of romance fiction. And yet, in the "Q&A with
Philippa Gregory" appended to the novel's conclusion, as elsewhere,
Gregory defends her narrative choices, a defense that I must quote
at length:

> My training as a journalist taught me to ask the awkward questions—and
> this pays dividends in historical research too. I love history. In almost any
> circumstances I always ask, 'But how did it get like this? How did it start?'
> These are questions which come naturally and automatically to a historian
> and that is what, by instinct and training, I am .... Most of my research is
> book based—the Tudors especially have a huge collection of histories writ-
> ten about them—and I find a lot of interesting material in very old history
> books [written] by some ... historians [who] look at aspects of their lives
> that modern historians neglect.... I like to know the specialized history of
> the period ... all those things that the reader should not know that I have
> researched, but [which] should [help them] feel at home in the detail of the
> Tudor world.[8]

In the "Author's Note" preceding the Q&A, Gregory claims to have
solved the mystery of Robsart's death, using as her proof evidence that
Elizabeth and William Cecil contracted Robsart's murder to look like an
accident, calling both characters "accessories" who "incriminate[d]"
themselves with their "indiscreet remarks ... to the Spanish ambassador
[Alvaro de la Quadra] in the days before Amy's death, which [de la
Quadra] recorded for his master, *just as I present them* in this fictional
account."[9] In her rhetorical framing, Gregory uses her position as a fiction
writer to make explicit claims that she is a "historian by training," a practice that she describes with some detail and with considerable scholarly
logic to her (primarily) nonacademic female readership.[10] This practice,

---

[8] Gregory, *The Virgin's Lover*, 448–450.

[9] Gregory, *The Virgin's Lover*, 439, emphasis added.

[10] Janice A. Radway notes the argument of reader-response critics, which suggests that "the
reader is responsible for what is made of the literary text." However, Radway points out that
this view ignores the "particular ideological power of [the] literary form" of romance (54,
55). Radaway finds that, primarily, romance readers are women—ranging from young adults
to advance middle ages—and are deft critics of what counts as "good" or "bad" in terms of
the romance genre, its plot, characters, and tropes. Still, she also explains that the audience
of romance novels "provided ample evidence that they ... learn and remember facts about
geography, historical customs, and dress from the books they read" (76, n. 16). It is this

especially Gregory's claim to have conducted extensive historical research, which appears in a bibliography at the novel's end, appears to challenge or negate the disclaimer of the novel's copyright page: "this book is a work of fiction. Names, characters, places, and incidents either are products of the author's imagination or are used fictitiously. Any resemblance to actual events or locales or persons, living or dead, is entirely coincidental."[11] Despite the copyright disclaimer, Gregory's emphasis on her historical writing in other paratextual moments are entirely in keeping with the practices of popular and academic published histories, as in the bibliographical essays appended to Carole Levin's *Heart and Stomach of a King* (1994), David Starkey's history, *Elizabeth: The Struggle for the Throne* (2001), or Christopher Haigh's historiography, *Elizabeth I* (1998).[12] What's more, Gregory's website indicates that she "was an established historian and writer when she discovered her interest in the Tudor period and wrote the novel, *The Other Boleyn Girl*, which was made into a TV drama and a major film," and the site further offers her university education and degrees to accredit her writing of history.[13] Noticeably, on the website, Gregory reverses the order of the process she describes in her novel's Q&A—on the website, history comes before fiction—an order that privileges and emphasizes her history training. Strikingly, Gregory is not unique; she is, simply, one among many women writers, like Maxwell, Miles, or Weir, producing romance novels and serious historical fiction about Elizabeth I's life, legends, and legacy. For the degree and rate at which these women depict Elizabeth while they also make claims to "do" history, theirs are claims that need to be given serious thought.

specific point on which my argument turns, as I suggest that women novelists, representing themselves as historians, count on their readers to remember and repeat the "facts" of their novels. See Radway, "Women Read the Romance: The Interaction of Text and Context, *Feminist Studies* 9, no. 1 (1983), 53–78.

[11] Radway, "Women Read the Romance," vi.

[12] Carole Levin, *The Heart and Stomach of a King: Elizabeth I and the Politics of Sex and Power* (Philadelphia: University of Pennsylvania Press, 1994); David Starkey, *Elizabeth: The Struggle for the Throne* (New York: HarperCollins Publishers, 2001); and Christopher Haigh, *Elizabeth I*, 2nd ed., Profiles in Power Series (Harlow: Pearson Education Limited, 1998).

[13] The website says, "Philippa graduated from the University of Sussex with a degree in History, and received a PhD in 18th century literature from the University of Edinburgh.... She holds an honorary degree from Teesside University and is a fellow of the Universities of Sussex and Cardiff, and a Regent for the University of Edinburgh. Her love for history and commitment to historical accuracy are the hallmarks of her writing." The site's headmast reads: "Philippa Gregory | *Established historian* & writer. International No. 1 best seller" (emphasis added). Philippa Gregory, "About Philippa," *Philippa Gregory*, last modified, December 14, 2017, http://www.philippagregory.com/biography

There is something very early modern about the ways in which contemporary novelists present their fictions, and I argue that contemporary novelists turn to and blend the theories and styles of two early modern traditions: first, the tradition of writing romances in the period, and next, the tradition of writing historical chronicles in the period. Originally considered the province of male writers, both early modern romance and history eventually became associated with women writers. More specifically, women writers like Mary Sidney, Anne Dowriche, Lady Mary Wroth, and Margaret Cavendish wrote in ways that blurred the generic conventions of imaginative literature and history. For early modern writers, both romances and histories alike "could articulate a political or religious position, comment on the vagaries of noble service and demonstrate how good breeding might lead to a virtuous life."[14] Even though early modern romances contained many fantastical elements, they also as often depended on details of the writers' autobiographies, so that, sometimes, romances were seen by their readers "as more history-like than novels."[15] For instance, both Wroth's *Urania* and Cavendish's *The Blazing World* are often described as pseudo- or semi-autobiographical texts that depend on both history and imaginative writing, or similarly, their biographies are interpretative keys to reading their romance writing.[16] Also, sixteenth- and seventeenth-century romances were linked to Elizabeth I, even in the most ancillary of associations. As Karen Britland notes, "romance writing in England increased in popularity from the Elizabethan period" and, in Stuart England, became "a cultural tool through which it … looked back to an Elizabethan golden age."[17]

[14] Karen Britland, "Women in the Royal Courts," in *The Cambridge Companion to Early Modern Women's Writing*, ed. Laura Lunger Knoppers (Cambridge: Cambridge University Press, 2009), 128.

[15] Looser, *British Women Writers*, 23.

[16] On Mary Wroth, see Barbara K. Lewalski, "Writing Women and Reading the Renaissance," *Renaissance Quarterly* 44, no. 4 (1991), 792–821; Josephine A. Roberts, "Labyrinths of Desire: Lady Mary Wroth's Reconstruction of Romance," *Women's Studies* 19 (1991), 183–192; and Heide Towers, "Politics and Female Agency in Lady Mary Wroth's *Love's Argument*," *Women's Writing* 13, no. 3 (2006), 432–447. On Margaret Cavendish, see Tessie Prakas, "'A World of her own Invention': The Realm of Fancy in Margaret Cavendish's *The Description of a New World, called The Blazing World*," *Journal for Early Modern Cultural Studies* 16, no. 1 (2016), 115–145; and Sandra Sherman, "Trembling Texts: Margaret Cavendish and the Dialectic of Authorship," *English Literary Renaissance* 24, no. 1 (1994), 184–210.

[17] Britland, "Women in the Royal Courts," 128.

With its nostalgic nature, then, romance writing seemed a natural progression for women to begin writing histories. Lori Newcomb writes, "as women claimed authority over and through fiction, each writer negotiated her way between ... the diffused international romance tradition and an equally diffused impulse towards history."[18] For early modern audiences, the romance was a mode ambivalently tied to female authorship, often downgraded to something "feminine" and "pejorative," a view of women's writing that ignored the "special self-consciousness" women employed.[19] In her study of late seventeenth- to mid-eighteenth-century women's writing, Looser demonstrates "modern history's early linkage to romance and to women" especially through its perceived "second-class, feminized status."[20] As Looser argues, early modern histories were downgraded because "history as a genre (like fiction) did not appear neatly defined and fully formed," also noting that both "fiction and history were contested and fluid categories throughout the long eighteenth century."[21] Still, Looser says, history was a more privileged genre than fiction or romance, and thus, late-seventeenth- and early-eighteenth-century fiction writers began to "liken[] their production [of fictional texts] to histories in order to achieve status through association with a more respectable genre."[22]

Concurrently, early modern male writers, chroniclers, and rhetorical theorists encouraged authors to use writing strategies typically linked to imaginative literature—or "poesy"—to make history more appealing to readers. For example, in his *Chronicles* (1577), Raphael Holinshed explains that "concerning the Historie of England," "no one can be eye witnesse to all that is written within our time, much lesse to those things whiche happened in former times, and therefore must be content with reportes of others."[23] Although Holinshed insists that he has been "so careful [and] spared no paynes or helpe of frendes to search out either written or printed auncient Authors, or to enquire of modern eye witnesses, for the true setting downe

---

[18] Lori Humphrey Newcomb, "Prose Fiction," in *The Cambridge Companion to Early Modern Women's Writing*, ed. Laura Lunger Knoppers (Cambridge: Cambridge University Press, 2009), 273.

[19] Humphrey Newcomb, "Prose Fiction," 273–274.

[20] Looser, *British Women Writers*, 10–11.

[21] Looser, *British Women Writers*, 21.

[22] Looser, *British Women Writers*, 21.

[23] Raphael Holinshed, *The Firste volume of the Chronicles of England, Scotlande, and Irelande* (London: John Hunne, 1577), iiii^r.

of that whiche I have here delivered," he also qualifies the *Chronicles*' "truth" as he cautions his readers that in some moments, he is bound to "shew ... fancie." For his use of imagination, Holinshed "crave[s] pardon."[24]

As Holinshed indicates, the writing of history, and indeed theorizing the writing of history, was never clearly distinguished from the writing of imaginative literature. Many writers seemed to think that imaginative techniques enhanced historiography and therefore participated in the academic exercise of *ars historica*, the classical tradition of history writing as an art form that is "lively, joyful, and entertaining as well as instructive."[25] However, early modern writers contributed new ways of thinking about the *ars historica* tradition, believing "poetry" (their catch-all term for a range of imaginative genres) was the most legitimate means of delivering history to the masses, thereby blurring the categories of "history" and "poesy" by frequently interchanging these terms. What's more, rhetorical theorists claim the poet is the best writer of history. According to George Puttenham's *Arte of English Poesie* (1589), the poet is "the meetest to register the lives and noble gests of Princes," "the great Monarkes of the world," and "other memorable accidents of time."[26] Similarly, in *Defense of Poesy* (1595), Sidney not only argues that poets were "the first ... deliverers of their knowledge to the posterity," but that "even historiographers ... have been glad to borrow both fashion and, perchance, weight of the poets."[27] Edmund Spenser, too, theorizes the role of the poet in an imaginative (re)telling of history. In his "Letter of the Authors" appended to *The Faerie* Queene (1590), Spenser writes that in his "historye of King Arthure," he will use "the Method of a Poet."[28] The historiographer, Spenser says, "discourseth of affaryes orderly as they were donne, accounting as well of the times as the actions, but a Poet thrusteth into the middest, even where it most concerneth him," which "maketh a pleasing Analysis of all."[29] Thus, Spenser privileges the work of the poet, whose

---

[24] Holinshed, *The Firste volume*, iiii^r–iiii^v.

[25] Lionel Gossman, "'Back to the Future': The *Ars Historica*," *History and Theory* 47 (2008), 454.

[26] Puttenham, *Art of English Poesy*, 99.

[27] Phillip Sidney, *The Defense of Poesie* (London: William Ponsonby, 1595), B3^r.

[28] Edmund Spenser, *The Faerie Queene*, in *The Norton Anthology of English Literature*, 9th ed., Vol. B: The Sixteenth Century/The Early Seventeenth Century, Gen. ed. Stephen Greenblatt (New York: W. W. Norton & Co., 2012), 779.

[29] Spenser, *The Fairie Queene*, 779.

"method" for writing about historical figures, he claims, is more "delight-full and pleasing to commune sence" and whose writing "is much more profitable and gratious" to the reader.[30] Or, to put it simply, as Puttenham does, in early modern England, "the Poet was ... the first Historiographer."[31] In sum, by carefully reading male chroniclers' theories of history writing alongside rhetoricians and poets' theories of writing historical imaginative works, what emerges is a consistent and dialectical understanding that history and fiction are mutually shaping and mutually reinforcing enterprises, not the antithetical projects we assume.

TRUE = FACT = TRUTH

In his history play, *All is True* (ca. 1613), Shakespeare, too, takes up this early modern *ars historica* tradition, which can be heard in its many and varied repetitions of "true" and "truth," beginning in the play's Prologue, which tells the audience, "such noble scenes as draw the eye to flow/ We now present ... such as give/ Their money out of hope they may believe/ May here find truth, too ... To make that only true we now intend."[32] In his final monolog, Archbishop Cramner draws clear links between the infant Elizabeth's future and what is true: "the words I utter/Let none think flattery, for they'll find 'em truth. This royal infant ... Truth shall nurse her ... Peace, plenty, love, truth, terror ... were the servants to this chosen infant."[33] The play itself interrogates what is true, including what makes a true wife or a true divorce, what defines a true and loyal subject, what accounts for true information. Working upon theories of the *ars historica* tradition, early modern chroniclers and rhetorical theorists similarly interrogate and complicate what is true and how to depict truth in history writing, while continuing to align history writing with the art of poesy. For example, in *The true order and Methode of writing and reading Hystories* (1574), Thomas Blundeville insists that the historian's "office [is] to tell things as they were done without either augmenting or diminishing them or swarving one iote from the truth" and "truely to reporte

---

[30] Spenser, *The Faerie Queene*, 779.

[31] Puttenham, *Art of English Poesy*, 99.

[32] William Shakespeare, *All is True (Henry VIII)*, in *The Norton Shakespeare*, 2nd ed., Gen ed., Stephen Greenblatt (New York: W. W. Norton & Co., 2008), Prologue1. 4–21.

[33] Shakespeare, *All is True*, 5.4.15–48.

every such speech, and deede, even as it was spoke, or done."[34] Yet other writers challenge whether or not this exacting truth is possible. Puttenham, for one, describes three types of history writing—"wholly true and wholly false and a third holding part of either"—which are meant for readers' "honest recreation and good example."[35] Sidney also suggests that historical "truth" is more complicated than the "plain" truths about which Blundeville writes; although Sidney admits "the historian ... is so tied, not to what should be, but to what is; to the particular truth of things," he also says that a "fayned example" can have "asmuch force to teach [historical truth] as a true example."[36]

Reading early modern chronicles and rhetorical treatises that prescribe the writing of history (and poesy), there appears to be a clear precedent by which historical genres borrow elements of fiction to produce readable, dynamic, engaging, edifying texts. And that early modern fictional techniques can be used to transform history seems to set a precedent for contemporary fiction writers to "do" history, that is, to present their fictions as "truths" or "facts." To be sure, the women writing fictional accounts about Elizabeth I take great liberties with historical chronologies, sometimes freely revising dates for events to fit their narratives, and they do so deliberately, assuming their readers have little to no knowledge of the early modern period or Elizabeth's life. Yet always in contemporary novelists' narratives is the early modern notion of "truth," the idea that it is perfectly acceptable to take creative license, as long as it is done to reveal such historical "truths." Sometimes, such attention to truth poses challenges to professional and scholarly histories, typically accepted as sources that are the "most true." For instance, in *The Queen's Bastard* (1999), Robin Maxwell takes issue with Levin's historical timeline in her monograph; according to Maxwell, it is impossible for historians' dating to be precise, a convenient way for Maxwell to then correct these "truths" and offer her novel's versions of events as "true."[37] Like Christian Grey says in *50 Shades*, "this stuff is just details."[38]

---

[34] Thomas Blundeville, *The true order and Methode of wryting and reading Hystories* (London: Willyam Seres, 1574), Eiv[v].

[35] Puttenham, *Art of English Poesy*, 130.

[36] Sidney, *Defense of Poesy*, E2[r].

[37] Maxwell, *The Queen's Bastard*, 434.

[38] James, *50 Shades*, 221.

Do → Doing → Done

Some of the most gleeful and utterly disturbing uses of sexual innuendo appear in Shakespeare's *Titus Andronicus*.[39] One example is found in Act 2 scene 3 when Quintus and Martius fall into a man-made pit: "What subtle hole is this," Quintus cries, "Whose mouth is cover'd with rude growing briers,/ Upon whose leaves are drops of new-shed blood/ As fresh as morning dew distill'd on flowers?/ A very fatal place it seems to me."[40] And then later, in Act 4, having learned of their mother's infidelities and the mixed race baby she's had with Aaron, Chiron laments to Aaron, "Thou hast undone our mother," to which Aaron proudly admits, "villain, I have done thy mother."[41] This early modern brand of sexual innuendo—which is indeed far more clever than that of the trite and taciturn Christian Grey ("You're not giving much away are you?" or "I can recollect some quite probing questions")[42]—is employed by female novelists in the paratextual materials framing their narratives as they explicitly describe how they have "done" history. Such descriptions depend on rhetoric that seems, on one hand, very much like the prefaces and introductory chapters of scholarly monographs, in which academic writers outline their theoretical approaches and methodologies in the study of history or analyses of historical literature. Yet on the other hand, these rhetorical descriptions also seem like the brand of "sexposition" associated with HBO's *Game of Thrones* series, where characters "reveal crucial information related to plot and character development during intimate scenes," a means to prompt viewers to think about "what role history plays in the heat of the moment."[43] As Estelle Paranque's chapter in this volume demonstrates, some fictional characters are a means of reincarnating historical characters in more sexualized ways; as I am suggesting in this chapter, characters are sexualized in such a way as to defend the reincarnations of Elizabeth I and the sexualized discourses women writers use to justify their portraits of her.

[39] William Shakespeare, *Titus Andronicus*, in *The Norton Shakespeare*, 2nd ed., Gen ed., Stephen Greenblatt (New York: W. W. Norton & Co., 2008), 399–463.

[40] Shakespeare, *Titus*, 2.3.197–202.

[41] Shakespeare, *Titus*, 4.2.75–76.

[42] James, *50 Shades*, 45.

[43] "Sexposition," *Wikipedia*, last modified September 2, 2017, https://en.Wikipedia.org/wiki/Sexposition; Myles McNutt, "*Game of Thrones*—'You Win or You Die'," *Cultural Learnings*, Word Press, May 29, 2011, https://cultural-learnings.com/2011/05/29/game-of-thrones-you-win-or-you-die/

Indeed, a close rhetorical analysis of the novels' paratextual materials reveal strategic uses of sexual innuendo and sexual slang that shape their historical "truths" for readers. In these moments, women novelists claim to "fill in the gaps" of history. For instance, in the Author's Note appended to *Virgin* (2001), the third novel in her Elizabeth trilogy, Maxwell tells her readers, "in any account of a history that goes back 450 years there are sure to be gaping holes—that is expected. But in the period spanning the death of Henry VIII (1547) and the execution of Thomas Seymour (1549), I found in most cases glaring omissions and inconsistencies, inadequate analyses and faulty conclusions."[44] "The most egregious omission," she goes on to say, is Catherine Parr's "state of mind during the period" following the Seymour affair. Maxwell suggests Parr's discovery of Elizabeth and Thomas Seymour's embrace "is one 'hole in history' that only writers of historical fiction are allowed to fill," and, even as she claims her indebtedness to historians, she also says that she has "always been astonished that this episode of the Tudor story has been largely ignored or given short shrift" by historians.[45] Notice how Maxwell simultaneously claims a historical authority for the fiction writer, while downgrading other writers' expertise, a rhetorically savvy move assuring her readers that she has revealed the "truth" of Elizabeth's doings with Seymour. Importantly, Maxwell becomes increasingly fond of and invested in such historical "gaps." In *The Secret Diary of Anne Boleyn* (1997), she says nothing, only including a brief acknowledgment note. Yet in her second novel, *The Queen's Bastard* (1999), she explains that the story of Arthur Dudley "had many gaps in its chronology" left by Elizabeth's historians and biographers who "ignored so interesting a personage."[46] Later, she says, "another superb hole in history ... was the explosion aboard the Spanish vessel San Salvador during the voyage of the Armada."[47]

Other ways in which sexual innuendo is used to defend fictional novels' truths include the sense that novelists can "go all the way" where historians and scholars can only get to first base (so to speak). For instance, in her Author's Note for *The Lady Elizabeth* (2008), Alison Weir writes, "for dramatic purposes, I have woven into my story a tale that goes against all

---

44 Maxwell, *Virgin*, 239.
45 Maxwell, *Virgin*, 241, 239.
46 Maxwell, *The Queen's Bastard*, 433.
47 Maxwell, *The Queen's Bastard*, 435.

my instincts as a historian!"[48] Nevertheless, she insists it is okay to do so because the novelist has the "heady freedom to ask: What if?" a point she makes again in her 2014 novel, *The Marriage Game*: "the 'what if' aspect of history is always fascinating," she says.[49] Having already written *The Lady Elizabeth*, which turns on gossip about the possibility that Elizabeth miscarried a child (a result of her affair with Thomas Seymour), Weir says she "felt obliged to remain" with this gossip in *The Marriage Game*.[50] In her novel, *Elizabeth* (2011), Margaret George says that for both history- and fiction writers, Elizabeth is "the supreme mystery woman" and although no one can truly know her, it's "not stopped everyone from try- ing … to solve that mystery," including George herself.[51] In any case, through such sexual innuendo, female novelists convey to their readers that they enter Elizabeth's life through deep research, while also fantasiz- ing for and with readers how to unlock Elizabeth's deep secrets.

One of the primary effects of this sexual slang is historical argument by innuendo. That is, women writers use such sexual language very strategi- cally, matching their vocabulary to Elizabeth's own bawdy banter and sexual play with her courtiers in the novels themselves, while suggesting very deliberate answers to questions about Elizabeth's virginity and sex life. Historical argument by sexual innuendo, then, resolves this particular mystery for readers. George admits that the "facts" of Elizabeth's life are confounding, especially when it comes to her intimate relations with men, explaining that Elizabeth "was a Virgin Queen who encouraged lovemak- ing (up to a point) and [showed] all the outward signs of rapturous love."[52] Weir might argue that she "firmly believe[s] that Elizabeth I was the Virgin Queen she claimed to be," but she also reminds readers that the "paucity of information" and the lack "reliable evidence" make it entirely possible to conjecture that Lady Elizabeth had sex with Thomas Seymour and had a miscarriage as a result.[53] After all, Weir insists, she is a historian "determined to stick to the facts as faithfully as possible in her books" and "what you come up with as a novelist must be credible and convincing within the known facts and cultural, social, and moral ethos of the

---

[48] Weir, *The Lady Elizabeth*, 475.
[49] Weir, *The Lady Elizabeth*, 475.
[50] Weir, *The Marriage Game*, 401.
[51] Margaret George, *Elizabeth* (New York: Viking, 2011), 665.
[52] George, *Elizabeth*, 665.
[53] Weir, *The Lady Elizabeth*, 476.

period."[54] Other writers, like Rosalind Miles and Maxwell do use innuendo, but are more explicit in their answers to the question, did Elizabeth have sex? Miles says, "I believe that [Elizabeth and Dudley] were lovers in the fullest sense of the word."[55] Maxwell echoes Miles: "my own opinion is that the two were intimate in the fullest sense of the word," telling her readers that Elizabeth's behaviors with Dudley were not those "of a chaste woman."[56]

Just as the Elizabeth in most of these novels is not a chaste woman, neither are the novelists themselves, especially in the ways they borrow and recycle materials from historical sources, literary scholars, and other novelists. Some writers append lengthy bibliographies to their novels: Susan Kay's bibliography includes nearly 30 sources she used to compose *Legacy* (2010); George lists almost 50 titles (and these are only the suggested supplementary readings for audiences) in her Afterword to *Elizabeth*. Including bibliographies makes it possible for readers to verify novelists' historical interpretations or readers can just take the writers at their words (which is more likely). In lieu of including a bibliography of sources as Kay, George and Gregory do, other writers instead generalize their borrowings or point to only their most useful sources. For instance, Maxwell opens her Author's Note to *Virgin* explaining that she is "deeply indebted to a number of excellent historians without whose research this book would have been impossible;" in *The Queen's Bastard*, she says she drew liberally from Elizabeth Jenkin's *Elizabeth and Leicester*, as well as David Howarth's *The Voyage of the Armada*.[57] Miles writes that she "owe[s] an enormous debt of gratitude to … all [of Elizabeth's] biographers, chroniclers, admirers and critics whose work [she drew] on in the preparation of this book," explaining to her readers that to list her sources would mean her "acknowledgements would be endless."[58] Novelists also liberally borrow ideas, plot points, dialogue, among other details, from each other and from other popular sources. One particularly remarkable example is the "fact" that Elizabeth had a child (or children), a pregnancy (or pregnancies) she cleverly covered through illnesses and countryside progresses—a claim made by Anne Clinard Barnhill, Maxwell, and Weir, as well as the

---

[54] Weir, *The Lady Elizabeth*, 487.
[55] Miles, *I, Elizabeth*, 636.
[56] Maxwell, *Virgin*, 434, 84.
[57] Maxwell, *Virgin*, 239; *The Queen's Bastard*, 434–435.
[58] Miles, *I, Elizabeth*, 631.

2011 film, *Anonymous*.[59] The effect of such borrowing from fiction is that plot details appear to readers as "true" precisely because they are repeated in multiple fictional sources.

As writers acknowledge or attribute source materials, they also present their sources as either (or simultaneously) "reputable" and/or "loose," in ways that, again, match depictions of their novels' Elizabeths as chaste and discreet *and* coy and wanton. For example, an excerpt from a *Romantic Times* review included on Gregory's book jacket argues that "no lover of Elizabethan history should be without this novel, nor will [anyone] be disappointed with [its] meticulous research."[60] In *Elizabeth*, George tells us that J. E. Neale's *Queen Elizabeth I* "is the granddaddy of all basic biographies, elegant, concise, and definitive"; she says that *Elizabeth I: Collected Works* edited by Leah Marcus, Janel Mueller, and Mary Beth Rose is the most reliable source she has because these editors allow "Elizabeth to speak in her own words"; and she suggests that Neil Hanson's *The Confident Hope of a Miracle* is perhaps somewhat impure because of its "unfavorable view of the English, particularly Elizabeth."[61] Maxwell, too, makes judgments about her sources as chaste or not, writing that William Seymour's *Ordeal by Ambition* is a "well researched account," but when it comes to the historical rumors that Thomas Seymour poisoned Catherine Parr, Maxwell says that perhaps this book relied too much on "loose talk at the time."[62]

Female novelists do not only describe their sources as promiscuous and chaste; the novelists themselves demonstrate their own tensions between about being promiscuous with historical details and being faithful to history. Many writers cop to taking license with the "facts" of Tudor history and Elizabeth's life, but again, like early modern historians and chroniclers, insist it's all done in the interest of revealing historical "truth." In *Virgin*, Maxwell demonstrates concerns with being faithful to history and with her presentation of historical truth, which depends on the audience. Maxwell says, "the readers of my first two novels in this series … have questioned me endlessly … about what in these stories is 'historical' and what is 'fiction.'"[63] To answer these questions, Maxwell explains that the

---

[59] *Anonymous*, directed by Roland Emmerich (2011; Los Angeles, CA: Columbia Pictures).

[60] Gregory, *The Virgin's Lover*, no page.

[61] George, *Elizabeth*, 668–671.

[62] Maxwell, *Virgin*, 240.

[63] Maxwell, *Virgin*, 242.

events in her fictional narrative "adhere very closely to the historical record." She admits that she has "taken literary license," but immediately downplays that license, writing, "I believe everything written is well within the realm of possibility."[64] After all, she concludes, "conjecture extrapolated from fact is … the very heart of historical fiction."[65] George says very similar things in her Author's Note: "I have tried, as always, to be true to historical facts," she insists, and while admitting that she invented some details, she also tells readers that her inventions "have some factual basis."[66] Like other novelists, George indicates, "I have allowed myself a little leeway in some of the timing of events."[67] Weir writes that she has "taken some dramatic license," "telescoped events here and there," "omitted one or two unimportant episodes," "tweaked minor facts," "taken out of context" certain "quotes" or put [them] into the mouths of others."[68] And while she admits to playing with these "minor" things, no matter, she says, "they are accurate in spirit."[69] What is so very striking is that while novelists acknowledge their unrestrained deployment of details like dates, timelines, people's age, and so on, they also unfailingly insist that they rarely, if ever, invent their characters' speeches and dialogue. Weir is a useful example of what most novelists suggest about dialogue; in *The Marriage Game*, she writes, "I have made extensive use of the recorded sayings and exchanges of Elizabeth I and the people surrounding her, although I have modernized their words slightly in places, so that they remain accessible and in keeping with the narrative."[70] Or, to return to a passage I quoted earlier, novelists often claim to transcribe dialogue from historical documents, as Gregory claims to do by including Elizabeth and Cecil's damning exchange about Robsart's "accident" in *The Virgin's Lover*, when she writes that these "indiscreet remarks" were said and recorded "just as I present them in this fictional account."[71]

Ultimately, female novelists' rhetorical strategies seek to romance, seduce, and satisfy readers, giving up elusive answers about Elizabeth's life that readers have been searching for. At least, that is what the novels'

---

[64] Maxwell, *Virgin*, 242.
[65] Maxwell, Virgin, 243.
[66] George, *Elizabeth*, 666.
[67] George, 668.
[68] Weir, *Lady Elizabeth*, 475; *The Marriage Game*, 399.
[69] Weir, *The Marriage Game*, 399.
[70] Weir, *The Marriage Game*, 399.
[71] Gregory, *The Virgin's Lover*, 439.

jacket blurbs and snippets from book reviews endorsing the novels claim. For instance, a quote from *Publishers Weekly* claims that *The Virgin's Lover* is "expertly crafted" and that readers will become "addicted to Gregory's intelligent, well-researched tales."[72] Maxwell's books are described by a variety of publications as "fascinating," "lurid," "electrifying," "riveting," and "so convincing."[73] On the front cover of Weir's *Lady Elizabeth*, *Booklist* writes that this is "a compelling, even irresistible, read," a review this magazine recycles on the back cover of Weir's *Marriage Game*, a novel other publications claim to be so "juicy" and so masterful in its "marrying historical fact with licentious fiction" that it "should be savored."[74] And in a telling Author's Note for *Virgin*, Maxwell writes, "I can only hope that my take on the subject is believable, satisfying, and as true to the facts as humanly possible."[75] In *Reading the Romance*, Janice Radway argues that "no writer can forsee or prescribe the way her book will develop, be taken up, or read" by her female readership, but she also believes that if romance readers will "believe in the possibility of a romantic relationship they have never experienced" through fiction, then it is also possible that "romance readers [will] believe assertions made about subjects they know nothing about."[76] Following this logic, I'd suggest that there is something very deliberate and crafty about the ways that female novelists present Elizabeth I in works of fiction only to then undermine those fictions with their para-textual materials.

In *50 Shades*, there's a moment when Ana and Christian joke about the "fact" of their relationship, examining their picture published in the *Seattle Times*: "it must be true," laughs Christian, since "it's in the newspaper."[77] As Frances Dolan has recently argued, early modern writers and readers demonstrated similar, nuanced relationships to printed texts, whether the texts were histories, poems, ballads, or plays.[78] To elaborate on Shakespeare, many early modern works consistently announce that "all that is in them is true," employing methods that "create the appearance of [truth] without

---

[72] Gregory, *The Virgin's Lover*, no page.

[73] Maxwell, *The Secret Diary*, no page; *The Queen's Bastard*, no page; *Virgin*, no page.

[74] Weir, *The Lady Elizabeth*, no page; *The Marriage Game*, no page.

[75] Maxwell, *Virgin*, 242.

[76] Radway, *Reading the Romance: Women, Patriarchy, and Popular Literature* (Chapel Hill: University of North Carolina Press, 1984), 2, 195.

[77] James, *50 Shades*, 312.

[78] Frances E. Dolan, *True Relations: Reading, Literature, and Evidence in Seventeenth-Century England* (Philadelphia: University of Pennsylvania Press, 2013), 177.

really constituting" that truth or even needing to.[79] As I've been arguing, these are also the same methods used by our contemporary novelists to convince their readers of their "true" histories about Elizabeth, histories that are meant to prove to readers that the novelists have "done" Elizabeth's life in the most authentic, accurate, and objective ways possible, just as "real" historians "do."

BIBLIOGRAPHY

PRIMARY SOURCES

Barnhill, Anne Clinard. *Queen Elizabeth's Daughter.* New York: St. Martin's Griffin, 2014.

Blundeville, Thomas. *The true order and Methode of wryting and reading Hystories.* London: Willyam Seres, 1574.

Brathwaite, Richard. *A Survey of History; Or, a Nursery for Gentry.* London: J. Okes, 1638.

Emmerich, Roland, dir. *Anonymous.* Los Angeles, CA: Columbia Pictures, 2011.

Gregory, Philippa. *The Virgin's Lover.* New York: Touchstone, 2004.

Harper, Karen. *The Poyson Garden.* New York: Dell Publishing, 1999.

———. *The Queen's Governess.* New York: New American Library, 2010.

———. *The Thorne Maze.* New York: St. Martin's Paperbacks, 2003.

Holinshed, Raphael. *The Firste volume of the Chronicles of England, Scotlande, and Irelande.* London: John Hunne, 1577.

James, E. L. *Fifty Shades of Grey.* New York: Vintage Books, 2011.

Kay, Susan. *Legacy.* Naperville: Sourcebooks Landmark, 2010.

Maxwell, Robin. *The Queen's Bastard.* New York: Scribner Paperback Fiction, 1999.

———. *The Secret Diary of Anne Boleyn.* New York: Scribner Paperback Fiction, 1997.

———. *Virgin.* New York: Scribner Paperback Fiction, 2001.

Miles, Rosalind. *I, Elizabeth.* New York: Three Rivers Press, 1994.

Puttenham, George. *The Art of English Poesy: A Critical Edition,* edited by Frank Whigham and Wayne A. Rebohrn. Ithaca: Cornell University Press, 2007.

Shakespeare, William. *All is True (Henry VIII).* In *The Norton Shakespeare.* 2nd ed. Edited by Stephen Greenblatt. New York: W. W. Norton & Co., 2008. 3119–3201.

———. *Titus Andronicus.* In *The Norton Shakespeare.* 2nd ed. Edited by Stephen Greenblatt. New York: W. W. Norton & Co., 2008. 399–463.

Sidney, Phillip. *The Defense of Poesie.* London: William Ponsonby, 1595.

---

[79] Dolan, *True Relations,* 177.

Smith, James Todd. *Mr. Smith*, Def Jam Recordings, 1996. compact disc. Originally recorded in 1996.

Spenser, Edmund. *The Faerie Queene*. In *The Norton Anthology of English Literature*. 9th ed. Vol. B: The Sixteenth Century/ The Early Seventeenth Century. Edited by Stephen Greenblatt. New York: W. W. Norton & Co., 2012. 775–984.

Weir, Alison. *The Lady Elizabeth*. New York: Ballantine Books, 2008.

———. *The Marriage Game*. New York: Ballantine Books, 2014.

SECONDARY SOURCES

Britland, Karen. "Women in the Royal Courts. In *The Cambridge Companion to Early Modern Women's Writing*, edited by Laura Lunger Knoppers. Cambridge: Cambridge University Press, 2009. 124–139.

Dolan, Frances E. *True Relations: Reading, Literature, and Evidence in Seventeenth-Century England*. Philadelphia: University of Pennsylvania Press, 2013.

Gossman, Lionel. "'Back to the Future': The *Ars Historica*." *History and Theory* 47 (2008): 453–457.

Gregory, Philippa. "About Philippa." *Philippa Gregory*, last modified, December 14, 2017, http://www.philippagregory.com/bibliography

Haigh, Christopher. *Elizabeth I*. 2nd ed. Profiles in Power Series. Harlow: Pearson Education Limited, 1999.

Levin, Carole. *The Heart and Stomach of a King: Elizabeth I and the Politics of Sex and Power*. Philadelphia: University of Pennsylvania Press, 1994.

Lewalski, Barbara K. "Writing Women and Reading the Renaissance." *Renaissance Quarterly* 44, no. 4 (1991): 792–821.

Looser, Devoney. *British Women Writers and the Writing of History, 1670–1820*. Baltimore: The Johns Hopkins University Press, 2000.

McNutt, Myles, "*Game of Thrones*—'You Win or You Die.'" *Cultural Learnings*. Word Press, May 29, 2011, https://cultural-learnings.com/2011/05/29/game-of/thrones-you-win-or-you-die

Newcomb, Lori Humphrey. "Prose Fiction." In *The Cambridge Companion to Early Modern Women's Writing*, edited by Laura Lunger Knoppers. Cambridge: Cambridge University Press, 2009. 272–286.

Prakas, Tessie. "'A World of her own Invention': The Realm of Fancy in Margaret Cavendish's *The Description of a New World, Called the Blazing World*." *Journal for Early Modern Cultural Studies* 16, no. 1 (2016): 115–145.

Radway, Janice A. "Women Read the Romance: The Interaction of Text and Context." *Feminist Studies* 9, no. 1 (1983): 53–78.

Roberts, Josephine A. "Labyrinths of Desire: Lady Mary Wroth's Reconstruction of Romance." *Women's Studies* 19 (1991): 183–192.

"Sexposition." *Wikipedia*, Wikimedia Foundation, last modified September 2, 2017, https://en.Wikipedia.org/wiki/Sexposition

Sherman, Sandra. "Trembling Texts: Margaret Cavendish and the Dialectic of Authorship." *English Literary Renaissance* 24, no. 1 (1994): 184–210.

Starkey, David. *Elizabeth: The Struggle for the Throne*. New York: HarperCollins Publishers, 2001.

Towers, Heide. "Politics and Female Agency in Lady Mary Wroth's *Love's Argument*." *Women's Writing* 13, no. 3 (2006); 432–447.

CHAPTER 15

Conniving Queen, Frivolous Wife, or Romantic Heroine? The Afterlife of Queen Henrietta Maria

Susan Dunn-Hensley

In a 2013 talk entitled *Royal Bodies,* author Hilary Mantel (*Wolf Hall* and *Bring Up the Bodies*) drew parallels between modern royalty and Tudor royalty. Most notably, she described Catherine (Kate), Duchess of Cambridge, as becoming "a jointed doll on which certain rags are hung."[1] Mantel expanded on this assertion, saying that the young duchess, whose "only point and purpose" is to give birth, "appeared to have been designed by a committee and built by craftsmen, with a perfect plastic smile and the spindles of her limbs hand-turned and gloss-varnished."[2] According to Mantel's unsparing critique, Kate seems perfectly constructed for her role of princess because she is "irreproachable: as painfully thin as anyone could wish, without quirks, without oddities, without the risk of the emergence

---

[1] Hilary Mantel, "Royal Bodies." London Review of Books. February 21, 2013. https://www.lrb.co.uk/v35/n04/hilary-mantel/royal-bodies
[2] Mantel, "Royal Bodies."

S. Dunn-Hensley (✉)
Wheaton College, Wheaton, IL, USA

© The Author(s) 2019
E. Paranque (ed.), *Remembering Queens and Kings of Early Modern England and France*, Queenship and Power,
https://doi.org/10.1007/978-3-030-22344-1_15

279

of character. She appears precision-made, machine-made, so different from Diana whose human awkwardness and emotional incontinence showed in her every gesture."[3]

This description of the Duchess was part of a nuanced discussion of the relationship between the English royal family and society. However, as Mantel would soon discover, critiquing queens long dead is one thing, calling a living woman "a jointed doll" is quite another.[4] The backlash against Mantel was swift and predictable. Numerous papers ran the story, frequently quoting the critique out of context and prompting readers in the comment sections and on social media to unleash the expected attacks—evoking Mantel's age and appearance as reasons for her animosity toward the duchess. Mantel could have made it clearer that she was commenting on the performance of queenship and not on the living woman who embodies that role. However, what was lost in all of the hand wringing was the real point that Mantel was making: queens consort have always been particularly vulnerable to both the state's attempt to construct them and to the opinions of the national audiences who are consuming their performance.[5] While Mantel's historical critique deals primarily with the Tudors, her analysis applies to queens consort throughout history, including Queen Henrietta Maria, wife of Charles I.

Scholars and popular writers have had almost 400 years to consider Henrietta Maria's life and her role in the English Civil War. Historians and biographers have fashioned Henrietta Maria into various stereotypical images: romantic heroine, frivolous wife, and conniving Catholic queen.[6] During this time, her history has been retold, molded, and shaped by the heirs of those who opposed her in the Civil War. As I discuss in the conclusion of my book *Anna of Denmark and Henrietta Maria: Virgins, Witches, and Catholic Queens*, the Glorious Revolution in 1688 would do more than just influence England's religious future; it would also rewrite

---

[3] Mantel, "Royal Bodies."

[4] Mantel, "Royal Bodies."

[5] Mantel, "Royal Bodies."

[6] In Chap. 8 of this book, Sarah Betts discusses representations of Henrietta Maria as romantic heroine. For representations of Henrietta Maria as frivolous wife and conniving queen, see Henrietta Haynes, *Henrietta Maria* (London: Methuen & Co, 1912); Carola Lenanton Oman, *Henrietta Maria* (London: Hodder & Stoughton, 1936); C.V. Wedgewood, *The King's Peace 1637–1641* (London: C. Nicholls & Company, 1966); Quinton Bone, *Queen of the Cavaliers* (Chicago: University of Illinois Press, 1972); Elizabeth Hamilton, *Henrietta Maria* (New York: Coward, McCann & Geoghegan, 1979).

England's past through the lens of a clear victor and from the perspective of a Whiggish narrative.[7] In this narrative, the Stuart queens could be erased, romanticized, and demonized, but they could never be presented in their complexity, for they represented the threat of the foreign Catholic "other" that Britain had to defeat in order to join the forward march of modernity.[8]

This chapter begins where my argument in the book left off, considering how Henrietta Maria's image fares in the late twentieth and early twenty-first centuries. Contemporary novelists have largely abandoned the image of Henrietta Maria as a scheming queen—most likely because the threat of Catholicism no longer informs that view. However, despite the influence of feminism, writers continue to present the queen in ways that flatten her character and contain her transgressive behavior. In this chapter, I consider Henrietta Maria as she appears in academic studies, as well as in two works of historical fiction: *Myself, My Enemy* (also published as *Loyal in Love*) by Jean Plaidy and *Cavalier Queen* by Fiona Mountain. As the title *Myself, My Enemy* suggests, Plaidy presents the queen as a weak woman whose mistakes cost the king his nation and his life. Mountain, by contrast, presents her as a sexually frustrated young woman who finds her sexual awakening and her sense of purpose in her relationship with her favorite, Henry Jermyn, Earl of St. Albans. Plaidy and Mountain's novels present the queen's transgressive behavior—advocating for her Catholic faith, advising her husband, and leading the Royalist army into battle—in ways that contain the threat of the powerful woman. The reductive way these texts represent Henrietta Maria raises the question of how much license fiction writers should take with history, particularly in the case of historical figures such as queens consort whose life stories may be unknown to the majority of readers.

QUEENSHIP AND HISTORICAL SCHOLARSHIP

In *The Last Medieval Queens: English Queenship 1445–1503*, Joanna Laynesmith argues that, through their participation in royal ceremonies of state (weddings, entries, and coronations) and personal rituals associated with birth and death, medieval queens consort complemented, legitimized,

---

[7] Susan Dunn-Hensley, *Anna of Denmark and Henrietta Maria: Witches, Virgins, and Catholic Queens* (Palgrave, 2017), 227.

[8] Dunn-Hensley, *Anna of Denmark*.

and enriched their husband's kingship, making them "an integral part of the king's public body."[9] Despite the importance of the queen consort to the continuation of dynasty, popular biographers and even scholars often ignore or minimize her contributions. One reason for this historical neglect is the obvious fact that the consort's purpose to the monarchy rests largely on her fertility. As such, scholars and biographers tend to discuss queens consort in terms of the domestic—sexuality, fertility, and intercessory roles, and, when scholars discuss the rituals of rule, they tend to privilege those rituals connected to power.[10] As Carolyn Harris observes, the domestic sphere receives "little attention within political histories because scholars frequently judge analysis of the activities of royal wives to be relevant only to histories of women and the family or of court life."[11]

Linda Woodridge and Edward Berry make a similar observation about studies of ritual, which "tend to stratify along gender lines."[12] Scholars who examine ritual have traditionally focused on rites connected to power, and, in patriarchal societies, those rites privilege the male experience. Thus, many historians focus on male initiation into adulthood and community, war, and ceremonies of international diplomacy rather than rites connected to the "female" and "promoting human and agrarian fertility."[13] According to Woodridge, the "exclusion of fertility from serious attention" and the "defining of ritual as rites of power" works in accordance with the "preference of a male-dominated society."[14] Queens regnant, such as Elizabeth I, can be discussed in terms of the same male-privileged rituals that scholars use to discuss kings. Queens consort require a different focus, one that does not always lie in the realm that scholars have traditionally privileged.

The consort's success as queen lay primarily in the fertility of her body, making it impossible for her to escape from misogynist imagery connected to the female body. Further, because the early modern consort's role as wife placed her in a subordinate position, any attempt to exert political power appeared as a subversion of good government and natural order.

[9] J.L. Laynesmith, *The Last Medieval Queens* (Oxford: Oxford UP, 2005).

[10] See Linda Woodbridge and Edward I. Berry, *True rites and maimed rites: ritual and anti-ritual in Shakespeare and his age* (Univ of Illinois Pr, 1992).

[11] Carolyn Harris, *Queenship and Revolution in Early Modern Europe* (Palgrave Macmillan, 2016), 3–4.

[12] Woodbridge, *True rites*, 8.

[13] Woodbridge, *True rites*.

[14] Woodbridge, *True rites*.

For Henrietta Maria, the problematic role of the consort combined with political and religious prejudices. Carolyn Harris suggests that English Catholics had hoped that the Catholic Queen would operate according to a medieval model of queenship, "in which the monarch dispensed justice but the consort had the ability to intercede for the condemned."[15] This model of queenship would have allowed Henrietta Maria to advocate for the English Catholics without appearing to subvert the power of the king. Unfortunately, for Henrietta Maria, the intercessory role of the medieval queen paralleled the intercessory role of the Virgin Mary, which Puritan writers rejected as a usurpation of God's authority.[16]

After the Glorious Revolution, the prospect of a Catholic England died, and the victorious Protestants wrote the history, a history in which not only Henrietta Maria but also the succeeding Catholic Stuart queens consort could be alternately marginalized or demonized. Years of venomous parliamentary attacks on the queen throughout the 1640s left lasting scars on her reputation. Despite her efforts to present herself as a force of peace and order in the kingdom, many continued to present the queen as a dangerous Catholic woman whose devotion to an idolatrous faith led the king and the nation into a bloody war. Continued religious turmoil over the next few decades would guarantee that the queen's legacy would remain inextricably connected to popular opinions of the Catholic Church.

By the early twentieth century, the threat of Catholicism no longer animated the English imagination, and scholars such as Quinton Bone and Elizabeth Hamilton attempted to defend the queen against accusations that her malignant influence brought down the dynasty.[17] Unfortunately, in doing so, they often ended up downplaying her influence altogether. As Michelle White points out, while Bone and Hamilton challenged the idea that Henrietta Maria exercised control over Charles I, their biographies nullify Henrietta Maria as an historical figure, suggesting that she did little of any real importance.[18] Interestingly, even those who suggest that she helped temporarily bring down the Stuart monarchy often deny her agency in that action, suggesting that in her frivolity she created tensions in the political world, all the while blithely staging her extravagant masques. For

[15] Harris, *Queenship*, 30.
[16] See Chapter 3: "The Virgin Mary and Protestant Reformers" in Diarmaid MacCulloch, *All Things Made New: The Reformation and Its Legacy* (Oxford UP, 2016).
[17] Bone, *Henrietta*; Hamilton, *Henrietta*.
[18] Michelle White, *Henrietta Maria and the English Civil Wars* (Ashgate, 2006), 2–3

example, Henrietta Haynes proclaims the queen a failure, arguing that she "failed to commend either her person, her religion, or her political ideas, and she brought her husband a degree of unpopularity which without her he might have escaped."[19] Haynes asserts that, had Henrietta Maria "been a Protestant and a woman of profound sagacity, she might have saved her husband"; unfortunately, she "lived at a great moment, and she had no greatness to meet it."[20] Clearly, the historical queen—lacking the benefit of hindsight—did at times misjudge the political climate. However, Haynes' denouncement of the queen as a complete failure reveals a simplistic reading of history, which reduces a complex human being to a mere stereotype of female incompetence and disorder.

In recent decades, contemporary scholars such as Caroline Hibbard, Alison Plowden, Erica Veevers, Karen Britland, Laura Lunger Knoppers, Carolyn Harris, and Michelle Anne White have marshaled the available primary sources and offered a much more nuanced view of the queen.[21] These writers have emphasized the ways in which the queen influenced Caroline culture through her court performances and patronage of artists.[22] Indeed, Sophie Tomlinson argues that Henrietta Maria's influence extends beyond the private world of court entertainment, suggesting that public acceptance of actresses and female playwrights in the Restoration can be traced in part to the queen's performances.[23] Further, a number of historians and literary critics argue that Henrietta Maria did not merely

[19] Haynes, *Henrietta*, xiv.

[20] Haynes, *Henrietta*, xv.

[21] Caroline Hibbard, "Translating Royalty: Henrietta Maria and the Transition from Princess to Queen." *Court Historian*. 5.1 (2000): 15–28; Alison Plowden, *Henrietta Maria: Charles I's indomitable queen*. (Sutton Publishing, 2001); Erica Veevers, *Images of Love and Religion: Queen Henrietta Maria and Court Entertainments* (Cambridge University Press, 1989); Karen Britland, *Drama at the courts of Queen Henrietta Maria* (Cambridge: Cambridge UP, 2006); Laura Lunger Knoppers, *Politicizing Domesticity from Henrietta Maria to Milton's Eve* (Cambridge University Press, 2011); White, *Henrietta Maria*, 2006.

[22] While scholars such as Melinda Gough and Barbara Ravelhofer argue that Henrietta Maria played a key artistic role in the masques that she sponsored, scholars such as Axel Stähler continue to present the queen's theatrical collaborators as the real creative force behind the masques. Gough, "'Not As Myself': The Queen's Voice in *Tempe Restored*," *Modern Philology* 101 (2003), 48–67; Ravelhofer, *The Early Stuart Masque: Dance, Costume, and Music* (Oxford: Oxford UP 2009); and Stähler, "Inigo Jones's *Tempe Restored* and Alessandro Piccolomini's *Della institution morale*," *The Seventeenth Century* 18 (2003), 180–210.

[23] Sophie Tomlinson, *Women on Stage in the Stuart Drama* (Cambridge: Cambridge UP 2006), 3.

concern herself with fashion and frivolity, but instead actively participated in English politics and diplomacy.[24]

Scholarship, however, is not the primary way that the public consumes information, and representations of Henrietta Maria in popular culture had a more significant influence on her image in the nineteenth and early twentieth centuries than academic works did. In Chap. 9 of this book, Sarah Betts examines a variety of nineteenth- and twentieth-century representations of Henrietta Maria in image, text, and performance. Betts shows that, despite the tendency of scholars to either dismiss or demonize Henrietta Maria, many popular representations cast the queen as a romantic heroine. These images, inspired by Antony Van Dyck's paintings of the royal family, focus on the queen's idyllic life before the Civil War, her great love for her husband, and her profound suffering at his death. Although these images of Henrietta Maria prove far more sympathetic than scholarly assessments of the queen as a foolish wife or Parliamentary representations of her as a malevolent plotter, they still tend to present the queen in terms of recognizable female stereotypes.

While contemporary fiction writers do not present the queen's attempts to exert power as part of a nefarious plot to overthrow Protestant England, as her enemies in the seventeenth century did, writers such as Plaidy, nonetheless, present the queen as a threat to the Stuart dynasty and to the nation. In her foolishness and frivolity, Plaidy's Henrietta Maria unknowingly sows the seeds of her husband's destruction and of civil war. In Plaidy's book, an older, wiser version of Henrietta Maria narrates her own story, primly dismissing her earlier behavior as foolish and unseemly. For example, after relating an argument between herself and Charles over his desire to appoint English women to her bedchamber, the more mature Henrietta tells the reader that Charles realized "that it was never any use trying to convince me. He believed now that I was the most illogical, unreasoning young woman imaginable, a creature of whims and fancies, lacking completely in control of my feelings."[25] The more mature queen agrees with Charles' assessment of her younger self, saying, "I know I was the main cause of all of the unhappiness of those years. I could not see it then."[26] Because the casual reader may well have read little about Henrietta

---

[24] See Michelle Dobbie, "Political Intrigue and Early Modern Diplomacy," *Lives and Letters* 2 (2010), 1–16.

[25] Jean Plaidy, *Myself My Enemy*, (G.P. Putnam's Sons, 1983), 91.

[26] Plaidy, *Myself My Enemy*.

Maria's life, Plaidy's novel—presented as it is in the queen's voice—takes on an air of authenticity despite its status as a fictional work.

In Plaidy's hands, young Henrietta becomes the embodiment of the stereotypes that contemporary society uses to diminish and silence teenage girls: she is moody, silly, impulsive, and vain. Indeed, the narrative presents Henrietta's previous attempts to exert authority as little more than the frivolity of youth. Further, Plaidy explicitly links Henrietta's failure as a queen to her failure as a wife. One would certainly be justified in presenting the personal as political in the life of a consort; as Harris argues, "The seemingly private activities of a queen consort became political acts when they conflicted with the expectations of her husband's subjects."[27] Plaidy's book, however, does not offer the kind of nuance that a discussion of the role of the domestic in politics requires. Instead, the book, which was published in 1983, reads almost like a nineteenth-century conduct book, placing blame on Henrietta Maria primarily because of her failure to be a good wife.

In Plaidy's telling, Charles is patient and longsuffering, while Henrietta is too spoiled and stubborn to see that she is undermining her marriage and her new nation. This point becomes particularly clear as Henrietta recounts Charles' decision to send her French attendants back to France. Henrietta tells the reader, "my trouble in those days was that I never looked beyond the immediate moment. If I scored a little victory I thought that I had won the war – though why there should be a war between husband and wife I cannot see now."[28] By presenting the conflict between Charles and younger self as unnecessary warfare, older Henrietta Maria erases her younger self's justification for opposing her husband, suggesting that any such resistance was both petty and dangerous. In addition, she makes the teenaged Henrietta Maria responsible for the failures in that marriage. Plaidy acknowledges that Buckingham held undue influence over Charles, but she offers little criticism for Charles' failures early in the marriage. For example, after describing the dismissal of her French retinue, older Henrietta marvels at Charles' kindness toward her despite her anger at his actions: "When Charles came to me I refused to speak to him. I see now how patient he was, how sorry that this had happened."[29] Plaidy might intend for this response to show mature Henrietta Maria's love for

[27] Harris, *Queenship*, 2.
[28] Plaidy, *Myself*, 109.
[29] Plaidy, *Myself*, 115.

her husband; however, it also manages to excuse Charles' behavior even as it minimizes the pain that young Henrietta Maria would have felt at Charles' aggressive disbanding of her household.

As the book progresses, Henrietta Maria becomes more dangerous as her influence moves from the domestic realm to the political. As Plaidy describes the nation's descent into civil war, she presents Henrietta Maria as a meddling wife whose attempts to help her husband only place him in greater danger. In recounting Charles' struggles with Parliament, Plaidy presents Henrietta Maria as a dangerous counselor to the king: "Impetuous, unworldly, without even the smallest understanding of the situation, I plunged in to save him."[30] In case the reader should miss Henrietta Maria's culpability, Plaidy presents Henrietta as explicitly blaming herself for Charles' troubles, even suggesting that she might have caused his death: "I know now that he would have done so much better without me. Who knows, he might even have been saved."[31] Plaidy's rhetoric is anything but subtle. She effectively places the criticism leveled against Henrietta Maria by scholars such as Haynes in Henrietta's own mouth. Henrietta, thus, utters lines such as "I have always been foolish; now I added recklessness to my folly" and "We did not at first realize how disastrously we – or rather I – had mismanaged that affair."[32] As Plaidy rarely delves into the complex causes of the war or the ways that Parliament manipulated images of the queen to cast her as a danger to the state, she leaves her reader with the impression that Henrietta Maria's incompetence doomed the king and the land.

By contrast, Mountain, writing in the twenty-first century, attempts to depict Henrietta Maria as a complicated, empowered woman. However, this representation also proves problematic, for Henrietta Maria's more empowered persona does not appear until very late in the novel, and, when it does appear, Mountain constantly undercuts it with an obsessive emphasis on Henrietta's sexual desire for Jermyn. The early part of the book introduces the reader to a teenaged Henrietta,[33] brimming with naïveté and youthful sexuality. Traditional representations of Henrietta Maria persist in Mountain's novel. The narrator refers to her "quick temper," informs that reader that "she did know how to flirt," and calls her

---

[30] Plaidy, *Myself*, 201.

[31] Plaidy, *Myself*.

[32] Plaidy, *Myself*, 201 and 231.

[33] Mountain refers to the queen as Henrietta.

"vain and giddy."[34] While authors often begin their books with naïve versions of their characters in order to reveal their increasing maturity over time, Mountain waits entirely too long to show Henrietta's maturity. In 1626, a year after Henrietta's marriage, Mountain describes her in ways that foreground her frivolity: "Like a child, Henrietta's mood could transform itself in an instant from abject misery to heady joy."[35] Ten years later, in 1636, Henrietta still lacks a sense of the seriousness of the political tensions building around her. As Jermyn discusses Ship Money, one of the early causes of tension between king and country, Henrietta must force herself to pay attention: "Concentrate, Henrietta chided herself. Taxes. They were talking again about damned taxes."[36] In this passage, Henrietta appears as dangerously ignorant of the political climate as Haynes' scholarship assumed her to be. Thus, even in a contemporary novel for women, the author seems reluctant to imagine a queen who would have understood the political world around her, leaving readers who are unfamiliar with the queen to imagine her as a silly woman driven primarily by her sexual appetites.

Even when Mountain's Henrietta does begin to take a mature, empowered role, her passion for Jermyn overshadows all other aspects of her character, including her faith. In giving Henrietta Maria a dispensation to marry a Protestant, Pope Urban VIII exhorted the young princess to be the Esther to her oppressed Catholic people. Because Mountain focuses so intently on developing the love triangle, she completely misses the opportunity to explore the problems that this commission would have created for the young queen. As soon as she stepped on English soil, Henrietta had to navigate the demands of two conflicting roles: queen of a Protestant nation and symbolic leader of her English Catholic subjects. Henrietta Maria's life bears testimony to her struggle to support her husband's dynasty while simultaneously pushing a religious agenda that threatened to undermine that dynasty. These conflicting loyalties haunted Henrietta Maria's life as queen, affecting every aspect of her royal performance including her coronation. Henrietta Maria remained an uncrowned queen because she feared that the English Catholics would be disheartened to see her kneeling before a Protestant bishop, and Charles refused to allow the Bishop of Mende to crown her.

---

[34] Fiona Mountain, *Cavalier Queen* (Arrow Books, 2011), 17, 27, and 73.
[35] Mountain, *Cavalier Queen*, 198.
[36] Mountain, *Cavalier Queen*, 325.

Considering the historical implications of the queen's faith, one might be surprised that Mountain spends so little time developing it. Despite frequent obligatory reminders that Henrietta's Catholicism put her in opposition to the Protestant court and Parliament, the majority of the text ignores the reality of the queen's faith. Even when Mountain introduces Henrietta's desire to restore Catholicism, which she refers to as the queen's "glorious destiny," she does so in a way that undermines Henrietta's agency.[37] According to the narrator, to the queen "it felt like a heavy responsibility to place on her frail shoulders and she was not sure she was equal to it. But it was such a worthwhile aim that she would not be daunted, would do her very best not to disappoint."[38] Mountain recognizes the heavy burden of Henrietta's commission, but manages to erase Henrietta's own agency, framing the queen's desire to restore Catholic worship as a desire to please others. Further, except for a few references to remind us of Henrietta's spiritual mission, most of the text focuses on Henrietta's more carnal mission. Only two pages after offering the reader this contemplation of the queen's destiny, the narrator reminds us of the queen's more pressing calling, bedding Jermyn: he "was the first man that she had seen naked and had kissed, and whom she secretly longed in her heart to see naked again, to kiss again."[39] Mountain's focus on Henrietta Maria's desires as opposed to her devotions makes sense. Contemporary culture tends to conflate mere sexual appetite with actual female empowerment and character development. Further, romance novels often foreground sexual desire, and forbidden desire creates more dramatic tension than licit married love. As such, we can understand why an historical romance novel would play up historical gossip to create a more compelling narrative. The problem with Mountain's take on Henrietta Maria is that she places this forbidden love plot above everything else. Henrietta Maria spends little time thinking about building dynasty, staging entertainments, or restoring Catholicism. Indeed, the majority of her thoughts center squarely on Jermyn and her desires for him.

Mountain's depiction of Henrietta's faith remains problematic throughout the text. While attending mass in her private closet with her children, Henrietta has one of her rare religious experiences: "Through her children's enthralled eyes, Henrietta experienced the miracle of the mass as if

[37] Mountain, *Cavalier Queen*, 83.
[38] Mountain, *Cavalier Queen*.
[39] Mountain, *Cavalier Queen*, 85.

for the first time. She felt afresh the beauty of the ancient rhythms that had soothed her soul since she was a little girl, the solemn reading of the gospels, the recitation of psalms and the creed through which God spoke."[40] Mountain's description of "ancient rhythms" and "solemn readings" may evoke the atmosphere of a mass. However, it reduces the queen's religious faith to window dressing. As the book progresses, Henrietta's response to her faith remains disappointingly superficial, particularly for someone who, prior to her marriage, had undergone a course of study with Father Berulle, founder of the Oratorian Order.[41] The narrator's description of Henrietta's response to the dedication of her Chapel, an event that brought Catholicism back to the heart of the court, provides a telling example: "She had made it happen. She had done it primarily for her mother, as well as for the Pope and for God, but for the first time she saw why it was so important to them."[42] This passage undermines Henrietta's agency even as it affirms it, for, while the passage serves to demonstrate Henrietta's success at restoring her religion to the court, it also makes clear that Henrietta's primary motivation for doing so is not based on firm conviction but instead on a desire to please other people. Even at this stage in her life, Henrietta still operates as an agent of her mother and the Pope. More disturbing, Henrietta apparently does not understand the importance of restoring Catholicism until the dedication of the chapel. This pattern of representation persists throughout much of the text, as the narrator presents this defining part of Henrietta's life as the literary equivalent of a stage prop—not intended to drive plot or characterization.

The problematic nature of Plaidy and Mountain's representation of Henrietta's faith becomes clear when we examine two key events presented in both texts: Henrietta Maria's disruption of an Anglican service and her "pilgrimage" to Tyburn. Many historians recount the story of Henrietta's disruption of an Anglican service as an example of her immaturity. To understand this incident, however, we must locate it the context of the Queen's difficult first months in England. Severe outbreaks of plague forced the royal family to move frequently from one location to the next. This constant movement made it difficult for the young queen to adapt to her surroundings, and separation from Charles left the queen,

---

[40] Mountain, *Cavalier Queen*, 318.

[41] Roger Lockyer, *The Early Stuarts: A Political History of England, 1603–1642* (Addison-Wesley Longman, 1999), 297.

[42] Mountain, *Cavalier*, 356–357.

who spoke little English, in the uncomfortable position of exercising her will over subjects who had no desire to accommodate her religious needs. Such was the case on August 12, 1625, when Charles I went hunting with Buckingham while Henrietta Maria went to Tichfield. Traditionally, when houses hosted the royal family, they would set up a chapel for the family's use. In this case, the queen's hosts ignored her request for a chapel in which to hear Mass, presenting her instead with Protestant services.[43] In response to this slight, Henrietta Maria performed an act of resistance, talking and laughing as she and her maids passed through the chapel in the middle of the Anglican minister's sermon.[44] While Pauline Gregg's assessment that Henrietta behaved "like a small child" does seem fair, we can see in Henrietta Maria's actions the same types of subversive performance often employed by those who lack power and aim to gain voice through disruption.

Plaidy presents Henrietta's actions as a willful subversion, a response to the Countess of Denbigh's holding the service without asking her permission. In Plaidy's account, Henrietta gathers her ladies and their dogs and parades them through the service as a reminder that to conduct such a service without the permission of the queen "was a breach of good manners."[45] Mountain also stresses that Henrietta interrupts the service to voice her displeasure—in this case as a response to the stress of Buckingham's criticism. However, while Mountain understands Henrietta's motivations, her word choice reduces the moment to silliness: "She took such delight in this simple act of revenge that one promenade was not enough."[46] On Henrietta's second walk through the service, Mountain describes her as "giggling at the thrill of such open rebellion," for she had "not had such fun in a long time."[47] Plaidy and Mountain rightly recognize the disruption of the service as a rebellious act; however, while Plaidy presents a Henrietta who understands the gravity of her actions, Mountain robs the scene of any deeper sense of subversion, ignoring the more serious reasons for Henrietta's actions.

Representation of Henrietta Maria's pilgrimage to the Tyburn gallows, the site at which many Catholics including Edmund Campion had been

---

[43] Gregg, *King Charles I*, 55.

[44] For a sociological overview of theories of resistance, see Jocelyn Hollander and Rachel Einwohner, "Conceptualizing Resistance" in *Sociological Forum* 19, no. 4 (2004): 533–554.

[45] Plaidy, *Myself*, 96.

[46] Plaidy, *Myself*, 165.

[47] Plaidy, *Myself*.

executed, proves even more problematic because neither author integrates this important and dramatically interesting scene into the overall structure of the novel. According to Michelle Anne White, "among the manuscript sources at the British Library only one reference to such a pilgrimage could be found."[48] According to this account, at 3 o'clock in the afternoon, on June 26, 1626, Henrietta Maria reportedly walked with five of her servants from St. James' palace and "kneeld before Tyburn gallows and prayed the space of five minutes."[49] Her performance proved particularly subversive, for it called into question the actions of recent monarchs, suggesting that those executed at Tyburn were not traitors, but martyrs.

Plaidy presents this moment of devotion as accidental and insignificant, avoiding the serious implications of the Tyburn visit by presenting Henrietta as happening upon Tyburn while taking a walk with Father Sancy. Henrietta reflects on the suffering of her people, and Sancy suggests that they "say a short prayer for their souls."[50] Thus, the "pilgrimage" is not premeditated, and Henrietta's investment is minimal. Henrietta's actions lead to rumors in which "the incident was embellished and distorted out of all proportion to what had actually taken place."[51] Henrietta reports, "I heard that I had done penance at Tyburn; I had walked barefoot carrying a candle. I had set up an altar there; I had said Mass; I had prayed to the Virgin and the saints for the souls of those I called Martyrs."[52] Plaidy downplays the religious significance of the event, using it instead to discuss the queen's vulnerability to scandal. While Plaidy does a good job of showing the dangerous political minefield that Henrietta Maria traverses, she simultaneously robs Henrietta of any sort of agency in the actions that caused such tension in the Caroline court.

Mountain presents the Tyburn visit as a pilgrimage, even placing it on Holy Thursday, to heighten the religious connections. Further, Henrietta performs the traditional role of penitent pilgrim, walking barefoot to Tyburn, "a place that had haunted and disturbed her since she had learned of it."[53] The rest of the description offers a picture of devotion that is largely missing from the rest of the novel:

[48] White, *Henrietta*, 25.
[49] White, *Henrietta*.
[50] Plaidy, *Myself*, 110.
[51] Plaidy, *Myself*.
[52] Plaidy, *Myself*.
[53] Mountain, *Cavalier*, 170.

> Henrietta knelt for a few moments at the centre of the triple tree where so many Catholic saints and martyrs had died the most agonising death.... Overcome with a sense of bravery and supreme self-sacrifice of the martyrs, Henrietta closed her eyes to whisper a prayer for their souls. "God give me the grace to die for my religion if I have to, as they have done," she whispered.[54]

If this passage were not so anomalous, this book could have been very compelling. Henrietta Maria's faith, a driving force in her life, placed her at odds with the king and his people. Rather than abandon her faith, she pushed forward with a zeal that would strike fear in the hearts of the king's Puritan subjects. The conflict between duty to her faith and duty to her king doomed her from the start in a way that evokes Sophocles' Antigone. Further, fighting to restore the faith while grappling with the reality of an adulterous liaison could have created some compelling drama. Mountain could have used this conflict to create richer, more complex characters. Unfortunately, Mountain does little to develop Henrietta's faith and these sentiments about martyrdom ring hollow when juxtaposed with Henrietta's general lack of concern with her religion.

Despite Henrietta's assertion that she desires to serve even to the point of martyrdom, the reader sees little evidence of this fervor in the novel. Indeed, the narrator relates the moral significance of Henrietta's relationship to Jermyn in decidedly flippant terms:

> It was not that Henrietta did not feel guilt. If Father de Berulle were there, she would have confessed everything to him. It would have been a relief to confess and be absolved. But she could not bring herself to tell Father Philip. She did not know him well enough.... She felt guilty but not sufficiently guilty to stop .... And when she knelt alone before the private altar in her closet and looked up at candles and the statue of Mary, she could not put aside the idea that he had been sent to her, given to her.[55]

Mountain's Henrietta has little understanding of the purpose of confession, viewing it primarily as a form of therapy that will provide "relief." From a narrative perspective, we cannot help but wonder why Mountain did not enhance the conflict in the story by having Henrietta experience an actual crisis of conscience where her love for Jermyn had to be honestly

---

[54] Mountain, *Cavalier*.
[55] Mountain, *Cavalier*, 216–217.

weighed against her love for the Church. Instead, Mountain offers a cop-out that extricates Henrietta from her moral problem: she sanctifies the affair, presenting it not as sin—but as a "gift" from God. As the novel continues, we find few additional references to Henrietta's relationship with Jermyn as adultery or sin. Thus, the queen's faith, a significant com-ponent of her character, remains unexamined as the narrator focuses on Henrietta's obsessive desire to possess Jermyn.

Henrietta Maria in Love: Problems of a Love Triangle

Plaidy presents the relationship between Charles and Henrietta Maria as a love match; nonetheless, she seems uncomfortable with Henrietta Maria's sexuality. The mature Henrietta Maria tells us that "I loved Charles so dearly, so intensely"; however, "I was not a sensual woman; my love for him was protective, almost maternal."[56] With these words, Plaidy domes-ticates Henrietta's desire in rather disturbing ways. Later, she asserts, "I thought of Charles as one of my children."[57] Mountain's Henrietta feels much the same way about Charles; however, unlike Plaidy's protagonist, Mountain's Henrietta does not lack sensuality. She simply directs all of her sexual desires toward Jermyn.

Mountain begins the novel with an aging Henrietta Maria speculating about her legacy: "A hundred years from now, two hundred, three hun-dred ... what would the history books say about her then? ... That she was Harry Jermyn's whore and her sons his bastards."[58] Fortunately for fic-tional Henrietta, most historians do not accept the idea that she had an affair with Jermyn. Mountain, however, influenced by Anthony Adolph's biography of Jermyn, *Full of Soup and Gold*, repackages anti-royalist pro-paganda and presents it to the reader as truth. Readers do not expect his-torical romance novels to operate as history textbooks, and one cannot fault Mountain for following the conventions of the romance, a genre which Pamela Regis calls "the most popular, least respected literary genre."[59] I do not wish to attack the genre or this book; instead, I am interested in what this particular rendering of the life of Henrietta Maria

---

[56] Plaidy, *Myself*, 201.
[57] Plaidy, *Myself*.
[58] Mountain, *Cavalier*, 3.
[59] Pamela Regis, *A Natural History of the Romance Novel* (U of Pennsylvania Press, 2007): xi.

tells us about twenty-first century attitudes toward powerful women and about the ways that popular culture packages history. After all, as Julia Novak observes, "contemporary biofictions about women speak as much about twenty-first century conceptions of femininity as to particular historical moments of female subjectivity."[60] We can allow for some creative license, particularly when changing history leads to more complex characterization. However, Mountain's portrayal of Henrietta and Jermyn's affair proves problematic because it not only changes the historical Henrietta's character, but also because it flattens it. Further, it fails on the level of dramatic plotting, for it introduces a love triangle that does not offer the protagonist two equally appealing options. Even though the love between Charles and Henrietta Maria is eternalized in letters, Van Dyck paintings, and even the propaganda of Parliamentary enemies who feared their closeness, Charles appears as a decidedly weak side in this love triangle.

While Jermyn provokes passion, Charles merely provokes Henrietta's sympathy, a pattern that begins the moment the narrator introduces each character. Mountain introduces Charles through a picture, reducing him to a two-dimensional surface as opposed to an embodied human. Further, Henrietta's first sight of Charles is mediated through Jermyn who shows her the king's picture. The narrator's initial description of Charles undermines the triangle from the outset: "[His eyes] were indeed sorrowful, unspeakably so. Large and slightly protuberant and sorrowful as Henrietta's beloved spaniel's. The saddest eyes she had ever seen in her entire life. His whole face was sad, positively tragic ... it made her feel sad too, just to look at him."[61]

This description of Charles proves particularly problematic when placed alongside Henrietta Maria's initial response to Jermyn, which appears a few pages earlier: He so "closely resembled the image of a tall, elegant, golden prince that Henrietta had come to nurture and cherish in her heart, that for one disorienting moment she was certain that the English were playing some great and clever trick upon them all and the prince himself had returned, incognito, to win *her* hand"[62] This confusion of future lover and bridegroom foreshadows the relationship of the future lovers—suggesting that their connection through fate supersedes her arranged marriage to Charles.

[60] Julia Novak, "Feminist to Postfeminist" in *Angelaki* 22, no. 1 (2017): 224.
[61] Mountain, *Cavalier*, 38.
[62] Mountain, *Cavalier*, 19.

In this love triangle, Charles continually comes out as the weaker side. While Charles' intimate relationship with his wife begins through a stilted diplomatic process, Jermyn's sexual relationship with Henrietta begins with a semi-erotic encounter in a garden. While in France with the delegation negotiating Henrietta's marriage to Charles, Jermyn gambles, loses his clothes, and ends up hiding in the garden. Henrietta, who apparently does not have any female attendants, overhears a conversation about his predicament and is inexplicably able to leave her room and go to the garden undetected. Although Henrietta is young and devoutly religious, when she comes upon the naked Jermyn, she covers him with her cloak and impulsively kisses him. Although this scene proves highly unrealistic in an early modern court setting where modern ideas of privacy would be anachronistic, the scene, nonetheless, proves pivotal to the development of Henrietta's character. In this scene of passion, Henrietta holds the power, and her connection with Jermyn involves her own sexual desires and choices in ways that her dynastic marriage does not.

Indeed, the marriage that Katie Whitaker refers to as "one of the greatest romances of all time: dramatic, emotional, and of vast historic importance" fades in comparison to Henrietta's passionate sex play with Jermyn.[63] Throughout the book, Henrietta's feelings for Charles rarely rise above the level of compassion. She feels sympathy for him, feels comfortable with him, but she never feels real sexual desire. This lack of passion not only undermines the construction of a compelling love triangle, but it also ignores a significant amount of historical information supporting a companionate marriage and an artistic partnership between the king and queen. While Whitaker presents Henrietta and Charles' union, particularly in the 1630s, as defining "British court culture" and "driving an exceptional flourishing of the arts,"[64] Mountain largely ignores the role that Henrietta Maria played in the artistic life of the court. In this text, Henrietta has little agency in the masques she commissions and little interest in patronage.

Henrietta Maria spends much of the novel obsessing over her relationship with Jermyn. At one point, the narrator tells us that, "at that moment, going to bed with Harry Jermyn was all that she wanted to do."[65] Such a

---

[63] Katie Whitaker, *A Royal Passion: The Turbulent Marriage of King Charles I of England and Henrietta Maria of France*. (W.W. Norton and Company, 2010): xvii.

[64] Whitaker, *A Royal Passion*.

[65] Mountain, *Cavalier*, 268.

flat depiction of Henrietta Maria is unfortunate. In a tale that takes place against the backdrop of the English Civil War, with a heroine who rides into battle as "Her She-Majesty, Generalissima," the reader might expect a stronger and more transgressive character. Indeed, one might have at least hoped for a Henrietta who would resemble a dystopian fiction heroine, both capable of human passion and able to look beyond her own desires. Mountain does present Henrietta as leading the army, camping with the men, and transgressing gender boundaries; however, she repeatedly normalizes and domesticates these transgressions by reminding the reader of Henrietta's heterosexual desire for a traditionally masculine character. Indeed, Mountain even includes a scene in which Henrietta relinquishes her royal authority over Jermyn in order to assuage his masculine pride. This scene encapsulates what is problematic with this text's representation of the queen. Jermyn and Henrietta have been engaged in a heated argument over Henrietta's attempts to restore Catholicism. Henrietta, however, is not upset "because of what he had said to her but because she wanted him ... wanted him to kiss her, to crush her in his arms."[66] Later, Jermyn returns to Henrietta, but Mountain makes clear that he does so "on his own terms and of his own free will," a move that fundamentally changes their relationship. As Mountain puts it, "he was, in effect, her equal now, an equality born out of need and love and respect."[67] This scene proves problematic on multiple levels. However, most disturbing is that Henrietta's sexual frustration proves a more powerful motivation than does her religious conviction, and she is clearly willing to give up her royal authority merely to satisfy her sexual desires.

Perhaps the most striking example of the domestication of the queen can be found in a scene where Parliamentary soldiers shell the house in which Henrietta is staying. As canons fire around them, Jermyn rescues the queen by pushing her in a ditch and throwing himself on top of her. The narrator tells us that Henrietta thought that "to lie with him on a bed of rocks in the cold, with cannon-shot raining down, was better than any feather mattress in a state bed in a palace."[68] We might have an easier time accepting this statement as realistic if only a page before (an hour earlier for Henrietta) Henrietta had not seen a Royalist soldier ripped apart by cannon fire. On the very same page that contains the description of Henrietta's

[66] Mountain, *Cavalier*.
[67] Mountain, *Cavalier*, 363.
[68] Mountain, *Cavalier*, 457–458.

joy at being under Jermyn, she sees a solider with a "youthful face beneath his feathered hat" hit by a cannonball that rips through his body: "Blood sprayed, black in the darkness. His legs crumpled, knees hitting the road before he fell down face first in the dirt."[69] Are we to believe that Henrietta can see a young man die and not think of her own young sons, who are fighting alongside their father? Are we to believe that Jermyn's body on hers is enough to make her forget her horrific introduction to war? Historical fiction can be passionate and compelling without reducing the female protagonist to a romantic stereotype.

If Mountain had wanted to invent a romantic backstory for Henrietta, she could have done so in the context of Henrietta's actual biography—focusing on the tension between Henrietta's desires and her religious beliefs or between her desires and the needs of the state. Instead, Mountain's book has the same problem that Gina Bellafante finds in the Showtime series *The Tudors*, which she says, "radically reduces the era's thematic conflicts to simplistic struggles over personal and erotic power."[70] Besides creating a reductive narrative, what is the cost of reducing a powerful woman to a stereotype? Reading the Goodreads reviews of Mountain's book offers some insights. Repeatedly, these reviews cited Mountain's book as their introduction to Henrietta Maria. Many reviewers admitted, "I have never learned about this time period," and "I was unfamiliar with this 'lesser known' queen." Historical facts are often a casualty when fiction masquerades as history. However, fictional representation becomes particularly problematic when the subject is a woman whose reputation for 400 years has been in the hands of people who have flattened her into a mold that fits their own needs and desires.

Reductive fictionalized narratives do great violence to the memory of historical figures, particularly when few other popular narratives exist to counterbalance them. Plaidy and Mountain could have presented Henrietta Maria as a complicated woman who wanted to protect her Catholic subjects through the type of intercessory role that had once been the prerogative of the queen. They could have shown her attempting to bolster her dynasty at a difficult moment in history. If Mountain had wanted to focus primarily on romance, she could have presented Henrietta as negotiating her desires for Jermyn against her strong religious beliefs. Plaidy and Mountain ignore these possibilities and downplay the queen's intelligence,

---

[69] Mountain, *Cavalier*, 457.

[70] William Robinson, *History, Fiction, and the Tudors: Sex, Politics, Power, and Artistic License in the Showtime Television Series* (Palgrave, 2016): 7.

power, and religion, flattening the historical truth about this complicated woman. Like writers in centuries past, Plaidy and Mountain focus so intently on the body of the consort and on her domestic role that they minimize her contributions in the realm of politics and culture. Thus, even in the late twentieth- and early twenty-first centuries, the queen consort cannot escape the culture's persistent desire to domesticate women who exercise authority in ways that transgress cultural expectations.

BIBLIOGRAPHY

PRIMARY SOURCES

Mountain, Fiona. *Cavalier Queen*. London: Arrow Books, 2012.
Plaidy, Jean. *Myself, My Enemy*. New York: G.P. Putnam's Sons, 1983.

SECONDARY SOURCES

Dunn-Hensley, Susan. *Anna of Denmark and Henrietta Maria: Virgins, Witches, and Catholic Queens*. New York: Palgrave Macmillan, 2017.
Gregg, Pauline. *King Charles I*. Berkeley: University of California Press, 1984.
Harris, Carolyn. *Queenship and Revolution in Early Modern Europe*. New York: Palgrave Macmillan, 2016.
Haynes, Henrietta. *Henrietta Maria*. New York: HardPress Publishing, 2016. (reprint)
Mantel, Hilary. "Royal Bodies." London Review of Books. February 21, 2013. https://www.lrb.co.uk/v35/n04/hilary-mantel/royal-bodies
Laynesmith, J.L. *The Last Medieval Queens: English Queenship 1445–1503*. Oxford: Oxford University Press, 2005.
Novak, Julia. "Feminist to Postfeminist." *Angelaki* 22, no. 1 (2017): 223–230.
Regis, Pamela. *A Natural History of the Romance Novel*. Pittsburgh: University of Pennsylvania Press, 2007.
Robinson, William. *History, Fiction, and the Tudors: Sex, Politics, Power, and Artistic License in the Showtime Television Series*. New York: Palgrave, 2016.
Whitaker, Katie. *A Royal Passion: The Turbulent Marriage of King Charles I of England and Henrietta Maria of France*. New York: W.W. Norton and Company, 2010.
White, Michelle Anne. *Henrietta Maria and the English Civil Wars*. Aldershot: Ashgate, 2006.
Woodbridge, Linda, and Edward I. Berry. *True rites and maimed rites: ritual and anti-ritual in Shakespeare and his age*. Champaign: University of Illinois Press, 1992.

CHAPTER 16

"Let them eat cake, she says": Assessing Marie-Antoinette's Image

Courtney Herber

Marie-Antoinette is one of those historical figures who everyone seems to *know*. She is *known* for her orgies and gambling and especially for her cal-loused dismissal and ignorance of the peoples' starvation to which she allegedly responded, "Let them eat cake." Whether these *facts* are indeed verifiable in the historical record, it is important to examine their origins. It is even more important to place their rise as rumors within the cultural consciousness of its own historical moment. My goal in this chapter is not to correct the historical inaccuracies that exist in the media or minds of the public. Instead, this chapter aims to identify some of the major works in which we meet Marie-Antoinette throughout the last century and to con-textualize each version of her that we meet within that historical moment.

In this chapter, I examine three historical moments in which Marie-Antoinette appears in mainstream popular culture. As Robert Brent Toplin writes, "Historical films help to shape the thinking of millions. Often the depictions seen on the screen influence the public's view of historical

C. Herber (✉)
University of Nebraska, Lincoln, NE, USA

© The Author(s) 2019
E. Paranque (ed.), *Remembering Queens and Kings of Early Modern England and France,* Queenship and Power,
https://doi.org/10.1007/978-3-030-22344-1_16

301

subjects much more than books do."[1] The moments that will book-end this short survey are the 1938 MGM feature film, "Marie-Antoinette," and the 2006 Sofia Coppola film *Marie Antoinette*. To provide context for these films, I provide analysis of the biographies which inspired them, Stefan Zweig's *Marie Antoinette: The Portrait of an Average Woman* for the 1938 film and Lady Antonia Fraser's *Marie Antoinette: The Journey* for the 2006 film. Inspired by the same biography as the 1938 film, I also incorporate the Japanese anime *The Rose of Versailles* into my analysis. Through these moments, I examine the use of her character with an eye for political, economic, and socio-cultural issues and contextualize the use of Marie-Antoinette's image within the various historical moments in which they arose.

"The Portrait of an Average Woman"

Born in Vienna to a Jewish family in 1881, Stefan Zweig was a prolific author. He spent the first part of his life in Austria-Hungary, but after the rise of fascism in Austria, he fled the Continent ultimately to settle in Brazil. Along the way, he befriended Sigmund Freud, who heavily influenced his writings. His biography on the tragic French queen was published in its original German in 1932 with an English translation in 1933.

The Austria in which Zweig crafted his biography of Marie-Antoinette was one of political strife and instability. Created in 1919 after the signing of the Treaty of Saint-Germain-en-Laye, the First Republic of Austria replaced the Austro-Hungarian Empire, which had officially existed as a political body since 1867.[2] While World War I reduced the landed aristocracy to genteel poverty, all citizens dealt with inflation.[3] Vienna was held politically by the Social Democrats who implemented sweeping social reforms designed to help working-class urban families, such as child care and schools, and free hospitals.[4] As much as they were designed to help ease

[1] Robert Brent Toplin, *History by Hollywood: The Use and Abuse of the American Past* (Urbana & Chicago: University of Illinois Press, 1996), vii.

[2] Of course, the kingdom of Austria-Hungary had existed prior to 1867. The Austrian Habsburgs had ruled in the area since the middle ages, but it was not until 1867 that the Austro-Hungarian Compromise was signed. The Austro-Hungarian Empire was broken up in 1919 by the Treaty of Saint-Germain-en-Laye, one of the many treaties crafted at Versailles after World War I.

[3] David Clay Large, *Between Two Fires: Europe's Path in the 1930s* (New York: W. W. Norton & Company, Inc., 1990), 60.

[4] Large, *Between Two Fires*, 61.

the financial situation for families, those programs were expensive and as there were no longer many truly wealthy in Austria, the middle class, divided between urbanites and rural folk, had to foot the bill. The rural countryside, which produced the food and other necessities for the nation to function, were represented by the conservative Christian Social party. In response to Social Democratic attempts to force their control over the unwilling "black" countryside, a homegrown paramilitary organization sprung up, the *Heimwehren*.[5] Another influential paramilitary movement on the right was the *Frontkämpfer Vereinigung* (Front Fighter's Association). To protect "red" Vienna, the *Republikanischer Schutzbund* were created. These paramilitary groups fought one another for territory through the 1920s, but they did not tend to draw civilians into their conflicts. This changed in 1927 on "Bloody Friday." The fractious politics of the conservative countryside and left-wing Vienna simmered at a fever-pitch until violence broke out in January of 1927. At a veteran's rally in Schattendorf, a Front Fighter sympathizer shot into a *Schutzbund* group killing two members, leading to the Schattendorf Verdict which incited people to riot in the streets of Vienna.[6] Protestors made their way to government buildings; the mob vandalized and set fire to police stations, University buildings, Parliament, and the Palace of Justice. To bring the mob under control, Johann Schober, the police chief ordered his men to shoot into the crowds if they continued to obstruct the fire brigade's work. The mob did not relent, and the police forces fired into the crowds killing nearly 100 people.[7] The right-wing forces at work during the July Revolt of 1927 grew more powerful in the aftermath. The Christian Social Party, who generally represented the rural "black" countryside, under Chancellor Engelbert Dollfuss took power in 1932, which set Austria on a path toward fascism and further violence, due to his desire to keep Austria independent from Hitler's Nazi Germany. While the rise of the Austrofascist Federal State of Austria was not politically similar to the rise of the French Third Estate and the Estates-General, both signified an upheaval of social and political order.[8]

It was in this upheaval that Zweig researched and wrote his biography of Marie-Antoinette. While there are natural comparison points between the France of the late eighteenth-century and Austria of the 1930s, Zweig keeps his feelings about the rising fascist regime to a minimum and instead

[5] Large, *Between Two Fires*, 63–64.
[6] Large, *Between Two Fires*, 65.
[7] Large, *Between Two Fires*, 66–74.
[8] Large, *Between Two Fires*, 74–77.

focuses on the Freudian analysis of the Queen.[9] However, to use a little Freudian-esque analysis on his text, his anxieties show through at a few points, especially when connected to moments of high tension within the Queen's story. While Zweig could not explicitly state his comparisons between his current situation and the Queen's a century and a half earlier, some of his experiences come out in his descriptions, such as "the pent-up excitement of the whole country was being spurted as from a fire-hose against an individual," a "violent thunder-clap," "As for the generals, they have never liked civilian interference in the conduct of war," and "Seen at close quarters and contemplated as the expression of our fallible humanity, every political movement looks confused and muddled."[10]

The "pent-up excitement...from a fire-hose" could recall how on Bloody Friday, the mob cut off the fire-hoses and the ability of the fire brigade to do its job in saving Vienna and the Palace of Justice from being subsumed by the arsonists' flames.[11] Zweig recalls the imagery when he describes another high-tension moment in Antoinette's story, just after the Affair of the Diamond Necklace is resolved, and the Queen goes out in public to the theater, she is shunned and derided by the public. Using the memory of the blazing flames to describe the icy treatment of the queen, Zweig brings together two moments when the populace made their feelings known through violence, either toward buildings in Vienna or verbal violence toward the Queen. He describes the incident as a "violent thunder-clap" which supposedly startled Marie-Antoinette "out of her arrogant indifference" regarding her household's budget and the economic situation outside of Versailles' grounds.[12] The effect that this had on the Queen was immediate and deep. She made economies in her household that saved over a million livre a year and she understood, for the first time, the power of public opinion.

"As for the generals," Zweig wrote, describing the Viennese reaction to the execution of Louis XVI, and the possibility of all-out war between Austria-Hungary and France, "they have never liked civilian interference

---

[9] There do not seem to be any documentary sources to point to why, exactly, he found Marie Antoinette so fascinating. There is little rhyme or reason to his biographies, as his own biographer pointed out, "The subjects he chose were a continual source of speculation and criticism." Elizabeth Allday, *Stefan Zweig* (London: W. & J. Mackay Limited, 1972), 16.

[10] Stefan Zweig, *Marie Antoinette: Portrait of an Average Woman*, trans. Eden Paul and Cedar Paul (New York: The Viking Press, 1933), 220, 203, 381.

[11] Zweig, *Marie Antoinette*, 203.

[12] Zweig, *Marie Antoinette*, 203.

in the conduct of war."[13] In this, just as in the description of late-eighteenth-century Vienna, he could just as easily have described the civilian involvement in the *Heimwehr* in his own Austria. The *Heimwehr* consisted of both volunteer and veteran soldiers, and perhaps it is to their involvement in the Bloody Friday and aftermath that he was reaching.

It was again to his Viennese past that Zweig beckoned when he described Antoinette's attitude toward the coming Revolution as something "confused and muddled." When looking at a moment of great social change, he off-handedly describes, it is difficult to see anything besides the big personalities involved. While Zweig goes on to list some of those involved in the Revolution with the Queen, such as the Duke of Orleans, Honore Mirabeau, and Charles-Maurice Tallyrand, it would not be hard to replace those names with Chancellor Dollfuss, Vienna Mary Karl Seitz, or Karl Renner.

While largely sympathetic to Marie-Antoinette and her plight, Zweig's approach to the Queen is one of tough-love. The representation of Marie-Antoinette in his biography is one who is impulsive, prone to flights of expensive fancy due to her need to be loved and lack of sexual satisfaction, and while not unintelligent her mind was not keen on academic pursuits. Several times throughout the book, Zweig refers to the Queen as that "average woman" who was "narrow-minded" and "indifferent." In his writing, Zweig brings Marie-Antoinette to life and paints her as an ordinary person until greatness is thrust upon her. Her nobility shines through at times of great peril, writes Zweig, and she becomes what France had needed all along: a prince to defend the monarchy.

It is easy to see how this biography inspired producer Irving Thalberg to adapt the text as a film. It is also easy to imagine how this film would have been quite popular and successful. The cinema, and the imaginative relief it provided to a beleaguered populace, was popular throughout the 1930s. MGM released up to 50 films a year and tickets cost generally between 10 and 25 cents throughout the United States. During the Great Depression, almost four times more Americans went weekly to the cinema than they did from the 1960s through to the 2000s.[14] "In 1930 (the earliest year from which accurate and credible data exists)," writes Michelle Pautz, "weekly cinema attendance was 80 million people, approximately

---

[13] Zweig, *Marie Antoinette*, 381.
[14] Michelle Pautz, "The Decline in Average Weekly Cinema Attendance: 1930–2000," *Issues in Political Economy* 11, Summer (2002): 54–65.

65% of the resident U.S. population. However, in the year 2000, that figure was only 27.3 million people, which was a mere 9.7% of the U.S. population."[15] Americans, during the hard times of the Great Depression, wanted to escape from their real lives and live, if only for a few hours, in a fantasy world where beautiful people had adventures, wore sumptuous costumes, went to exotic locations, and enjoyed happy endings.[16] Movies gave them that escape, and MGM was one of the largest and most successful of Hollywood's movie studios. *Marie Antoinette* had a massive budget and combined the prestige and period drama genres. There had been much excitement for the film, the production of which was followed closely by the *New York Times*. The *Times* ran pieces when the film began casting for its 152 speaking parts, concentrating on the drama surrounding who was going to be cast as Louis XVI opposite Norma Shearer, who played Antoinette, when filming with Shearer began, two years after Thalberg's death, and describing some of the work of recreating the halls of Versailles, as they were not allowed to film in the actual palace.[17] *The New York Times* reported that there had been "an unusual number [of sets] even for such a spectacle as this."[18] The crew of the film attempted to recreate as much of the rich visual landscape of pre-revolutionary France, down to costuming. Marie-Antoinette's wedding gown in the film reportedly weighed more than 100 pounds. It is unfortunate, then, that the movie was not filmed in Technicolor, but in black and white. What set this film apart from other narratives of Marie-Antoinette was that it was such a big production and it drew heavily from the Zweig biography as its inspiration for how to reincarnate such a controversial figure in the modern age.[19]

The movies of MGM in the Great Depression were about escaping the modern world back to a different time, place, or set of circumstances. *Marie Antoinette* was no exception to that and was successful in representing, but

[15] Pautz, "The Decline in Average Weekly Cinema Attendance," 1.

[16] Important to note—Television significantly contributed to a decline of movie attendance, as media consumers could simply achieve that escape in the comfort of their own homes.

[17] Although they did recreate the French royal residence, they did so on a much larger scale, especially for the ballroom scenes. Douglas W. Churchill, "Hollywood Cake," *The New York Times*, May 22, 1938, sec. Screen. Douglas W. Churchill, "Hollywood Turns Back the Clock," *The New York Times*, August 15, 1937, sec.

[18] Screen. "Casting Started on Shearer Film," *The New York Times*, October 8, 1937, sec. Amusements.

[19] "Van Dyke, The Trouble-Shooter," *The New York Times*, August 14, 1938.

still downplaying, the brutal truths of pre-Revolutionary France... so why focus a movie on an ill-fated queen and her execution? Firstly, while she may have been wealthy beyond the imaginings of many American filmgoers, that wealth, or the physical trappings of it, caught the imaginations of those who were going without. Secondly, it showed her caught in those trappings, and once she was freed of them, she became the person she was meant to be, the good and noble queen who goes to her death as a symbol of an institution. While Marie-Antoinette was the main character, the biggest draw could have been the beauty of the movie and its captivating drama. The film succeeds in both counts and it is engaging to watch Shearer's Marie-Antoinette grow up from a young teenager to the woman she becomes at the end of her life, facing the guillotine. The thrills of her love affair with Fersen, the sexual trials with her husband, the rise of the revolutionaries, and the fall of the monarchy all were exciting, foreign, and in some ways, also familiar to movie-going audiences who fell in love with the impulsive, kind, and loyal queen.

In both the Zweig text and the 1938 film, Marie-Antoinette's childlessness and lack of marital sexual fulfillment is the root cause of her gambling, dancing, and other irresponsible behaviors. "I liked the script because the story was told simply," Director W. S. Van Dyke told *The New York Times*, in a 1938 interview:

> not so much in terms of history as in terms of the people who made history. I could understand the people and their motives: Antoinette, a woman made emotionally unstable by a marriage that failed to be consummated; King Louis XVI, a psychopathic case because of a physical disability... I kept only one major purpose constantly in mind: that was to make my characters as little like kings and queens and princes and as much like ordinary human beings as possible.[20]

It is unsurprising then that the film's focus would be on her transformation from gay girl to serious mother. As Marie-Antoinette's motherhood was a fulcrum upon which the film and book centered, the role of mothers outside the realm of fictionalized history was also hotly debated. The film's production began in 1933, at a time when an increasing number of women were choosing to work outside the home.[21] As the Great Depression deepened, it

---

[20] "Van Dyke, The Trouble-Shooter," *The New York Times*, August 14, 1938.

[21] Alice Kessler-Harris, *In Pursuit of Equity: Women, Men, and the Quest for Economic Citizenship in 20th Century America* (Oxford: Oxford University Press, 2001), 35.

became harder for women to justify why they should continue to be employed while men, supposed to be the breadwinners, could not get or keep their jobs.[22] "The American standard," wrote Abraham Epstein, "assumes a normal family of man, wife, and two or three children, with the father fully able to provide for them out of his own income."[23] Wives and mother's places, in the minds of some lawmakers, were to be in the home and tending to children, not out in industry or other gainful employment, especially when men were less and less able to demonstrate their abilities in providing for their families, as was evidenced by the U. S. 1932 Economy Act. The Act, which included a clause that "required that in any reduction of civil service personnel, married persons whose spouses were also employed by the federal government should be dismissed first," made it easier to lay off women who had been employed for the sake of keeping their husbands on the payroll.[24] The Act only pertained to federal jobs, but the practice was nothing new in the private sector.[25] In the film, the audience would see both a glorification of motherhood and celebration of the family, as well as a cautionary tale of childless, reckless youth. In both Zweig's text and VanDyke's film, Marie-Antoinette's motherhood is essential to the story. While her first child was "alas, a daughter," the act of giving birth to a child brought "the woman's torment" to a close "and the mother's happiness" to the fore.[26] As much as the girl was a disappointment to some, her birth pushed Marie-Antoinette into her destiny and allowed her to become "a happy, serious-minded, and conscientious woman."[27] Giving birth allowed Marie-Antoinette to retreat from her gay life and devote herself to her family. The emphasis on the queen's son is quite evident in Zweig's text as even though Marie-Therese was born almost three years before Louis-Joseph, she merits four paragraphs to herself as only child before Zweig moves on to the birth of the *dauphin*.

Both the text and film, and indeed *The Rose of Versailles*, Coppola's *Marie Antoinette* and Fraser's *Marie Antoinette: The Journey* hinge on Marie-Antoinette's motherhood. While that is partly due to the historical record and the Queen's desire to have a child to cement her place at the

---

[22] Kessler-Harris, *In Pursuit of Equity*, 59.

[23] Abraham Epstein, *Insecurity, a challenge to America; a study of social insurance in the United States and abroad* (New York: H. Smith and R. Haas, 1933), 101.

[24] Kessler-Harris, *In Pursuit of Equity*, 59.

[25] Kessler-Harris, *In Pursuit of Equity*, 59–60.

[26] Zweig, *Marie Antoinette*, 139.

[27] Zweig, *Marie Antoinette*, 140.

French court and to have someone to love and nurture. Marie-Antoinette had always gotten along well with children, even from her first days at the French court when she met her two young sisters-in-law, Clothilde and Elisabeth (nine and six years old to the *dauphine's* 14).[28]

Motherhood was important to Marie-Antoinette and her fertility was important to the succession and kingdom. Motherhood was vaunted and respected in pre-Revolutionary France, as Enlightenment thinkers and novelists, such as Marie-Jeanne Roland wrote that it was a "woman's suffering in childbirth [that] made her the ethical subject *par excellence*."[29] By her suffering, it was thought that women taught men to pity, which according to Lesley H. Walker, was the very bedrock of ethical thinking in eighteenth-century France. Motherhood, the very act of giving birth, was seen as giving women a certain knowledge of morality, as it was expected that they would impart Christian values to their children. Royal motherhood, for Marie-Antoinette, was no different in that regard, which is why one of her most iconic portraits, that painted by Vigee Lebrun, *Marie-Antoinette and her Children* of 1787, features a queen full of worries and anxiety, surrounded by her adoring children, an empty cradle to the side most likely signifying the death of one of her daughters a few months before the painting was completed.[30] This portrait, symbolizing the Queen's love for her children as well as her domesticity, came on the heels of the Affair of the Diamond Necklace, a tension-filled moment in history when the Queen needed to repair her broken public image. She did so partly through portraits such as Lebrun's, which attempted to show her to be as much the "everymother" as other French mothers. It was partly through visual means that she waged a public relations campaign to connect her image with the idea of motherhood, rather than extravagance and luxury.

The 1938 film, especially, relies on those images. While Zweig wrote about the Queen as a tragic princess and as a mother, the film can show that transformation. The main difference between the film and Zweig's biography is necessarily the emphasis on visuals. While Zweig relies on his captivating prose to tell the queen's story, the filmmakers had to incorporate much more to draw in the media consumer. My impression of the film

---

[28] Antonia Fraser, *Marie Antoinette: The Journey* (New York: Doubleday, 2001), 68–69.

[29] Lesley H. Walker, *A Mother's Love: Crafting Feminine Virtue in Enlightenment France* (Cranbury, NJ: Associated University Presses, 2008), 15.

[30] Walker, *A Mother's Love*, 130.

is that there is a progression in the sumptuousness of the visuals as the story moves from its introduction to its sanitized conclusion. The Austrian court which opens the film is beautifully filmed. The French court, where the young Antoinette spent her formative years, is also stunningly recreated in the MGM studio lot, but as the queen grows up, becomes a mother and a bulwark of monarchy against the rising tide of popular sentiment, her costumes and the scenery become simpler. Without the trappings of wealth and privilege, she becomes a regular, ordinary woman, but one both resigned and noble. This is evidenced at both the end of the film and Zweig's biography. At her end, we see Marie-Antoinette driven through the crowds to the scaffold, silent and upright. She mounts the scaffold and as she stands, awaiting her death, we see a visual overlay of the young archduchess we met at the beginning of the film excitedly proclaiming that she would be the queen of France. Both versions of the character exist on the screen simultaneously, and behind the younger we see the heavy blade of the guillotine rise. The scene jarringly cuts to Fersen, who is on a nearby rooftop watching the execution of his lover. The crown cheers and he looks down, grief-stricken.

The 1938 film ends with the death of the queen. We do not see the moment of her death, and this was intentional, otherwise it would have been part of the film. By not showing the gruesome aftermath of her execution, the fantasy still plays on for the audience. With its conspicuous absence, the audience can possibly ignore the fact that she died. While Van Dyke made the scene as real as possible, including a real guillotine and directing Shearer to place her neck under it, by not focusing on the actual moment of her death, the verisimilitude of the scene is maintained.[31] The cohesion of the story is maintained, as is the illusion that maybe, just maybe, it allows for the audience to remember her as she was alive, and not to simply know her from her death. They do not have to confront the awful fate of Marie-Antoinette. They can sit and stretch as the lights turn on and fill the theater, in awe of the majesty and pomp that was in much of the film they just watched. Because there is only the brief glimpse of the guillotine blade, the queen's end is not viscerally communicated to the audience; only the facial expressions of Fersen and the cheers of crowds put "the end" onto the tragic tale of Marie-Antoinette, a woman who, but for a very unfortunate series of events and ill-thought out decisions, could

---

[31] Bosley Crowther, "The Queen was in her Parlor-at the Waldorf," *The New York Times*, August 21, 1938.

have lived a fairy tale. There was no happily ever after for Marie-Antoinette, but the audience had the opportunity to live vicariously the ups and downs of her life without having to grapple with her story's abrupt end.

Marie-Antoinette, for Zweig, was the perfect representation of an ordinary woman ennobled by the terrible circumstances of fate and a symbol of what the monarchy was supposed to be: a timeless institution that represented the dignity, honor, and pride of the French people. In going so resolutely to her death, her blood gave birth to the troubled Republic, as well as foreshadowed the deaths of many others, "No one troubles about the blood which is slowly soaking into the ground."[32] Not much is made of her actual moment of death, "a flash of the falling knife; a dull thud; and by the hair, Samson [the executioner] picked up a bleeding head and lifted it high for the multitude to gloat upon."[33]

What did invoking the queen's image do for MGM in 1938? What did the filmmakers hope to achieve with Marie-Antoinette that they could not with another ill-fated queen, such as Mary Stuart or Lady Jane Grey? All three were executed queens. What made MGM choose Marie-Antoinette? Partly, there already had been films on Mary Stuart and Lady Jane Grey, released in 1936. Importantly, Mary and Jane met their ends at the hands of other queens, namely Elizabeth and Mary Tudor. Perhaps MGM went with Marie-Antoinette because her story would allow for a grander budget costume drama; Versailles was known to be one of the grandest palaces in Europe and the extravagances of the eighteenth-century French court were legendary. Perhaps MGM went with the Austrian-French queen, instead of the English or Scottish-French ones, because Marie-Antoinette's struggles are ones which are easier to relate to as a twentieth-century audience. While dynastic struggles make interesting drama, what is far more relatable is finding social acceptance in peer groups, marriage troubles, childlessness, and the desire to protect one's family, especially against circumstances out of one's control.

The world of the Great Depression was no longer the hopeful or prosperous Roaring Twenties. In both Europe and in the Pacific, anti-democratic regimes were gaining power and a foothold in government. Adolf Hitler had seized control of the reins of government in Germany in 1934, ushering in an ever-more-horrific doctrine of fascist dictatorship, police states,

---

[32] Zweig, *Marie Antoinette*, 454.
[33] Zweig, *Marie Antoinette*, 454.

and genocide.[34] Japan had grown ever-more-powerful after the beginning of the Second Sino-Japanese War, and the Rape of Nanking was in the newspapers in the months preceding *Marie Antoinette*'s release.[35] Austria, France, Italy, and Spain were battling fascist movements in their own borders. The world was a dangerous and uncertain place. All the political unrest was exacerbated by economic uncertainty. So why did Marie-Antoinette's story need to be told again, at this very specific moment in time? While it was a welcome distraction from the dangers outside of the theater, her fate was also a warning. While to some Marie-Antoinette would always represent the "Let them eat cake" attitude of the ultra-wealthy during the French Revolution, as well as in their own time, she was also a victim of an angry populace and populist movement. Against the backdrop of the Great Depression and concerns about growing fascist movements in Europe, Marie-Antoinette's story told the possible dangers of populist movements and of the desperation of the common man, but it did so through the opulent lens of the privileged, in whose shoes the audience had an opportunity to dance a gavotte.

"THE ROSE OF VERSAILLES"

Born in 1947 in Osaka, Japan, Ikeda Ryoko is a *manga-ka* who rose to fame in the early 1970s.[36] Since then, several of her manga have been translated for European audiences. Her most popular was *Bara no Versailles*, or the Rose of Versailles. Inspired by the Zweig biography, the historical fiction *shoujo*, or girls', manga series was serialized 82 installments in the magazine *Margaret* from 1972 to 1973. It has since been collected into ten volumes of the *manga* and been adapted into a television *anime* of the same name. The *manga* has never been officially translated into English. The *anime*, though, has been professionally translated and released.[37] *Bara no Versailles* was originally intended to focus entirely on the character of Marie-Antoinette. However, after early fan polling (as is frequently done with Japanese *manga*), it was found that the clear favorite character was not Marie-Antoinette but a fictionalized addition

---

[34] Robert O. Paxton, *The Anatomy of Fascism* (New York: Alfred A. Knopf, 2004), 96.

[35] "Japan in Nanking," *The New York Times*, December 19, 1937.

[36] *Manga* is a Japanese comic, and a *manga-ka* is the writer/artist who creates *manga*.

[37] As of the time of this publication, *The Rose of Versailles* anime series was available at http://www.crunchyroll.com/

Ikeda created named Oscar Francois de Jarjayes. Lady Oscar is a girl who was raised as a boy and is skilled in swordsmanship. Eventually, when the *dauphin* is set to wed Marie-Antoinette, Oscar is called upon, because of her noble background and fighting skill, to head the Royal Guard.

Just as in the Zweig biography and the 1938 film, Marie-Antoinette in *The Rose of Versailles* is a likable character. Antoinette is shown to grow from a sweet and kind but spoiled young woman into a noble mother and queen. Her first appearance in the anime shows her chasing a beautiful butterfly and laughing in a fountain, her gown soaked, with her governesses trailing not too far behind her. She is vivacious and kind, but also mischievous and reluctant to meet her destiny as *dauphine*. Her mother, Maria Theresa, narrates an inner-dialogue expressing her concerns about her daughter, and foreshadowing a bit as well, "Marie, she's just 14 years old. Marie is still a carefree and playful tomboy. Perhaps the Royal Crown and the position of Queen will only bring her misfortune? Could I have made a terrible mistake?"[38] Soon after, the Empress tearfully says goodbye to her daughter, embracing her one last time. Sending her off with a wound scroll of advice, Maria Theresa sends her daughter to her new family and new husband in France. Along the way, the audience is made privy to a scheme by the Duke of Orleans, who plans to abduct the princess and kill her and replace her with a look-alike. The plan is foiled by Oscar, who single-handedly incapacitates or kills at least five henchmen of Orleans. She brings Antoinette to a nearby palace, where, even in the same hall as the look-alike, charms the king and court with her natural beauty and goodness. Initially, Oscar does not want to serve as the head of Antoinette's palace guard, calling her a "shrew" repeatedly, but over the course of the first season, Antoinette impresses Oscar with her noble bearing and kind disposition.

In her first introduction to court society at Versailles, at first Antoinette chafes at the strict protocols in place but learns to deal with them as she grows into her role as *dauphine*. When she enters into the great hall, wearing a pink and white gown, the crowd murmurs their approval of the new princess. One woman comments, "Look at how light and elegant her steps are."[39] Another says, "She certainly carries herself like an Austrian princess born from royal lineage." This, while complimentary, is in jarring contrast to how her Austrian lineage is portrayed later, as well as in other works like

---

[38] *The Rose of Versailles*, DVD (1979: Japan: Nozomi Entertainment, 2015), Episode 2.
[39] *The Rose of Versailles*, DVD (1979; Japan: Nozomi Entertainment, 2015), Episode 3.

the live-action films I examine in the chapter. The King himself, after retiring to Madame du Barry's chambers for the evening, comments on how well Antoinette carried herself in her first public appearance as the *dauphine*, "Antoinette," he tells an angry and jealous Jeanne du Barry, "has captured the hearts of everyone in the palace in just one day!"[40]

While she had captured the hearts of all those at court, excepting Madame du Barry, it is because of Antoinette's handling of the du Barry affair that helps Oscar to see her honorable nature and dignified behavior. Du Barry serves as Antoinette's first foil and enemy at court, and du Barry's underhanded scheme of implicating Oscar's mother in a murder plot put the *maitresse en titre* firmly in Antoinette's circles. The du Barry affair is simply the first in a long line of trials for Antoinette over the course of the series, and up until the very end of the series, Oscar proudly takes her place as head of Antoinette's guard. While Oscar's personal feelings toward Antoinette do not change, Oscar, once she sees how the people of France clamor for revolution, resigns her post as head of Antoinette's guard to join the Revolutionaries. "The Royal Family should never point a gun at its people," Oscar tells Antoinette at their final meeting, tears streaming from her eyes. While she was loyal to Antoinette, her loyalty to France was greater, and they bid one another *au revoir*. Oscar spends the remaining episodes battling consumption as well as the monarchist forces, dying from her wounds in the storming of the Bastille.

The revolutionary narrative would have been appealing to post-war Japanese audiences, as Anne McKnight writes "*Rose of Versailles's* dynamic and exuberant formal articulation and its pioneering 'bubble' language of character consciousness, the manga is structured by a historicist narrative: the demise of the court and the emergence of the 'people.'"[41] McKnight contextualizes the Japan of the 1970s in which Ikeda wrote and drew her *manga* and calls attention to the issues with which Ikeda grapples in her storyline, like issues of class, gender, citizenship and "a subjectivity grounded in the conditions of labor."[42] All of this is done through the examination of the French Revolution through the eyes of the characters of the young queen, Lady Oscar, and Oscar's disciple, Rosalie. Ikeda's focus on women was no accident. She was writing for the *shoujo* genre,

[40] *The Rose of Versailles,* DVD (1979; Japan: Nozomi Entertainment, 2015), Episode 3.

[41] Anne McKnight, "Frenchness and Transformation in Japanese Subculture, 1973–2004," *Mechademia* 5, Fanthropologies (2010): 118–137, 120.

[42] McKnight, "Frenchness and Transformation...," 120.

which is typically defined by its focus on character-driven story and romance, but Ikeda shifted the genre and incorporated the historical narrative which examined not only constructions of femininity and masculinity but also could have been inspired by the blossoming women's movement in Japan.

A reflection of the Second Wave Feminism that swept the world in the 1960s and 1970s, the *uman ribu* of Japan was one in which many of the activists were also supporters of the New Left movements, anti-Vietnam protests, or Red movements also sweeping Japan.[43] Women's rights to make decisions about their own fertility was one of the most important causes and tenants of the *uman ribu*. "Some of their [the *uman ribu*]," as Setsu Shigetsu writes, "most significant and sustained campaigns were directed against the state's attempts to restrict access to abortion, emphasizing instead 'the creation of a society' where 'women could decide' whether 'they wanted to give birth.'"[44] This ideal is embodied in the characters of both Marie Antoinette and Oscar. Both are born to the highest echelons of society and each follows her own heart when it comes to decisions regarding her fertility. The Queen seeks to have children, for herself and for the good of France. Oscar, until the very end of the series, denies herself physical romantic entanglements so she can choose to focus on her duties.

Both McKnight and Nobuko Anan situate the revolutionary narrative of *Rose of Versailles* against the background of the post-war rise of the new leftist socialist movements, exemplified by the United Red Army and of the women's movement. This is evident in the popularity of the character of Oscar, who demonstrating some feminine qualities, also challenges stereotypes and expectations, especially in her sympathy for the revolutionaries and her androgyny. Marie-Antoinette does not challenge gender or class expectations. She embodies them. Once she becomes a mother, Marie-Antoinette seeks only to foster her family and to protect those she loves. This is evidenced a few times after the series time-slides from when Fersen leaves to when she gives birth to the *dauphin*. She still performs her duties to see petitioners, but only does so half-heartedly. Her burning desire to be with her family and children causes her to move out to Petit Trianon, saying "If I stay here [at Versailles Proper], I'll be pressed by my

---

[43] Setsu Shigematsu, *Scream from the Shadows: The Women's Liberation Movement in Japan*, (Minneapolis: University of Minnesota Press, 2012), xvi.

[44] Shigematsu, *Scream from the Shadows*, xx.

duties and won't have time to play with the children."[45] Oscar, after visiting her at Trianon, remarks to her comrade, Andre, that the Queen was never happier, and she had truly become the mother of France.

Oscar, however, defies those gender stereotypes and pushes against the expectations of motherhood. Anan theorizes the queen was not as popular because, "One reason why readers did not care about Marie is because she does not try to turn the confined, surveilled space [the home] into that of resistance. She simply shifted to Mother as demanded by the royalists. On the other hand, Oscar represents disobedience."[46] Marie-Antoinette, as soon as she gives birth to her second child, moves to Petit Trianon, her own private villa on the grounds of Versailles. There, she does not attend to any business of the Crown, only raising her children in peace and happiness. She hides herself, and her children, away from the brewing storm of discontent outside of Versailles' bounds. Oscar tries to convince the Queen to return to her duties, but she cannot make herself destroy Marie's happiness. Her inability to confront Marie with the dangerous situation that was brewing in the poorer classes marked the beginning of the end for Oscar and Marie. Eventually, both went to their deaths because of it.

Not only did Oscar represent disobedience to monarchical authority, in giving up her role as the head of the Queen's Guard, she also strove for an egalitarian society where class was not a barrier to achievement. Oscar loved and was loved by royalty and commoners alike, man or woman, it did not matter. While Marie-Antoinette went stoically to her death, Oscar ran bravely into hers, fighting all the way. Ikeda intended to tell the story of "the inner revolution of the Japanese women," and did so through the life and death of Lady Oscar, rather than Marie-Antoinette.[47] Through *The Rose of Versailles*, Ikeda brought to life the French Revolution as well as the social revolutions Japan experienced in the post-war period. According to Anan, "*The Rose of Versailles* reflects not only the desire of the girl readers, but also the collective voice of the women who could not find their space in the revolution sought after by male activists."[48] Just as in the Zweig book and the 1938 film, Marie-Antoinette's destiny (alongside her eventual death) is to become a mother. In *The Rose of Versailles,* that positive portrayal of motherhood

---

[45] *The Rose of Versailles*, DVD (1980; Japan: Nozomi Entertainment, 2015), Episode 22.

[46] Nobuko Anan, "*The Rose of Versailles:* Women and Revolution in Girls' Manga and the Socialist Movement in Japan," *The Journal of Popular Culture* 7, no. 1 (2014): 41–63, 48.

[47] Riyoko Ikeda. *Berusaiyu no bara daijiten.* (Tokyo: Shueisha, 2003), 146. Translated by Nobuko Anan.

[48] Anan, "*The Rose of Versailles,*" 52.

was not enough to save her life or popularity. The viewing demographic of *The Rose of Versailles* did not want to see motherhood as the ultimate goal for a woman. They wanted to see a complicated woman fight for her beliefs and whose worth was not tied to her ability to bear children. This was why Ikeda shifted the story to focus on Oscar instead of Marie. Japanese *manga* readers are well acquainted with character polls—they are regularly asked who their most favorite characters are in given series. These polls can change the future make-up of the story or encourage creators to focus on the most popular character, as was the case with the hit *shoujo* anime of the 1990s, *Bishoujo Senshi Sailor Moon*. The most popular character was Sailor Mercury, or Mizuno Ami. Because of that continued popularity, she was given her own solo short animated feature that was shown before the Sailor Moon SuperS movie in cinemas. Ikeda used knowledge of which character was most popular, her fictionalized insertion, Oscar de Jarjaryes, to shift the story to feature her and her gender-challenging and -bending trials. This sort of character, a woman who defines herself, rather than letting others define her, was what audiences wanted to see, which was why Lady Oscar went on to be featured in other ventures, such as the live-action film or the musical. Marie did not challenge gender norms, rather, she embodied them.

"MARIE ANTOINETTE"

Born in 1932, Lady Antonia Fraser is the oldest daughter of Frank Pakenham, Earl of Longford and his wife, Elizabeth. Antonia was educated at Oxford University. She has received awards for her historical non-fiction such as the James Tait Black Memorial Prize and the Enid McLeod Literary Prize for *Marie Antoinette: The Journey*.[49]

Marie Antoinette: The Journey was published in 2001. Like the relationship between *The Rose of Versailles*, the 1938 film, and Zweig's biography, Sophia Coppola's 2006 "Marie Antoinette" film was inspired by Fraser's biography. The Marie-Antoinette of *The Journey* is, much like Zweig's, a sympathetic character. Fraser emphasizes Antoine's transformation from a naïve girl into a confident woman. While, like in Zweig, a major part of that transformation is her motherhood, Fraser works to find the woman herself in letters and other documents that simply were not available to Zweig. This meticulous approach to Marie-Antoinette charts the woman's growth over her lifetime, evident in her joys, her fears, and her sorrows.

[49] Fraser, *Marie Antoinette*.

The earlier film and biography pin Marie-Antoinette's spending habits, gambling, and partying squarely on the lack of sexual contact with her husband. While her motherhood was important in the newer stories, Fraser and Coppola emphasize the young woman's loneliness and her struggle to create a place for herself in the French court. This is evident from the very beginning when we see the changeover of Antoine's clothing from her native Austrian style to that of the French. Antoinette, played by Kirsten Dunst, is forced to leave behind everything she has ever known.

Antoinette's welcome to Versailles is mostly devoid of dialogue. The only characters who speak to her are children. The adult characters bow and curtsy as she walks past, acknowledging her rank, but not her as an individual. While she happily accepts flowers from children and walks the gauntlet toward the relative safety of indoors, the scene focuses on her point of view. We as the audience see how everyone is looking at her, waiting for her to walk past and sneering, looking blankly at her, or simply just bored. While the murmurs in the background are still indistinct, the sound of a horse's hooves fills the silence in Marie's head, subtly filling the scene. This can evoke the feeling that Marie feels as though she is on display, much like a prized mare.[50] This continues as the scene shifts from her exploration of her chambers to her wedding to the *dauphin*. She is seen and judged for her beauty and status but not as herself. Much of this feeling is conveyed without dialogue, but through the facial expressions of onlookers in each of these major events in the film.

The 2006 film also tries to tell Marie-Antoinette's story from her imagined point of view, which emphasizes the *dauphine*'s emotional separation from the world around her. This film is not intended to be historically accurate but is instead a coming-of-age story and an exploration of feminine self-representation.[51] Coppola intertwines the story of the queen with Versailles itself, and the film ends as the royal family leaves the grand palace for their safety. The final moment of the film, after Marie-Antoinette looks wistfully out of her carriage at the sunrise, again saying goodbye to a place she called home, is a view of the once supremely beautiful bedchambers of

---

[50] *Marie Antoinette.* DVD, directed by Sofia Coppola (2006; USA: Columbia Pictures, 2007).

[51] Christina Lane and Nicole Richter, "The Feminist Poetics of Sofia Coppola: Spectacle and Self-Consciousness in Marie Antoinette (2006)," in *Feminism at the Movies: Understanding Gender in Contemporary Popular Culture,* ed. Hilary Radner and Rebecca Stringer (New York: Routledge, 2011), 190.

the *dauphine*.[52] The room, once pristine, is ravaged by the invading mobs of the peasantry. Chandeliers litter the floor, tapestries are ripped, and it is empty of the *joie de vivre* that Marie-Antoinette brought to it. The ephemeral nature of life at Versailles in Marie-Antoinette's life is well represented by that wrecked bedroom. It was the first set of rooms that she explored when she first arrived at Versailles. It was where she made many attempts to seduce her husband, where she gave birth to her children, and did all of her infamous shopping. Indeed, it is where we see her at her most real, her most vulnerable.

All that glitters is not gold and the tides of boom and bust are showcased within that frame. As a royal, the *dauphine* was watched carefully for her fashion choices and behaviors. In the films especially, her struggles at court did not allow her any time or emotional bandwidth with which to care about the French people and their troubles. While portrayed as a kind person to those she loved, the Queen of the films did not have many opportunities for interactions with the French people. This showed her to be, while full of good intentions, out of touch with the realities of the lives of the many.

The perceptions of the Queen as insensitive to the struggles of others was also embodied by a young woman in the 2000s who has continued to receive criticism for a similar perceived lack of understanding of the lives of those less fortunate than herself. Paris Hilton, a hotel heiress, has been compared to a modern-day Marie-Antoinette many times in recent history.[53] This was especially so when her reality television program *The Simple Life* began airing in 2003. The premise of the show was to take Hilton and another privileged socialite, Nicole Richie, and put them into situations that are everyday to much of American society, such as working a 9-to-5 or buying groceries. The two young women, quite predictably, struggled

---

[52] It was also in this bedchamber that Antoinette learned the rigors of French court ritual and the utter lack of privacy that would mark her life as *dauphine*, "This is ridiculous," says the *dauphine*, after waiting in the cold, nude, for her dressing gown, "This, Madame, is Versailles," replies the Comtesse de Noailles. Sofia Coppola, *Marie Antoinette* (Sony Pictures, 2006).

[53] Chris Tookey, "Pssssst: You're the Paris Hilton of Versailles," accessed December 11, 2017, http://www.dailymail.co.uk/tvshowbiz/reviews/article-411588/Pssssst-Youre-Paris-Hilton-Versailles.html; Susan Grigsby, "Paris Hilton, the Marie Antoinette of Our Era," last modified April 22, 2014, https://www.dailykos.com/stories/2014/4/22/1293903/-Paris-Hilton-the-Marie-Antoinette-of-Our-Era; Victoria Moorhouse, "Paris Hilton's Beauty Routine Isn't What You'd Expect—It's Better," last modified May 05, 2016, http://www.instyle.com/beauty/paris-hilton-interview

with the quotidian tasks of middle-class Americans. The privileged bubble in which Hilton lives could be a parallel to that of Marie-Antoinette, where she does not need to engage with those who do not hold any interest for her and where her excesses are something of which to be proud, rather than signifying moral decay.[54] Coppola and Fraser's depiction of the Queen was of a kind but a lonely and sheltered young woman who did the best with the admittedly highly privileged hand that was dealt to her. They sought to show that there was more to Marie-Antoinette than her fashion sense or her extravagant spending, that Marie-Antoinette was both set free by and trapped within her wealth. Even with that depiction entering the mainstream consciousness, the popular understanding of Marie-Antoinette is one which keeps her in her gilded cage, her chambers at Versailles being a visual reminder of just how such beauty and luxury could indeed be stifling and seem like a monotonous prison of duties, obligations, and hierarchical decorum. In essence, Marie-Antoinette has been "memeified."

CONCLUSION

Even with the positive portrayals of her over the last century, Marie-Antoinette still seems to inhabit a negative space within cultural consciousness. Her memory is invoked as a criticism of super-wealthy women who are seen to be out of touch with the lives of the middle and lower classes. There have been substantial efforts by artists and scholars to complicate the portrayal of the Queen in the last century, to bring nuance and sympathy to the "Let them eat cake she says, just like Marie Antoinette" of popular culture.[55] Each of the periods in which artists produced major works to humanize the Queen: the rise of fascism and the beginnings of the Austrian Civil War, the Great Depression, Post-War Japan, the Roaring Nineties, and early 2000s have something in common. Social, political, and economic upheaval mark each of these periods, and in each of these times of instability, Marie-Antoinette pops up as an icon. Perhaps this is because we are all still looking for our scapegoat, just as Thomas Jefferson did when he blamed the Queen for the French

---

[54] Paris Hilton (@ParisHilton), "My dogs live in this two-story doggy mansion…," Tweet, August 25, 2017, https://twitter.com/ParisHilton/status/901082063922769921. Such as this two-story house which she had built for her dog. It also has heating and air conditioning.

[55] Yes, this is the line from Queen's song "Killer Queen."

Revolution, and it is easier to blame a long-dead woman.[56] Perhaps we keep being drawn back to her story because we know there must be something more than the parties and gambling, something more than the "let them eat cake" moment. I can only guess the whys, but the fact of the matter is that Marie-Antoinette is a figure who has managed to capture our imaginations centuries after her death and the continued use of her image raises meaningful questions about how women, wealth, and revolution are portrayed in popular culture.

BIBLIOGRAPHY

PRIMARY SOURCES

Fraser, Antonia. *Marie Antoinette: The Journey*. New York: Doubleday, 2001.
Grigsby, Susan. "Paris Hilton, the Marie Antoinette of Our Era." Last modified April 22, 2014. https://www.dailykos.com/stories/2014/4/22/1293903/-Paris-Hilton-the-Marie-Antoinette-of-Our-Era
Haberman, Maggie, and Mikayla Bouchard. "Mnuchin's Wife Mocks Oregon Woman Over Lifestyle and Wealth." *The New York Times*, August 22, 2017, sec. Politics. https://www.nytimes.com/2017/08/22/us/politics/mnuchin-louise-linton-treasury-instagram.html?_r=0
Hilton, Paris. "My dogs live in this two-story doggy mansion..." Twitter, August 25, 2017. https://twitter.com/ParisHilton/status/901082063922769921
Ikeda, Ryoko. *Berusaiyu no bara daijiten*. (Tokyo: Shueisha, 2003), 146.
Jefferson, Thomas. *Autobiography of Thomas Jefferson, 1743–1790*. New York and London: The Knickerbocker Press, 1914.
Marie Antoinette. Directed by W. S. Van Dyke. USA: MGM Studios, 1938.
Marie Antoinette. Directed by Sofia Coppola. USA: Columbia Pictures, 2006.
Moorhouse, Victoria. "Paris Hilton's Beauty Routine Isn't What You'd Expect – It's Better." Last Modified May 05, 2016. http://www.instyle.com/beauty/paris-hilton-interview
Nagahama, Tadao, dir. "The Rose of Versailles." Animax, 1979–1980. crunchyroll.com
Tookey, Chris. "Psssss: You're the Paris Hilton of Versailles." Accessed December 11, 2017. http://www.dailymail.co.uk/tvshowbiz/reviews/article-411588/Psssssst-Youre-Paris-Hilton-Versailles.html
Zweig, Stefan. *Marie Antoinette: Portrait of an Average Woman*. Translated by Eden Paul and Cedar Paul. New York: The Viking Press, 1933.

[56] "I have ever believed," wrote Jefferson in his autobiography, "that had there been no queen, there would have been no revolution," Thomas Jefferson, *Autobiography of Thomas Jefferson, 1743–1790* (New York and London: The Knickerbocker Press, 1914), 149, 150.

SECONDARY SOURCES

Anan, Nobuko. "The Rose of Versailles: Women and Revolution in Girls' Manga and the Socialist Movement in Japan." *The Journal of Popular Culture* 7, no. 1 (2014): 41–63.

"Casting Started on Shearer Film." *The New York Times*. October 8, 1937, sec. Amusements.

Churchill, Douglas W. "Hollywood Cake." *The New York Times*. May 22, 1938, sec. Screen.

———. "Hollywood Turns Back the Clock." *The New York Times*. August 15, 1937, sec. Screen.

Doyle, William. *The French Revolution: A Very Short Introduction*. Oxford: Oxford University Press, 2001.

Epstein, Abraham. *Insecurity, a Challenge to America; a Study of Social Insurance in the United States and Abroad*. New York: H. Smith and R. Haas, 1933.

Kessler-Harris, Alice. *In Pursuit of Equity: Women, Men, and the Quest for Economic Citizenship in 20th Century America*. Oxford: Oxford University Press, 2001.

Lane, Christina, and Nicole Richter. "The Feminist Poetics of Sofia Coppola: Spectacle and Self-Consciousness in Marie Antoinette (2006)." In *Feminism at the Movies: Understanding Gender in Contemporary Popular Culture*, edited by Hilary Radner and Rebecca Stringer. New York: Routledge, 2011.

Large, David Clay. *Between Two Fires: Europe's Path in the 1930s*. New York: W. W. Norton & Company, Inc., 1990.

McKnight, Anne. "Frenchness and Transformation in Japanese Subculture, 1973–2004." *Mechademia* 5, no. Fanthropologies (2010): 118–37.

Pautz, Michelle. "The Decline in Average Weekly Cinema Attendance: 1930–2000." *Issues in Political Economy* 11, no. Summer (2002): 54–65.

Setsu Shigematsu. *Scream from the Shadows: The Women's Liberation Movement in Japan*. Minneapolis: Minnesota University Press, 2012.

Toplin, Robert Brent. *History by Hollywood: The Use and Abuse of the American Past*. Urbana & Chicago: University of Illinois Press, 1996.

Walker, Lesley H. *A Mother's Love: Crafting Feminine Virtue in Enlightenment France*. Cranbury, NJ: Associated University Presses, 2008.

Index[1]

[1] Note: Page numbers followed by 'n' refer to notes.

© The Author(s) 2019
E. Paranque (ed.), *Remembering Queens and Kings of Early
Modern England and France*, Queenship and Power,
https://doi.org/10.1007/978-3-030-22344-1

Printed by Printforce, United Kingdom